MAKING SENSE OF THE
Vietnam Wars

NATIONAL
HISTORY
CENTER

REINTERPRETING HISTORY
Wm. Roger Louis, series editor

The series Reinterpreting History is dedicated to the historian's craft of challenging assumptions, examining new evidence, and placing topics of significance in historiographical context. Historiography is the art of conveying the ways in which the interpretation of history changes over time. The vigorous and systematic revision of history is at the heart of the discipline.

Reinterpreting History is an initiative of the National History Center, which was created by the American Historical Association in 2002 to advance historical knowledge and to convey to the public at large the historical context of present-day issues.

Making Sense of the Vietnam Wars: Local, National, and Transnational Perspectives ■ EDITED BY Mark Philip Bradley and Marilyn B. Young

MAKING SENSE OF THE
Vietnam Wars

*Local, National, and
Transnational Perspectives*

EDITED BY

Mark Philip Bradley and Marilyn B. Young

OXFORD
UNIVERSITY PRESS
2008

OXFORD

UNIVERSITY PRESS

Oxford University Press, Inc., publishes works that further
Oxford University's objective of excellence
in research, scholarship, and education.

Oxford   New York
Auckland   Cape Town   Dar es Salaam   Hong Kong   Karachi
Kuala Lumpur   Madrid   Melbourne   Mexico City   Nairobi
New Delhi   Shanghai   Taipei   Toronto

With offices in
Argentina   Austria   Brazil   Chile   Czech Republic   France   Greece
Guatemala   Hungary   Italy   Japan   Poland   Portugal   Singapore
South Korea   Switzerland   Thailand   Turkey   Ukraine   Vietnam

Published by Oxford University Press, Inc.
198 Madison Avenue, New York, New York 10016

www.oup.com

Oxford is a registered trademark of Oxford University Press

Library of Congress Cataloging-in-Publication Data
Making sense of the Vietnam Wars: local, national, and transnational
perspectives / edited by Mark Philip Bradley and Marilyn B. Young.
p. cm. — (Reinterpreting history)
Includes bibliographical references and index.
ISBN 978-0-19-531513-4; ISBN 978-0-19-531514-1 (pbk.)
1. Indochinese War, 1946–1954.   2. Vietnam War, 1961–1975.
3. Vietnam—History—1945–1975.   I. Bradley, Mark, 1961–
II. Young, Marilyn Blatt.
DS553.1.M355 2008
959.704'1—dc22   2007029903

Printed in the United States of America
on acid-free paper

ACKNOWLEDGMENTS

We are delighted that this volume will be the first in the National History Center's book series Reinterpreting History. These essays examine the conceptual and methodological shifts that have marked scholarship on the Vietnam wars and provide innovative and fresh interpretations of critical issues and events. Their geographical and interpretative sweep is exceptionally wide, exploring American and Vietnamese dimensions of the conflict as well as its global inflections and high policy along with histories from below. No single volume can do justice to the full complexities of the Vietnam wars and its deeply contested meanings. But taken together we hope these essays will fulfill the goal of the series to provide students and the public with a better understanding of how and why historical thinking changes over time.

The volume grew out of a panel at the 2006 annual meeting of the American Historical Association organized by the National History Center to survey the field of Vietnam War scholarship. We are grateful to William Roger Louis and Susan Ferber for encouraging us to put the volume together and for their support as we sought out additional contributors. We, and the authors, would like to thank members of the AHA audience for their lively interventions, the external readers for Oxford University Press for their incisive critiques, and the Department of History at the University of the Kentucky for bringing us all together for a stimulating workshop in the final stages of this project. A special thanks goes to An-My Lê for allowing us to use her brilliant photograph as our cover image. Finally our thanks to Susan Ferber, Stacey Hamilton, Jennifer Kowing, and Merryl Sloane at Oxford University Press for the care they have given to the editorial and production processes for the volume, and to Sarah Miller-Davenport for her indexing.

                                        Mark Philip Bradley and Marilyn B. Young

CONTENTS

EDITORS AND CONTRIBUTORS

Editors

MARK PHILIP BRADLEY is Associate Professor of History at the University of Chicago. He is the author of *Imagining Vietnam and America: The Making of Postcolonial Vietnam, 1919–1950* (2000), which won the Harry J. Benda Prize from the Association for Asian Studies. He is currently working on a global history of the Vietnam wars and on a study of the place of the United States in the global human rights revolutions of the twentieth century.

MARILYN B. YOUNG is Professor of History at New York University. She is the author of *The Vietnam Wars, 1945–1990* (1991), which won the Berkshire Women's History Prize, and is the coeditor of numerous anthologies on U.S. foreign policy, including, with Lloyd Gardner, *The New American Empire: A 21st Century Teach-in on U.S. Foreign Policy* (2005) and *Iraq and the Legacies of Vietnam; or, How Not to Learn from History* (2007). She is currently working on a project that explores American memories of the Korean War.

Contributors

MICHAEL J. ALLEN is Assistant Professor of History at North Carolina State University. His work explores how war reshaped American politics and international relations in the twentieth century and how it offered ordinary Americans powerful new ways to participate in both. He is currently completing a book manuscript entitled *Until the Last Man Comes Home: Body Recovery and the Politics of Loss in Post-Vietnam America*.

DAVID W. P. ELLIOTT is Professor of International Relations and Politics at Pomona College. He is most recently the author of *Vietnamese War: Revolution and Social Change in the Mekong Delta, 1930–1975* (2003).

DAVID HUNT is Professor of History at the University of Massachusetts at Boston. He is writing a book entitled *Vietnam's Southern Revolution, 1959–1968*.

SETH JACOBS is Associate Professor of History at Boston College. He is the author of *America's Miracle Man in Vietnam: Ngo Dinh Diem, Religion, Race, and U.S. Intervention in Southeast Asia* (2004), which received the Stuart L. Bernath Book Prize from the Society for Historians of American Foreign Relations, and *Cold War Mandarin: Ngo Dinh Diem and the Origins of America's War in Vietnam, 1950–1963* (2006). He is currently working on a book that explores U.S.–Lao relations in the Eisenhower and Kennedy periods.

HEONIK KWON is a Reader in Social Anthropology in the School of Social and Political Studies at the University of Edinburgh. He held a research fellowship at the Economic and Social Research Council for a project on comparative Cold War cultural histories, focusing on Vietnam and Korea. Among his recent publications are *After the Massacre: Commemoration and Consolation in Ha My and My Lai* (2006) and *The Ghosts of War in Vietnam* (2007).

MARK ATWOOD LAWRENCE is Associate Professor of History at the University of Texas at Austin. He is the author of *Assuming the Burden: Europe and the American Commitment to War in Vietnam* (2005), which won the American Historical Association's George Lewis Beer Prize for European international history and the Paul Birdsall Prize for strategic and military history. He is now working on a study of U.S. policy making toward the Third World in the 1960s.

FREDRIK LOGEVALL is Professor of History at Cornell University. His books include *Choosing War: The Lost Chance for Peace and the Escalation of War in Vietnam* (1999), *The Origins of the Vietnam War* (2001), and, as coauthor, *A People and a Nation: A History of the United States* (2007). He is currently at work on a study of the French Indochina War and its aftermath and, with Campbell Craig, on an interpretive history of America's Cold War.

EDWARD MILLER is Assistant Professor of History at Dartmouth College. His work has appeared in the *Journal of Southeast Asian Studies* and the *Journal of Vietnamese Studies*. He is currently at work on a book titled *Grand Designs: The Making and Unmaking of America's Alliance with Ngo Dinh Diem, 1954–1963*.

LIEN-HANG T. NGUYEN is Assistant Professor of History at the University of Kentucky. Her doctoral thesis from Yale University is entitled "Between the Storms: An International History of the Vietnam War, 1968–1973." Her work has appeared in the *Journal of Vietnamese Studies*.

GARETH PORTER is an independent investigative historian and journalist specializing on U.S. national security policy. From 1974 through 1976, he was Co-director of the Indochina Resource Center, an antiwar lobbying organization in Washington, D.C. His most recent book is *Perils of Dominance: Imbalance of Power and the Road to War in Vietnam* (2005).

SOPHIE QUINN-JUDGE is Senior Lecturer in History at Temple University and Associate Director of Temple's Center for Vietnamese Philosophy, Culture, and Society. She first worked in Southeast Asia and Russia as a volunteer and journalist before receiving her Ph.D. from the School of Oriental and African Studies in London. She is the author of *Ho Chi Minh: The Missing Years* (2003).

MAKING SENSE OF THE
Vietnam Wars

INTRODUCTION

Making Sense of the Vietnam Wars

MARK PHILIP BRADLEY AND MARILYN B. YOUNG

In the late summer of 2005, even as a real war raged in Iraq, a group of men in surplus military gear moved out on patrol through the scrub of central Virginia, hunting for Viet Cong. Hiding somewhere out there, men and women in black pajamas waited in ambush. "To get to Vietnam," Phuong Ly, a reporter for the *Washington Post* explained, "follow Interstate 64 to Louisa, V[irginia].... Signs show the way: 'To the Nam,' 'Phou Bai—2 km.' " The encampment, and the battles, took place on a fifty-acre clearing where some scorched forest land added a "nice touch." As one participant observed: "Looks like it's been napalmed."[1]

The American war in Vietnam has joined the roster of war reenactments, from the Revolutionary and Civil wars to World War II, which enliven the summers of thousands of Americans. Most of those involved, Phuong Ly wrote, think of playing war, including the war in Vietnam, as a "hobby, like golf or collecting model trains, but more educational." One of the organizers worried about "turning the war into a game or parody" and of having fun when they were meant to feel "scared and somber." But some of those on that hot August day in Virginia were there for more personal reasons: "It gives me a mental picture of what our dads did," one explained. Another hoped to understand her father better, to find a way to "open up a conversation" with him. He, in turn, had initially expressed concern that the exercise would "trivialize" the war. Later, he said he was pleased that his war had "finally been treated like other wars." In this, he was mistaken. As Phuong Ly observed, military reenactments as a genre are usually "staged to make history come alive for generations who know it only dimly from books." Vietnam, on the other hand, "isn't quite history. To many people, it's a painfully current event."[2] The reenactors hoped to lay it to rest.

It is, we think, a forlorn hope. Many Vietnamese believe that the spirits of the unquiet dead—those who failed to receive proper burial at the time of death—continue to wander the earth. Restless and unhappy, they haunt the living. In the United States, Vietnam itself is a wandering ghost whose proper burial awaits a full understanding of what happened between the two countries. Making sense of the wars for Vietnam has had a long history. The question "why Vietnam?" dominated American political life for much of the length of the Vietnam wars. It has continued to be asked in the more than three decades since they ended.

As it does for the Virginia reenactors, the question implies a desire not just for an answer but also for a justification. In the view of most Americans, including many historians, the question centers on the United States itself, and the simplest answer that both explains and justifies U.S. involvement in Vietnam has been "the Cold War." For many critics of the war, the Cold War was the source of the failed American intervention in Vietnam. For others, the Cold War's end in 1991 became a retroactive vindication of U.S. policies in Vietnam and elsewhere in the world, and somehow it made more acceptable the American lives lost. But the Cold War in and of itself actually offers little by way of explanation. Rather, its relationship to the wars in Vietnam remains the very thing that must be explained.

Even if one finds a satisfactory answer to the questions revolving around the Cold War, approaching Vietnam through U.S. history makes invisible the Vietnamese presence in that war. Indeed, until recently, American narratives of the war have seldom found a place for the Vietnamese—northerners and southerners, men and women, soldiers and civilians, urban elites and rural peasants, radicals and conservatives—and how they came to understand the thirty years of war that unfolded around them. It wasn't always easy for the Virginia reenactors to find people to play the enemy. A Vietnamese-American photographer, An-My Lê, was willing to play along as she made pictures of the reenactments like the one on the cover of this volume. "[T]hey would often concoct elaborate scenarios around my character," Lê says. "I have played the sniper girl...the lone guerrilla left over in a booby-trapped village...the captured prisoner." Despite the odd disjunctures—Lê was born in 1960 of Vietnamese parents in a Francophile home in Saigon and came to the United States in 1975—she saw herself and the reenactors in a similar way. "[M]any of them had complicated personal issues they were trying to resolve, but I was also trying to resolve mine. In a way, we were all artists trying to make sense of our own personal baggage."[3] The respectful and empathetic gaze of her photographs nonetheless also conveys a sense of irony and the unsettling valences of Vietnam War reenactments.

The reenactors, with or without the participation of Vietnamese like An-My Lê, are tied to a narrative of the past that cannot illuminate the war but can only play at reproducing it. Without the specific presence of the

Vietnamese who made a revolution or resisted it, who fought the Americans or cooperated with them, or who endured and survived a war that engulfed the world around them, accounts of the war go no deeper than that walk in the Virginia woods.

This volume brings together a group of distinguished scholars who address the question "why Vietnam?" as if it had never been asked before. They come to the subject through very different routes and cross several scholarly generations. Some lived through the war (fighting in it or fighting against it), others were born just as it came to an end. Some see themselves largely as historians of either the United States or Vietnam, others as both. Their chapters exemplify and foreground conceptual and methodological shifts in the field, from top-down reconsiderations of critical decision-making moments in Washington, Hanoi, and Saigon to microhistories of the war that explore its meanings from the bottom up. Some draw on recently available Vietnamese-language archival materials. Others mine new primary sources from the United States, France, Great Britain, the former Soviet Union, China, and Eastern Europe. Collectively, their essays do not point toward nor even seek synthesis. Rather, they map the contested history of the Vietnam wars and suggest future trajectories for scholarship in the field. They also raise questions about larger meanings and the ongoing relevance of the wars for Vietnam in American, Vietnamese, and international histories of the twentieth and twenty-first centuries.

We begin with a set of chapters that reexamine how the United States came to be involved in the Vietnam wars. These essays confront a massive historical literature. The scholarly books and articles on the American presence in Vietnam—not to mention more popular recountings in memoirs, fiction, and film and on television—number in the many thousands. Initially, historians focused on the decisions for war in the Kennedy and Johnson years, seeking to explain how the Johnson administration ultimately came to launch the air war and to make an open-ended commitment of American ground troops in Vietnam. But over time, a broader decision-making arc emerged in the historiography. Scholars began to explore Franklin Roosevelt's plans for an international trusteeship to manage the decolonization of French Indochina and the ways in which that vision gradually eroded, so that by 1950 the United States under President Harry S Truman had moved, slowly but inexorably, to support the French in their eight-year war against Ho Chi Minh's fledging independent Vietnamese state. Historians also looked to the place of Vietnam in Dwight Eisenhower's foreign policy, noting both Eisenhower's reticence to come to the military aid of embattled French forces at Dien Bien Phu in 1954 and his vigorous efforts in the aftermath of French defeat to construct an anticommunist South Vietnamese state under the leadership of Ngo Dinh Diem.

The particulars of U.S. perceptions and policies toward Vietnam from Roosevelt to Johnson have been sharply debated among American historians. Did trusteeship mark a lost opportunity for a very different postwar pattern of Vietnamese-American relations? Was Truman's embrace of the French war, rather than the Kennedy-Johnson decisions of the 1960s, the real turning point for U.S. engagement in Vietnam? Did the failure of Eisenhower's massive support for the Diem regime in South Vietnam produce the subsequent escalation of American military involvement in Vietnam? Would John F. Kennedy, had he lived, have taken the United States out of Vietnam? Could Lyndon B. Johnson have made different choices? Or was the Kennedy-Johnson era intervention inevitable, given the historical patterns that had shaped the Vietnamese-American encounter since 1945? To what extent were these even presidential decisions, rather than those of an increasingly powerful national security bureaucracy? These questions and the sharply different answers that scholars have given to them are ably traced by the authors of the initial four essays.

Hovering over such questions and debates, however, are interpretive frameworks that have sought to account for the larger forces shaping U.S. intervention in Vietnam. In them, the Cold War has occupied a central analytical presence. As George C. Herring argued, in what remains one of the single most important accounts of the American war in Vietnam, "The United States intervened to block the apparent march of a Soviet-dominated Communism across Asia, enlarged its commitment to halt a presumably expansionist Communist China, and eventually made Vietnam a test of its determination to uphold world order." These decisions, Herring continued, were the "logical, if not inevitable, outgrowth of a world view and a policy, the policy of containment, which Americans in and out of government accepted without serious question for more than two decades."[4] For Herring and for historians who shared his critique of American intervention in Vietnam, the Cold War rendered U.S. policy makers blind to the powerful local forces of decolonizing revolutionary nationalism in Vietnam, which determined the situation on the ground.[5] Other critics, operating in a realist mode, who viewed the strategies of containment that shaped American policy in postwar Europe in favorable terms, have argued that Vietnam simply wasn't the place to apply such Cold War axioms: it held a low strategic value for the United States, and the potential costs of involvement were too high.[6]

Some Cold War arguments took more exculpatory directions. The well-known quagmire thesis, exemplified by Arthur Schlesinger's 1966

Bitter Heritage, saw the Vietnam War as a series of misguided steps shaped by a Cold War prism.[7] If the result for Schlesinger was tragedy, it was also one largely without villains. An influential competing explanation by Leslie Gelb and Richard Betts in their 1979 *Irony of Vietnam* argued that American presidents and their advisors knew what they were getting into and had few illusions of success. But like Schlesinger, they took refuge in the Cold War: it purportedly shaped the choices American policy makers made and provided no real alternative in Vietnam other than a willed stalemate.[8]

The apotheosis of Cold War defenses for American intervention in Vietnam came in the writings of Guenter Lewy, Harry Summers, and more recently Michael Lind and Mark Moyar.[9] Given popular expression by Ronald Reagan in a speech before the 1980 Veterans of Foreign Wars convention in Chicago, when he called Vietnam "a noble cause,"[10] Vietnam emerges in these works as a winnable and necessary war. The central premise joining them is that a Cold War frame was just the right lens for policy makers to view developments in Vietnam. Far from a civil or revolutionary conflict, the wars in Vietnam, they argue, were acts of aggression by North Vietnam against the South, fully supported by the international communist world. Some of these works focus on the military dimension of the war, arguing that politicians in Washington, the antiwar movement, and the media undermined the tactics and strategies that could have brought American victory in Vietnam. Others are keen to assert that the American war in Vietnam was critical to the larger Cold War struggle against the Soviet Union and that South Vietnam was a viable and democratic alternative to the communist North. In its strongest iteration, the noble-war proponents argue that in fact the United States ultimately won the war after 1975, pointing to the absence of falling dominoes in Southeast Asia, the Vietnamese move toward a market economy, and the collapse of the Soviet Union.[11]

The essays here offer cold comfort for Cold War apologists and triumphalism. More important, they challenge central aspects of the Cold War framework upon which much of the more critical work on American intervention has rested. Mark Lawrence's approach is transnational, rendering Vietnam and the United States not in solely bilateral terms but through the ways in which they were embedded in a larger world. His exploration of historical writings on American policies toward Vietnam from Roosevelt to Eisenhower foregrounds their global dimensions and the necessity of multiarchival research to fully understand them. In part, he points to work that has placed early Vietnam decision making in the context of Western liberal capitalism and the structures of the world economy. In this view, concerns in Washington over the postwar economic reconstruction of Great Britain and

Japan and their need for access to raw materials and markets in Southeast Asia shaped Truman's policy toward Vietnam. The Cold War may have lent urgency to these concerns, Lawrence suggests, but the policies that flowed from it had their sources in a separate range of issues. At the same time, Lawrence charts the ways in which the British and French governments played a leading role in getting the United States to make its commitment to the French war in Vietnam in 1950. It was the common effort among like-minded conservative officials in all three countries, he argues, that brought the Cold War to Vietnam.

Lawrence also notes the place of Euro-American racialized perceptions of the Vietnamese in early American policy making, a theme that is at the heart of Seth Jacobs's essay on U.S. policy toward Laos in the late 1950s and early 1960s. Reflecting a broader cultural turn in the work of some U.S. diplomatic historians and the use of popular cultural sources as well as state papers, Jacobs focuses on how race, rather than geopolitics, shaped Eisenhower and Kennedy era perceptions and policies toward Laos. He argues that prevailing derisive attitudes toward the Lao as "indolent," "primitive," and "inert"—at one point, the American ambassador to Laos told President Kennedy that the Lao king was "a real zero"—prompted American policy makers to back away from a militarized showdown with the local communist insurgency, the Pathet Lao, and to support a neutralist government at the Geneva Conference of 1962. Jacobs's account also restores the significance of Laos, largely ignored in the existing scholarly literature, for American Cold War efforts in Vietnam and Southeast Asia. He suggests that Kennedy's decision to cut American losses in Laos only added to pressures to draw the line against international communism elsewhere in the region and contributed to the subsequent escalation of American involvement in Vietnam. But here too, Jacobs argues, a perceived hierarchy of Asian races, in which the Vietnamese were seen as considerably more able than the Lao, played a central role in this reorientation of U.S. policy.

Gareth Porter and Fredrik Logevall's essays are centrally concerned with the decisions by the Johnson administration to escalate the American war in Vietnam. Both authors push against a more static Cold War framework for understanding these decisions, but in somewhat different ways. Porter takes issue with what he calls the "Cold War consensus" among American diplomatic historians, particularly its assumption of a bipolar balance of terror between the Soviet Union and the United States and belief that containment necessitated taking seriously a communist threat anywhere in the world. Porter up-ends these familiar claims, arguing that in reality the United States enjoyed a preponderance of power, one recognized by the weaker Soviets and Chinese, which gave American decision makers from Eisenhower to Johnson considerable latitude in crafting a forceful policy toward Vietnam. Logevall too argues against the hegemonic power of a Cold War consensus in the early and mid-1960s among American political elites. But in his view, a reduction in Cold War tensions in this period rather than global power imbalances shaped a considerably more permissive climate for decision makers than the older scholarly literature would have us believe.

If Porter and Logevall share an impatience with Cold War verities, their differing conceptions of the meanings of fluidity and contingency in super-power relations, as well as their contrasting understandings of presidential decision making, lead them to radically divergent explanations for American escalation in 1965. For Porter, an indefatigable group of leading national security officials ultimately pressured a reticent President Kennedy and a reluctant President Johnson to use force in Vietnam. In Logevall's case, the primacy of presidential decision making remains central. He suggests that U.S. allies in Europe, the Congress, the press, and public opinion were at best ambivalent about an escalation of American involvement in Vietnam and in some cases believed it would harm the broader contours of American foreign policy. In the end, Logevall argues, it was Johnson's concern with domestic and personal credibility, not the coercion of his advisors, which led him to choose war.

The sharp interpretive divisions that separate Porter and Logevall suggest the ways in which the new scholarship on Vietnam remains usefully contentious rather than moving toward grand synthesis. The interpretive weight of the essays by Jacobs and Lawrence reinforces that sensibility. Neither Porter nor Logevall direct the kind of attention that Jacobs does to how larger cultural frames of meaning might have shaped Kennedy's and Johnson's decision making on Vietnam. And, as Lawrence argues, the contingencies that Porter and Logevall emphasize may mask the lingering potency of patterns of thought that first emerged in the late 1940s in which the Cold War intersected with shared European and American concerns about the global forces of decolonization and the international economy. But their collectively probing and critical spirit nonetheless brings us closer to an understanding of the complexities of the Cold War and its impact on American intervention in Vietnam.

The second group of essays explores Vietnamese perspectives on the coming of war in similarly layered ways, but their starting points are some-what different. In contrast to the sustained and, some have argued, excessive historiographical attention directed toward American intervention, scholar-ship on the Vietnamese dimensions of the war has only very recently come into its own. During the war itself, the nature of the United States' "enemies" and "allies" in Vietnam tended to be rendered in monochromatic and unidimensional tones. For U.S. decision makers from Truman to Nixon, the leadership of North Vietnam was often seen as surrogates of Moscow and Beijing and the National Liberation Front (NLF) in turn as a puppet of the North. South Vietnam's political and military leaders were either lionized as anticommunist saviors or sometimes dismissed as hopelessly corrupt incompetents (though, at least for public consumption, a new savior was usually in the making—or waiting in the wings). Many opponents of the war saw the key Vietnamese players in almost diametrically opposed terms: they were severely critical of the South Vietnamese state and strongly supportive of what they saw as the struggle for national liberation by the North and the NLF. If their understanding of Vietnamese actors marked a welcome departure from official invocations of international communist conspiracies, they nonetheless advanced a unitary and almost timeless rendering of the Vietnamese past. The nature and tenacity of the North and the NLF were mapped onto a singular Vietnamese identity shaped by traditions of fierce resistance to foreign invaders, which began with the Vietnamese struggle against China as early as the first century BCE.

It is striking how little most Americans in and out of the corridors of power really knew about Vietnam itself during the war. Very limited scholarly attention in the American academy was directed toward Vietnamese history throughout the period of the war and in its immediate aftermath; nor was much attention paid to French scholarship, colonial or otherwise. Only a handful of universities taught the Vietnamese language. Courses on the full sweep of Vietnamese history and culture were few and far between. Those few that existed had to rely on a slender base of historical research informed by interpretive frameworks that often transcended space and time. If some looked to the resistance tradition foregrounded by the antiwar movement to construct narratives about the inevitability of the present-day Vietnamese state, others emphasized the enduring Confucian legacies of the centuries-long relationship between Vietnam and China to decode the more recent past. The very few popular works giving some attention to Vietnamese history that appeared during the war itself, such as Joseph Buttinger's *The Smaller Dragon* and Frances Fitzgerald's *Fire in the Lake*, tended to see Vietnam as a smaller China whose contemporary politics and culture remained rooted in the shared Sino-Vietnamese Confucian sensibilities of the past.[12] In Fitzgerald's traditionally minded telling, for instance, the indigenous legitimacy of Ho Chi Minh and the North Vietnamese state rested on these enduring purported commonalties. Like the emperors who ruled Vietnam in previous centuries, Fitzgerald argued, Ho enjoyed the mandate of heaven.

In the aftermath of the war, the field of Vietnamese studies in the West slowly began to grow. With a few important exceptions, including the work of David Elliott and Jeffrey Race,[13] the wartime period attracted little historical attention. Instead, scholarship which drew on deep engagement with Vietnamese-, French-, and Chinese-language sources primarily focused on precolonial and colonial Vietnamese history. In the late 1970s and early 1980s, some of the most sophisticated and important work in Asian history came from historians studying Vietnam, including Keith Taylor, John Whitmore, Alexander Woodside, Hue-Tam Ho Tai, Jayne Werner, and David Marr.[14] But despite the increasing richness of the field, the main interpretive lines did not fully break out of what several scholars have recently termed the "grand narrative of national struggle against China, France and America."[15] Cracks, however, were starting to emerge. As David Marr argued in his magisterial *Vietnamese Tradition on Trial*, the "cumulative effect of the stress on traditional strengths," including "relative ethnic and linguistic homogeneity, ancient civilization, and a proud record of struggle against northern invaders," served to "downgrade the historical significance of major transformations occurring during the colonial period in Vietnam."[16] And yet, as his title suggested, Marr too continued to perceive a tradition against which a variety of elite Vietnamese anticolonial discourses took shape.

The nationalist scaffolding of Vietnamese history began to more fully collapse in the 1990s as both senior and younger scholars questioned the basic premises of the more traditional narratives. They pushed against the nation as the appropriate frame for Vietnamese history and opened up the local, multiethnic, regional, and global complexities and contestations of the Vietnamese past. These newer perspectives were part of a larger scholarly move aimed at "rescuing history from the nation,"[17] itself very much a product of the boundary-crossing historical moment of the 1990s. They were also the result of a changing research climate in Vietnam and the ebbing of Cold War era tensions. In the wake of the *doi moi* reforms of the late 1980s, which brought the market economy to Vietnam, Western scholars were for the first time since the war able to work in Vietnamese archives and libraries and to undertake oral history and ethnographic research. The desire to reorient scholarship toward more contingent and capacious approaches to the Vietnamese past emerged with particular force in a 1998 essay by Keith Taylor, who was sharply critical of existing Vietnamese historiography for obscuring the diversity of "what peoples we call Vietnamese were doing at particular times and places in the material and cultural exchanges available to them."[18] A younger generation of historians of Vietnam in the West—such as Nhung Tuyet Tran, Peter Zinoman, Shawn McHale, and Patricia Pelley—has increasingly mounted even more far-reaching challenges to existing nationalist paradigms in the early modern, colonial, and postcolonial eras.[19] But until very recently, the wartime period remained largely untouched by Western scholars of Vietnam.

Perhaps the most sustained postwar effort to think in different ways about the war as it unfolded in Vietnam itself came not from historians but from contemporary Vietnamese authors and filmmakers, many of whom were veterans. Throughout its wars against the French and the Americans and in their aftermath, the Vietnamese state crafted an official narrative of sacred war (*chien tranh than thanh*) that celebrated the heroic resistance of soldiers, workers, and peasants in a seamless narrative that sought to link Vietnamese resistance against the Chinese to the state's twin goals of national liberation and socialist revolution. In the cultural loosening that accompanied the *doi moi* reforms, an outpouring of popular novels and films powerfully questioned the Vietnamese state's portrayal of the war. They highlighted the corruption and venality of wartime and postwar party cadres, the suffering of individual soldiers, and the spiritual and material poverty of the postwar era. Their shared sensibilities have emerged in the claims of the veteran narrator of Bao Ninh's *Sorrow of War (Noi buon chien tranh)*, one of the most popular of these works, who after recounting his disillusionment over his wartime service, says, "The ones who loved war were not the young men but the others like the politicians, middle-aged men with fat bellies and short legs. Not the ordinary people. The years of war had brought enough suffering and pain to last them a thousand years....So much blood, so many lives were sacrificed—and for what?"[20] But if creative artists have been willing to revisit the Vietnam wars in fundamentally new ways, Vietnamese historians of Vietnam have not: the state's master narrative in the historical realm has largely remained intact.

The long-standing reticence of Western and Vietnamese historians of Vietnam to direct more critical attention toward the war makes the essays in this volume on the war's Vietnamese dimensions particularly exciting. They are among the first to take up this important work. Enabled by opportunities since the 1990s for scholars to undertake research in Vietnam, these essays are directly informed by the emergence of new sensibilities about the Vietnamese past, and they cut across a range of issues from elite politics to histories of the everyday. In recovering a variety of Vietnamese actors largely ignored in the existing historiography, they point toward the multiple meanings the war held for the Vietnamese people as well as to the local and transnational frames that shaped those apprehensions.

Sophie Quinn-Judge's essay reminds us how little we have known about decision making among the top leadership in Hanoi and demonstrates the complexities of writing new narratives of their thought and action. As Quinn-Judge notes, scholarship on wartime North Vietnam has portrayed the communist leadership as if it had been immune to ordinary politics of the sort familiar in the West and has minimized the importance of internal policy debates on the North's political evolution. Quinn-Judge draws on new archival materials, many of them drawn from Eastern European archives, to reconsider the political fortunes of such leading figures as Ho Chi Minh and Vo Nguyen Giap and highlights the ideological and regional cleavages that produced sharp differences at the highest levels of the party from the 1940s to the 1960s over the appropriate strategies and tactics toward the French and American wars. Her essay charts the direction of a more fully developed picture of the wartime North Vietnamese state.

In exploring the rise of Ngo Dinh Diem to power and the construction of the South Vietnamese state in the mid-1950s, Edward Miller's essay shifts our attention from northern to southern Vietnam. If, as Quinn-Judge suggests, our knowledge of elite politics in North Vietnam has been limited, serious scholarship on South Vietnam drawing on Vietnamese-language sources has been almost nonexistent. Miller is among the first scholars to redress this imbalance by mining new archival materials in Ho Chi Minh City.[21] Against prevailing scholarly perceptions of Diem as a puppet of his American supporters and an inflexible autocrat lost in the Confucian traditions of the Vietnamese past, Miller seeks to accord Diem the agency denied to him in these cartoon narratives. He is not uncritical of Diem but emphasizes the active role Diem played in the postcolonial politics of the French war period and the idiosyncratic vision of Vietnamese modernity that animated Diem's rule. In doing so, Miller makes a pioneering contribution to our emergent understanding of the cultural politics of South Vietnam.

The essays by David Hunt and Heonik Kwon are microhistories that adopt bottom-up rather than top-down perspectives to explore the interior worlds of war and revolution in Vietnam. Both of their chapters bring social and cultural history into the study of the Vietnam wars and illuminate what national and international histories often obscure. Hunt's essay tells how ordinary rural Vietnamese in the southern delta province of My Tho lived their lives in the midst of war. With a particular focus on the ways in which gender mediated peasant experiences, Hunt demonstrates how war, poverty, and unstable households pushed many peasants into constant movement between urban centers and their own villages. Through these processes, he argues, peasant actors transformed their sense of self and community as they encountered and navigated between the NLF's project for socialist revolution and the American-backed South Vietnamese government's competing vision of capitalist modernity.

Kwon's essay draws upon his ethnographic research in what he calls the Tiger Temple, a residential neighborhood at the margins of the central Vietnamese city of Danang, to explore the competing formal and informal social networks that emerged during the war. One set of connections is relatively familiar: the purposeful political structures that animated the Cold War divide in Vietnam and that were manifested in the Tiger Temple by agents of the NLF and the South Vietnamese regime. The other, Kwon suggests, has been hidden by Cold War narratives. In this world, labels like communist and noncommunist, or patriot and collaborator, quickly fell away. Instead, there was a liminal world shaped by a dense mesh of crosscutting and informal ties among local actors. Kwon roots his claims in the life history of Lap, an unemployed amputee, and the ways in which Lap's story of "same-same" (readers will want to look closely at Kwon's marvelous account of how Lap himself tells this narrative) reveal the vital presence of networks suspended between the traditional family and high politics, which mediated the destructive impact of the war and ensured individual and familial survival for many ordinary Vietnamese.

Like the contributions by historians of the American war, these essays also exhibit productive tensions. Quinn-Judge, for instance, is sympathetic to the aims of microhistory but worries that local accounts offer only a partial reconstruction of the Vietnamese past and may crowd out rather than complement efforts to better understand the high politics of the government and the party. These essays also usefully probe the limits of what American-centric narratives can offer for the study of the wars in Vietnam. As Kwon suggests, the Cold War discourses of balance of power, containment, and the domino theory were a palpable force in the Tiger Temple. But so too were bifurcated families, divided identities, and the hidden histories of survival whose meanings and significance were both shaped by and themselves reshaped the Cold War's local presences. In similarly provocative ways, Quinn-Judge raises the possibility of a blowback effect of American decisions on the contours of northern Vietnamese politics. Ironically, she contends, the United States' decisions to distance itself from the Ho Chi Minh regime in the 1940s and to escalate the ground war in the 1960s may have strengthened the hand of radicals in the party leadership who favored policies of revolutionary violence and class warfare over the less confrontational approaches of socialist nationalism that characterized the thinking of Ho and other more moderate leaders.

The final group of essays considers the ending of the war in historical time but also the beginnings of the endless war in scholarly and popular discourse over its larger meanings. The eight years between the Tet Offensive of 1968 and the fall of Saigon in 1975 remain among the most controversial of the Vietnam wars. In considerable measure, however, the scholarship on this period—and its almost exclusive focus on the Nixon administration—has operated in a kind of interpretive vacuum, disconnected both from larger global forces and their roots in domestic politics and society. The new scholarship on the American and Vietnamese dimensions of the war has just begun to address these issues. Essays by Lien-Hang T. Nguyen and Michael J. Allen in this closing part of the volume are among the first efforts to combine transnational and local frameworks to initiate what we anticipate will become a sweeping reconceptualization of the final years of the war. Nguyen opens her essay with a brief but deft sketch of the debates among American diplomatic historians over policy toward Vietnam under Richard Nixon. But the bulk of her chapter is an original and transformative account of the global context that shaped the diplomacy of North Vietnam, South Vietnam, and the Nixon administration between 1969 and 1973. Nguyen combines research for this later period in newly available Vietnamese archival materials in Hanoi and Ho Chi Minh City never before used by scholars and a wide international canvas to reveal how the shifting patterns of the East-West confrontation, the Sino-Soviet split, and the North-South divide shaped and constrained the policies of Vietnamese and American actors. As she does so, Nguyen provides a definitive demonstration of the way in which, on both sides of the ideological divide, "small-power diplomacy" negotiated the shoals of superpowers intent on the pursuit of their own self-interests.

Michael Allen's essay explores the vigorous disputes over American prisoners of war (POWs) and those missing in action (MIAs) in Vietnam during the Nixon period and after. As Allen suggests, the central question for most American historians of the post-Tet years has been why the United States was so slow to accept defeat and fought on until 1973. Virtually all agree that concern for American POW/MIAs was key to prolonging the war. One explanation is the success with which Nixon, in 1969, was able to redefine the war as a fight to free U.S. POWs, thus causing needless deaths and spawning a virulent myth of Americans languishing in Vietnamese prisons that haunts U.S.–Vietnamese relations to this day. Allen challenges this received narrative, arguing that Nixon was joined by the North Vietnamese, the antiwar movement, and POW/MIA families in his attempts to use American POWs and MIAs to sway public opinion and that he never controlled the purposes to which they were put. Though Nixon successfully muddied the politics of the POW/MIA issue, Allen suggests, the campaign by grass-roots activists and international actors did constrain Nixon's options and deepened popular disillusionment with the war.

The rancor and bitter divisions of the Nixon years over Vietnam so skillfully conveyed by Allen spilled over into the postwar period and continue to this day. The rapidity and ease with which decades-old passions continue to rise to the surface in public and scholarly debates over the war is remarkable. No matter the changing interpretations of this war without end, the anger and sorrow it provokes can feel as immediate and palpable today as it did during the period of the war itself. The final essay in this volume, by David Elliott, is an especially measured intervention into these wars over memory, lessons, and meanings. Elliott's encounter with Vietnam began in 1963 when he arrived with the U.S. Army in Saigon. In the more than four decades since, as he moved from army intelligence officer to eminent senior scholar, Elliott has produced some of the most important work on both the Vietnamese and American dimensions of the war. In his chapter here, Elliott brings together many of the central interpretive issues and problems threaded throughout the volume to take stock of where the historical literature on Vietnam has been, to foreground the problems with the resurgence of the "noble war" gloss on American intervention in Vietnam, and to suggest the kinds of questions and problems that might usefully engage the next generation of historians of the war.

Elliott is especially concerned with the processes through which we might get to this new interpretive space, ones he suggests are best articulated in the classical Vietnamese historical practice of *da su*, or wild history. A spatial, temporal, and conceptual chasm separates the fluid terrain of Elliott's wild histories from the inert simulacrum of the Vietnamese jungles that form the contested ground of American reenactors of the war and the wandering ghosts of Vietnam in the American imagination. Its aim is not to lay the past to rest nor to accord the war an imagined retrospective glory but to recover the contingent, submerged, ambiguous, and fragmentary dimensions of its lived realities. For us, the probing and critical spirit of wild history is exemplified by the essays in this volume and offers the most promising way forward in making sense of the wars for Vietnam.

NOTES

1. Phoung Ly, "Vietnam Buffs Bring War to VA," *Washington Post*, 8 August 2005, A1.
2. Ibid.

3. Anh-My Lê, *Small Wars* (New York: Aperture, 2005), 121, 122.

4. George C. Herring, *America's Longest War: The United States and Vietnam, 1950–1975* (New York: Wiley, 1979), x.

5. See also George McT. Kahin and John Lewis, *The United States in Vietnam* (New York: Dial, 1967); Kahin, *Intervention: How America Became Involved in Vietnam* (New York: Knopf, 1986); Robert Schulzinger, *A Time for War: The United States and Vietnam, 1941–1975* (New York: Oxford University Press, 1997); and Marilyn B. Young, *The Vietnam Wars, 1945–1990* (New York: HarperCollins, 1991).

6. See, for instance, Hans J. Morgenthau, *Vietnam and the United States* (Washington, D.C.: Public Affairs Press, 1965).

7. Arthur M. Schlesinger, Jr., *The Bitter Heritage: Vietnam and American Democracy* (Boston: Houghton Mifflin, 1966).

8. Leslie H. Gelb and Richard K. Betts, *The Irony of Vietnam: The System Worked* (Washington, D.C.: Brookings, 1979).

9. Guenter Lewy, *America in Vietnam* (New York: Oxford University Press, 1978); Harry G. Summers, *On Strategy: A Critical Analysis of the Vietnam War* (New York: Dell, 1984); Michael Lind, *Vietnam: The Necessary War* (New York: Free Press, 1999); and Mark Moyar, *Triumph Forsaken: The Vietnam War, 1954–1965* (Cambridge: Cambridge University Press, 2006).

10. Ronald Reagan speech, 18 August 1980, cited in Lou Cannon, "Reagan: 'Peace through Strength,'" *Washington Post*, 19 August 1980, A1.

11. For a quick introduction to recent exchanges between proponents of the noble cause (sometimes termed "Vietnam revisionists") and their critics, see Melvin R. Laird, "Iraq: Learning the Lessons of Vietnam," *Foreign Affairs* 84 (November–December 2005): 22–43; K. W. Taylor, "How I Began to Teach about the Vietnam War," *Michigan Quarterly Review* 43.4 (Fall 2004): 637–47; Robert Buzzanco, "Fear and (Self) Loathing in Lubbock: How I Learned to Quit Worrying and Love Vietnam and Iraq," *Counterpunch*, 16–17 April 2005 (http://www.counterpunch.org/buzzanco04162005); K. W. Taylor, "Robert Buzzanco's 'Fear and (Self) Loathing in Lubbock,'" *Journal of Vietnamese Studies* 1.1–2 (February–August 2006): 436–52; and Edward Miller, "War Stories: The Taylor-Buzzanco Debate and How We Think about the Vietnam War," *Journal of Vietnamese Studies* 1.1–2 (February–August 2006): 453–84.

12. Joseph Buttinger, *The Smaller Dragon: A Political History of Vietnam* (New York: Praeger, 1966); and Frances Fitzgerald, *Fire in the Lake: The Vietnamese and the Americans in Vietnam* (Boston: Little, Brown, 1972). Fitzgerald in particular drew her analysis of traditional Vietnamese society from the work of French scholars, most notably Paul Mus, *Viêt-Nam: Sociologie d'une guerre* (Paris: Seuil, 1952).

13. David W. P. Elliott, *Pacification and the Viet Cong System in Dinh Tuong, 1966–67* (Santa Monica, Calif.: Rand, 1969); Elliott, *Documents of an Elite Viet Cong Delta Unit* (Santa Monica, Calif.: Rand, 1969); and Jeffrey Race, *War Comes to Long An: Revolutionary Conflict in a Vietnamese Province* (Berkeley: University of California Press, 1972).

14. Keith Weller Taylor, *The Birth of Vietnam* (Berkeley: University of California Press, 1983); John K. Whitmore, *Vietnam, Ho Quy Ly and the Ming, 1371–1421* (New Haven, Conn.: Yale Southeast Asian Studies Series, 1985); Alexander Woodside, *Community and Revolution in Modern Vietnam* (Boston: Houghton Mifflin, 1976); Jayne Werner, *Peasant Politics and Religious Sectarianism: Peasant and Priest in Cao Dai Vietnam* (New Haven, Conn.: Yale Southeast Asian Studies Series, 1981); Hue-Tam Ho Tai, *Millenarianism and Peasant Politics in Vietnam* (Cambridge, Mass.: Harvard University Press, 1983); David G. Marr, *Vietnamese Tradition on Trial, 1920–1945* (Berkeley: University of California Press, 1981). Although published somewhat earlier, Woodside's *Vietnam and the Chinese Model: A Comparative Study of Nguyen and Ch'ing Civil Government in the First Half of the Nineteenth Century* (Cambridge, Mass.: Harvard University Press, 1971) and Marr's *Vietnamese Anticolonialism, 1885–1925* (Berkeley: University of California Press, 1971) are also among these foundational works.

15. Nhung Tuyet Tran and Anthony Reid, "Introduction: The Construction of Vietnamese Historical Identities," in Tran and Reid, eds., *Viet Nam: Borderless Histories* (Madison: University of Wisconsin Press, 2006), 3.

16. Marr, *Vietnamese Tradition on Trial*, x.

17. Prasenjit Dura, *Rescuing History from the Nation: Questioning Narratives of Modern China* (Chicago: University of Chicago Press, 1995). See also Dipesh Chakrabarty, *Provincializing Europe: Postcolonial Thought and Historical Difference* (Princeton, N.J.: Princeton University Press, 2000); Thongchai Winichakul, *Siam Mapped: A History of the Geo-body of a Nation* (Honolulu: University of Hawaii Press, 1994); and Victor B. Lieberman, *Strange Parallels: Southeast Asia in a Global Context, c. 800–1830* (Cambridge: Cambridge University Press, 2003).

18. Keith W. Taylor, "Surface Orientations in Vietnam: Beyond Histories of the Nation and Region," *Journal of Asian Studies* 54.7 (November 1998): 949–78.

19. Nhung Tuyet Tran, "Bilateralism Reconsidered: The Endowment of Local Succession in Early Modern Vietnamese Society," *Journal of Asian Studies* (forthcoming); Peter Zinoman, *The Colonial Bastille: A History of Imprisonment in Vietnam, 1862–1940* (Berkeley: University of California Press, 2001); Shawn Frederick McHale, *Print and Power: Confucianism, Communism and Buddhism in the Making of Modern Vietnam* (Honolulu: University of Hawaii Press, 2004); and Patricia M. Pelley, *Postcolonial Vietnam: New Histories of the National Past* (Durham, N.C.: Duke University Press, 2002). See also George Edson Dutton, *The Tây Son Uprising: Society and Rebellion in Eighteenth-Century Vietnam* (Honolulu: University of Hawaii Press, 2007); and Christoph Giebel, *Imagined Ancestries of Vietnamese Communism: Ton Duc Thang and the Politics of Memory and History* (Seattle: University of Washington Press, 2004).

20. Bao Ninh, *The Sorrow of War* (New York: Pantheon, 1993), 75, 42; originally published in Hanoi in 1991. On the contestations over war memory in contemporary

Vietnam, see Hue-Tam Ho Tai, ed., *The Country of Memory: Remaking the Past in Late Colonial Vietnam* (Berkeley: University of California Press, 2001).

21. Along with Miller's work on Diem, Philip Catton and Jessica Chapman have also recently explored the Diem period, drawing on Vietnamese-language sources; see Catton, *Diem's Final Failure: Prelude to America's War in Vietnam* (Lawrence: University of Kansas Press, 2002); and Chapman, "Staging Democracy: South Vietnam's 1955 Referendum to Depose Bao Dai," *Diplomatic History* 30.4 (September 2006): 671–703. Robert K. Brigham examines the experiences of ordinary soldiers in the South Vietnamese army in his *ARVN: Life and Death in the South Vietnamese Army* (Lawrence: University of Kansas Press, 2006). Important work in progress by Van Nguyen-Marshall and Nu-Anh Tran promises to address the seriously understudied dimensions of southern Vietnamese cultural politics during the war; see, for instance, Nguyen-Marshall, "Oral History and Popular Memory in the Historiography of the Vietnam War," in Michael Zeitlin and Paul Burda, eds., *Soldier Talk: The Vietnam War in Narrative* (Bloomington: Indiana University Press, 2004), 141–66; and Tran, "South Vietnamese Identity, American Intervention and the Newspaper *Chinh Luan [Political Discussion]*, 1965–1969," *Journal of Vietnamese Studies* 1.1–2 (February–August 2006): 169–209.

PART I

*American Intervention
and the Cold War Consensus*

EXPLAINING THE EARLY DECISIONS

The United States and the French War, 1945–1954

MARK ATWOOD LAWRENCE

"All men are created equal; they are endowed by their Creator with certain unalienable rights; among these are Life, Liberty, and the pursuit of Happiness." So proclaimed Ho Chi Minh on 2 September 1945, at the outset of his epochal speech declaring Vietnam's independence from French colonial rule.[1] The Vietnamese leader, speaking before thousands in Hanoi's Ba Dinh Square, chose his words carefully. By quoting from America's 1776 Declaration of Independence, Ho hoped to draw parallels between U.S. and Vietnamese history and thereby to encourage Americans to back the Vietnamese revolution. Above all, he wanted the United States, clearly destined to be the preeminent power in Asia after the Second World War, to block any French effort to reclaim the territory. Ho Chi Minh was, of course, badly disappointed. Over the next decade, Washington not only permitted the restoration of French colonialism in Indochina but also spent $3 billion trying to help the French military crush Ho's fledgling state, the Democratic Republic of Vietnam (DRV). In 1954, Washington grudgingly accepted its failure in that effort, but it hardly gave up the fight against the Vietnamese revolution. On the contrary, the United States stepped into the role of the defeated French and worked strenuously over the next two decades to create a viable Vietnamese state capable of resisting Ho Chi Minh and all that he represented.

How could Ho's effort to attract American sympathy have failed so miserably? Why, to put the problem differently, did U.S. leaders choose, during the decade after the Second World War, to commit themselves ever more strenuously to the counterrevolutionary cause in Vietnam despite their country's anticolonial traditions? Like most matters connected to Vietnam, this question has attracted a tremendous amount of interest from scholars, memoirists, journalists, and other commentators. For the most part, these authors have explored the period after the Second World War in order to elucidate the origins of America's full-fledged embroilment in the 1960s and 1970s. To be sure, historians have disagreed sharply over the degree to which early U.S. decisions made the later American war inevitable. But not even those who most strongly emphasize the contingent nature of policy making in the 1960s dispute the notion that American behavior in the 1940s and 1950s established patterns of thought and action that would shape later decisions.[2] Some authors have also focused on the early years in order to understand how U.S. leaders handled an acute dilemma that confronted them around the world in the first decade of the Cold War: how to balance their desire to win the favor of anticolonial nationalists in Asia and Africa against their determination to form partnerships with Western European governments that wished to preserve their strong influence, if not outright control, in those same places. The competing demands of colonizer and colonized in Vietnam posed the dilemma more urgently than anywhere else, and the solutions that Americans offered helped to set patterns that would play out globally throughout the Cold War.

In grappling with these themes, scholars have focused overwhelmingly on three moments that marked crucial steps in the development of U.S. policy. First, they have sought to explain why Washington, at some point between mid-1944 and mid-1945, abandoned Franklin Roosevelt's insistence that Indochina be taken away from France and placed under an international trusteeship to prepare it for independence. Why, they have asked, did the United States instead stand aside and permit the French to do as they wished? Second, historians have attempted to explain why the Truman administration decided in 1949 and early 1950 to throw American aid behind the French military effort to destroy Ho Chi Minh's DRV and to establish an alternative Vietnamese state subservient to France. American aid marked a decisive turn away from the passive nonobstruction of French aims toward active collaboration with Paris, a key step by which the United States definitively rebuffed the Vietnamese revolution and embraced the challenge of creating a Western-oriented Vietnam. Third, historians have tried to explain the Eisenhower administration's refusal four years later to intervene as French forces were being overrun at the epic battle of Dien Bien Phu. That defeat marked the end of French colonialism but also the beginning of Washington's effort, free of its discredited ally, to prevent further losses by transforming South Vietnam into a Western bulwark.

This chapter explores the evolution of scholarly thinking about U.S. calculations at each of these critical junctures. Interpretations have changed partly as a result of new theoretical and methodological insights that historians have brought to bear on the history of U.S. decision making. Interpretive shifts have also occurred due to the increasing accessibility of documentary records and the passage of sufficient time to allow the digestion and redigestion of their complexities. These developments have produced a body of scholarship that has achieved remarkable complexity and nuance, even as lively debate has continued.[3] On one point, however, consensus has endured: Vietnam was a mere abstraction for the Americans who crafted policy toward it—a repository of the anxieties and dilemmas that bedeviled U.S. officials around the world, rather than a country to be understood on its own terms. In the first decade of the Cold War, as in later years, U.S. leaders took little account of the social and economic realities in the country. Instead, they made decisions on the basis of Vietnam's apparent connections to the strategic, political, ideological, and economic objectives that they considered their most urgent priorities in making foreign policy. From this striking disjunction between American calculations and the Vietnamese context sprang years of frustration and, ultimately, defeat for the United States.

FDR, Truman, and Trusteeship

Since U.S. records on the Second World War first became available, historians have been struck by Franklin Delano Roosevelt's hostility toward French colonialism in Southeast Asia. A man usually known for the ambiguity of his opinions, Roosevelt was categorical when the question of Indochina's postwar status came before his administration in 1943 and 1944. "The case of Indochina is perfectly clear," he declared to his secretary of state in January 1944. "France has milked it for one hundred years," he complained. "The people of Indochina are entitled to something better than that."[4] The "something better" that Roosevelt had in mind was trusteeship, a scheme that entailed taking Indochina away from France and placing it under an international directorate that would prepare it for independence. The president believed that Western tutelage had achieved excellent results in the Philippines, to which the United States was due to grant independence in 1945. "There is no reason why it should not work in the case of Indochina," he mused.[5] Roosevelt acknowledged that the British government staunchly opposed trusteeship, but he drew confidence from the fact that both Soviet leader Josef Stalin and Generalissimo Chiang Kai-shek approved the idea at the Tehran conference of Allied leaders in late 1943.

With such support at the highest levels, trusteeship stood out as the leading idea for Indochina as the Allied powers began intensive postwar planning for Southeast Asia in 1944. And yet, by the late summer of 1945, the scheme lay dead, with American officials reassuring the French government that they had no intention of blocking the recovery of French rule in Indochina. How can we explain this remarkable shift? The question has attracted a good deal of scrutiny over the years partly because the decision to scrap trusteeship marked the first move down the slippery slope toward actively backing French policy in Southeast Asia. But it has generated interest as well because of fascination with a related question that has weighed on Americans ever since the extent of Roosevelt's anticolonial enthusiasm first became known. Was there a "lost opportunity" in 1944 and 1945 to head off disaster in Vietnam if Washington had stuck to Roosevelt's trusteeship idea and, in doing so, had at least partially gratified Vietnamese nationalism? This tantalizing possibility was articulated in the 1960s and 1970s by journalists and memoirists, most notably former Office of Strategic Services agents who had parachuted into Vietnam and observed Ho Chi Minh's pro-American posturing at close range during 1945.[6] Historians were less comfortable engaging in explicit counterfactual analysis, but the question nevertheless hung in the background as they sought to understand the puzzling collapse of the trusteeship plan.

Some authors have contended that Roosevelt himself had quietly soured on the plan in the months leading up to his death on 12 April 1945. In this view, articulated as Roosevelt era materials became available in the 1970s, the president became discouraged by a variety of unwelcome developments in late 1944 and early 1945, all of which convinced him that there was no alternative to the restoration of French rule. The most important supposed change in the president's thinking concerned the ability of China to act as one of the "four policemen" that Roosevelt hoped would manage international affairs in the postwar period. Roosevelt, argues historian Walter LaFeber, watched with deepening disappointment as China succumbed to political chaos during the final stages of the war, a development that drove home the impossibility of relying on China to play the leading role that Roosevelt had scripted for it as guardian of U.S. interests in postcolonial Southeast Asia.[7] But Roosevelt, according to this line of argument, saw other problems too. He grew discouraged by the practical problems of preventing Charles de Gaulle's new Free French government from sending military forces to the Far East to participate in the war against Japan and perhaps even in the liberation of Indochina itself. And he may have been frustrated by the fact that, at the Yalta Conference in February 1945, he had seen no choice but to accept the principle that UN trusteeships would be established over the territories of friendly colonial powers only with their consent. After that, it would presumably have seemed impossible to make an exception of Indochina.[8]

Other scholars, taking account of a wider body of documentation, located the shift in American policy not in the Roosevelt period but in the first months of the Truman administration. These authors acknowledged that many State Department and Pentagon officials strongly opposed trusteeship as early as 1943. But they argued that Roosevelt successfully resisted pressure from those bureaucracies and clung to trusteeship all the way to his death.[9] Above all, they noted that Roosevelt's final comments about Indochina in March 1945 show persistent determination to block a French recovery despite the general policy on trusteeships agreed at Yalta.[10] Only after Harry S Truman ascended to the White House, the argument continues, were the critics—by now a dominant block within the national security bureaucracy—able to get their way, partly by withholding from the new president the extent of Roosevelt's dedication to trusteeship and partly by framing the issue in a way certain to win approval from a new chief executive with little interest in colonial problems. Top advisors were thus pushing on an open door at the White House when they insisted that Washington reorder its priorities. State Department officials argued that the deterioration of U.S.–Soviet relations made it dangerous for Washington to alienate France, which they saw as a key partner for the United States in an increasingly uncertain postwar era. Military officials, meanwhile, worried that obstructing European colonialism might create an awkward precedent and jeopardize their plans to establish bases on strategically located Japanese islands, which seemed ever more essential as international tensions mounted. With these concerns in mind, Secretary of State Edward Stettinius told French foreign minister Georges Bidault on 8 May 1945 that Washington had no intention—and, incredibly, had never had any intention—of challenging French sovereignty in Indochina.[11]

It is impossible, of course, to resolve when exactly the United States abandoned trusteeship since to do so would require reading Roosevelt's mind. His final comments on Indochina make it difficult to argue that he had definitively changed his position before his death, yet it is hard to imagine that he was not at least having second thoughts as he watched the world situation evolve. The best way to reconcile the conflicting evidence may be to follow Lloyd C. Gardner's nuanced reading of Roosevelt. The president, Gardner writes, may not have fully believed in his "dream" of trusteeship by the end of his life, but he clung to it anyway. "Even when none of the pieces had fallen into place," argues Gardner, "he still held out hope that an atmosphere could be created that would help move things along to a more decent world order than had prevailed before the war."[12] This interpretation meshes with Roosevelt's overall leadership style, which encompassed a remarkable willingness to push at the outermost limits of what seemed politically and bureaucratically possible. Truman, who lacked Roosevelt's confidence in foreign affairs, followed a safer path charted by his advisors.

It may be, however, that it is not ultimately very important to pinpoint the timing of U.S. decision making on trusteeship. While this debate unfolded in the 1970s and 1980s, other historians suggested the existence of deeply rooted economic and ideological imperatives that made a change in U.S. policy almost certain, no matter who occupied the White House. The first authors to argue in this vein were part of a school of historians that came to prominence in the 1960s and 1970s by asserting that U.S. foreign policy was fundamentally driven by the need of the American economy for overseas markets and raw materials. Those interests, argues historian Gabriel Kolko, made it impossible for American leaders, no matter how sentimentally attached to anticolonialism, to tolerate the triumph of leftist revolutionaries who championed autarkic economic policies that clashed with American plans for a new international order based on free trade and open markets. "American support for the restoration of France to Indochina was a logical step toward stopping the triumph of the Left everywhere," Kolko writes. American leaders, he suggests, believed that the reimposition of French rule would kill two leftist birds with one stone: it would eliminate the radical threat in Indochina and ease the risk of a communist takeover in France, where the Left seemed positioned to gain from the political upheaval likely to result from the disintegration of the French empire.[13]

In more recent years, younger scholars have picked up on a new fascination within the historical profession—the study of attitudes about race and gender—to make a different argument emphasizing the importance of deeply rooted ideas and assumptions, rather than the particular decisions of specific individuals. Above all, Mark Philip Bradley, drawing on a wealth of insights developed by cultural historians, contends that Americans embraced French policy in Indochina partly because of a shared set of demeaning assumptions about the character and capabilities of the Vietnamese people, whom they derided as lazy, effeminate, irrational, and duplicitous. Although Roosevelt and other Americans often criticized French colonialism, Bradley contends that the differences between the two countries ultimately were far less significant than the powerful prejudices that they held in common as heirs to centuries of Western thinking about non-Europeans. The step from advocacy of trusteeship to tolerance of French rule was, then, neither as long nor as difficult as historians have often suggested. Both policies, Bradley observes, assumed that the Vietnamese were unfit to govern themselves, and neither contemplated independence within the foreseeable future. Heavy

American reliance on French reporting about conditions within Vietnam, according to Bradley, only heightened the chance that Washington would come to regard French control as the only realistic means of imposing order and stability in a region that would yield precious little of either if left to its own devices.[14]

Internationalizing the War

Deciding among the various arguments about the abandonment of trusteeship ultimately depends on one's basic approach to understanding the past: do individuals make history, or are individuals merely the instruments of deeply embedded structural forces that leave them little scope for choice? If the latter, are material or ideological currents more significant? The second major question connected to U.S. policy making in the first decade of the Cold War—why did Washington back the French war against the DRV in 1950?—poses no such profound dilemmas. In dealing with this matter, historians have not so much disagreed with each other as repeatedly added new, complementary arguments that over time have produced an ever more elaborate and comprehensive explanation of American behavior. By the early twenty-first century, scholars had developed no fewer than five lines of interpretation that, taken together, suggest that the Truman administration's decision was motivated by a series of overlapping calculations that all led in the same direction. Debate lies almost entirely in determining the relative importance of the variety of considerations that pushed U.S. policy makers toward supporting France.

This is not to say that the decision was easy or uncontested for those who made it. Indeed, recent scholarship has made the point, largely lacking from earlier studies, that American officials clearly understood as early as 1949 that in backing France they were undertaking a risky venture. Internal critics of U.S. decisions became especially vocal in June 1949, when the Truman administration made its first public statement of support for Bao Dai, the one-time Vietnamese emperor under whom the French government was attempting to create a new state subservient to Paris. In backing the French political and military strategy, American critics complained, Washington was supporting a sham government that would never be able to challenge Ho Chi Minh for the mantle of Vietnamese nationalism. The Bao Dai regime was "merely a puppet government of the French," complained Edwin Stanton, the U.S. ambassador in Thailand. Charlton Ogburn, Jr., an expert on Southeast Asia in the State Department's Office of Far Eastern

Affairs, concurred, adding prophetically: "I think we are heading into a very bad mess in the policy we are now following toward Indochina."[15] Even those who supported the decision to throw American aid fully behind the French war effort understood that they risked emboldening the enemy while damaging the United States' reputation among anticolonial nationalists if they backed Paris. Increasingly mindful of such dissent within the U.S. bureaucracy, historians have had to explain not only why Americans supported France but also why they did so in the face of abundant warnings of the dangers that lay ahead.

The first school of thought, developed during the 1970s, held that the U.S. decision to back the French war constituted merely one prong of a worldwide drive to contain the expansion of communism as the Cold War intensified in the late 1940s. According to this interpretation, U.S. alarm about Soviet aggression focused on Europe and the Middle East during the first years after the Second World War. With the communist victory in China in 1949, however, the Truman administration came to see the challenge as global. Washington policy makers extended to Asia the policy— active support for forces working to contain Soviet power—that they had developed to meet the threat elsewhere and had proclaimed in the Truman Doctrine speech in March 1947. Some U.S. analysts warned that Vietnamese forces led by Ho Chi Minh were driven at least as much by a desire for independence from French colonialism as by any dedication to communism or subservience to Moscow. But the complexities of Vietnamese motives faded from view as the Truman administration, alarmed by the rapidly deteriorating global situation, readily viewed Vietnam as yet another front in the metastasizing Cold War. The U.S. commitment to Vietnam, asserts historian George C. Herring, "was a logical, if not inevitable, outgrowth of a world view and a policy, the policy of containment, which Americans in and out of government accepted without serious question for more than two decades."[16]

A second explanation, elaborated around the same time, shared this concern with strategic calculation but focused on American fears of communist advances in France rather than in Asia. In this view, U.S. leaders were convinced that the United States needed to do everything possible to bolster the power and reliability of France. Policy makers had made a similar calculation around the end of the Second World War, but at that time they were concerned mainly about the ominous strength of the French Communist Party. By permitting France to recover its position in Indochina, they hoped to head off a political crisis that might strengthen the communists' appeal. By 1949, the internal communist danger had largely passed, but Americans still worried about preserving a robust and cooperative France, particularly its ability to contribute to Western defenses against Soviet aggression in Europe. The Truman administration calculated that buttressing France in Vietnam would help to achieve this goal by bolstering the political parties most favorable to close cooperation with the United States and by helping France to end a severe drain on its limited military resources.[17] "If we can help France get out of the existing stalemate in Indo-China, France can do something effective in Western Europe," Charles E. Bohlen, a high-ranking State Department advisor, reasoned in 1950.[18]

The third explanation, developed mainly during the 1980s, shifted the focus from geostrategy to domestic politics. In this view, the Truman administration focused its attention on Southeast Asia and backed the French war in order to defend itself from critics at home. Central to this interpretation is the contention that Truman's narrow reelection in 1948 left an angry Republican Party searching for an issue that it could use to attack the president and to ensure that it would capture the White House the next time around. The administration's failure to prevent the communist victory in China, despite vast expenditures under two Democratic presidents, provided the golden opportunity. As Mao Zedong's forces completed their triumph in 1949, Republicans attacked Truman and Secretary of State Dean Acheson for doing nothing while the world's most populous country succumbed to communism—one of the opening shots of what would become the full-fledged McCarthyite assault in the early 1950s. In this perilous political climate, the argument runs, Truman saw no choice but to go along with Republican demands that the United States make a stand against further communist expansion in Asia. The president not only feared being branded as soft on communism, but he also understood that he had to act in Asia in order to win congressional approval of his top foreign-policy priorities, the North Atlantic Treaty and the transatlantic security partnership more generally. When Congress demanded in December 1949 that the administration spend $75 million to fight communism in Southeast Asia, Truman accepted the task without quibble as the price of attaining his cherished European objectives.[19]

The fourth explanation of U.S. decision making centered on economic motives. This interpretation flowed from the insights of the materialist historians who revolutionized the field of American diplomatic history in the 1960s and 1970s but was fully articulated only in the 1980s by a younger generation of scholars with fuller access to the American record. Almost no one, it is important to note, has argued that U.S. policy makers were motivated by a desire to obtain markets or resources of direct value to the

American economy. Over decades of colonial rule, the French government had successfully excluded the United States from all but a trickle of investment and trade in Indochina. Approaching the matter in a different way, however, historians have successfully argued that economic considerations were crucial to Washington. Many U.S. officials, they contend, calculated by 1950 that Indochina mattered a great deal to the economies of key American allies, especially Britain and Japan. Vietnam's importance lay, then, not in its direct contribution to the U.S. economy but in its significance to other industrialized states whose vitality U.S. policy makers considered vital to the establishment of a new global economic order that would ensure prosperity over the long term.

Studies focusing on the British dimension have contended that U.S. policy toward Vietnam was driven by the Truman administration's conviction that Britain's postwar recovery—a matter of paramount importance to Washington—hinged on undiminished access to the natural resources of Southeast Asia, especially Malayan rubber and tin. These commodities were nothing short of lifeblood to the devastated British economy in the late 1940s because of their ability to earn U.S. dollars at a time of catastrophic trade imbalances vis-à-vis the United States. Even though Malaya lay a good distance from the war in Indochina, argues historian Andrew J. Rotter, Washington saw a connection between the two territories, especially after a communist insurgency led by ethnic Chinese erupted in Malaya in June 1948. A communist triumph in Vietnam, American officials reasoned, would embolden the Malayan insurgents, greatly complicating the British effort to maintain control there and possibly threatening Western interests in Thailand, Indonesia, Burma, India, and possibly even Australia. Increasingly fearful of a domino effect, the Truman administration believed that it was crucial to buttress the French in Vietnam, where the fight against Chinese expansion was hottest.[20]

Other scholars have emphasized the centrality of Japan in American perceptions of Indochina's economic value. Immediately following the Second World War, U.S. policy makers generally agreed on the necessity of creating a weak and compliant Japanese state that could never again threaten the international order. But by mid-1947, historians suggest, the Truman administration had changed its mind. American policy makers feared that a demoralized Japan might succumb to communism, but above all they became convinced that the impending Nationalist defeat in China made it necessary to look elsewhere for a powerful ally in the Far East. Once restored as a major industrial power, Japan promised to provide a new bulwark of U.S. power in the Far East. But how was this new power to be created and sustained? American planners determined that Japan would require broad access to markets and resources on the Asian mainland. China, on its way to communist takeover, obviously could not satisfy Japanese needs, so America looked elsewhere—to Southeast Asia. "In a strong parallel to Tokyo's actions in 1940–1941," writes historian Michael Schaller, "American policy-makers hoped to resolve or escape their dilemmas in China by adopting a 'southern strategy' that would contain China even as it opened a new economic zone for Japan."[21] Vietnam, the Southeast Asian territory most vulnerable to Chinese expansion, naturally became the focus of U.S. concern. Its abundance of rice, rubber, and coal made it a potentially important contributor to the Japanese economy, while its geographic position along the Chinese border suggested that it was the place where the West should make its stand to safeguard Southeast Asia as a whole.[22]

A final explanation for U.S. behavior takes even heavier account of the outlooks and interests of other nations by going so far as to suggest that they—especially the governments of France and Britain—played crucial roles in leading the United States to make its commitment to Vietnam. The point is not, it is important to note, that clever Europeans fooled or blackmailed the United States, a claim that some U.S. leaders have made in attempting to escape blame for their own questionable decisions.[23] Rather, the point is that European officials, who had a vested interest in a bold U.S. commitment to a common Western policy in the region, worked closely with like-minded policy makers in Washington to produce such an outcome. Drawing on European archives—and thus reflecting a resurgent interest in using foreign sources to elucidate American behavior—this line of interpretation emphasizes the deep frustration felt in Paris and London as the United States, despite its decision to permit the recovery of French colonialism, remained aloof from Indochina between 1945 and 1949. Both European governments recognized that they could achieve their goal of a stable Southeast Asia only if the United States put its enormous resources behind their plans to quell unrest and to rebuild the region's war-shattered economy. Vietnam inevitably became the focus of European desires for American aid because it was there that instability was most advanced. As the French-DRV war ground on painfully with no end in sight, French and British diplomats pressed harder for greater American involvement.[24]

The problem they confronted in Washington was a persistent deadlock within the national security bureaucracy. On one side were officials who believed that the United States must avoid any close association with France in order to stay true to its liberal principles and to cultivate a cooperative relationship with Asian nationalists. On the other side were those who believed that the United States should actively support France in order to advance American interests in Europe, which, in this view, easily trumped American interests in Southeast Asia. This stalemate was broken only in 1948 and 1949 by a common effort among like-minded French, British, and U.S. officials to recast the political situation in Vietnam in a way that would overcome the objections of those Americans who remained hostile to the French war effort. Advocates of a united Western front in Southeast Asia made headway in part by emphasizing that the Democratic Republic of Vietnam was a tool of Soviet expansionism. Although there was virtually no evidence linking the Kremlin to Ho Chi Minh's movement, the rapidly mounting anticommunist mood in Washington inclined U.S. policy makers to view instability anywhere in the world either as the work of communists or as an opportunity that communists would eagerly exploit.

Advocates of Western solidarity gained even more from their efforts to implement the Bao Dai solution, the plan to establish the former emperor as head of a new "state of Vietnam" that would enjoy nominal independence within a French imperial structure known as the French Union. The scheme failed utterly to achieve its stated goal of creating a viable Vietnamese regime that could challenge Ho Chi Minh. It succeeded, however, in providing a basis on which the U.S., British, and French governments could form a common front in Vietnam. While many officials from all three countries doubted that Bao Dai had the necessary leadership qualities to rally his people, Western governments nevertheless found the new state's partial independence sufficient to claim that the French war was no longer being waged simply to reimpose colonialism; it was by 1950 a fight to protect an independent, noncommunist Asian state from communist aggression. With the war reframed in this way, few Americans could resist the logic of lending support for France, which now seemed to be defending not French dominance but common Western interests.[25]

Dien Bien Phu and U.S. Nonintervention

Whatever balance one strikes among the various calculations that led to the U.S. decision in 1950, there is little question that they added up to one of the most important decisions of the entire three-decades-long U.S. involvement in Vietnam. In choosing to back the French war, American officials locked into place the three key assumptions that would underpin U.S. policy making toward Vietnam thereafter. They accepted that the DRV amounted to a fundamentally communist movement that served the Kremlin's interests;

they accepted that the collapse of Vietnam to the communists would be an intolerable setback that would inevitably imperil Western interests throughout Southeast Asia, if not throughout all of Asia; and they accepted that the United States had the expertise and material wherewithal to turn the situation to the advantage of the West. A few American officials continued to voice doubts about some or all of these notions as shipments of U.S. materiel began to arrive in Saigon, but before long those doubts were almost completely silenced amid surging McCarthyism. Although Americans often questioned the dedication or capability of France during the peak years of the Franco–U.S. partnership, virtually no one questioned whether the United States was serving its larger Cold War interests by helping to prevent a DRV victory.

It is therefore remarkable that in the spring of 1954, as French forces faced catastrophic defeat in the remote valley of Dien Bien Phu, U.S. leaders chose not to intervene directly in the war to prevent the outcome they had worked so hard to avoid for four years. In this curious behavior lies the third major question about U.S. decision making: how can we account for this restraint when the prevailing logic of U.S. support for France dictated that Washington do everything possible to keep the war going? In addressing this issue, scholars have agreed that the answer lies in assessing the motives and machinations of President Dwight D. Eisenhower. But over the years, they have explained his behavior in markedly different ways. Some have viewed Eisenhower as a hawk who was frustrated in his desire to use American forces to rescue French forces at Dien Bien Phu and revitalize the war effort. At the opposite end of the spectrum, others have depicted Eisenhower as a closet dove who cleverly managed to avoid U.S. intervention without losing face with the many hawks who surrounded him in American decision-making circles. Finally, a third group has charted a middle ground, arguing that Eisenhower displayed ambiguous and contradictory behavior that makes it impossible to categorize him one way or the other.

Attempts to understand U.S. decision making during the Dien Bien Phu crisis began even as the guns were cooling off. On 7 June 1954, the *Washington Post* published a front-page exposé in which correspondent Chalmers M. Roberts reported that the Eisenhower administration had made extensive preparations in April to intervene on the French side. No one contemplated sending U.S. ground forces, according to Roberts, but the administration strongly advocated using bombers based in the Philippines and on aircraft carriers in the South China Sea. The administration even at one point set a date, 28 April, for an air strike at Dien Bien Phu. Only congressional insistence that Britain participate in the intervention, and the British government's subsequent refusal, prevented Washington from going ahead, Roberts reported.[26] The *Post*'s vision of a hawkish administration restrained only by Congress and London became entrenched as historical orthodoxy. This status resulted partly from the assumption, strongly encouraged by Roberts, that he had enjoyed special access to high-level decision makers who knew the truth. (Only much later did he reveal that these were mainly congressional Democrats with an interest in tarnishing the administration.)[27] The story's authoritativeness also stemmed from Roberts's publication later the same year of an expanded version of the story, entitled "The Day We Didn't Go to War," in the *Reporter*, a news weekly.[28] But it received its most powerful affirmation from the memoirs of French, British, and American policy makers published in the 1950s and 1960s. French memoirists go furthest by suggesting that Secretary of State John Foster Dulles and Admiral Arthur Radford, the chair of the Joint Chiefs of Staff, had even proposed the loan of U.S. atomic weapons to save French forces at Dien Bien Phu before they reneged, thus ensuring France's ultimate defeat.[29]

As new evidence became available, some historians stuck to this line of argument, usually depicting Eisenhower as a hawkish if passive chief executive who did little to obstruct the machinations of even his more aggressive subordinates, Dulles and Radford. But other scholars, influenced by a significant new departure in the study of the Eisenhower administration, have drawn sharply different conclusions. In his revealingly titled *The Hidden-Hand Presidency*, political scientist Fred I. Greenstein argues that Eisenhower was anything but a passive, simple-minded cold warrior who deferred to Dulles on national-security issues. Rather, insists Greenstein, Eisenhower was a remarkably shrewd and peace-minded leader who quietly exercised tight and generally sagacious control over policy making.[30] For this school of Eisenhower revisionists, Vietnam has offered a particularly striking example of the president's cautious wisdom, which seems to contrast sharply with Lyndon Johnson's plunge into Vietnam in 1965.

Focusing on the Dien Bien Phu crisis, historian Melanie Billings-Yun developed this theme in a 1988 book contending that Eisenhower practiced ingenious "subterfuge" in 1954 to avoid intervention in Vietnam.[31] According to Billings-Yun, Eisenhower feared that an air strike would lead to a ground war that the United States could not win at an acceptable cost. Moreover, he believed that intervention risked damaging the administration politically with an electorate that, after three grueling years of war in Korea, had little tolerance for further embroilment in Asia. Yet Eisenhower, argued Billings-Yun, also feared the political risks of appearing to be weak in the face of communist aggression—a danger that weighed heavily on Republicans as well as Democrats ever since the "who lost China?" imbroglio a few years earlier. Beset by conflicting pressures, Eisenhower cleverly devised a solution that created the impression of bold dedication to fighting communism in Indochina while in fact establishing conditions under which his administration could back down without serious political damage. More specifically, contended Billings-Yun, the president insisted that the United States would intervene in Vietnam only if three conditions were met: the French had to grant fuller independence to Indochina; Congress had to approve of the intervention; and the British government had to agree to participate alongside the United States and other countries in what Dulles dubbed "united action." All the while, Billings-Yun insisted, Eisenhower expected neither Paris nor Congress nor London to comply, thus ensuring that his bluff would not be called. Indeed, on 3 April 1954, the administration encountered opposition from congressional leaders, who feared another unpopular, Korea-like embroilment in Asia. A few days later, British leaders made clear that they opposed intervention and hoped for a resolution at the conference table in Geneva. Eisenhower could, then, blame others for producing an outcome that he secretly favored.

Some scholars rejected Billings-Yun's argument, contending that Eisenhower showed a genuine desire during the critical days of April 1954 for intervention.[32] Among other evidence, they cite Eisenhower's harsh criticism of Winston Churchill's position and the president's blunt invocation of the domino theory during a news conference on 7 April.[33] Influenced by Billings-Yun, however, the bulk of scholarly opinion has moved toward a middle ground that emphasizes complexity and inconsistency in the administration's behavior. George C. Herring and Richard H. Immerman present this view in a seminal article subtitled " 'The Day We Didn't Go to War' Revisited." Eisenhower, they suggest, was less committed to an air strike at Dien Bien Phu than Roberts had argued but more willing to intervene than Billings-Yun had claimed. Insistence on united action may have been "part bluff," Herring and Immerman assert, but the administration was prepared to intervene "if conditions warranted it and if the proper arrangements could be made."[34] Historian David Anderson concurs in his broad analysis of the Eisenhower administration's decision making on Vietnam, suggesting that although the president understood that his conditions made intervention unlikely in the short run, he never ruled out the option and never doubted that a noncommunist Vietnam was crucial to American interests.[35]

Ultimately, of course, it is no more possible to know precisely what Eisenhower and Dulles were thinking in 1954 than to pin down Roosevelt's calculations in 1945. "If they had made up their minds what to do," as Herring puts it, "Eisenhower and Dulles covered their tracks so skillfully that they confounded contemporaries and baffled future scholars."[36] There is no such uncertainty, however, on another—ultimately much more important—matter. In the second half of 1954 and over the next two years, the Eisenhower administration, far from abandoning Indochina as a lost cause, firmly recommitted the United States to Vietnam, now as the protector of South Vietnam, a new entity created by the Geneva accords of July 1954. As many historians have chronicled, Washington installed Ngo Dinh Diem to lead the Saigon regime, helped him to survive fierce challenges in the early months of his rule, established the Southeast Asia Treaty Organization to defend against new communist encroachment, spurned the agreement negotiated at Geneva to hold elections in 1956 for a unified Vietnamese government, and provided tremendous amounts of material aid over the following years in a quixotic bid to build South Vietnam into a viable nation.[37] By the end of the Eisenhower years, the country ranked as the world's fifth largest recipient of U.S. assistance.

All of these steps make it difficult to conclude that the Eisenhower administration marked any kind of important break in the flow of U.S. policy making toward Vietnam after 1945. Indeed, there is no evidence that Eisenhower ever questioned the fundamental assumptions that had guided U.S. decision making since at least 1950: Ho Chi Minh's movement, now installed as the government of North Vietnam, served the interests of international communism; a unified Vietnamese state under communist domination would imperil Western influence across Asia; and the United States could deploy its know-how and resources to prevent that outcome. In acting on these ideas, the administration laid into place a new, heavily publicized commitment to Vietnam that engaged American prestige even more fully than before and limited the options available to the administrations that followed. In 1961, John F. Kennedy inherited a Vietnam policy "rich in rhetoric and momentum," as Leslie Gelb and Richard Betts put it.[38] Nonintervention in 1954 is best understood, then, not as a decision that fundamentally altered the American approach in Vietnam but as a narrow verdict on the bankruptcy of French policy. After Dien Bien Phu and the division of Vietnam in 1954, Americans made it a priority to eliminate French influence from South Vietnam and to take over themselves as the principal Western influence in the area. The ultimate effect was to postpone intervention for a decade.

Conclusion

The three U.S. administrations that made policy toward Vietnam from the end of the Second World War through the mid-1950s did so amid rapidly changing domestic and international contexts. Moreover, they confronted sharply different political and military situations in Vietnam. In at least one key respect, however, they acted in remarkably similar ways. Each administration made decisions about Vietnam according to abstract calculations of strategic, economic, ideological, or political advantage that took little account of the complexities of Vietnamese society. This is not to say that American diplomats stationed in Southeast Asia and Washington-based analysts did not work throughout these years to understand the sources of the Vietnamese insurgency and to craft policy solutions that might help to resolve the grievances and tensions that underlay instability. Just as in later years, the U.S. bureaucracy was hardly as ignorant of social conditions within Vietnam as former policy makers and some historians would sometimes later claim as they attempted to explain U.S. embroilment in Vietnam as the result of faulty understanding of a distant and alien culture.[39] What is striking is not the lack of investigation or expertise about Southeast Asia so much as the unwillingness of top decision makers to draw on that knowledge in making policy decisions. Across the Roosevelt, Truman, and Eisenhower years, Vietnam mattered to U.S. leaders because it seemed connected to the issues that preoccupied them on the grandest level—how to contain communist expansion or construct a new global political and economic order—or on the most mundane, including how to fend off criticism and get reelected.

In 1944 and 1945, Roosevelt viewed Vietnam as the quintessential embodiment of all that was wrong with European colonialism. By placing Indochina under international trusteeship, he hoped to end colonial repression and move toward his goal of creating a liberal postcolonial order based on free interchange among independent nation-states. Admirable as those goals may have been, Roosevelt's thinking did not flow from any sophisticated understanding of the social transformation occurring in Vietnam. On the contrary, Roosevelt held a remarkably shallow view of the Vietnamese people, dismissing them in one meeting as a "people of small stature, like the Javanese and Burmese, [who] were not warlike."[40] Truman and his senior aides were even less inclined to consider Vietnam on its own terms. They viewed the country almost entirely in terms of its significance to the strategic, economic, and political goals that topped their foreign-policy agenda. The only exception to this pattern came in the spring of 1954, when

Eisenhower opted not to intervene in Vietnam partly because he understood the perilous battlefield situation and the depths of French mismanagement. But Eisenhower's decision reflected merely a momentary flash of under-standing—and only about issues that required no deep sensitivity to the nuances of Vietnamese society. Within a couple of months, the administration had reverted fully to the long-standing pattern. It committed the United States to South Vietnam on the basis of strategic, economic, political, and ideological goals that it had inherited from the Truman administration and never seriously questioned.

In this disjunction between the reasons for instability in Vietnam and the reasons for American intervention lay the seeds of defeat for the United States. In this disjunction also lie innumerable opportunities for new research into the early phases of U.S. involvement in Vietnam. As this essay has indicated, historians have repeatedly examined American deci-sion making and produced a sophisticated body of work rooted in the vast U.S. archival record. Scholars have done less to set these decisions within their larger, international context—a vital task in order to gain critical dis-tance on U.S. behavior. One can, after all, fully judge U.S. decisions only in light of the ways in which they were constrained or enabled by decisions elsewhere and the effects they produced on others. Opportunities abound for new research in Britain and France, whose governments did a great deal to shape American perceptions of developments in Vietnam.[41] Even greater opportunities lie in China and Russia, where new archival releases make it possible to examine U.S. decisions as part of an escalatory process involv-ing the communist powers that produced ever-shifting diplomatic, politi-cal, and military realities in Vietnam.[42] But most of all, opportunities lie in exploring Vietnam itself, where recent archival openings make it possible for the first time to write with authority about the 1945–1954 period.[43] Only by more fully understanding the complexities of Vietnamese history can we appreciate the implications of the decisions made in Washington.

NOTES

1. Ho Chi Minh speech, 2 September 1945, in Robert J. McMahon, ed., *Major Problems in the History of the Vietnam War*, 2nd ed. (Lexington, Mass.: Heath, 1995), 36.

2. Two key works that emphasize contingency over inevitability are David Kaiser, *American Tragedy: Kennedy, Johnson, and the Origins of the Vietnam War* (Cambridge, Mass.: Harvard University Press, 2000), and especially Fredrik

Logevall, *Choosing War: The Lost Chance for Peace and the Escalation of War in Vietnam* (Berkeley: University of California Press, 1999). For a brief rebuttal, see my *Assuming the Burden: Europe and the American Commitment to War in Vietnam* (Berkeley: University of California Press, 2005), 2–4, 281–87. For the older inevitability thesis, see especially Leslie H. Gelb and Richard K. Betts, *The Irony of Vietnam: The System Worked* (Washington, D.C.: Brookings Institution, 1979).

3. For another up-to-date overview of scholarship on the Franco–Viet Minh war, see Mark Philip Bradley, "Making Sense of the French War: The Postcolonial Moment and the First Vietnam War, 1945–1954," in Mark Atwood Lawrence and Fredrik Logevall, eds., *The First Vietnam War: Colonial Conflict and Cold War Crisis* (Cambridge, Mass.: Harvard University Press, 2007), 16–40.

4. Roosevelt to Cordell Hull, 24 January 1944, in U.S. Department of State, *Foreign Relations of the United States: The Conferences at Cairo and Teheran, 1943* (Washington, D.C.: U.S. Government Printing Office, 1961), 872.

5. Roosevelt's comments at the meeting of the Pacific War Council, 21 July 1943, quoted in Mark Philip Bradley, *Imagining Vietnam and America: The Making of Postcolonial Vietnam, 1919–1950* (Chapel Hill: University of North Carolina Press, 2000), 76.

6. For a journalist's account, see Robert Shaplen, *The Lost Revolution: The U.S. in Vietnam, 1946–1966*, rev. ed. (New York: Harper, 1966), especially chapter 2, revealingly entitled "Ho Chi Minh—The Untried Gamble." For the OSS point of view, see especially Archimedes L. A. Patti, *Why Vietnam? Prelude to America's Albatross* (Berkeley: University of California Press, 1980). For skeptical views of the "lost opportunity," see Dixie Bartholomew-Feis, *The OSS and Ho Chi Minh: Unexpected Allies in the War against Japan* (Lawrence: University of Kansas Press, 2006), and Bradley, *Imagining Vietnam and America*, especially chapter 4.

7. Walter LaFeber, "Roosevelt, Churchill, and Indochina, 1942–45," *American Historical Review* 80 (1975): 1277–95.

8. See ibid., as well as Edward R. Drachman, *United States Policy toward Vietnam, 1940–1945* (Rutherford, N.J.: Fairleigh Dickinson University Press, 1970); William Roger Louis, *Imperialism at Bay: The United States and the Decolonization of the British Empire* (Oxford: Clarendon, 1977); and Christopher Thorne, "Indochina and Anglo-American Relations, 1942–1945," *Pacific Historical Review* 45 (1976): 73–96.

9. Key works include Lloyd C. Gardner, *Approaching Vietnam: From World War II through Dienbienphu* (New York: Norton, 1988); Gary R. Hess, *The United States' Emergence as a Southeast Asian Power, 1940–1950* (New York: Columbia University Press, 1987); and George C. Herring, "The Truman Administration and the Restoration of French Sovereignty in Indochina," *Diplomatic History* 1 (1977): 97–117.

10. For an analysis of these meetings, see Stein Tønnesson, "Franklin Roosevelt, Trusteeship, and Indochina: A Reassessment," in Lawrence and Logevall, *The First Vietnam War*, 56–73.

11. Joseph Grew to Jefferson Caffery, 9 May 1945, *Foreign Relations of the United States, 1945* (Washington, D.C.: U.S. Government Printing Office, 1969), 6:307.

12. Gardner, *Approaching Vietnam*, 52.

13. Gabriel Kolko, *The Politics of War: The World and United States Foreign Policy, 1943–1945* (New York: Random House, 1968), 610. For a broader articulation of the revisionist thesis, see William Appleman Williams, *The Tragedy of American Foreign Policy*, rev. ed. (New York: Dell, 1962).

14. Bradley, *Imagining Vietnam and America*, especially chapter 3. Bradley draws on the insights of Edward Said, among other recent cultural theorists. See Said's *Orientalism* (New York: Viking, 1979). For a similar analysis, see Seth Jacobs, *America's Miracle Man in Vietnam: Ngo Dinh Diem, Religion, Race, and U.S. Intervention in Southeast Asia* (Durham, N.C.: Duke University Press, 2004).

15. Quoted in Lawrence, *Assuming the Burden*, 232. For persistent American doubts, see ibid., chapters 4 and 5.

16. George C. Herring, *America's Longest War: The United States and Vietnam, 1950–1975* (New York: Wiley, 1979), x. The Defense Department study known as the Pentagon Papers largely backed this interpretation. See U.S. Department of Defense, *United States–Vietnam Relations, 1945–1967*, 12 vols. (Washington, D.C.: U.S. Government Printing Office, 1971).

17. George McT. Kahin, *Intervention: How America Became Involved in Vietnam* (New York: Anchor, 1986), 5; Hess, *The United States' Emergence as a Southeast Asian Power*, 213; Anthony Short, *The Origins of the Vietnam War* (New York: Longman, 1989), 68–70; Marilyn B. Young, *The Vietnam Wars, 1945–1990* (New York: Harper, 1991), 21–22.

18. Quoted in Joyce Kolko and Gabriel Kolko, *The Limits of Power: The World and United States Foreign Policy, 1945–1954* (New York: Harper & Row, 1972), 561.

19. Robert M. Blum, *Drawing the Line: The Origins of the American Containment Policy in East Asia* (New York: Norton, 1982), chapter 1; Gelb and Betts, *The Irony of Vietnam*, 40–46; Robert Mann, *A Grand Delusion: America's Descent into Vietnam* (New York: Basic, 2001), chapters 1–2; and Short, *The Origins of the Vietnam War*, chapter 2.

20. Andrew J. Rotter, *The Path to Vietnam: Origins of the American Commitment to Southeast Asia* (Ithaca, N.Y.: Cornell University Press, 1987), and Rotter, "The Triangular Route to Vietnam: The United States, Great Britain, and Southeast Asia, 1945–1950," *International History Review* 6 (1984): 404–23. See also Ritchie Ovendale, "Britain, the United States, and the Cold War in South-East Asia," *International Affairs* 63 (1982): 447–64.

21. Michael Schaller, "Securing the Great Crescent: Occupied Japan and the Origins of Containment in Southeast Asia," *Journal of American History* 69 (1982): 401.

22. See ibid., as well as William S. Borden, *The Pacific Alliance: United States Foreign Policy and Japanese Trade Recovery, 1947–1955* (Madison: University of

Wisconsin Press, 1984), and Michael Schaller, *The American Occupation of Japan: The Origins of the Cold War in Asia* (New York: Oxford University Press, 1985).

23. For Senator J. William Fulbright's claim, see Short, *The Origins of the Vietnam War*, 72. For John Foster Dulles's, see Gardner, *Approaching Vietnam*, 53. For Dean Acheson's, see Acheson, *Present at the Creation: My Years at the State Department* (New York: Norton, 1969), 673.

24. This argument is developed in Lawrence, *Assuming the Burden*.

25. Ibid., especially chapters 5 and 6. For divisions between "Asianist" and "Europeanist" officials within the U.S. bureaucracy, see also William J. Duiker, *U.S. Containment Policy and the Conflict in Indochina* (Stanford, Calif.: Stanford University Press, 1994), chapter 3; and Robert J. McMahon, *Colonialism and Cold War: The United States and the Struggle for Indonesian Independence, 1945–1949* (Ithaca, N.Y.: Cornell University Press, 1981), 140–43.

26. Chalmers M. Roberts, "U.S. Twice Proposed Indochina Air Strike," *Washington Post*, 7 June 1954, 1.

27. Chalmers M. Roberts, *First Rough Draft: A Journalist's Journal of Our Times* (New York: Praeger, 1973), 114–15.

28. Chalmers M. Roberts, "The Day We Didn't Go to War," *Reporter* 11 (14 September 1954), 31–35.

29. Henri Navarre, *Agonie de l'Indochine (1953–1954)* (Paris: Plon, 1958); Joseph Laniel, *Le drame Indochinois: De Dien-Bien-Phu au pari de Genève* (Paris: Plon, 1957); and Paul Ely, *Mémoires: L'Indochine dans la tourmente* (Paris: Plon, 1964). For a discussion of these and other memoirs, see George C. Herring and Richard H. Immerman, "Eisenhower, Dulles, and Dienbienphu: 'The Day We Didn't Go to War' Revisited," *Journal of American History* 71 (1984): 343–44.

30. Fred I. Greenstein, *The Hidden-Hand Presidency: Eisenhower as Leader* (New York: Basic, 1982). For an overview of the Eisenhower revisionism initiated by Greenstein, see Richard H. Immerman, "Confessions of an Eisenhower Revisionist: An Agonizing Reappraisal," *Diplomatic History* 14 (1990): 319–42.

31. Melanie Billings-Yun, *Decision against War: Eisenhower and Dien Bien Phu, 1954* (New York: Columbia University Press, 1988), xii.

32. A powerful statement of this view is John Prados, "Assessing Dien Bien Phu," in Lawrence and Logevall, *The First Vietnam War*, 226–31. For an older rendition, see James R. Arnold, *The First Domino: Eisenhower, the Military, and America's Intervention in Vietnam* (New York: Morrow, 1991).

33. See Prados, "Assessing Dien Bien Phu," 227–28.

34. Herring and Immerman, " 'The Day We Didn't Go to War' Revisited," 363. See also Immerman, "Between the Unattainable and the Unacceptable: Eisenhower and Dienbienphu," in Richard A. Melanson and David Mayers, eds., *Reevaluating Eisenhower: American Foreign Policy in the 1950s* (Urbana: University of Illinois Press, 1987), 120–54.

35. David Anderson, *Trapped by Success: The Eisenhower Administration and Vietnam, 1953–1961* (New York: Columbia University Press, 1991), 33. For a

similar nuanced position, see Kathryn C. Statler, *Replacing France: Alliance Politics and the American Commitment to Vietnam, 1950–1960* (Lexington: University of Kentucky Press, 2007).

36. Herring, *America's Longest War*, 44.

37. See, for example, Anderson, *Trapped by Success*; Jacobs, *America's Miracle Man in Vietnam*; and Statler, *Replacing France*.

38. Gelb and Betts, *The Irony of Vietnam*, 67.

39. The most egregious example of this claim is the 1995 memoir by Robert S. McNamara, the U.S. defense secretary who presided over the escalation during the Kennedy and Johnson presidencies. See McNamara, *In Retrospect: The Tragedy and Lessons of Vietnam* (New York: Times Books, 1995). For the most famous statement of the "quagmire thesis" by a historian, see Arthur M. Schlesinger, Jr., *The Bitter Heritage: Vietnam and American Democracy, 1941–1966* (Boston: Houghton Mifflin, 1966).

40. Memorandum of conversation, Roosevelt and Stalin, 8 February 1945, in U.S. Department of State, *Foreign Relations of the United States: Conferences at Malta and Yalta, 1945* (Washington, D.C.: U.S. Government Printing Office, 1955), 770.

41. Examples to date include Lawrence, *Assuming the Burden*; Rotter, *The Path to Vietnam*; and Statler, *Replacing France*.

42. Examples to date include Chen Jian, *Mao's China and the Cold War* (Chapel Hill: University of North Carolina Press, 2000), especially chapter 5; Ilya V. Gaiduk, *Confronting Vietnam: Soviet Policy toward the Indochina Conflict, 1954–1963* (Stanford, Calif.: Stanford University Press, 2003), especially chapters 1–3; and Qiang Zhai, *China and the Vietnam Wars, 1950–1975* (Chapel Hill: University of North Carolina Press, 2000), especially chapters 1–2.

43. The best example to date of a study that sheds light on U.S. decision making by using Vietnamese records is Bradley, *Imagining Vietnam and America*.

"NO PLACE TO FIGHT A WAR"

Laos and the Evolution of U.S. Policy toward Vietnam, 1954–1963

SETH JACOBS

The presidential transition from Dwight D. Eisenhower to John F. Kennedy occurred during one of the tensest periods in the history of American foreign policy. Many crises competed for the chief executive's attention: Fidel Castro had established a communist beachhead ninety miles from Florida; Washington and Moscow clashed over a UN-sponsored peacekeeping mission to the Congo; and Nikita Khrushchev was threatening to force the Western allies out of Berlin. Most portentously, Ngo Dinh Diem had just barely survived a coup attempt that exposed the precariousness of the South Vietnamese government despite six years of lavish American support. Yet Eisenhower and Kennedy did not talk much about Cuba, the Congo, Berlin, or Vietnam when the outgoing president briefed his successor the day before Kennedy's inauguration. Instead, the two men discussed Laos. A three-sided civil war in that country among the U.S.–backed Royal Lao regime, the communist Pathet Lao, and a neutralist front seemed about to conclude with the communists on top—an outcome which, Eisenhower warned, would make it impossible to prevent the rest of Southeast Asia from slipping behind the iron curtain.

Just what Eisenhower counseled Kennedy to do about Laos is unclear. Some officials present at the meeting claimed afterward that Eisenhower had advocated unilateral U.S. military intervention, while others remembered him urging caution. All agreed, however, that Eisenhower and Kennedy spent the lion's share of their conference focused on Laos, that both men considered conditions there the most important business facing the new administration, and that other Cold War flashpoints like Vietnam barely registered as immediate concerns. Kennedy later remarked to a friend that "Eisenhower never mentioned the word Vietnam to me." That was untrue—Eisenhower had referred to Vietnam in passing—but Laos topped his agenda. Robert McNamara, who attended the transition

45

talks as Kennedy's secretary of defense-designate, recalls that "[w]e were left... with the ominous prediction that if Laos were lost, all of Southeast Asia would fall.... The meeting made a deep impression on Kennedy and us all. It heavily influenced our subsequent approach to Southeast Asia."[1]

Historians would do well to bear McNamara's words in mind when assessing the early advisory stages of the Vietnam War. While the decade from Dien Bien Phu to Diem's assassination has been the subject of numerous monographs, scholars have been inclined to treat U.S. policy toward Southeast Asia during this time as though it involved only Vietnam, not all of the former French Indochina. American-Lao relations in particular tend to be marginalized. This is understandable, given that neither Eisenhower nor Kennedy ever made a direct military commitment to Laos, and few American soldiers died in Laos on Eisenhower's or Kennedy's watch. Yet U.S. policy toward Laos did much to shape America's approach to Southeast Asia during the Cold War. The Eisenhower administration set the precedent for future "free" elections in South Vietnam by encouraging its Lao viceroys to rig the electoral process; Eisenhower launched the Central Intelligence Agency's proprietary airline, Air America, on its twenty-year involvement in Southeast Asia when he ordered its planes to drop supplies to anticommunist forces in Laos; and Kennedy deployed the first official U.S. combat troops to Southeast Asia in response to Pathet Lao aggression, ordering marines to take up positions across the Lao border in Thailand. Incongruous as it seems, Laos occupied more of Eisenhower's and Kennedy's time than did Vietnam.[2]

The most compelling reason for closer scrutiny of Washington's Laos policy in the Eisenhower/Kennedy period is that the capstone to that policy bound America more tightly to its client state of South Vietnam and, by extension, to its longest war. Laos was critically important in transforming America's role in the Vietnamese civil conflict from advice and support to cobelligerency. When Kennedy repudiated Eisenhower's endorsement of the Lao right wing and accepted a neutralist government in Laos, this political solution to a Southeast Asian crisis made a military solution in Vietnam harder to avoid. In other words, Kennedy's dovishness in Laos paradoxically dictated hawkishness in Vietnam. Some months after taking office, Kennedy decided that while it was necessary to stem the red tide in Southeast Asia, Laos was a singularly unpropitious site to make a stand. Vietnam, the president calculated, would be a better battleground. Thus, Kennedy threw his weight behind Souvanna Phouma, a neutralist Lao prince acceptable to both Left and Right, and agreed to American participation in an international conference organized to guarantee Laos's nonalignment.

But Kennedy assured South Vietnamese president Diem that these moves in no way lessened U.S. determination to take up arms in Vietnam should the communists seek to extend their sphere below the 17th Parallel. "[T]he strategy best calculated to preserve Vietnamese independence and enable your brave people to build a better future," Kennedy wrote to Diem, "is clearly very different from the strategy required for Laos."[3]

Why was it different? Most scholars who have examined U.S. policy toward Laos in this period argue, in effect, that geography was destiny, that Laos—a landlocked nation made up of deep valleys, triple canopy jungle, and some of the highest mountains in Southeast Asia—presented American policy makers with what one historian calls "a logistical nightmare" that overwhelmingly favored the communists. Not only were China and North Vietnam closer to Laos than was the United States, which made it easier for them to send troops across the Lao border, but the communist doctrine of "people's war" was suited to countryside both rugged and lacking in railroads, air strips, and all-weather roads. By contrast, America's mechanized forces would be nearly impossible to supply, defend, or transport in such terrain. Better to confront the communists in Vietnam, with its long coastline, deep-draft harbors, modern airports, and paved road system.[4]

These considerations played a role in Kennedy's choice to content himself with a "draw" in Laos, but they were not the decisive factors. Indeed, Laos possessed some topographical and positional advantages over South Vietnam that made a determination based solely on logistics unlikely. First, much of the fighting between the American-sponsored Royal Lao Army (RLA), the neutralists under rebel Captain Kong Le, and the Pathet Lao in the early 1960s took place in the Plain of Jars, a 500-square-mile plateau of rolling grasslands that an observer aptly described as "a sort of giant-sized golf course," where enemy guerrillas would not have the kind of natural cover they could use in South Vietnam. Furthermore, there was a pro–U.S. country on Laos's western flank. Laos and Thailand share a border of 1,090 miles, and conservative Thai premier Sarit Thanarat was willing to allow American forces to use his nation as a base from which to attack the Pathet Lao. It was in Sarit's interest to maintain Laos as an anticommunist buffer between his country and North Vietnam. Also, Phoumi Nosavan, America's Lao strongman, was Sarit's cousin; the two men often coordinated their political and military strategies. Washington thus had an ally, contiguous to Laos, where American troops could be stationed and to which those troops could retreat. South Vietnam offered no such conveniences.[5]

More significant than strategic assessments of the Lao landscape were ethnocentric perceptions of the Lao people. U.S. policy toward Laos in the 1950s and early 1960s cannot be understood apart from the traits that Americans ascribed to inhabitants of that country, the manner in which American statesmen and the American media constructed a putative Lao national character that differed from South Vietnam's and that made Lao chances of withstanding communist pressure appear negligible. As several works of diplomatic history taking the so-called cultural turn have shown, it is not sufficient to accuse Americans of generalized "racism" in their Cold War dealings with countries like Vietnam, Indonesia, and China. Policy makers and press lords may have mouthed the domino theory's rhetoric of interchangeability, but they never believed that one Asian nation was much the same as any other. Rather, conceptualization of Asia in the American popular imagination was complex, positing a hierarchy of "good" and "bad" Asians, as Kennedy demonstrated in the above-cited letter to Diem when he contrasted Lao "ineffectiveness" with "the fierce desire of your people [the Vietnamese] to maintain their independence and their willingness to engage in arduous struggle for it." Americans at midcentury considered some Asians "tough" and therefore dependable anticommunist allies while consigning others to the ranks of those who, in the words of a State Department working paper, "will not fight for themselves," much less for the free world. No Asians rated lower in American eyes than the Lao.[6]

The record of policy-making deliberations under Eisenhower reveals numerous complaints about how difficult it was to get Lao soldiers and politicians to behave like cold warriors, or even to recognize that there was a war on. In one of the earliest discussions of an American policy for Laos, Foreign Service desk officer Robert McClintock noted the former colony's strategic value—it could "open or interdict the most direct land route from China to the Gulf of Siam"—but also listed its shortcomings: "the indolence of the inhabitants, their political apathy, and their inability thus far to be counted as a real military force." Laos, McClintock observed, was "inhabited by lotus eaters." This impression did not improve after Eisenhower sent the first U.S. ambassador to Laos in September 1954. For the remainder of the decade, embassy cables from Laos's administrative capital of Vientiane to Washington variously described the Lao as "lackadaisical," "indifferent," "soft," "spongy," and "apathetic," and on one occasion advised the president to "always remember [the] Lao inherent reluctance to fight." Perhaps the most vocal critic of Laos in the Eisenhower administration was CIA director Allen Dulles, who vented his contempt for the Lao during National Security Council meetings. There were "few people of any courage" in Laos, he informed the NSC; the Lao were "not much given to fighting" and had "a long tradition of not liking bloodshed." This explained why, whenever the

RLA employed "hit-and-run tactics against the communists," it was "not clear whether there was more hit or more run."[7]

Yet Dulles did not advocate abandonment of Laos, believing, along with Eisenhower, that the country must be denied to the communists. Its loss, policy makers reasoned, would not only give Moscow a strategic wedge into the heart of Southeast Asia but a psychological victory over all nations vacillating between communism and freedom. Unfortunately, the accords generated by the 1954 Geneva Conference on Indochina forbade the introduction of additional foreign military personnel into Laos. While no American had signed the accords, Eisenhower had pledged, for public relations purposes, not to violate them, which meant that he could not dispatch American troops to fight the Pathet Lao. Instead, Eisenhower reached for the U.S. checkbook, channeling hundreds of millions of dollars to the Royal Lao government through an aid organization called the Program Evaluation Office. By Eisenhower's second term, over 80 percent of the $40 million America spent annually in Laos went to the RLA, and Laos became the only foreign country in the world where Washington paid 100 percent of the military budget.

The money never translated into victory. Even though the RLA was superior in numbers to its challenger and better supplied with planes, tanks, guns, and ammunition, the Pathet Lao won almost every skirmish. The "key factor," according to CIA operatives stationed in Vientiane, was the "actual will of individual soldiers to fight," and this was virtually nonexistent. A typical CIA situation report lamented the "Lao disinclination to combat, natural tendency to effect compromise, and desire to live [an] easy life without unnecessary stresses or strains." J. Graham Parsons, U.S. ambassador to Laos from 1956 to 1958, told Eisenhower that "most" RLA units did "little more than wring their hands." Eisenhower remained convinced that a pro-Western Laos was essential to America's security, but his disrespect for Lao martial skills became evident when members of the incoming Kennedy administration sought his advice. In one top-secret discussion, Eisenhower remarked that "obviously, the Laotians didn't like to fight." In another, he referred to the RLA as "a bunch of homosexuals."[8]

Policy makers' disgust with the Lao intensified after Kennedy assumed office. Robert Dean has shown how the Kennedy White House pulsed with a "stoic, boundary-defining masculinity"; it is not surprising that this most macho of presidents and his two-fisted advisors should have considered the RLA's blasé approach to warfare proof that Laos did not deserve to remain part of the free world. "As a military ally, the entire Laos nation is clearly inferior to a battalion of conscientious objectors from World War I," Ambassador John Kenneth Galbraith wrote to Kennedy from New Delhi.

Arthur Schlesinger, Jr., special assistant to the president, asked why Americans should "fight for a country whose people evidently could not care less about fighting for themselves," and speechwriter Theodore Sorenson argued that a "bastion of Western strength on China's border could not be created by a people quite unwilling to be a bastion for anyone." Averell Harriman, Kennedy's roving ambassador, told an interviewer in 1965 that the RLA "wouldn't fight at all," noting that it was considered "a great improvement" when RLA battalions that had previously "thrown down their weapons and run" in the face of Pathet Lao attacks remembered to "carry their weapons with them" while retreating.[9]

Even Secretary of State Dean Rusk, the New Frontiersman most inclined to continue Eisenhower's hard-line policy in Laos, was exasperated by the RLA's lack of fighting spirit. Two months into the Kennedy administration, Rusk informed the president that "we could not guarantee the steadfastness of any Lao, even Phoumi." Although RLA troops were among the highest paid in the world, Rusk observed that Phoumi had been unable to galvanize his men and that the United States "missed having government troops who were willing to fight." When the RLA commander visited Washington in June 1961, Rusk spoke to him with what the secretary himself described as "a frankness which went beyond traditional diplomatic practice." "If the U.S. is to call on its young men to go and fight to defend the freedom of another country," Rusk lectured, "it must be quite certain of the desire of that country for freedom." Consequently, Washington had to be "certain that the will to defend freedom...exists in Laos," and such certainty required more evidence than had been "apparent" of the "readiness to accept sacrifice on the part of the Laotian people." Rusk's concerns were echoed by the Laos Task Force, an ad hoc body set up to produce recommendations for Kennedy. "Despite the magnitude of our aid program and the large number of Americans working with the Lao," the task force reported:

> we did not succeed in developing any real sense of motivation among these people.... We generally assumed that the Lao were vitally concerned with the communist threat and were eager to preserve their country's independence. Instead, we have found ourselves dealing with an almost total lack of motivation. We have spent large sums to support the Lao Army and employed a large force of Americans to assist in its training, but we have not instilled into the armed forces the necessary discipline and will to fight.[10]

American journalism reinforced these views. The Lao whom Americans encountered in mainstream magazines and newspapers were quintessential antiwarriors, "pacifist Buddhists who frequently make jokes about how their country has never won a war," in the words of the *New York Times*. Apart from occasional backhanded compliments about Lao "tolerance" and "innocence," the major American press outlets had little positive to say with respect to the Lao, and their criticisms often verged on disdain. Standard qualifying terms included "diffident," "drowsy," "docile," "torpid," "unenterprising," and "soporific"—adjectives unlikely to inspire confidence.[11]

The first multipage article on Laos in a prominent American magazine appeared in 1956, when the *Saturday Evening Post* ran Oden Meeker's account of his work as head of a relief mission in that "unbelievable Asiatic kingdom." Unlike most American reporters, Meeker liked the Lao, whom he described as "gentle" and "utterly charming." Daily life in Laos, Meeker noted, was "tranquility just this side of Rip Van Winkle." By the time Meeker expanded this article into a book, Pathet Lao activity had increased and the Eisenhower administration had designated Laos a vital piece of strategic real estate. Meeker therefore placed his "magical kingdom" more obtrusively within the context of the Cold War, warning readers that "[i]n Laos the Americans and their allies are faced with trying to instill a sense of economic and political urgency in a group of people who may well be the least urgent souls on earth." The Lao, he explained, were "far more interested in decorating things with curlicues than in getting ahead in the world." This might have the happy result that "in Laos no one ever suffered a nervous breakdown," but it made these "dreamy, gentle, bucolic, nonaggressive people" unpromising material for crusaders. "The Lao are still Lao," he wrote. "They aren't really very angry with anybody" and, moreover, "they are reluctant to kill any living thing." American attempts to "create in Laos a nation strong enough to resist the attractions and pressures across the communist frontiers" were likely to shatter on the rocks of an omnipresent "drowsiness and passivity" that made "*mañana* sound dynamic."[12]

The *Providence Journal* drew from the same grab-bag of signifiers when it tried to explain why "American hustle to bring progress to this lazy land...has failed to have much impact on the fun-loving, unambitious people or their officials." Reporter David Lancashire argued that the Lao "frown on hard work" and were loath to emulate the example of eager-beaver Westerners sent to assist them. "During the recent communist offensive," Lancashire wrote, "lights burned nightly in the American aid offices,...but Laotian military headquarters closed for weekends and Buddhist holidays, and regular three-hour noon siestas prevailed." Lancashire described "an American financial expert work[ing] long hours" in a "hotbox office at the Laos national bank" while native "bank employees sat idly flipping elastic bands at lizards scurrying across the ceiling." Readers could be forgiven for concluding, along with the *Washington Post*, that the United States was "galloping off on a white charger to save people who don't want to be saved."[13]

At least, the Lao did not seem willing to fight for their salvation. R. H. Shackford, billed by the *Washington News* as "one of America's outstanding foreign correspondents," affirmed that "Laotian soldiers often resemble Ferdinand the Bull, who wanted only to smell the flowers." *U.S. News and World Report* assured readers that "the Lao is a wonderful person,...a gentle person," but that, sadly, "[h]e does not like to fight. He is not like a German—a German has a strong will." The *Baltimore Sun* looked closer to home for its analogy: the Lao, it claimed, possessed "no such vigor as drives, say, a farmer living in Maine." How, then, could Washington ask that farmer to leave his plow and fight alongside the RLA?[14]

Firsthand media accounts of the RLA in action rendered the prospect even less inviting. "[T]wo hundred million dollars' worth of military aid has not made government troops capable of vanquishing the jungle-tough rebels," understated the *Christian Science Monitor* in early 1961. In fact, those troops seemed more likely to vanquish themselves: the *New York Herald Tribune* portrayed RLA soldiers as so incompetent that they forgot where they planted American-supplied land mines and wound up "blow[ing] their own feet off." According to the *New York Times*, "The typical Laotian soldier is a laughing young peasant who...abhors killing....He sings, dances, and plays music at every break as his 100-man company moves toward the front, often with a plucked jungle flower sticking out of the muzzle of his ill-kept rifle." The performance of such simple souls under fire was predictable. "They just aren't fighting," complained *Newsweek*. "The Pathet Lao can take over all the country if they want it." American advisors stationed in Laos did not attempt to conceal their low opinion of the RLA when interviewed by reporters. "This is war, dammit," one colonel fumed, "but the Laotians are just not willing to risk getting killed." To the suggestion that a ceasefire might give the RLA a chance to improve discipline, another U.S. military official sourly responded, "They've been observing a ceasefire for some time now, anyway."[15]

Even Time Inc., the multimedia empire created by Henry Luce and dedicated to promoting an activist U.S. foreign policy, was unenthusiastic about the free world's chances in Laos. While Luce initially considered Laos an important Cold War battleground, he soon lost interest; as early as 1956, his most influential publication, *Time* magazine, dismissed the nation as a "lotus land" in "habitual half-slumber" whose "sleepy government" never "stirred itself to anger." Tellingly, *Time*, that champion of global interventionism, pre-dated the White House in its willingness to accept Laos's nonalignment. "Scarcely any country on earth is less fitted to serve as a pivotal point in the struggle against communism than Laos," it asserted in 1959, citing Lao king Sisavang Vong's proclamation that "my people do not know how to fight; they know only how to sing and make love." *Time*'s portrayal of the RLA read as black comedy. "Royal Lao soldiers tossed hand grenades in the Nam Song River and jumped in afterward to scoop up the stunned banana fish that floated to the surface," one article related. "They swam, roasted pigs and fish over open fires, and drank plenty of Mekong rice whisky....Laotian soldiers...can seldom bring themselves to fire at any enemy they can actually see,...though one lieutenant shot himself in the foot."[16]

When Kennedy began making noises after his inauguration about safeguarding Lao self-rule, Luce, for once, proved disinclined to charge at the sound of the trumpets. Instead, he got his Hong Kong bureau chief Stanley Karnow and correspondents Jerry Schecter and James Wilde to compose what *Time* advertised as "the only comprehensive story of Laos's history and current crisis that exists anywhere." This effort, which must rank among the most sneering works of Orientalia produced during the Cold War, was *Time*'s cover feature for 17 March 1961. It described Laos as "landlocked, lackadaisical, and so primitive that the currently favored adjective 'underdeveloped' would be an unwarranted compliment." While the Lao themselves were "pleasant," they were also, readers learned, "bone lazy" and their "favorite phrase" was "*bo pen nyan*, a vaguely negative phrase that means everything from 'too bad' to 'it doesn't matter.'" In other "backward lands," *Time* noted, "it is popular to write this quality off to malnutrition, liver flukes, and intestinal parasites, but in Laos...lethargy extends to the highest ranks of princelings raised on French cuisine." Worst of all was the Lao king, whose "most striking characteristic politically is a lethargy so profound that it is almost spectacular." Like his subjects, he had "sunk into a torpor that could not be shaken by the fast-paced world around him," and the RLA was beyond hope: "What could serious cold warriors do with soldiers who set up tiny clay images of Buddha to shoot at,...[and] then deliberately missed?" Those millions of Americans for whom *Time* was required reading doubtless asked themselves the same question.[17]

Life magazine, Luce's other publishing sensation, ran a number of articles blasting the "primitive inefficiency and shattering inertia" of the Lao. "In Laos, it is downright bad taste to work more than is absolutely necessary," the prolific Karnow asserted in a September 1959 full-page spread. Evidence of this lack of initiative was everywhere: "Years ago, someone ambitiously built a railroad station at the town of Savannakhet, but the railroad itself has yet to be started. The main highway...is paved for only eight miles....[Laos's] best hotel...is a dilapidated bungalow." No institution more perfectly reflected the nation's shortcomings than its army, which, Karnow noted, had recently captured a Pathet Lao battalion only to let the communists escape, unharmed. When asked to "explain how this had happened," Laos's defense minister had shaken his head and responded, "That is an extremely difficult question." Such attitudes contributed to a situation in which, by Karnow's reckoning, the communists had "only about 4,000 men" but nonetheless "held the initiative in both guerrilla and psychological warfare." *Life*'s follow-up story informed readers that Laos was an "indolent little country," that the "unwarlike Lao army" had exhibited "a notable...reluctance to shoot," and that "Laotian civilians" were "even less warlike than the soldiers."[18]

Americans advanced three main theories to account for Lao unassertiveness. The most common explanation blamed Buddhism, "with its strong emphasis on harming no living creature," according to *Time*. Southeast Asia's dominant religion did not enjoy a positive reputation in America during the early years of the Cold War—a recent study of U.S.–Vietnamese relations under Eisenhower demonstrates that Buddhism was "invariably linked with passivity...and moral relativism"—and the Lao, lacking a militantly Catholic commander like Diem to give them backbone, seemed condemned by their faith to wave a white flag. The *New York Times* made this point in early 1961, arguing that "Laotians...are a people who do not want to fight because they are so deeply Buddhist they abhor killing of any kind." Other newspapers and magazines also found in Buddhism a convenient scapegoat. "The royal Laotian soldier's lack of eagerness for fighting stems from...his Buddhist religion," declared the *Washington Star*. *Newsweek* observed that "Laotians, being Buddhists, are notoriously unwilling to fight," and the *Denver Post* attributed the free world's string of reverses in Laos to the fact that Washington was allied with "a Buddhist people who don't want to fight back."[19]

Elite figures in the Kennedy administration accepted this analysis. "As Buddhists, the Lao favored contemplation and disliked killing," Schlesinger recalled in a 1965 account of Kennedy's presidency. Roger Hilsman, director of the State Department's Bureau of Intelligence and Research, noted in his memoirs that the Lao were "Theravada Buddhists, among the most gentle, peace-loving, and serene people in the world." John Holt, counselor of the American embassy in Laos, advised newly appointed Ambassador Winthrop Brown that "Lao Buddhist troops do not like to fire bullets except to frighten.

This is a known fact." The Lao royal family inadvertently contributed to such caricatures when they appealed to Washington for support. Prince Souvanna Phouma wrote Kennedy in February 1961 to reassure him that it was "unthinkable" that a "peaceful people, fervently Buddhist...like [the] Lao people should wish [to] become communist." The Americans needed to appreciate a distinction, Souvanna claimed: "I know my people and can assure you it [is] *socialist* by reason [of] its religion...[but] that it does not desire [to] become communist." Kennedy was unlikely to take solace in this hairsplitting, or in the Lao king's pronouncement that "the Lao people, dedicated to peace, have never ceased...to practice the teachings of Buddha, which ordain forgiveness, meekness, and charity." To a realist like Kennedy, these teachings were poor preparation for combat with fanatical jungle fighters.[20]

Americans dissatisfied with the Buddhist explanation cited another reason for Lao reluctance to wield the sword: the absence of any feeling of national unity. According to this argument, Laos's tortuous terrain, scarcity of overland communications, diversity of people and languages, and scattered population made genuine patriotism impossible. The Lao had no sense of being part of a sovereign country and therefore were unwilling to fight to defend that country against communism. "Laos was hopeless," Ambassador Brown recalled in 1968. "It had no national identity. It was just a series of lines drawn on a map." A State Department briefing paper prepared for Kennedy a week after his inauguration advised the president, "Laos has never been a national entity....Its people lack a sense of national loyalty....As a result, no strong, effective non-communist leadership has emerged." The Laos Task Force concurred. "U.S. policy in Laos," it insisted, "has...suffered from a general assumption that we are dealing with a nation." Not so: "Laos is merely a loosly [*sic*] organized assortment of peoples with tribal-like loyalties...over which the Lao monarch exercises only a vague sort of hegemony." Appeals to national allegiance were bound to fail under such conditions.[21]

The ministers of information made the same case, but in more vivid language. "Report from Laos," a *Saturday Review* cover story, asserted that the Lao "are living in the third century"; that "there is no sense of ethnic unity," much less any "sense of a nation"; and that many "tribes are not only cut off completely from the outside world; they are hardly aware of the existence of tribes less than fifty miles away." The *Washington Post* went further, noting that most Lao "do not even know that they are citizens of a country known as Laos." *Time* argued that nationhood was too sophisticated a concept for inhabitants of this "land of love and laughter." "90% of all

Laotians," the magazine reported, "think the world is flat—and populated mainly by Laotians." No wonder they had difficulty conceiving of a world divided into two hostile blocs![22]

Another notion that received a surprising amount of play in the American media held that promiscuity sapped Lao martial spirit. This theory was for the most part inferred rather than asserted, but the passages devoted to Lao sexuality in publications like *Time* and *Life* were invariably accompanied by accounts of the RLA's bungling performance, and the connection was difficult to miss. For example, the same *Time* story that ridiculed RLA soldiers as "small, laughing men" who "dislike the idea of shooting at anybody" also described Lao "fertility rites...when the men wave bamboo poles topped with phallic symbols and copulating puppets and the girls look on and giggle." In another feature, *Time* noted that "a 17th century Dutch visitor...complained that he could not stroll at night in Laos because of the 'horrible fornications' all around. Things have changed very little." The magazine then proceeded to lament "the lack of aggressiveness among Laotians" and remarked that "many of the Laotian army's 25,000 men are still incompetent." *Life* devoted considerable space to discussing the "Laotians' amiable attitude toward sex," revealing that Lao "festivals...are not complete without love courts" where native girls "wait in 'sacred groves' to bestow themselves on any passing male, strangers included." Perhaps this was why the "Lao army, kept alive by U.S. aid, is not in good shape."[23]

One of the most remarkable sex-themed articles concerned the Lao elections of 1958, which Washington hoped would freeze the Pathet Lao out of the government. The Eisenhower administration had tried to build up support for conservative Lao politicians with Operation Booster Shot, a village-aid program that flooded rural Laos with food and medical and other supplies. Predictably, the program resulted in widespread corruption, and the elections saw communists increase their number of seats in the assembly. In its postmortem on this foreign-policy disaster, *Time* explained the result by noting that "the day before elections was *Balung Fai*, the annual spring Fertility Festival." Everyone in Vientiane, even "the most respected males," had been "out from dawn to late at night...carrying phallic symbols, hoisting up bamboo poles atop which puppets were shown in the act of sexual intercourse." And that was not all: "French postcards were pinned on men's sleeves, and men dressed up like women submitted to mock rape while the women stood by giggling." The next morning, the Lao staggered to the polling stations and voted red. Readers could draw their own conclusions.[24]

Had Americans not been so locked into their cartoonish conception of Laos, they might have grasped a hard fact which, in retrospect, seems

manifest: not *all* Lao were battle shy; only the RLA forces were. The Pathet
Lao fought with valor—as, for that matter, did the neutralists; in August
1960, neutralist Captain Kong Le and his single paratrooper battalion seized
Vientiane, which was not recaptured by Phoumi's American-trained divisions until December of that year. History indicated that the Lao did not suffer from some pathological distaste for warfare; it was just those Lao asked
to fight for Washington's puppet who threw in the towel. Yet Americans
ascribed U.S. reverses in Laos to flaws in the Lao national character rather
than to blind spots in U.S. foreign policy.

No one did more to encourage this perceptual confusion than Tom
Dooley, the "jungle doctor of Asia" whose 1956 bestseller *Deliver Us from
Evil*, according to his biographer, "quite literally located Vietnam on the
new world map for millions of Americans." Overlooked in scholarship on
Dooley is the extent to which he also located Laos on the map for a mass
audience. If *Deliver Us from Evil* dealt with conditions in war-torn Vietnam,
Dooley's two subsequent books concerned his experiences in Laos, where
he spent the last years of his life operating clinics under the auspices of the
International Rescue Committee. Those texts, *The Edge of Tomorrow* and
The Night They Burned the Mountain, attracted almost as wide a readership
as Dooley's debut. Moreover, it was during his sojourn in Laos that Dooley
made the tape recordings that were shipped to America and broadcast as the
Saturday dinner-hour program "That Free Men May Live." For many listeners, Dooley was their only source of information on Laos, and the images he
conveyed about this far-off kingdom did much to shape their understanding
of what the United States could accomplish there.[25]

Dooley's broadcasts and books fortified American notions of Lao
passivity. "The people of Laos are philosophically resigned to fate," he
informed his radio audience. "They become apathetic in the face of severe
crisis.... Why, I can't even get some of my nurses to kill a fly in the operating room because of their religious beliefs!" Chai, the native interpreter
whom Dooley cast as his sidekick in *The Edge of Tomorrow*, was, readers
learned, typically Lao in that "he would not kill anything." When patients
paid "for an operation with a live chicken or duck," Dooley recalled, "Chai
could not kill the birds for our dinner." Dooley was fond of the Lao—"their
simplicity is delightful"—and he related many heart-tugging anecdotes
of Lao patients rescued from "the depths of misery" by "the white man's
miraculous medicines," but he was not optimistic about the capacity of
this "drowsy people" to hold the line against communist expansion. "The
villagers... have no idea of the rift the world has suffered," he wrote. "They
understand nothing of the two camps of ideas, the God-loving men and

the godless men." These were "big issues far beyond their knowledge or understanding."[26]

The Vietnamese, on the other hand, seemed made of sterner stuff. After Kong Le captured Vientiane and compelled the National Assembly to install a new prime minister, Dooley remarked on the air, "It is amazing that a few men could overthrow a government which has been supported by a tremendously generous flow of American dollars." "However," he added, "Vietnam has simply been magnificent." In another broadcast, Dooley noted that "Vietnam, with Ngo Dinh Diem at the helm, has no queasy moments like in Laos....One is either for or against international communism, and he and his country are against it!" Had Dooley been in a position to advise Kennedy as to which Southeast Asian country was better equipped to serve as a link in the chain of defense Washington was trying to forge, there is little doubt what his recommendation would have been.[27]

Like Dooley, America's fourth estate frequently contrasted Lao stagnancy with Vietnamese dynamism. *Newsweek*'s dismal account of the RLA partying "while Laos burns" featured a sidebar that praised "tough President Diem" for mastering "the tactics that defeated the communists in Malaya." Diem's "military campaign against the guerrillas," the magazine noted, had "become increasingly effective." The *New York Times* flatly stated that "[t]he people of Laos lack the resolution of the Thais or the free Vietnamese." Another *Times* feature declared, "Laotians are uninterested in political or ideological conflict and, in contrast to the Vietnamese, will not fight." Kennedy, who read several newspapers every morning and who cultivated close relationships with many of America's leading journalists (particularly those who wrote for the *Times*), could not have failed to take note of such portrayals, and this may have disposed him to receive sympathetically UN advisor William Sullivan's admonition that while the Lao were "not fighters," the South Vietnamese were "tigers and real fighters," and that "therefore the advantages would be on our side to have a confrontation and showdown in Vietnam and not get sucked into this Laos operation."[28]

The precise moment when Kennedy decided to disavow Eisenhower's policy toward Laos is impossible to determine. Ironically, he at first assumed a more pugnacious stance than his predecessor, perhaps because he felt the need to prove his toughness. He ordered 500 marines to a base near the Thai border and upgraded Eisenhower's Program Evaluation Office into an overt military mission; from now on, Kennedy instructed, American advisors were to wear uniforms in the field with the RLA—an important symbolic shift. As if to convince the communists he meant business, Kennedy appeared on television with three maps showing Pathet Lao advances in recent months and announced that Laos's fate "will tell us something about what kind of future our world is going to have." The White House seemed to be gearing up for war.[29]

But Kennedy had moderated his tone by April 1961, supporting British prime minister Harold Macmillan's proposal for a ceasefire in Laos and indicating that he would accept Souvanna as head of a coalition government. Kennedy also agreed with Cambodian prince Norodom Sihanouk that the Geneva Conference should be reconvened to deal with the Laos crisis. When that conference began in May, Harriman headed the American delegation, and Kennedy's instructions to his representative were straightforward: "I want a settlement. I don't want to send troops." The president mollified the hawks in his administration by assuring them, "If we have to fight for Southeast Asia, we'll fight in South Vietnam."[30]

Several factors brought about this change in policy. Kennedy's humiliation at the Bay of Pigs left him wary of plunging into another military misadventure. Macmillan and French president Charles de Gaulle made clear to Kennedy their reluctance to participate in any joint offensive to save Phoumi and their preference for a political solution built around Souvanna. Logistical concerns, to be sure, weighed on Kennedy's mind. Laos was a poor locale for the employment of modern conventional forces: landlocked and 10,000 miles away, it had almost no communications and supply lines and its climate fostered tropical diseases. Without question, war in the mountains and jungles of Laos was a specter to trouble the sleep of any American commander.

Most important in persuading Kennedy to neutralize Laos, however, was the assumption that the Lao were incorrigible pacifists who, in the words of the Laos Task Force, "demonstrated little desire, willingness, or ability to defend themselves." Everything Kennedy read or heard confirmed this image. His uniformed military advisors exceeded even their civilian counterparts in heaping scorn upon the Lao. Major General Ruben Tucker, chief of the newly formed Military Assistance Advisory Group in Laos, described the RLA as "worthless," with "no stomach and no real capability" of engaging the communists, and warned Kennedy that if he committed U.S. troops to defend the Lao government, "American blood would certainly be spilled for a gutless group." Joint Chiefs of Staff chairman General Lyman Lemnitzer expressed his frustration with the RLA in an outburst redolent of the hubris that characterized U.S. policy making in the post–World War II, pre-Vietnam era. "We made good soldiers out of the Koreans," he declared. "Why can't we make good soldiers out of the Laotians?"[31]

Two encounters in particular seem to have influenced Kennedy's policy shift, and both indicate that his acceptance of a neutralist solution in Laos owed less to the issue of whether Laos's terrain lent itself to military operations than to American perceptions of the Lao as fighters. First was a report from Ambassador Winthrop Brown, who had been summoned home from Vientiane for consultations. As Brown recalled years later, Kennedy wanted to see him in private. The president got right down to business, asking, "What kind of people are these people [i.e., the Lao]?" Brown responded, "Well, sir, the policy is..." He got no further. "That's not what I asked you," Kennedy interrupted. "I said, 'What do you think, *you*, the ambassador?'" Brown then became, as he remembered, "exceedingly indiscreet and said a great many things which were critical." He expressed his "very low opinion of the Laotian army," which he described as "a feeble lot." As for the king, Brown considered him a "total zero," a "weak man" who "cried several times when he talked to me." Brown believed that most Lao were in favor of neutralism—"to the extent that there were thinking Laotians about these problems," and "there weren't too many of them." The Lao, Brown reported, felt that "if they could establish a neutral position,...all these problems would go away and they would be left alone to be peaceful." Although Washington might condemn this view as naïve, that was where the Lao stood. "They're charming, indolent, enchanting people," Brown concluded, "but they're just not very vigorous." In short, they were just about the poorest candidates imaginable to thwart the march of Southeast Asian communism.[32]

Then there was the 27 April 1961 meeting among Kennedy, the National Security Council, and the congressional leadership at which the extent of hostility toward the Lao on Capitol Hill became apparent. Kennedy wanted to gauge how much congressional support he could count on if he were to put American troops into Laos, and he arranged for the NSC to brief such legislators as Majority Leader Mike Mansfield (D-MT), Minority Leader Everett Dirksen (R-IL), Majority Whip Hubert Humphrey (D-MN), and Foreign Relations Committee chairman J. William Fulbright (D-AR); also present were Senators Richard Russell (D-GA), Styles Bridges (R-NH), and Bourke Hickenlooper (R-IA). Secretary of Defense McNamara offered a gloomy assessment of "our military capabilities" in Laos, noting that it was the "opinion of the Joint Chiefs of Staff that if United States forces became engaged...and the North Vietnamese or Chinese communists came to the aid of the Pathet Lao, we would not be able to win by conventional weapons alone." Kennedy quoted a JCS estimate that "the communists could put into Laos five men to our one," which made American victory in a limited war unlikely. Acting Secretary of State Chester Bowles added that the Chinese had "stated that they would enter Laos if we did." Kennedy then asked the assembled lawmakers for their views.

Unsurprisingly, the congressmen rejected intervention, but their verdict seemed to have little to do with the logistical issues the briefers had raised. Indeed, Russell snapped, "Logistics be damned!" What was important, in his opinion, was that America fought "where we have an ally that will fight for himself," and that did not appear to be the case in Laos. Russell, leader of the southern Democratic bloc, called Laos "an incredible fantasy." He advised the president to "write Laos off." Dirksen agreed. "[T]hese people have no fighting heart," he declared. "They do not want to kill each other, and there seems to be no fighting heart present." The senator referred to the "low casualty rates" suffered by the RLA in battle to underscore his point. Admiral Arleigh Burke, chief of Naval Operations, asked where America was going to fight "if we don't fight here," to which Bridges responded that "it is quite apparent that we have to take a firm stand somewhere, but not...where the people won't fight for themselves." Russell told Burke, "If you think Thailand and South Vietnam will fight, let's put our troops in Thailand and South Vietnam and take our stand there." Hickenlooper concurred, stating that while he "liked the idea of our taking a stand in Thailand and South Vietnam," Laos was "no place to fight a war."

There was some discussion about America's hesitant SEATO allies, the risk of igniting war with China, and the utility of nuclear weapons in a Southeast Asian theater. The topic that really pressed the congressional leadership's emotional buttons, though, was Lao unwillingness to fight, or what Mansfield termed "Laotian values." Mansfield summarized the views of his colleagues when he said that he had been thinking about Laos for a long time and that "the worst possible mistake we could make would be to intervene there." Deputy Undersecretary of State Alexis Johnson, who attended the meeting, later called it the "turning point on Laos." 27 April 1961, he affirmed, was "the date on which...the die was cast." From then on, "it was quite clear in the minds of all of us that, whatever happened, we were not going to militarily intervene." Kennedy may have decided against intervention earlier, but now he knew that senior Democrats and Republicans in Congress would support his policy.[33]

Eight days after this meeting, RLA and Pathet Lao leaders agreed upon a ceasefire, paving the way for the 1961–1962 Geneva Conference on Laos. The conference opened a week later. Representatives of the rival Lao factions and various international participants, including the United States, negotiated for fourteen months before reaching an arrangement whereby

Souvanna would head a coalition government, all foreign troops would leave Laos, and Lao territory would no longer be used as an avenue for the infiltration of neighboring countries. This was not an ideal outcome from Washington's perspective, even assuming the provisions of the agreement were carried out in good faith, but it was better than large-scale American intervention or Pathet Lao victory. Kennedy has been deservedly praised by historians for obtaining a negotiated settlement in Laos.[34]

The president chose this course, however, not because he questioned the prevailing view that America needed a noncommunist stronghold on the Asian mainland—indeed, he expanded America's role in South Vietnam while Harriman bargained at Geneva—but because he considered the Lao miserable allies. Like his fellow policy makers, and like the journalists who helped set the boundaries within which policy could be made, Kennedy reduced the Lao to a set of stereotypes: childlike, lazy, submissive, unfit to fight the free world's battles. "Because of...the Laotians' own gentle nature," Rusk recalled, "we concluded that an American stand against communist aggression in Laos would have been frustrated by the Laotians themselves." This perception, and not any insight into the virtues of nonalignment or desire to ease Cold War tensions, led Kennedy to determine that a neutralist government in Vientiane was the best result he could obtain.[35]

More important, Kennedy's Laos policy came with a hidden trip wire. He did not believe he could retreat any further in Southeast Asia. If the Viet Cong pressed their advantage against the U.S.–sponsored Saigon regime, America would have to fight. By cutting his losses in Laos, Kennedy narrowed the range of options for himself and future presidents attempting to cope with Vietnam.

NOTES

1. Kennedy cited in Walt W. Rostow, *The Diffusion of Power: An Essay in Recent History* (New York: Macmillan, 1972), 264; Robert S. McNamara, *In Retrospect: The Tragedy and Lessons of Vietnam* (New York: Random House, 1995), 37. For discrepancies in first-person accounts of the Eisenhower-Kennedy briefing, see Fred I. Greenstein and Richard H. Immerman, "What Did Eisenhower Tell Kennedy about Indochina? The Politics of Misperception," *Journal of American History* 79 (September 1992): 568–87.

2. For studies of America's pre-1963 Vietnam policy, see David L. Anderson, *Trapped by Success: The Eisenhower Administration and Vietnam, 1953–1961* (New York: Columbia University Press, 1991); James R. Arnold, *The First Domino: Eisenhower, the Military, and America's Intervention in Vietnam* (New York:

Morrow, 1991); Ronald H. Spector, *Advice and Support: The Early Years of the U.S. Army in Vietnam, 1941–1960* (New York: Free Press, 1985).

3. President of the United States to President of Viet-Nam, 9 July 1962, *Foreign Relations of the United States* [hereafter *FRUS*], 1961–1963 (Washington, D.C.: U.S. Government Printing Office, 1990), 2:511.

4. Lawrence Freedman, *Kennedy's Wars: Cuba, Berlin, Laos, and Vietnam* (New York: Oxford University Press, 2000), 298. For other works stressing logistical costs and risks, see Robert Dallek, *An Unfinished Life: John F. Kennedy, 1917–1963* (Boston: Little, Brown, 2003), 350–52; David K. Hall, "The Laos Neutralization Agreement, 1962," in Alexander L. George, Philip J. Farley, and Alexander Dallon, eds., *U.S.–Soviet Security Cooperation: Achievements, Failures, Lessons* (New York: Oxford University Press, 1988), 442; David Kaiser, *American Tragedy: Kennedy, Johnson, and the Origins of the Vietnam War* (Cambridge, Mass.: Belknap, 2000), 39–57.

5. Observer cited in Bernard B. Fall, *Anatomy of a Crisis: The Laotian Crisis of 1960–1961* (Garden City, N.Y.: Doubleday, 1969), 51. For the collaboration between Sarit and Phoumi, see Daniel Fineman, *A Special Relationship: The United States and Military Government in Thailand, 1947–1958* (Honolulu: University of Hawaii Press, 1997), 243, 247.

6. For representative works exploring how cultural biases influenced the formulation and implementation of U.S. policy toward Asia, see Mark Bradley, *Imagining Vietnam and America: The Making of Postcolonial Vietnam* (Chapel Hill: University of North Carolina Press, 2000); Melani McAlister, *Epic Encounters: Culture, Media, and U.S. Interests in the Middle East* (Berkeley: University of California Press, 2001); Andrew J. Rotter, *Comrades at Odds: The United States and India, 1947–1964* (Ithaca, N.Y.: Cornell University Press, 2000); President of the United States to President of Viet-Nam, 9 July 1962, *FRUS*, 1961–1963, 2:511; Memorandum for the President: Plan for Possible Intervention in Laos, 30 May 1961: National Security Files, Regional Security: Box 231, John F. Kennedy Library, Boston, Massachusetts (hereafter JFKL).

7. McClintock to Undersecretary: A U.S. Policy for Post-Armistice Indochina, 12 August 1954, Records of the Policy Planning Staff—1954, Lot 65D101, Record Group 59, General Records of the Department of State, National Archives II, College Park, Maryland; Legation in Laos to Department of State, 3 May 1955, *FRUS*, 1955–1957 (Washington, D.C.: U.S. Government Printing Office, 1990), 21:641–42; Embassy in Laos to Department of State, 8 January 1957, ibid., 21:875; Embassy in Laos to Department of State, 29 May 1957, ibid., 21:921; Embassy in Laos to Department of State, 6 October 1960, *FRUS*, 1958–1960 (Washington, D.C.: U.S. Government Printing Office, 1992), 16:884; Embassy in Laos to Department of State, 5 October 1960, ibid., 16:878; Dulles cited in Memorandum of Discussion at 455th Meeting of National Security Council, 12 August 1960, *FRUS*, 1958–1960, 16:788; Memorandum of Discussion at 456th Meeting of National Security Council, 18 August 1960, ibid., 16:809–10; Editorial Note, ibid., 559.

8. CIA Information Report, 26 November 1960: White House Office, Office of the Staff Secretary, International Series: Box 11, Dwight D. Eisenhower Library, Abilene, Kansas (hereafter EL); CIA Situation Report, 31 August 1960: White House Office, Office of the Staff Secretary, International Series: Box 10, EL; Embassy in Thailand to Department of State, 16 October 1960, *FRUS*, 1958–1960, 16:910; Notes by General Eisenhower on Luncheon Meeting with President Kennedy at Camp David, 22 April 1961: Post-presidential Papers, August-Walter Reed Series: Box 2, EL; Eisenhower cited in Michael M. Beschloss, *The Crisis Years: Kennedy and Khrushchev, 1960–1963* (New York: Burlingame, 1991), 397.

9. Robert Dean, *Imperial Brotherhood: Gender and the Making of the Cold War* (Amherst: University of Massachusetts Press, 2001), 32; Galbraith to Kennedy, 10 May 1961: President's Office Files, Special Correspondence: Box 29a, JFKL; Arthur Schlesinger, Jr., *A Thousand Days: John F. Kennedy in the White House* (Boston: Houghton Mifflin, 1965), 332; Theodore Sorenson, *Kennedy* (Old Saybrook, N.Y.: Konecky and Konecky, 1965), 641; Averell Harriman, Oral History, 17 January 1965, JFKL.

10. Rusk cited in Memorandum of Conversation, 12 March 1961: National Security Files, Countries: Box 130, JFKL; Memorandum of Conversation, 29 April 1961: National Security Files, Countries: Box 130a, JFKL; Record of Secretary's Conversation with General Phoumi Nosavan, 29 June 1961: ibid.; Task Force Memorandum: Critique of U.S. Policies in Laos and South Vietnam, n.d.: ibid.

11. Jacques Nevard, "Reverses in Laos Laid to 'Myth' of 'Invasion' by Powerful Foes," *New York Times*, 21 April 1961; Nevard, "Laotians Purging Vice in Vientiane," *New York Times*, 23 April 1961; "Laos: The Alarmed View," *Time* 76 (24 October 1960): 36; "Embattled Laos: Into the Slithering Jungle," *Newsweek* 57 (16 January 1961): 34; Keyes Beech, " 'Our Man in Laos' a Big One," *Philadelphia Inquirer*, 16 September 1959; Arthur Edson, "The Land of Gentle, Courteous People," *Washington Post-Herald*, 27 August 1959; "Laos: Green Confusion," *Time* 77 (31 March 1961): 15; Peggy Durdin, "The Grim Lesson of Laos," *New York Times Magazine*, 21 May 1961.

12. Oden Meeker, "Don't Forget Madame's Elephant," *Saturday Evening Post* 269 (14 January 1956): 30, 64–65, 68; Meeker, *The Little World of Laos* (New York: Scribner's, 1959), 38, 78, 14, 93, 207–8, 39.

13. David Lancashire, "Laos Important to Free World," *Providence Journal*, 29 November 1959; Warren Unna, "Laos Capital Pursues Happiness amidst Threats to Life, Liberty," *Washington Post*, 5 April 1961.

14. R. H. Shackford, "Crisis Involves Much More than Tiny Laos," *Washington News*, 27 March 1961; "Red War in Southeast Asia: An Eyewitness Account," *U.S. News and World Report* 30 (11 June 1962): 78–80; Mark S. Watson, "Rebels Rely on Discipline in Laos War," *Baltimore Sun*, 3 May 1961.

15. "Laos—The Struggle Shifts," *Christian Science Monitor*, 28 March 1961; "Truce—But Laotian Troops Lose Feet to Own Mines," *New York Herald Tribune*, 10 May 1961; Nevard, "Reverses in Laos Laid to 'Myth' of 'Invasion' "; "The Cruelest Decision," *Newsweek* 57 (8 May 1961): 42; advisors cited in "Laos: Americans

at Work," *Time* 77 (7 April 1961): 26; "Laos: Toward Nirvana," *Time* 77 (28 April 1961): 34.

16. "Laos: On the Road to Chaos," *Time* 68 (20 August 1956): 23; "Laos: The Turnip Watchers," *Time* 67 (25 March 1956): 33; "Laos: Trouble in the Hills," *Time* 66 (25 July 1955): 25; "Laos: The Unloaded Pistol," *Time* 74 (21 September 1959): 33; king cited in "Laos: The Long Reign," *Time* 74 (9 November 1959): 30; "Laos: Unattractive Choice," *Time* 77 (27 January 1961): 23.

17. "A Letter from the Publisher," *Time* 77 (17 March 1961): 3; "Laos: The White Elephant," ibid., 20–25.

18. Stanley Karnow, "The Tale of a Troubled Paradise," *Life* 47 (7 September 1959): 22–23; "President Warns of Our Peril in Laos," *Life* 50 (31 March 1961): 19–26.

19. "Laos: The Unloaded Pistol," 33; Seth Jacobs, *America's Miracle Man in Vietnam: Ngo Dinh Diem, Religion, Race, and U.S. Intervention in Southeast Asia, 1950–1957* (Durham, N.C.: Duke University Press, 2004), 190; "Americans in Laos Distressed over Apparent Failures," *New York Times*, 25 March 1961; "Laotians Fighting Reds Show 'Battle Shyness,'" *Washington Star*, 18 March 1961; "Laos: What Went Wrong," *Newsweek* 57 (15 May 1961): 44; William Ryan, "Laos Fall to Reds to Mean Perilous Days for Americans," *Denver Post*, 7 May 1961.

20. Schlesinger, *Thousand Days*, 324; Roger Hilsman, *To Move a Nation: The Politics of Foreign Policy in the Administration of John F. Kennedy* (Garden City, N.Y.: Doubleday, 1967), 96; Holt to Brown, 24 February 1961: National Security Files, Countries: Box 130, JFKL; Souvanna Phouma to Kennedy, 8 February 1961: ibid. (emphasis added); Text of King of Laos's Speech as Received in Vientiane Telegram, 18 February 1961: ibid.

21. Winthrop Brown, Oral History, 1 February 1968, JFKL; Laos—Background and Current Situation, 30 January 1961: President's Office Files, Countries: Box 121, JFKL; Critique of U.S. Policies in Laos and South Vietnam, n.d.: National Security Files, Countries: Box 130a, JFKL.

22. Norman Cousins, "Report from Laos," *Saturday Review* 51 (18 February 1961): 13, 47; Chalmers Roberts, "Laos Is a Story of Change," *Washington Post*, 26 March 1961; "Laos: The White Elephant," 21–22.

23. "Laos: Test of U.S. Intentions," *Time* 77 (17 March 1961): 22; "Laos: The Unloaded Pistol," 33; Karnow, "Tale of a Troubled Paradise," 22–23.

24. "Laos: The Nameless Menace," *Time* 71 (19 May 1958): 26.

25. James T. Fisher, *Dr. America: The Lives of Thomas A. Dooley, 1927–1961* (Amherst: University of Massachusetts Press, 1997), 34–35.

26. "That Free Men May Live" (hereafter TFMML), 25 May 1957, Thomas A. Dooley Papers, Western Historical Manuscript Collection, University of Missouri, St. Louis, Series VII—Tapes; Thomas A. Dooley, *The Edge of Tomorrow* (New York: Farrar, Straus, and Cudahy, 1958), 32; Dooley, *The Night They Burned the Mountain* (New York: Farrar, Straus, and Cudahy, 1960), 87; *Edge of Tomorrow*, 41, 53; *Night They Burned the Mountain*, 112; *Edge of Tomorrow*, 107, 126.

27. TFMML, 23 November 1960, Thomas A. Dooley Collection, Pius XII Library, St. Louis University, Missouri, Teresa Gallagher File; TFMML, 22 June 1957, Dooley Papers, Series VII—Tapes.

28. "While Laos Burns," *Newsweek* 57 (3 April 1961): 22–24; Drew Middleton, "Geneva Talks: Laos Roadblocks," *New York Times*, 11 June 1961; "New Look at Laos," *New York Times*, 12 May 1962; Sullivan cited in Timothy N. Castle, *At War in the Shadow of Vietnam: U.S. Military Aid to the Royal Lao Government, 1955–1975* (New York: Columbia University Press, 1993), 41.

29. President's News Conference, 23 March 1961, in *Public Papers of the Presidents: John F. Kennedy, 1961* (Washington, D.C.: U.S. Government Printing Office, 1962), 214.

30. Kennedy cited in Freedman, *Kennedy's Wars*, 304; A. J. Langguth, *Our Vietnam: The War, 1954–1975* (New York: Simon & Schuster, 2000), 132.

31. Task Force Memorandum: Arguments against Any Military Action in Laos, n.d.: National Security Files, Countries: Box 130a, JFKL; Tucker cited in Memorandum for the President, Subject: Capabilities of the Royal Laotian Government Forces, 21 February 1962: National Security Files, Countries: Box 131, JFKL; CHMAAG (chief of the U.S. Military Assistance Advisory Group) Laos to CINCPAC (commander in chief of the U.S. Pacific Command), Joint Chiefs of Staff, 16 May 1962: President's Office Files, Countries: Box 121, JFKL; Lemnitzer cited in Winthrop Brown, Oral History, 1 February 1968, JFKL.

32. Winthrop Brown, Oral History, 1 February 1968, JFKL.

33. C. V. Clifton, Meeting of Congressional Leaders with the President, 27 April 1961: National Security Files, Chester V. Clifton Series, Conferences with the President: JFKL; U. Alexis Johnson, Memorandum on the President's Meeting with Congressional Leaders, 27 April 1961: ibid.; U. Alexis Johnson, Oral History, 11 April 1967, JFKL.

34. For an especially positive assessment of Kennedy's Laos policy, see Edmund F. Wehrle, " 'A Good, Bad Deal': John F. Kennedy, W. Averell Harriman, and the Neutralization of Laos, 1961–1962," *Pacific Historical Review* 67 (August 1998): 349–77.

35. Dean Rusk, *As I Saw It* (New York: Penguin, 1990), 428–29.

EXPLAINING THE VIETNAM WAR

Dominant and Contending Paradigms

GARETH PORTER

In every field of study in the physical sciences, the dominant framework or paradigm for carrying out research on a given problem is not subject to critical debate until it begins to break down. As Thomas Kuhn showed in analyzing the process of establishing scientific paradigms, a dominant paradigm begins to weaken only after researchers find that it has failed to account for too many "anomalies"—i.e., contradictions between paradigmatic assumptions and empirical realities of significance.[1]

Obvious structural differences separate the relationship between paradigmatic assumptions and research in the physical sciences from that same relationship in the social sciences. Whereas in the physical sciences, the basic assumptions which constitute the dominant paradigm are explicit and universally known, in historical interpretation they are more likely to be implicit rather than explicit. And there is never complete unanimity on those paradigmatic assumptions among historians, because heterodox countercurrents of interpretation inevitably spring up even when a dominant paradigm is at its peak of influence.

Nevertheless, historical research and interpretation also take place within something like paradigmatic frameworks, and historical writings on the U.S. path to war in Vietnam are no exception. The interpretation of U.S. policy making toward Vietnam up to mid-1965 has been shaped by certain assumptions about the nature of world politics of the period, about the ways of thinking and motivations of U.S. policy makers, and about how the policy-making process in national security works in the U.S. government. Despite differences of view among historians over many questions surrounding the broad issue of Vietnam policy, commonly held—and unexamined—assumptions about those questions can be viewed as a paradigmatic framework for interpretation, which has influenced the literature on U.S. Vietnam policy.

In this chapter, I analyze and critique that dominant paradigm, which may be called the "Cold War consensus" paradigm, regarding the explanation for the U.S. march to war in Vietnam.[2] I will identify what I regard as its fundamental weaknesses: the historical facts for which it has failed to account. In the final section, I introduce an alternative to the dominant paradigm, which I call the "power imbalance" paradigm, because the impact of U.S. military dominance is central to the dynamic that I believe underlay the policy-making process on Vietnam.

In suggesting that paradigmatic assumptions have shaped the historical narrative of the road to war in Vietnam, I am not arguing that historians have consciously adopted such a paradigm—or any other paradigm—as the framework for their account of policy making. The purpose of most of these works has not been to explain *why* the United States fought a war in Vietnam but to fashion a narrative highlighting certain features of the policy or the policy-making process. In *Planning a Tragedy*, published in 1982, Larry Berman wrote, "I have no grand theory for explaining the failure of Vietnam decision-making, nor do I believe that one is necessary."[3] Two works that are extremely critical of U.S. policy, *Intervention* by George McT. Kahin and *The Vietnam Wars, 1945–1990* by Marilyn Young, were not aimed at an overarching explanation for the U.S. war in Vietnam but at elucidating the contradictions inherent in the policy and its consequences.[4]

The influence of paradigmatic assumptions on historical writing does not operate through any conscious decision to stay within any specific parameters. It is precisely the absence of a conscious paradigmatic framework in the studies of Vietnam policy that has allowed what I argue is the dominant paradigm on the road to war in Vietnam to influence the narrative line. In selecting the issues, episodes, and documents to be used in a narrative as well as in interpreting their meaning, a historian without an alternative explanatory hypothesis to guide research inevitably reflects certain commonly held assumptions about such questions as the relationship of the Vietnam issue to the broader distribution of power in the world and the way in which national security policy works in the United States.

There is a well-established pattern in the literature on Vietnam of citing public statements and official national security documents on the threat to Southeast Asia as evidence of the thought processes and even motivations that are presumed to have driven U.S. policy. Thus, speeches with combative Cold War rhetoric or statements in interviews that define the U.S. strategic interest in South Vietnam by John F. Kennedy have long been considered to demonstrate his commitment to defeating the communist insurgents in South Vietnam. The documentation now available about Vietnam policy making, however, suggests that national security officials had motives for advocating war that were quite unrelated to the official definitions of threat—motives that would be less acceptable if they were acknowledged. And those motives and interests were not the same as the interests of the president. The policy-making process on Vietnam that is revealed by the full range of documentary sources was a sharp political struggle between conflicting interests in the executive branch. Because of the power of the dominant paradigm, an unrealistic picture of the policy-making process on Vietnam has prevailed. That contradiction is part of the reason that a paradigm shift is needed.

The Cold War Consensus Paradigm

The Cold War consensus paradigm has been based on three central assumptions:

- The power relationship between the United States and the communist world was irrelevant to the making of U.S. policy toward Vietnam.
- National security policy makers, from the president on down, were under the sway of a U.S. Cold War ideology of "containment" of communism, which considered a possible communist takeover anywhere in the world as a serious threat.
- Presidential personalities and attitudes are the primary driving forces in going to war, because decisions on the use of military force are ultimately made on the president's absolute constitutional authority.

The evidence for the first assumption underlying the Cold War consensus paradigm—the irrelevance of the power relationship between the United States and the Communist world to the making of U.S. policy—is the almost complete absence of any discussion of power relations at the global or regional levels in the literature on Vietnam policy. A partial exception to this generalization might be made in regard to some discussions of the period of 1949–1952, when the official U.S. perception was that the regional balance of power in Southeast Asia had begun to tip toward the communist side—and that it threatened the global power balance as well.[5] But in the accounts of policy making from the Eisenhower administration through the big U.S. troop buildup in 1965, the power relationship between the United States and the communist world simply disappears from the literature.

It is not surprising that historians have assumed that global power relations were irrelevant to Vietnam policy making. For decades, both historians of the Cold War and students of international politics have shared the view that the international system during the 1954–1965 period was a bipolar balance of power, or at least a "balance of terror", between the superpowers. The literature on the period is dominated by a focus on policies of "containment" and "deterrence," which were based on the assumption that the two superpowers were indeed roughly comparable in their power.[6]

The second assumption—that policy was shaped primarily by the beliefs of policy makers about the threat from communism—follows logically from the first assumption. The belief about the imperative of responding to the threat by using force, if necessary, has been reflected in a large number of works reflecting different attitudes toward the war. Some of these works reflect an obvious sympathy with the assumed Cold War consensus, whereas others have regarded it as a case of highly distorted thinking that brought disastrous consequences. The first variant is represented by the viewpoint underlying the narrative in the Pentagon Papers, and in a subsequent book coauthored by Leslie Gelb, a primary author of the Pentagon Papers, and Richard Betts. They argued that national security policy makers, from the president on down, were unwilling to withdraw from Vietnam because they consistently feared that the strategic consequences of defeat in the Vietnam were too great to risk. Gelb and Betts asserted that the "domino theory" was "at the heart of the matter" and had "held sway over U.S. strategic thinking for twenty years." Gelb and Betts further argued that this strategic belief was "persuasive" and even "sound" as a basis for policy making.[7] Herbert Y. Schandler argued in an early study of Vietnam policy making in the Johnson administration that the belief of U.S. policy makers that South Vietnam was vital to U.S. security was reasonable under the circumstances.[8]

The more prominent tendency in the literature, which is exemplified by Stanley Karnow's popular history of the war, is to argue that the domino theory and the Cold War strategic beliefs it encapsulated were sadly misguided but were nevertheless driving forces.[9] The theme of a lack of critical reflection on Cold War doctrines unites a number of historical accounts. Michael H. Hunt referred to "a firm Cold War consensus amounting almost to a religion among the nation's best and brightest" and to McGeorge Bundy's "deeply held, largely unexamined, and untested Cold War faith." Hunt described a key 1964 McNamara memo as reminding Johnson of "how Cold War axioms applied to Vietnam."[10] Similarly, George C. Herring wrote in the preface to the first edition of *America's Longest War* that the U.S. involvement in Vietnam "was a logical, if not inevitable outgrowth of a world view and a policy, the policy of containment, which Americans in and out of government accepted without serious questions for more than two decades."[11] Robert D. Schulzinger echoed that interpretation, observing that the "depth of the U.S. leaders' commitment to the principles of containment" make it hard to believe that Kennedy would not have gone to war had he lived.[12]

David Kaiser also appears to accept the Cold War consensus framework, if only by implication. He writes that virtually all of the senior civilian and military leaders of the Kennedy and Johnson administrations were part of a "GI generation" that had a "great capacity for teamwork, and consensus and a relentless optimism," but whose weaknesses "included an unwillingness to question basic assumptions, or to even admit the possibility of failure."[13]

A notable exception to the acceptance of the assumption that unquestioned adherence to Cold War principles drove the Vietnam policy makers is Fredrik Logevall, who devotes an extensive section in *Choosing War* to refuting the alleged power of what he calls the "Cold War Consensus that emerged in the early postwar period" on thinking about Vietnam. In the U.S. political system of the early 1960s, Logevall argues, the consensus was no longer unchallengeable in Congress and the media, because "the Cold War itself had changed." He expresses doubt that "geostrategic considerations" were actually driving the policy makers who advocated the U.S. war in Vietnam, suggesting instead that "domestic political credibility and even personal credibility" were more important factors. He even advances an individual political "sunk costs" theory—that some of those who had committed themselves to a course of war in Vietnam early on became subject to "individual careerist considerations."[14]

The third assumption—that U.S. policy reflected the authority of the president over decisions to make war—appears to be even more deeply entrenched in the literature than the other two, because it is related to a fundamental belief about American democracy. The idea that the president is the commander in chief of the U.S. military forces and has full power over any decision to use military force is one that is shared across the political spectrum in regard to foreign policy, and it has been both reinforced by and in turn reinforces the assumption that the Cold War presidents were central to the Cold War consensus. Thus, a very large literature has portrayed Dwight D. Eisenhower, John F. Kennedy, and Lyndon B. Johnson as adopting the Cold War beliefs that have been viewed as driving forces on the road to war in Vietnam. Eisenhower's policy in the 1954 Indochina crisis has been interpreted as one of readiness to go to war, which was frustrated by the insistence of congressional leaders on British and French commitments to "united action" and the unwillingness of the British and French to support a U.S. military intervention in the war as an alternative to the Geneva settlement. Eisenhower's articulation of the domino theory in April 1954, following by only a few days Secretary of State John Foster Dulles's "United Action" speech, has been generally viewed as a crystallization of the strategic beliefs that drove U.S. policy toward Vietnam. The Eisenhower-Dulles engineering in September 1954 of the Southeast Asia Treaty Organization (SEATO), which would be cited by subsequent administrations as a commitment to South Vietnam's security, completes the basic outline of the narrative of Eisenhower's Vietnam policy that has been accepted by many historians.[15]

For decades, Kennedy was viewed by virtually every historian who has written on the period as determined to hold on to South Vietnam and rejecting any negotiated solution.[16] Works by John M. Newman, David Kaiser, and Howard Jones have begun to revise that picture of Kennedy, showing that he was skeptical of a full military commitment to South Vietnam and even tried to withdraw U.S. troops from South Vietnam on a timetable. Most of these works conclude that it is impossible to know what Kennedy might have done had he lived, but that his policy may well have been different from the one pursued by the Johnson administration.[17]

None of these studies challenges the paradigmatic assumption that the president was fully in charge of Vietnam policy, however. By pointing to an interest on Kennedy's part in the idea of a neutralist settlement and asserting that he did intend to withdraw, however, John M. Newman's *JFK and Vietnam* comes close to suggesting the need for a fundamentally different understanding of the dynamics underlying Vietnam policy making. But Newman argues that deceptively optimistic presentations of the situation in South Vietnam persuaded Kennedy not to pursue a settlement.[18]

Nevertheless, Newman's argument that Kennedy probably would have withdrawn from Vietnam—which is sharply at odds with the Cold War consensus paradigm—provoked a counterattack from a number of historians who remained convinced that there was no fundamental break with the consensus. These historians have cited the absence of internal documentation of such a policy until October 1963, Kennedy's public statements suggesting a determination to stay in South Vietnam, his alleged rejection of peace negotiations on South Vietnam, and Robert F. Kennedy's denial in a 1964 oral history that JFK had seriously considered such a withdrawal as evidence against the Kennedy withdrawal thesis.[19]

If the Cold War consensus view of Kennedy's role in Vietnam policy has become the weakest link in the dominant paradigm, the interpretation of Lyndon Johnson's role has remained its strongest link. The literature has overwhelmingly laid the responsibility for going to war squarely on the shoulders of Johnson. In large part, that interpretation reflects the assumption that the "central figure in the policy making" is the president, as Logevall puts it.[20] Herring's account of the 1963–1965 period reflects the paradigmatic assumption of presidential power by referring repeatedly to "the administration," making no distinction whatever between the role of Johnson's advisors and LBJ's own role in policy making.[21]

But apart from presidential power over the use of force, Johnson has undoubtedly been seen as the driving force in the march to war in large part because his personality and style have appeared to historians to be so congruent with a belligerent stance on Vietnam. Johnson was an insecure bully whose crude macho way of communicating and lack of comfort with the use of diplomacy distinguished him sharply from Kennedy.[22] Departing from the dominant view of Johnson as the main force for war in his administration, works by Kahin and H. R. McMaster document significant resistance by LBJ to recommendations for moves toward war.[23] However, the authors of two major studies of U.S. policy making, Logevall and Kaiser, do not deal with the evidence presented in these earlier works of serious conflict between Johnson and his advisors over their advocacy of war. Instead, they make no distinction at all between Johnson and his advisors, portraying Johnson as not only the formal decision maker but also the leading advocate of the use of force in Vietnam. Indeed, Logevall relies heavily on a theme from some of the early literature on Vietnam policy—the importance of Lyndon Johnson's personal insecurity as a factor in his alleged preference for military force in Vietnam.[24]

Historical accounts of the policy making that led to war in Vietnam, with the few exceptions noted, have reflected these three paradigmatic assumptions: the irrelevance of the power relations, the adherence of policy makers to Cold War doctrines, and the primacy of the presidents in policy making. Although the interpretation of Kennedy's role in the policy making as falling within the Cold War consensus has been challenged in recent years, this element of the dominant paradigm has also been reaffirmed both by vigorous counterattack on the Kennedy withdrawal thesis and by a renewed focus on Johnson as having primary responsibility for leading the country into war.

Anomalies of the Cold War Consensus Paradigm

Although the Cold War consensus paradigm appears to have maintained its dominant position among historians of U.S. national security policy, the narratives of U.S. policy-making making based on the three key assumptions outlined above have failed to account for some major, well-documented historical facts. To put it in the language of paradigm shift, the historical record now available has yielded a number of "anomalies"—phenomena which should not have occurred, according to the paradigmatic assumptions. I find four major patterns in the historical record that can be considered to be anomalous in terms of the dominant paradigm:

- U.S. perceptions of Soviet and Chinese weakness were the dominant factor in the initial phase of U.S. political-military involvement in South Vietnam.
- Leading national security officials put pressure on the presidents to go to war in Vietnam from 1961 to 1965, but Presidents Kennedy and Johnson put up significant resistance to that pressure.
- The arguments about strategic interests at stake in the Vietnam conflict that were used for political purposes were not the ones actually discussed by national security officials among themselves.
- National security officials repeatedly emphasized the favorable opportunities presented by the U.S. power advantage, rather than the threat from the communist world, in their advocacy of the use of force in Vietnam.

Each of these anomalies is outlined briefly here, summarizing the research in my own study of the road to war in Vietnam.[25]

Perceptions of Communist Weakness and Eisenhower's Vietnam Policy

The Cold War consensus explanation for the U.S. road to war assumes that the policy decisions made by President Dwight D. Eisenhower and Secretary of State John Foster Dulles from 1954 to 1955, which catapulted the United States into the position of major power patron in South Vietnam, were prompted by adherence to Cold War beliefs about the necessity to respond to the dire threat from communism in Southeast Asia.[26] What the records of that period reveal, however, is quite different: ignoring Cold War doctrines, Eisenhower and Dulles refused even to consider using military force to try to prevent a communist takeover of Vietnam. Eisenhower told a meeting of the National Security Council in early January 1954 that there was "no sense in even talking about United States force replacing the French in Indochina" and concluded by saying, "with vehemence," according to the notes of the meeting, "I cannot tell how bitterly opposed I am to such a course of action." He repeated that he was "bitterly opposed" to U.S. military intervention in the region at a 10 February press conference and again in his press conference of 31 March 1954.[27]

As an alternative to military intervention in Indochina, Eisenhower and Dulles relied on the knowledge that the United States held strategic dominance over the communist world for a strategy of coercion of the Viet Minh aimed at the Soviet Union and China.[28] Based on intelligence analysis that the Soviets and Chinese would not be willing to "invoke serious risk of attacks on the Chinese mainland," Dulles believed that China could be induced by the use of strategic threats to drop its support for the Viet Minh, thus affecting the outcome of the negotiations in Geneva. That was the purpose of Dulles's "United Action" speech, as well as Dulles's proposal to Britain and France for a "deterrent action" to intimidate China—not a move to prepare for an actual joint intervention in Indochina.

After the Soviets and Chinese had forced the Viet Minh to accept a division of the country with a promise of an election within two years, Dulles considered the strategy of exploiting U.S. strategic dominance to have been a spectacular success, and he concluded that the communist powers would continue to pursue a defensive posture in Indochina for the indefinite future. An intelligence estimate in November 1954 suggested that the communist bloc's global strategy probably would sacrifice "the ambitions of local Communist parties," if necessary, to preserve peace with the United States. The knowledge that the Soviets and Chinese would not allow the North Vietnamese to violate the Geneva truce gave Eisenhower and Dulles the confidence to authorize a covert operation in South Vietnam beginning in early 1955, using South Vietnamese troops and CIA-sponsored "civic action" teams to destroy the powerful but now virtually disarmed communist movement through mass arrests and summary executions.

The new intelligence assessment of the Soviet posture in Vietnam as defensive also encouraged Dulles to make the fateful decision in mid-June 1955 to dispense completely with the Geneva accords' provisions for national elections, in the confident belief that this action would not result in any serious challenge from Hanoi. That decision resulted in a reversal of South Vietnamese president Ngo Dinh Diem's position on the elections. Diem had previously offered to negotiate with North Vietnam on the terms for such an election, in the belief that the United States was planning to take that position.

The historical record on the policy decisions made by Eisenhower and Dulles in 1954–1955 represents a direct challenge to the Cold War consensus paradigm. Those decisions should have been made under the influence of Cold War doctrines of threat, according to the paradigmatic assumptions, but they were not. And the Eisenhower administration's policy should not have been encouraged by evidence of Soviet and Chinese weakness on Vietnam, according to the assumption that the East-West power balance was irrelevant to Vietnam policy making. But, in fact, the primary factor shaping those policy decisions was the perception that U.S. military dominance over the communist powers had caused the Soviets and Chinese to accommodate U.S. power in Vietnam.

Kennedy and Johnson Resisted Pressures from the National Security Bureaucracy

According to the assumptions of the Cold War consensus paradigm, the major policy decisions on Vietnam from 1961 to 1965 should have reflected the policy preferences of the president rather than those of the national security bureaucracy. The historical record reveals, however, that the policy-making process during that period was driven by the policy preferences of key national security officials for the use of U.S. military force in Vietnam.[29] It also shows that Kennedy and Johnson repeatedly resisted the pressures for a U.S. war in Vietnam.

Since the declassification of the documents on the crucial NSC meetings in 1961, Kennedy's refusal to send troops, as recommended unanimously by his top advisors, has been acknowledged in all historical accounts. What has not been reflected in the literature, however, is the degree to which Kennedy's national security team put pressure on him to send troops to Southeast Asia. The national security bureaucracy made five separate proposals to JFK for either the deployment of troops or for a study of options for the deployment of U.S. combat troops to Laos or Vietnam in just seven months (2 May, 12 May, 28 July, 11 October, and 6–14 November). In the first three cases, Kennedy deflected the pressure by attaching to any possible future combat deployment a diplomatic condition which he knew could not be achieved. But he also showed by the care with which he handled each case that he was aware of the potential political cost of having the entire national security bureaucracy oppose his policy in Southeast Asia. Under relentless pressure, in October he began to make some small and partial accommodations with his advisors, first by agreeing to send an air force squadron to South Vietnam on a training mission and then to send Walt W. Rostow and White House military advisor Maxwell Taylor to South Vietnam to make recommendations. Kennedy's agreement in November to a large increase in the number of U.S. advisors and the deployment of aircraft to South Vietnam did not represent any change in JFK's view of Vietnam, because he made it very clear in the crucial NSC meeting on 15 November that he did not regard holding on to South Vietnam as comparable to other Cold War interests over which the United States had been willing to use force.

The fact that Kennedy had to struggle to regain control over his administration's Vietnam policy is underlined by his effort over a period of more than eighteen months, from the spring of 1962 to his death in November 1963, to reverse that decision both by opening up a diplomatic channel to Hanoi and by initiating a policy of withdrawing U.S. troops from South Vietnam by the end of 1965. In April 1962, Kennedy ordered Harriman to send instructions to Ambassador John Kenneth Galbraith in New Delhi to communicate to Hanoi through the Indian Foreign Ministry a willingness to talk about mutual deescalation in South Vietnam. Harriman scotched that JFK diplomatic initiative, however, by sitting on the draft telegram which had been prepared by his deputy for Southeast Asia.

Then Kennedy, in direct contradiction to the assumption underlying the Cold War consensus paradigm, began to pursue a policy of a phased withdrawal of U.S. military personnel by the end of 1965. The policy initiative was introduced by McNamara at a conference on Vietnam in Honolulu on 8 May 1962, and, in July, the decision for the training of South Vietnamese to replace all U.S. advisors "during the next three year period" was officially adopted. That initiative could only have come from Kennedy himself, first, because it was far too sensitive a decision to have been taken by anyone except the president, and second, because McNamara had been on the side of the JCS *against* JFK's resistance to the presence of U.S. combat troops, both in November and again in a 1 March meeting with Kennedy and the Joint Chiefs of Staff.

Contrary to the argument by some historians that the phased withdrawal plan was contingent on an optimistic view of the prospects for defeating the communist movement in three years, the Military Assistance Command Vietnam (MACV) rejected the three-year timetable. Instead, it submitted a plan in March 1963 that would have left in Vietnam as many as 12,200 U.S. advisors by mid-1965. Nevertheless, McNamara not only insisted that the withdrawal should be completed by the end of fiscal year 1965 (i.e., mid-1965), but said he wanted the first 1,000 U.S. troops to be withdrawn by the end of 1963—and that the withdrawal should not be contingent on success in the counterinsurgency war but based upon "the assumption that such a course of action would be feasible."[30]

In July, the commander in chief of the U.S. Pacific Command (CINCPAC), Admiral Harry Felt, again pushed back, insisting that the first withdrawal should take place "only if progress in the counterinsurgency campaign warrants such action." After the Diem regime stumbled into a political crisis in August, the JCS agreed with the CINCPAC position, agreeing to support the first withdrawal only if it still seemed warranted after they had reevaluated the situation around 31 October.

This sharp conflict between JFK and the military leadership over the issue of withdrawal from Vietnam represents a major anomaly for which the Cold War consensus paradigm cannot account. If there were no fundamental conflict in the executive branch over war policy, then Kennedy should not have been advocating a policy of withdrawal that was unacceptable to the military leadership. And if the president were really unchallenged, not only legally but also politically, Kennedy's Machiavellian maneuvering through McNamara and outside the NSC channels should have not have occurred.

The bureaucratic politics of Vietnam in the Johnson administration also contradict the paradigmatic assumptions about absolute presidential primacy in Vietnam policy. There is surely no parallel in modern history to the thirteen separate attempts by the national security bureaucracy over a fourteen-month period, from late November 1963 to February 1965, to get Johnson to authorize the use of military force against North Vietnam. Significantly, Johnson rebuffed every one of them except for the alleged second Tonkin Gulf, when he was not informed by McNamara on the afternoon of 4 August of the serious doubts of commanders in the Pacific about whether an attack had actually occurred after a strike had been approved by Johnson at a luncheon meeting.

Contrary to the paradigmatic assumption, Johnson's opposition to the option proposed by his advisors—bombing North Vietnam to gain leverage in South Vietnam—actually grew stronger after that incident, because Johnson quickly realized that he had been misled. Thus, an early September plan, on which all parts of the national security bureaucracy agreed, for provoking a North Vietnamese attack on U.S. ships in order to justify further bombing of the North had to be abandoned after a meeting between the president and the ambassador to Saigon, Maxwell Taylor. And in mid-September, when McNamara and Rusk tried to tell him that there had been a third North Vietnamese naval attack on U.S. vessels in the gulf and urged a retaliatory response, Johnson demanded proof of the attack and chided McNamara for his claim of an attack in August, which Johnson now knew had been false. His often-quoted antiwar speeches during the presidential campaign were not a cover for planning for future war in Vietnam, as has been long assumed, but paralleled Johnson's private expressions of irritation with McNamara over his advocacy of the bombing program.

Yet another pivotal event that should not have happened, according to the paradigmatic assumption, was LBJ's rejection of the unanimous recommendation of his national security team after his election in November 1964 of a policy of "graduated pressures" against North Vietnam aimed at eliciting a "sign of yielding by Hanoi." When the recommendation came back from the White House, the beginning of that campaign was made contingent on the establishment of political stability in South Vietnam—the position which LBJ had been taking since September and which his advisors had been determined to change.

The relationship between Johnson and his advisors in the weeks that followed that rebuff by LBJ contrasts even more starkly with the paradigmatic assumptions about the relationship between the president and his national security advisors. McGeorge Bundy, William Bundy, Taylor, and McNamara were increasingly disturbed by Johnson's unwillingness to stem the tide of defeatism and neutralism rising in Saigon, about which they had persistently warned the president, by beginning a bombing campaign. Both Bundy brothers concluded that LBJ was "stalling" in the hope that just such a neutralist solution would allow him to avoid going to war and that he was thus prepared to lose South Vietnam.

McGeorge Bundy and McNamara finally confronted Johnson directly on 27 January, telling him that the "essentially passive role" he was playing would "only lead to eventual defeat and an invitation to get out in humiliating circumstances." Johnson could hardly have failed to note the implicit political message underlying that warning—that if he did nothing to avert such a "humiliating" defeat, he could no longer count on their support against the inevitable political attacks. It was a clear expression of the power of national security advisors to exert political leverage on the president on politically sensitive issues involving the use of U.S. military power.

Johnson began to cave in to the advocates of bombing, reversing his position on the political precondition for the "graduated pressures." But after the embassy reported a "likely trend toward neutralism and anti-Americanism" under the new government of General Nguyen Khanh, Johnson insisted once more that "a stable Saigon government is an essential prerequisite to other activities." He agreed to retaliatory strikes only after McGeorge Bundy employed a ruse to convince him that a Viet Cong sapper attack on the U.S. base at Pleiku had been planned by Hanoi in collusion with Moscow to test the U.S. reaction to an attack while Bundy was in South Vietnam. In an administration in which the president was driving the policy toward war in Vietnam and was convinced of the need to prevail in South Vietnam whatever the cost, that ruse would have been unnecessary.

Policy Makers Expressed Different Concerns Privately

According to the assumptions of the dominant paradigm, U.S. officials should have been preoccupied primarily with the threat of communism in Southeast Asia. The threat of a domino effect from the loss of Vietnam or just South Vietnam has been generally regarded as the essence of official thinking about U.S. strategic interests at stake in the Vietnam conflict. But a closer examination of what policy makers were saying among themselves reveals that their real concern was not a rising tide of communism in the region but the possibility that failing to use force in Vietnam could lead to the collapse of the overarching U.S. East Asia Cold War strategy of pressure on the communist regime in China.[31]

When Eisenhower first suggested that the loss of Indochina would cause a "falling domino" effect in Southeast Asia in a press conference in early April 1954, it was part of an administration strategy to make the USSR and China worry that the United States might well take military action if the Viet Minh war effort against the French in Indochina was not brought to a halt. In treating it as a touchstone of strategic thinking, historians have ignored the fact that Dulles and Undersecretary of State Walter Bedell Smith had explicitly backtracked in congressional testimony on an earlier argument that there would be a "chain reaction" in Southeast Asia if the Viet Minh were to drive the French out of Indochina. They have also generally forgotten that, a little over a month after Eisenhower's presentation of the domino image, Dulles publicly rejected the "so-called domino theory," as he presented his plan for a security pact in the region.

One searches the record of the Kennedy and Johnson administrations' deliberations in vain for an internal discussion of the threat of communism in the region or for evidence that any senior policy maker believed that such an eventuality was realistic. What one finds instead is that policy makers were cynical about using whatever argument they calculated would serve to advance their cause, even when they knew it was a vast exaggeration, if not completely false. The Taylor-Rostow mission to Southeast Asia in 1961 was given a briefing at the U.S. embassy in Thailand that made it absolutely clear that the country faced no threat from the indigenous communist movement, which they learned was "small and did not have much handle to use for its work." But in writing their report, they ignored what they were told and argued that, with success in South Vietnam, communism would "gather momentum throughout Southeast Asia."

In May 1964, Johnson complained that Rusk, Bundy, and McNamara were trying to convince him that Vietnam would be "a domino that will kick off a whole list of others." Johnson then asked the CIA for its view on whether Southeast Asia would "necessarily fall if Laos and South Vietnam came under North Vietnamese control." The agency's analysts promptly debunked that idea as well as the argument that noncommunist Southeast Asia would "bandwagon" to the side of China. And even after he had renounced the use of the domino theory within the executive branch, William Bundy had no scruples about recommending that it be used to sell an aggressive policy in Vietnam to the public during the 1964 congressional election campaign.

Key national security advisors were not concerned about the rise of communism or loss of independence in Southeast Asia but about the increased likelihood that noncommunist Southeast Asian states—particularly Thailand—would be more inclined to opt out of the U.S. strategy for surrounding, isolating, and pressuring China by the implicit threat of military attack, which was often referred to as "containment" of China. That strategy had been reaffirmed as recently as November 1962, when the State Department drafted a paper warning against any action that would "reduce the pressures operating on the regime," including "pressures from our military presence in the Taiwan Strait, Korea and Southeast Asia."

The ultimate concern of the president's principal advisors was that Japan would succumb to what William Bundy called "the growing feeling that Communist China must somehow be lived with." The immediate concern, however, was Thailand, a military ally which had allowed the United States to build air bases, which could be used to bomb North Vietnam or China. As CIA director John McCone told McNamara in mid-1962, Bangkok had a "historical propensity to adjust to the prevailing trends in the area" and would "move toward neutralism and seek accommodation with the Communist bloc should the U.S. position in Southeast Asia show additional signs of weakness." When William Bundy proposed a negotiated withdrawal from South Vietnam in November 1964, McNamara and Rusk called him to tell him that was unacceptable. Their argument, according to Bundy, was that "the problems of carrying on" after the loss of South Vietnam—meaning, carrying on the existing U.S. Cold War strategy of "containing" China—would be "nearly insuperable" if the United States did not use force in Vietnam. Seven months later, in the final internal debate over whether to have an open-ended commitment of ground combat forces in South Vietnam, Bundy warned his colleagues that, if the United States didn't "make a try" with more combat troops in South Vietnam, the Thais would "cash in their chips" either by accommodating with China or by establishing a "left neutralist" government.

The concern that animated the principal national security officials in the Kennedy-Johnson era, therefore, was not that communism would spread through Southeast Asia, as the Cold War consensus paradigm suggests. Rather, it was that accommodation with China would have threatened existing U.S. policy and forced those officials to adopt a policy based on the premise that China would have to be "lived with." This anomaly suggests that the Cold War consensus paradigm has been leading historians down a blind alley, by focusing them on the wrong reason for the national security advisors' readiness for war in Vietnam.

The Rationale for War Was Related to U.S. Power Advantage

The Cold War consensus paradigm has long directed the attention of historians to the few pieces of documentary evidence, such as Johnson Administration's NSAM [National Security Action Memorandum] 288, that refer to the dire strategic consequences of a failure to use force to prevent a communist victory in South Vietnam. A closer examination of the reasoning underlying the proposals for war by key national security advisors shows, however, that they were attracted to the use of force in Vietnam in 1961 and again in 1964 as a low-cost, low-risk option, precisely because of the lopsided U.S. power advantage over the Soviet Union and China.[32] When Kennedy entered the White House, the National Security Council staff briefed Kennedy on the dramatic military weakening of China because of starvation conditions and concluded that its weakness, combined with the "problematic nature of Soviet support" would make for "a cautious Communist approach in Southeast Asia." The explicit premise of the recommendation to JFK to make a commitment to the defeat of the insurgency with U.S. forces, if necessary, in November 1961, embraced by the JCS, McNamara, and Rusk, was that an initial force commitment, combined with a public commitment to victory and a warning to Hanoi that it must cease and desist, would probably make it unnecessary to send large numbers of troops. Taylor had assured the president that North Vietnam would be afraid to send troops to the South because it was "highly vulnerable" to air attacks and to China.

McNamara's March 1964 recommendation to LBJ for a program of bombing North Vietnam to coerce Hanoi to end—or at least dramatically to reduce—its support for the war in the South was also based quite directly on the confidence that it was a low-risk strategy, because of U.S. military dominance over the communists. William Bundy's draft trip report for McNamara revolved around the same central rationales as those that had been used with Kennedy in 1961: Soviet and Chinese passivity in the face of the possibility of war with the United States and Hanoi's fear of potential devastation would inhibit North Vietnamese escalation in the South. The JCS and the CIA agreed that the Soviet Union would not make a move, because of its fear of provoking a crisis with the United States, and an interagency study concluded that Moscow probably would not do anything to defend North Vietnam as long as the regime itself was not directly threatened. The principals also agreed that China, unable to count on Soviet support in any confrontation with the United States, did not want to "face our power," as Rusk put it.

As LBJ's advisors prepared to make their formal recommendation for an air war against North Vietnam following the 1964 presidential election, their previous argument for war was further bolstered by a new CIA estimate that declared, "We are almost certain that both Hanoi and Peiping are anxious not to become involved in the kind of war in which the great weight of U.S. weaponry could be brought against them." It went on to suggest that a campaign of bombing North Vietnam might well succeed in forcing Hanoi to pull back in the South out of fear of suffering "the destruction of their major military facilities and the industrial sector of their economy." The estimate asserted confidently that North Vietnamese leaders could not even be certain that the United States would not use nuclear weapons against the North.

That estimate became part of the analysis supporting the recommendation for striking North Vietnam, and Johnson's principal advisors were attracted to that option both in the hope that Hanoi would relent under U.S. military pressure and with the confidence that there was little or no risk getting into a major ground war in the South, as William Bundy later recalled in his unpublished account of the policy-making process.

This calculation by the national security policy makers of a low-cost, low-risk option that might yield a victory constitutes the final anomaly in regard to the Cold War consensus paradigm. The national security team was pulled by perceived opportunities created by U.S. dominance over its foes, for which the dominant paradigm fails to account.

An Alternative: The Power Imbalance Paradigm

These four anomalies are not related to marginal issues but go to the heart of how and why the United States went to war in Vietnam. They indicate that the basic assumptions that have guided efforts to reconstruct the history of U.S. policy making on Vietnam need to be replaced by a new paradigm. The new paradigm must account for the observed pattern of national security policy makers focusing on the weakness and passivity of the communist states and the freedom of action this provided for the United States. It must also account for the acute conflicts between the presidents and their national security advisors over the issue of using force.

An alternative paradigm should first deal with the question of the relationship between power relations at the global and regional levels and the policy-making process on Vietnam. Based on the evidence already accumulated, the new paradigm should incorporate the assumption that power relations do indeed make a significant difference in the policy-making process if there is a clear-cut power advantage of one side over the other. And it should be based on the reality that the United States held a position of strategic dominance over the Soviet Union and China from 1953 to 1965, and that both sides in the Cold War were well aware of that power imbalance.[33]

The alternative paradigm would assume that the U.S. power advantage significantly influenced the definition of the situation by U.S. policy makers and the choice of options available to them in regard to Vietnam. By constraining the communist powers in an obvious way, the clear-cut power imbalance made the option of using force in Vietnam appear to be both low risk and low cost. It did so by making the United States far too confident in its ability to deter North Vietnam from escalating its involvement in the South. Thus, what appeared to be a decisive U.S. power advantage provided a perverse incentive for the United States to be more assertive and to rely more on military force on the issue of Vietnam than would have been the case in a setting of true mutual deterrence.

To account for the fact that Kennedy and Johnson resisted the urgings of their national security advisors to go to war, two additional alternative assumptions are proposed:

The first is that the institutional and personal interests of the national security officials were much more oriented toward the use of force in Vietnam than were those of the presidents. Contrary to the assumption that national security officials are essentially servants of the president, the alternative paradigm would be based on an insight that former national security official Morton Halperin offered as the conceptual basis for a book on how national security policy is made:

> Organizations have interests. Career officials in these [national security] organizations believe that protecting these interests is vital to the security of the United States. They therefore take stands on issues which advance these interests and maneuver to protect these interests against other organizations' senior officials, including the President.[34]

Because the interests of the institutions in the U.S. government lie in maintaining the existing U.S. power positions abroad and extending them wherever possible, the national security advisors in the Kennedy and Johnson administrations were very much influenced by the incentives created by the global power imbalance to use military power to consolidate the U.S. position in South Vietnam and East Asia more generally. Kennedy and Johnson, on the other hand, were motivated by a broad mix of political interests in which the advancement of U.S. power was balanced by other concerns which would not be served by war in Vietnam.

The second alternative assumption about the politics surrounding Vietnam policy making is that the president's constitutional authority to determine foreign policy and to wage war does not necessarily mean that he is free to do whatever he wants on issues of national security. On the contrary, when the issue is one that involves potential political hazards to the president from political attack for having "lost" a country by failing to fight, the politics of the policy-making process inevitably involve a need on the president's part for political support—or at least an assurance of nonhostility—from key national security officials. That need is a political constraint on the president and an enabling factor for his national security team. In this instance, it gave key national security officials—especially the Joint Chiefs of Staff and the secretary of defense—a degree of leverage over the president that encouraged them to pressure him to adopt their preferred policy on Vietnam.

For both presidents, their worst political nightmare was that the Joint Chiefs of Staff, possibly joined by some senior officials, would accuse them openly or covertly of selling out a U.S. ally in South Vietnam if they refused to go along with the use of force to prevent defeat in South Vietnam. Both Kennedy in 1961 and Johnson in 1964 had information suggesting that a refusal to do something militarily about Vietnam would be regarded by the Joint Chiefs of Staff as equivalent to another Bay of Pigs—a reference to Kennedy's refusal to authorize U.S. bombing in support of the anti-Castro invasion, which seriously strained relations between the military leadership and JFK in 1961–1962.[35]

Adopting this assumption of political conflict between national security officials and presidents as part of the framework for interpreting the policy-making process would require that historians give up the traditional approach of basing the reconstruction of a president's policy essentially on the basis of the public record and official documentation process (i.e., records of discussions in cabinet or NSC meetings, memorandums of conversations with the president, etc.). Based on that traditionalist approach to historical evidence, historian Edwin E. Moise has argued that the absence of internal evidence shows that Kennedy was not pursuing a policy of withdrawal from 1962 to the end of his life. Moise and Logevall also insist that statements by Kennedy in meetings should be interpreted only on the basis of their literal meanings rather than on the basis of a reading of the complete pattern of behavior revealed by all available evidence.[36]

These rules for selecting and interpreting documents make sense if one stays securely within the comforting assumptions of the dominant paradigm. But if there were a political struggle behind the scenes over Vietnam policy, and Kennedy and Johnson were afraid of saying anything or putting anything in writing that those in their administration who were trying to maneuver them into war could use to attack them, the usual categories of official documentation obviously would not reveal the presidents' real intentions. Given the evidence that has now come to light about the policy-making struggle over Vietnam, I would argue that the only appropriate methodology for research is one that examines the totality of the evidence in light of the proposed alternative paradigmatic framework. Historians must piece together what was really going on, I submit, by comparing and analyzing all of the pieces of the puzzle rather than adopting a narrow focus on each piece of archival evidence apart from the whole.

The alternative paradigm proposed here offers a new clarity in regard to a question that has haunted Americans over the past few decades. It addresses a set of anomalies that could become more troubling to historians of the war over time. But there is no guarantee that such a shift will take place: no law of development says a dominant paradigm must fall if it fails to address anomalies that have been discovered. In the end, the fate of the dominant paradigm and of the possible alternative will be determined by sociopolitical currents and countercurrents that may or may not create a strong demand for a paradigm shift on the Vietnam War.

NOTES

1. Thomas Kuhn, *The Structure of Scientific Revolutions* (Chicago: University of Chicago Press, 1962).

2. For an earlier discussion of this explanatory framework, which did not use the term "paradigm," see Robert J. McMahon, "U.S.–Vietnam Relations: A Historical Survey," in Warren I. Cohen, ed., *Pacific Passage: The Study of American East-Asian Relations on the Eve of the Twenty-first Century* (New York: Columbia University Press, 1996), 317.

3. Larry Berman, *Planning a Tragedy: The Americanization of the War in Vietnam* (New York: Norton, 1982), xiii.

4. George McT. Kahin, *Intervention: How America Became Involved in Vietnam* (New York: Knopf, 1986); Marilyn B. Young, *The Vietnam Wars, 1945–1990* (New York: HarperPerennial, 1991).

5. See, for example, Kahin, *Intervention*, 28–32; and Young, *The Vietnam Wars*, 23–26.

6. Two works that strongly influenced the thinking of post–Vietnam War generations of historians about that period of the Cold War are Alexander L. George and Richard Smoke, *Deterrence in American Foreign Policy: Theory and Practice* (New York: Columbia University Press, 1974); and John Lewis Gaddis, *Strategies of Containment: A Critical Appraisal of Postwar American National Security Policy* (Oxford: Oxford University Press, 1982).

7. Leslie H. Gelb and Richard K. Betts, *The Irony of Vietnam: The System Worked* (Washington, D.C.: Brookings Institution, 1979), 24–26. The authors are "more royalist than the king" in turning the domino theory into a general rule of using worst-case scenarios as prudential rules of statesmanship. They liken it to the idea that, "if you let your daughter come home late from a date without punishment, the next thing you know she will be pregnant." Ibid., 199.

8. Herbert Y. Schandler, *The Unmaking of a President: Lyndon Johnson and Vietnam* (Princeton, N.J.: Princeton University Press, 1977), 339–40, 197.

9. Stanley Karnow, *Vietnam: A History* (New York: Viking, 1983), 20, 43–44. Karnow also suggests that the U.S. occupation of Vietnam was a "crusade" and links it with American "exceptionalism" and even "Manifest Destiny," but makes no effort to show how those ideas were reflected in U.S. policy making.

10. Michael H. Hunt, *Lyndon Johnson's War: America's Cold War Crusade in Vietnam, 1945–1968* (New York: Hill and Wang, 1996), 10, 82.

11. George C. Herring, *America's Longest War: The United States and Vietnam: 1950–1975* (New York: Knopf, 1986), xii.

12. Robert D. Schulzinger, *A Time for War: The United States and Vietnam, 1941–1975* (New York: Oxford University Press, 1997), 334.

13. David Kaiser, *American Tragedy: Kennedy, Johnson, and the Origins of the Vietnam War* (Cambridge, Mass.: Belknap, 2000), 8.

88 *American Intervention and the Cold War Consensus*

14. Fredrik Logevall, *Choosing War: The Lost Chance for Peace and the Escalation of War in Vietnam* (Berkeley: University of California Press, 1999), 385–90.

15. The literature reflecting this understanding of Eisenhower's Indochina policy is too extensive to be cited in full here. For some of the leading works in this literature, see Herring, *America's Longest War*, 29–40; Richard Immerman, "Between the Unattainable and the Unacceptable: Eisenhower and Dienbienphu," in Richard A. Melanson and David Mayers, eds., *Reevaluating Eisenhower: American Foreign Policy in the 1950s* (Urbana: University of Illinois Press, 1987); George C. Herring and Richard H. Immerman, "Eisenhower, Dulles and Dien Bien Phu: 'The Day We Didn't Go to War' Revisited," in Lawrence Kaplan, Denise Artaud, and Mark Rubin, eds., *Dien Bien Phu and the Crisis of Franco-American Relations, 1954–1955* (Wilmington, Del.: SR Books, 1990); Melanie Billings-Yun, *Decision against War: Eisenhower and Dien Bien Phu* (New York: Columbia University Press, 1988); David L. Anderson, *Trapped by Success: The Eisenhower Administration and Vietnam, 1953–1961* (New York: Columbia University Press, 1991). For one study stating flatly that Eisenhower rejected any military intervention in Indochina, see Hunt, *Lyndon Johnson's War*, 12.

16. See Louise FitzSimons, *The Kennedy Doctrine* (New York: Random House, 1972); Richard J. Walton, *Cold War and Counter-Revolution: The Foreign Policy of John F. Kennedy* (Baltimore, Md.: Johns Hopkins University Press, 1972); Gelb and Betts, *The Irony of Vietnam*, 69–95; Stephen E. Pelz, "John F. Kennedy's 1961 Vietnam War Decisions," *Journal of Strategic Studies* 4 (1981): 128–81; Kahin, *Intervention*, 126–45; Lawrence J. Basset and Stephen E. Pelz, "The Failed Search for Victory: Vietnam and the Politics of War," in Thomas G. Paterson, ed., *Kennedy's Quest for Victory: American Foreign Policy, 1961–1963* (New York: Oxford University Press, 1989); James Giglio, *The Presidency of John F. Kennedy* (Lawrence: University of Kansas Press, 1991), 239–54; Herring, *America's Longest War*, 73–107; Hunt, *Lyndon Johnson's War*, 42–71; Robert Buzzanco, *Masters of War: Military Dissent and Politics in the Vietnam Era* (Cambridge: Cambridge University Press, 1999), 81–151; Schulzinger, *A Time for War*, 97–123.

17. The first study to challenge the conventional view of policy making in the Kennedy administration was John M. Newman, *JFK and Vietnam: Deception, Intrigue and the Struggle for Power* (New York: Time Warner, 1992). Later works arguing that Kennedy was interested in withdrawal from Vietnam include Kaiser, *American Tragedy*, and Howard Jones, *Death of a Generation: How the Assassinations of Diem and JFK Prolonged the Vietnam War* (New York: Oxford University Press, 2003).

18. Newman, *JFK and Vietnam*, 454–56. Newman's suggestion in the last two pages of the book that there might be a link between the assassination of Kennedy and the Vietnam War did not help the credibility of his case for a different view of Kennedy.

19. For works arguing explicitly against the thesis that Kennedy was withdrawing U.S. forces from South Vietnam, see Lloyd Gardner, *Pay Any Price: Lyndon*

Johnson and the Wars for Vietnam (Chicago: Dee, 1995), 542; Schulzinger, *A Time for War*, 123; William C. Gibbons, "Lyndon Johnson and the Legacy of Vietnam," and Larry Berman, "NSAM 263 and NSAM 273: Manipulating History," both in Lloyd C. Gardner and Ted Gittinger, eds., *Vietnam: The Early Years* (Austin: University of Texas Press, 1989), 138–39 and 177–203; Edwin Moise, "JFK and the Myth of Withdrawal," in Marilyn B. Young and Robert Buzzanco, eds., *A Companion to the Vietnam War* (New York: Oxford University Press, 2002), 162–73; Kai Bird, *The Color of Truth: McGeorge Bundy and William Bundy, Brothers in Arms* (New York: Simon and Schuster, 1998), 259; Fredrik Logevall, "Vietnam and the Question of What Might Have Been," in Mark J. White, ed., *Kennedy: The Frontier Revisited* (New York: New York University Press, 1998), 19–61; Logevall, *The Origins of the Vietnam War* (Harlow, U.K.: Longman, 2001), 39–57; Logevall, *Choosing War*, 68–74; Noam Chomsky, *Rethinking Camelot: JFK, the Vietnam War, and U.S. Political Culture* (Boston: South End, 1993).

20. Logevall, *Choosing War*, 389.

21. Herring, *America's Longest War*, 2nd ed., 108–41.

22. For accounts emphasizing these points, see Berman, *Planning a Tragedy*, 3–7; Gardner, *Pay Any Price*, 98, 124, and 258; Doris Kearns Goodwin, *Lyndon Johnson and the American Dream* (New York: St. Martin's Griffin, 1991), 19–45, 176; Hunt, *Lyndon Johnson's War*, 75–78; Karnow, *Vietnam*, 321.

23. Kahin, *Intervention*; H. R. McMaster, *Dereliction of Duty: Lyndon Johnson, Robert S. McNamara, the Joint Chiefs of Staff, and the Lies That Led to Vietnam* (New York: HarperCollins, 1997).

24. Logevall, *Choosing War*, 389–95; Kaiser, *American Tragedy*, 284–483.

25. Gareth Porter, *Perils of Dominance: Imbalance of Power and the Road to War in Vietnam* (Berkeley: University of California Press, 2005).

26. The discussion of this anomaly is based on Porter, *Perils of Dominance*, 89–107.

27. *Public Papers of the Presidents of the United States: Dwight D. Eisenhower*, vol. 2: *1954*, 250, 366.

28. On the Eisenhower-Dulles strategy outlined here, see Porter, *Perils of Dominance*, 70–86.

29. The discussion of this anomaly is based on ibid., 143–79.

30. Citations for this and subsequent non-footnoted quotations can be found in Gareth Porter, *Perils of Dominance: Imbalance of Power and the Road to War in Vietnam* (Berkeley: University of California Press, 2005).

31. The discussion of this anomaly is based on ibid., 229–58.

32. This discussion is based on ibid., 143–44, 149–52, 185–88, 204–5, 218–20.

33. The evidence for this central premise is documented in ibid., 1–31.

34. Morton Halperin, *National Security Policy-Making: Analyses, Cases and Proposals* (Lexington, Mass.: Lexington Books, 1975), 14.

35. On Kennedy's concern about a second Bay of Pigs, which he believed would cause some military leaders to regard him as unfit to be president, see Paul B. Fay, Jr.,

The Pleasure of His Company (New York: Harper & Row, 1966), 190. On the warn-ing to Johnson by his own military aide in March 1964 that a refusal by LBJ to put stronger pressure on North Vietnam would be regarded by the Joint Chiefs of Staff as an "Asian Bay of Pigs," see McMaster, *Dereliction of Duty*, 86.

36. See Moise, "JFK and the Myth of Withdrawal"; reviews by Fredrik Logevall and Edwin E. Moise in "A Roundtable on Gareth Porter's *Perils of Dominance*," *Passport* 37.2 (August 2006): 4–21.

"THERE AIN'T NO DAYLIGHT"

Lyndon Johnson and the Politics of Escalation

FREDRIK LOGEVALL

For a man who led his country into what is widely seen as a disastrous war, Lyndon Baines Johnson has enjoyed surprisingly gentle treatment from historians. He has had his detractors over the years, to be sure, but most authors have been at once critical of his Vietnam policy and sympathetic to his plight. Johnson made the wrong decision in 1965, they in essence argue, but how can you blame him? After all, with the exception of poor old George Ball, the undersecretary of state, all of the president's senior advisors advocated a military solution in the key months of decision, while in the broader foreign policy bureaucracy, the pressure was all in the direction of escalation. On Capitol Hill and in elite public opinion generally, so it is implied, the mood in the same period was likewise hawkish, or at least unquestioning. An all-powerful "Cold War consensus"—never much analyzed in this literature—reigned supreme in American opinion and dictated that the commitment to South Vietnam had to be maintained, through major military escalation if necessary. In real political terms, therefore, so the argument goes, LBJ had no choice but to expand the war. (To the extent that he had a choice, it was whether or not to move faster and harder militarily, along the lines suggested by a few military analysts.) He was thus not really personally responsible, he cannot fairly be held accountable, for his "nonchoice" to escalate the fighting. No one else in his position would have done differently.

Viewed from the context of the time, moreover, Johnson and his top Vietnam lieutenants understandably believed that the new military measures would work, that the Rolling Thunder bombing campaign and the dispatch of combat troops would compel Hanoi to give up the game. Add to all this the intransigence of North Vietnam on the subject of negotiations, and it becomes clear that there existed no realistic way of averting the war.

This "inevitability thesis," as I've called it elsewhere, is attractive at first glance, even comforting on some level (if it was all bound to happen, there's no need to lose sleep over what might have been).[1] Its power results in good measure from the unfortunate tendency of authors to focus much of their attention on the high-level discussions in July 1965—by then, the momentum for large-scale war really was more or less unstoppable—and by their assumption that because public and congressional support for the war effort was high after the so-called Americanization, it must have been high before as well. Some historians have also equated Johnson's undoubted skepticism and caution regarding Vietnam with dovishness, and concluded that he must have been forced into a war he didn't want.

The Wider Context

The more one examines these various components of the inevitability thesis, however, the more dubious they become. At no point from his ascension to the White House in November 1963 through the winter of 1965, it turns out, was Lyndon Johnson confined to a certain course of action in Vietnam. He inherited a difficult Vietnam problem from John F. Kennedy, and his choices ranged from bad to worse. But exist the choices did, at least through February and March 1965. Neither domestic nor international considerations compelled him to escalate the war. At home, Johnson confronted not an all-powerful Cold War mindset, fully committed to thwarting communist designs in Southeast Asia, but a pronounced fluidity in non-official thinking about the conflict. The general public, to the extent it paid attention at all, was ambivalent, not wanting to lose in Vietnam but also not wanting to send America's young men to fight and die there; in early 1965, large majorities voiced support for negotiations and for maintaining the present level of commitment to Saigon. (In such times of uncertainty, one U.S. official would later concede, the natural inclination for people is to follow the government's lead, whichever way it chooses to go.)[2] In the intelligence community, skepticism about the prospects for any U.S.–led war in Vietnam was widespread. The same was true on Capitol Hill and in the mainstream press, including on the editorial pages of the *New York Times*, the *Washington Post*, and the *Wall Street Journal*. Significantly, many of these observers said that the United States had more than fulfilled its obligation to a South Vietnamese government so patently unwilling to do its part in its own defense.

Consider, in particular, the mood in Congress, where the Democrats held large majorities in both houses in early 1965. The near-unanimous passage a few months prior of the Gulf of Tonkin Resolution—which gave

Johnson wide latitude to wage war in Southeast Asia as he saw fit—should not obscure (though it often does) the essential point: the most respected, most senior Democratic law makers in the country opposed an escalation of U.S. military involvement in Vietnam. This group included Armed Services Committee chair and Johnson mentor Richard Russell (Georgia), Majority Leader Mike Mansfield (Montana), Foreign Relations Committee chair J. William Fulbright (Arkansas), and Vice President–elect and then Vice President Hubert H. Humphrey (Minnesota). All four were widely respected for their foreign policy expertise. They were also politically savvy, arguably no less so than the presumed master of partisan strategizing, Lyndon Johnson. Each of them held well-founded concerns about how opinion leaders in the press and in Congress as well as voters in middle America would react to a long and inconclusive Asian war; each of them doubted the importance of Vietnam to U.S. security. Nor were they the only law makers to hold these views. Exact numbers are hard to come by, but certainly in the Senate a clear majority of Democrats and moderate Republicans were either downright opposed to Americanization or were ambivalent; meanwhile, vocal proponents of taking the war to North Vietnam were strikingly few in number. (Congressional support would rise in the spring and summer, after Americanization had commenced in earnest, in a textbook example of the rally-around-the-flag effect.)

Nor were America's allies abroad clamoring for escalation. On the contrary, by the end of 1964, the United States was largely isolated on Vietnam on the world stage. Most friendly governments in Asia and Europe were sympathetic to what Washington sought to achieve in Vietnam—to preserve an independent, noncommunist government in the South—and they shared the U.S. desire to check possible Chinese expansion in the region. Nevertheless, with a few exceptions, these governments resisted what in some cases was strong and persistent American pressure to become actively involved in the defense of South Vietnam. Deeply skeptical that a lasting military victory against the Viet Cong could be achieved—especially in view of the perceived politico-military weakness of the South Vietnamese government and the apathy and war weariness of the southern populace—many allied leaders also possessed doubts that the outcome in Vietnam really mattered to Western security. Some also feared the political implications at home of committing manpower to an overseas struggle whose importance to national security was open to question.[3]

China and the Soviet Union, meanwhile, were supporters of North Vietnam, but both were anxious to avoid a direct military confrontation with the United States. All too aware of their military weakness vis-à-vis the

Americans, both communist powers made clear to the Hanoi leadership that it could not necessarily count on their material support in the event of a large-scale U.S. intervention.[4] For the Soviets, in particular, major war in Vietnam would be a disaster, risking a conflagration in an inconsequential area of the world and likely halting the momentum toward Soviet-American détente begun in 1963. Kremlin leaders thus hoped for a political solution to the conflict, perhaps by way of a great-power conference, and they cautioned both Hanoi and Washington against escalation. What is more, it now seems quite clear that neither Moscow nor Beijing nor most American allies believed that the United States would suffer a crippling blow to its global prestige if it failed to stand firm in South Vietnam, particularly given the chronic ineptness of the Saigon government.

More than anything, it was this bleak political situation in South Vietnam, and the apparent unwillingness of southern leaders to work to rectify it, that gave Johnson maneuverability on the war. Dedicated and courageous anti-communists willing to fight for the cause certainly existed in the South, but never in sufficient numbers. Overall, incompetence, corruption, and infighting characterized the political leadership in Saigon, while the Army of the Republic of Vietnam (ARVN) was plagued by a general reluctance among officers to engage the enemy and alarming rates of desertion among soldiers. Among the larger South Vietnamese population, war weariness, induced by two decades of fighting, was widespread. And underneath it all percolated a latent, but potentially powerful, anti-Americanism. For large numbers of independent observers, the implications were clear: absent a much greater commitment to the struggle on the part of both the Saigon leadership and the mass of the population—an unlikely prospect, at best—there would be no hope for any U.S. military intervention, no matter how large. Americans would fail just as the French before them had failed.

Close analysis of North Vietnam's posture in 1964–1965 lies beyond the scope of this chapter, but certainly it can be said that Hanoi leaders looked with satisfaction on these developments in the South. They saw the struggle moving in their direction and were in no mood to make significant compromises. At the same time, Hanoi officials, though determined to match any U.S. escalation with one of their own, were anxious to avert any major escalation of the fighting—no one needed to convince them of America's awesome military might—and they hoped that Washington might instead opt for withdrawal. They did not, however, do much to push the Americans in that direction by way of some kind of diplomatic offensive, and in hindsight one must consider this a major tactical blunder. Still, there seems little doubt that they were prepared to negotiate an agreement that would have allowed the United States a face-saving means of disengagement from the war.[5]

Official Realism

A crucial question in historical terms is whether U.S. officials at the time were aware of these attitudes: the deep misgivings among informed observers at home and abroad, the severity of the politico-military problems in South Vietnam, the thinking in Hanoi. The answer can be stated unequivocally: they were. At the start of 1965, they knew full well that backing for the Vietnam commitment among the American people was broad but also shallow and that the support presumed a level of U.S. involvement that stayed more or less the same. They knew that Johnson had won raucous applause on the campaign trail the previous fall when he vowed not to send American boys to fight an Asian war. And they understood that influential voices in American society, including leading newspapers, were urging that the American presence in Vietnam be reduced rather than increased. Policy makers worried about the opposition to escalation among Senate Democrats such as Mansfield, Russell, and Fulbright, and among respected commentators such as Walter Lippmann, Hans Morgenthau, Reinhold Niebuhr, and the *New York Times* editorial page. In 1965, they worked hard to woo these critics, to convert them to the administration's position, or at least to induce them to be quiet.

Thus, in early 1965, the White House embarked on a low-key but determined campaign to shore up congressional support for the Vietnam commitment. In February and early March, senior officials held ten White House briefings and made sure every law maker was invited to at least one. Johnson himself frequently attended these sessions, as did Secretary of Defense Robert McNamara and Secretary of State Dean Rusk. Special care was taken to make sure Senate doves showed up and to convince them that talk of negotiations was premature and dangerous and that America could not now abandon its Vietnam commitment. Senate hawks, meanwhile—such as Minority Leader Everett Dirksen of Michigan and Democrats Thomas Dodd of Connecticut and Paul Douglas of Illinois—were quietly urged to trumpet their advocacy.

In terms of international opinion, policy makers were all too cognizant of the opposition to escalation and the desire for early negotiations on the part of key allied governments, and of the misgivings about the war evident even in Asia itself. In the lead-up to the Americanization of the war in 1965, the administration worked hard to get allied involvement in the military defense of South Vietnam, partly through an effort known as the "More Flags" program. Originally the program, which was launched in May 1964, sought only noncombat-related aid for South Vietnam, but in short order it was expanded to include also fighting troops. The campaign yielded meager results. A handful of countries eventually committed soldiers—though most drove a hard bargain in doing so, which is to say, their forces were mercenaries more than allies—but most, including all of the European allies, declined. By mid-1965, when large-scale war began, Washington's More Flags campaign had become, one might say, a "few flags" problem.[6]

Most important, policy makers in Washington generally had a sound grasp of the situation on the ground in South Vietnam and—to a lesser but significant degree—of the thinking in Hanoi. Secretary of Defense Robert McNamara would later claim, in his memoirs and a subsequent coauthored book, that he and his colleagues were largely ignorant of the dynamics of the struggle in Vietnam, the obstacles to a military solution, and Hanoi's openness to negotiations. "If only we had known" is the mantra in these works.[7] He sells himself short. He was hardly an expert on Vietnam in 1964 and 1965, but neither was he unaware of the chronic problems in the war effort, or the thin nature of domestic and allied support for the war, or the deepening Sino-Soviet split. As early as October 1963, he can be heard on the Kennedy White House tapes telling colleagues that "we need a way to get out of Vietnam," and at several points in early 1964 he expressed deep concerns about the state of the war and the prospects for victory. In late June 1965, as more American ground troops were arriving in South Vietnam, McNamara told a British official that the trends in the South pointed the wrong way. In the short term, the United States could hold on militarily, but over the long haul it was doubtful. "None of us at the center of things [in U.S. policy making] talk about winning a victory," McNamara confessed.[8]

Much more than they later admitted, senior U.S. officials understood that they faced long odds in Vietnam, even as they Americanized the war. The hubris so often ascribed to them is seldom seen in the vast internal record, at least with respect to the prospects in the fighting. (The hubris *is* evident in their presumed right to be in Vietnam and to tell the Vietnamese what kind of society they ought to create.) Lyndon Johnson and his chief lieutenants fully agreed that the military picture was worsening each month, and though they liked to say that bombing North Vietnam would make a major difference to the situation in the South, privately they were doubtful. They were not optimistic that Hanoi would succumb to this form of coercion and cease its support of the insurgency, and they knew that, regardless, success or failure would hinge on developments below the 17th Parallel. Even as they sent the first contingent of U.S. ground troops to the war, the president and his lieutenants understood that it would bring resentment from many southerners, including some of the leaders in Saigon, and generate charges of "colonialism" from elsewhere in Asia and around the world. As for the quality of the government in South Vietnam, policy makers were anything but sanguine: they knew it was less capable and less popular than ever, permeated with dissension, and—in some quarters at least—not altogether unsympathetic to an early end to the war through a deal with the Viet Cong.

Very well, the skeptical reader could respond, but lack of optimism regarding outcomes need not necessarily be a barrier to action. Couldn't policy makers decide that the preservation of America's global commitments demanded a large-scale effort in Vietnam, even if the odds pointed against long-term success? Couldn't they perceive the United States as needing to be the "good doctor" (as McNamara deputy John McNaughton put it), who had to be seen as trying to save the patient even if the chances for recovery were slim or nonexistent?[9] Yes, and that kind of thinking certainly did exist at the highest levels in the fateful months of late 1964 and early 1965. Even here, however, the analysis was more nuanced than is generally understood. In their estimations of the regional and global implications of a defeat in Vietnam, many senior policy makers did not differ all that much from most of the dissenters—especially if the defeat occurred because of the perceived ineptitude or apathy of the South Vietnamese themselves. Officials worried about possible Chinese expansion in the wake of such a defeat but, like the critics, they understood that historic Sino-Vietnamese friction and current Sino-Soviet friction reduced the chances of that happening. They were concerned about the possible increase in the appeal of Maoist revolutions in other newly emerging nations should Ho Chi Minh's be allowed to succeed, but they knew that the internal conditions that made Vietnam so ripe for a communist takeover did not exist in many other nations in the region. With regard to the likely Soviet reaction to an early U.S. disengagement, it cannot be considered to have been a major concern among senior planners. Most of them believed that Moscow would want to continue steps toward improved bilateral relations with Washington regardless of the outcome in Vietnam, and they do not appear to have worried a great deal about increased Soviet penetration in other Third World areas.

On the matter of diplomacy, American officials knew prior to Americanization that Hanoi had not closed the door to early negotiations. They were aware in late 1964 that UN secretary-general U Thant had won assurances from Hanoi earlier in the fall that it would enter bilateral talks with

Washington and that Burmese leader Ne Win had agreed to serve as host for the talks. And there were other signs. In early December, for example, Undersecretary of State William P. Bundy told Canadian officials that Hanoi had in recent weeks been putting out hints in various quarters that it was interested in pursuing a negotiated settlement to the war. Robert McNamara, in his coauthored book, *Argument without End*, makes much of Washington's misreading of Premier Pham Van Dong's "Four Points" statement of April 1965; no one in Washington, the book claims, realized that the statement might present an opening for talks. In fact, several officials thought precisely that. National Security advisor McGeorge Bundy, for example, after describing North Vietnam's statement as "quite unacceptable to us," acknowledged to LBJ that Hanoi had referred to the Four Points as "a basis for discussions" and that he, Ray Cline (acting CIA director), and Ambassador Llewellyn Thompson all agreed that there existed "at least a hint of real interest from Hanoi in eventual discussions." In late July 1965, a State Department intelligence report put it bluntly: "Has Hanoi shown any interest in negotiations? Yes, repeatedly."[10]

In sum, the Americanization of the war in Vietnam in 1965 cannot remotely be considered foreordained, at least not in any structural sense. Severe doubts both at home and abroad about Vietnam's importance to American and Western security; a South Vietnamese ally incapable and apparently unwilling to live up to its end of the bargain; pessimism among senior American policy makers about the prospects in the conflict and about the importance of the outcome; and an adversary seemingly open to negotiations—all of these suggest that Americanization was not overdetermined. One could indeed conclude the opposite, that the action is difficult to explain, perhaps even incomprehensible on some level. Regardless, it seems undeniable that Johnson, fated to be president when the key Vietnam decisions had to be made, could have chosen differently. He could have avoided this war.

The Price to Be Paid

This is not to suggest that disengagement was risk free, that it would not have cost Johnson anything politically. Such a course would have brought a domestic political cost, even if disguised through some kind of agreement leading to a coalition government in Saigon and a "decent interval" before any Hanoi takeover. The question is how big a cost. The president would have been branded an "appeaser" by Cold War hawks such as Richard

Nixon and journalist Joseph Alsop, but in response he could have called on his own team of heavy hitters to defend the decision. A distinction must be made, moreover, between being called names by your opponents and actually losing significant political power as a result. In view of the constellation of forces in Congress and in the press, especially after Johnson's landslide election victory in 1964, there is little reason to believe that a decision against war would have exacted an exorbitant political price. His margin of victory in the election was so huge, it could have withstood some erosion—if indeed any occurred. It bears remembering, moreover, that Republican nominee Barry Goldwater had run as a hawk in the campaign and had been trounced, his belligerence on Vietnam as thoroughly repudiated as it could have been.

Some historians and Johnson acolytes speculate that the president's cherished Great Society program would have been scuttled by congressional hawks if he had opted against escalation. Dixiecrats and many Republicans, according to this view, would have banded together to filibuster the civil rights and social legislation if he could have been made to appear soft on communism in Southeast Asia. But who were these supposed hawks? How much clout did they have? And what exactly did they say, either publicly or behind closed doors, to support this line of argument? The proponents of this interpretation don't tell us. The evidence suggests strongly that Vietnam hawks in Congress were a small and timid lot in the spring of 1965, and although their number and volubility might have grown later in the year had Johnson chosen to begin disengagement, it's hard to see how this would have changed the overall dynamic. Much more persuasive is the assessment made by McGeorge Bundy in 1994: "If [Johnson] had decided that the right thing to do was to cut our losses, he was quite sufficiently inventive to do that in a way that would not have destroyed the Great Society."[11]

What's more, the costs of getting out must be judged against the costs the president could have been expected to incur if he chose what by early 1965 had become the only other real option: major escalation. Here, the critics of the escalation have not received enough credit. Many of them perceived these costs to be very considerable indeed, if not in the short term, then certainly in the medium and long term. They grasped what Johnson and the Democrats could expect to face on the home front in the event of a large-scale war thousands of miles from America's shores. Many were political veterans, shrewd tacticians with decades of campaigning under their belts.

Take Hubert Humphrey, vice president–elect and then vice president during the key period of decision making. Here was a man whose understanding of recent American political history, and the Democratic party's fortunes in that history, was every bit as sound as Johnson's, if not more so. Humphrey had risen to political prominence during the early Cold War. He was steeped in the politics and ideology of the conflict, having helped lead the attack on communist-led unions after World War II. No one needed to lecture him on the problems that could befall politicians seen as lacking sufficient toughness in foreign affairs, as being "soft on communism."

Yet here we find Humphrey in February 1965—arguably the most important month of the whole quarter-century of U.S. involvement in Vietnam— telling Johnson in a carefully written memo that 1965 would be the best time to incur these risks and that the risks of escalation were far greater. A large-scale war, Humphrey warned, would risk "gravely undermining" other U.S. foreign policies, including relations with Moscow and with the European allies, and would encourage an end to the Sino-Soviet rift. It would also cut into the funding for the Great Society programs. The American people, meanwhile, would soon lose patience, because the administration had not made clear why the defense of South Vietnam was a vital "national interest." The public, Humphrey wrote, "can't understand why we would run grave risks to support a country which is totally unable to put its own house in order." Disengagement was the only answer and was both politically possible and advantageous:

> It is always hard to cut losses. But the Johnson administration is in a stronger position to do so now than any administration in this century. 1965 is the year of minimum political risk for the Johnson administration. Indeed, it is the first year when we can face the Vietnam problem without being preoccupied with the political repercussions from the Republican right.... The best possible outcome a year from now would be a Vietnam settlement which turns out to be better than was in the cards because the President's political talents for the first time came to grips with a fateful world crisis and so successfully. It goes without saying that the subsequent domestic political benefits of such an outcome, and such a new dimension for the President, would be enormous.

Even if such a settlement did not result, Humphrey concluded, disengagement would still be far preferable to a risky escalation. "If, on the other hand, we find ourselves leading from frustration to escalation and end up short of a war with China but embroiled deeper in fighting in Vietnam over the next few months," he wrote:

> political opposition will steadily mount. It will underwrite all the negativism and disillusionment which we already have about foreign involvement

generally—with direct spill-over effects politically for all the Democratic internationalist programs to which we are committed—AID, UN, disarmament, and activist world policies generally.[12]

It was a tour de force, a lucid and unsparing assessment of the choice facing the administration at that critical moment. It would have won quiet nods of approval had copies of it circulated among Humphrey's former Senate colleagues, not least among the Democratic leadership. We do not have a Humphrey-type memorandum by Mansfield, Russell, or Fulbright from this period, but we know that all three of them feared the domestic implications of a long and bloody war. Such a war, they surely understood, could put Johnson and the Democrats in serious trouble as the campaigning began for the 1968 election. The party could be in the same position as it had been in 1952: facing a tough battle, and probable defeat, in the election. It is critical to keep in mind, in this context, that few if any military advisors were offering even a chance of a swift victory in Vietnam. Even as they advocated escalation, virtually all of them were predicting a war on the scale of Korea, which in three years would be large and not close to being won. To achieve victory would take "five years—plus 500,000 troops," Marine Corps commandant General Wallace Greene told Johnson on 22 July 1965; five months earlier, Army chief of staff General Harold K. Johnson had given essentially the same estimate.[13] Where would this put LBJ as the campaigning began for the 1968 election? With hundreds of thousands of troops in combat, large numbers of American casualties, and victory still years away.

In other words, it would be a repeat of Korea. At the start of that war, the public had rallied around the flag and around Harry Truman, but enthusiasm waned once it became clear that victory would not come swiftly and cleanly. Though Lyndon Johnson would later claim that the "fall of China" in 1949 lost the 1952 election for the Democrats, this was a dubious reading of history. More likely, what lost it for them was what Truman did after that loss. That is, he entered into a large and inconclusive war in Asia. Accusations regarding China certainly flew in the 1952 campaign, but very probably they resonated—as likely would have been the case in 1968 in the absence of war—with voters who were not going to vote Democratic anyway. Certainly, these accusations affected fewer votes than did the frustrations caused by the stalemated fighting in Korea. Truman had learned firsthand the difficulty of sustaining popular support for a limited war far from America's shores, one entered without a declaration of war and without popular understanding of the possible obstacles ahead.

The Decision

Johnson now set about doing the same thing. In 1965, he refused to seek a declaration of war, and he rejected the plea from several top civilian and military advisors to fully prepare the nation for the struggle ahead. He opted, as George C. Herring has put it, to wage war in "cold blood."[14] There would be no national debate on Vietnam, no call-up of the reserves, no declared state of emergency. The United States would go to war on the sly. Historians have usually explained these decisions by pointing to LBJ's fear that a full-fledged debate on Vietnam would have jeopardized major pieces of Great Society legislation then pending in Congress, and to his belief that a low-key, gradual escalation reduced the chance of a major conflagration involving China and perhaps the Soviet Union. He may well have held these beliefs (though, in the case of the former, with dubious justification), but very likely he also had a third concern: that a public debate would bring out into the open the extent of the concerns in Congress and in the press and thereby undermine the shaky national consensus that existed on the conflict. Johnson knew as well as anyone that formidable players in Congress and elsewhere opposed Americanizing the war; it was not at all certain that his side would win a debate. And so he gambled—on a short-term strategy. He gambled that, without taking exceptional measures, he could hold public support long enough to achieve his objectives.

Here then, we find a principal reason that Lyndon Johnson took the nation into war in 1965. In the short term, military escalation represented the path of least resistance for him. At the start of 1965, the United States had been actively involved in the Vietnam struggle for some fifteen years, first in support of the French war effort, and then, after 1954, in trying to create and sustain an independent, noncommunist South Vietnam. At each point during that span when a decision had to be made regarding whether to expand or contract U.S. involvement, presidents had chosen to expand it. Though there is a qualitative difference between these earlier decisions and the one LBJ now faced (none was as committing, as costly, as irreversible, as controversial, as dangerous in terms of domestic politics), it stands to reason that he, too, would give serious consideration to escalation. It is never easy for people in positions of authority to acknowledge the failure of an existing policy and embark on a new course; for those at the pinnacle of the political system, who have had to publicly defend that policy time and time again, it must be harder still. The president and his top Vietnam aides had put themselves in a box with their repeated affirmations of South Vietnam's importance to U.S. security (in the case of top advisors McNamara, Bundy, and Rusk, all of them holdovers from JFK, the affirmations went all the way back to 1961), and one can see why they might stay the course in the hope that the new measures would work.

The issue was credibility and the concern that it might be irreparably harmed by a failure to stand firm in the war. As most often interpreted by scholars, this imperative had to do with the credibility of America's commitments abroad—the fear that if the United States failed to prevail in Vietnam, friends and foes around the world would respect it less. American power would be much less credible, causing allies to lose heart and adversaries to become emboldened. But it was not merely a question of U.S. national credibility abroad: for at least some key players, including the president, also important were concerns about domestic political credibility and, especially, personal credibility. Call it credibility[3] (cubed). Johnson worried about the harm that failure in Vietnam could do to his domestic agenda; even more, he feared the personal humiliation he imagined would inevitably accompany a defeat (and for him, a negotiated withdrawal constituted defeat). Top aides, meanwhile, feared for their reputations and careers should they abandon their previous support for a staunch commitment to South Vietnam's survival.[15]

Idealism, too, entered into the equation, even if it did not drive the policy. Johnson believed—with what degree of conviction can be debated—that the United States could be a force for good in Vietnam, helping the Vietnamese to achieve a better way of life. He spoke of creating a Tennessee Valley Authority–type project on the Mekong River, which would bring benefits to both Vietnams. The same belief was held by many intellectuals in the foreign policy bureaucracy, who maintained that the United States could modernize Vietnam using the tools of foreign aid, development planning, and technical assistance. Vietnam, that is to say, could be made more like the United States. Or, as LBJ put it, "I want to leave the footprints of America in Vietnam."[16]

Sympathetic authors emphasize that Johnson was often cautious and skeptical on Vietnam. Indeed he was, on occasion more so than his aides. From an early point, he grasped the weakness of his South Vietnamese ally, sensed the limits of American power in that part of the world, knew that the odds against success were long, wondered if the outcome really mattered to U.S. security. In September 1964, for example, he said of the hapless Saigon leaders: "I mean, if they can't protect themselves, if you have a government that can't protect itself from kids in the streets, what the hell can you do about an invading army?" In the wake of the Pleiku attack in February 1965, he dejectedly noted that "a man can fight if he can see daylight down the road somewhere. But there ain't no daylight in Vietnam, there's not a bit."[17]

But this gloomy realism did not make him dovish. Up through the winter of 1965, Johnson walked the middle of the road on Vietnam, but always closer to the escalation side than to the withdrawal side. He had declared already in late 1963 that he would not be the president who lost Vietnam, and he never wavered from that vow in the year and a half that followed. Time and again during that period, he framed his Vietnam choices in such a way that standing firm appeared to be the only option. The alternative of disengagement was dismissed by him, in characteristic (and telling) language, as "cutting and running," as inevitably meaning a retreat to Hawaii or San Diego. Few challenged Johnson on these claims, in part because his obsessive fear of leaks led to a cloistered decision-making environment that effectively excluded contrarian voices from the deliberations and discouraged indepth reexamination of the fundamental issues among those who remained. Recalled Chester Cooper, then a midlevel official on the NSC staff, of the "dark and forbidding mood" in the White House in the spring of 1965: "One had to be careful about expressing doubt about either the prospects of victory or the wisdom of our Vietnam policy."[18]

It should not be concluded from the foregoing that Johnson shunned all talk of diplomacy on Vietnam. After the spring of 1965, he constantly pressed George Ball and others for new negotiating ideas—though, as Ball later said, "he really meant merely new channels and procedures." The administration, Ball recalled telling colleagues, was " 'following the traditional pattern for negotiating with a mule; just keep hitting him on the head with a two-by-four until he does what you want him to do.' But that was useless with Hanoi; the mule's head was harder than the two-by-four." Said Chester Cooper: "Johnson's call [in July 1965] for a political settlement was largely, but not wholly, a public relations gambit. He was ready to negotiate, but only if the terms would provide the United States and its South Vietnamese ally with, in effect, a clear-cut victory."[19]

Silent Doves

Could the many influential voices warning against Americanization have done more to make themselves heard in 1964–1965? Unquestionably. Internationally, major allied leaders who foresaw a calamity ahead should escalation occur failed to work hard to keep it from happening. Thus, while the French government of Charles de Gaulle forcefully disputed the administration's position at every turn (Johnson was embarking on an "absurd war," de Gaulle said), the more important American ally in London consistently refrained from doing so, despite the fact that Prime Minister Harold Wilson and other British officials largely shared the French leader's views.[20] And even de Gaulle cannot be considered an agitator per se on negotiations in 1964–1965; for the most part, he was content to state his position—in that haughty and superior tone that drove U.S. officials to distraction—and see what the Americans chose to do.

Congress, meanwhile, in these months accorded the executive branch wide latitude in decision making, in terms of both the broad contours and narrow particulars of policy. The Gulf of Tonkin Resolution of August 1964 gave Johnson broad power to wage war in Vietnam more or less as he saw fit. In early 1965, Democratic leaders in the Senate, though prescient in foreseeing problems in any attempt to Americanize the conflict, were unwilling to say forcefully what they really believed: that Vietnam was not worth the price of a major war and that a face-saving negotiated settlement was the best that could be hoped for. White House officials, all too aware of the deep misgivings on Capitol Hill—especially in the Senate—were relieved when no genuine debate on the war ever occurred in the first half of 1965. They noted with satisfaction that Majority Leader Mansfield, the closest thing in the Senate to a Vietnam expert (by virtue of his long-term interest in the conflict there and his having taught Asian history), concluded one cautionary memo by vowing to back the president publicly on the war, whatever the policy. "I want you to know," Mansfield wrote, "that you have my support on a personal as well [as] an official basis."[21]

Just how to account for this congressional reticence about speaking up is not altogether easy. Surely it mattered that Mansfield took a deferential and compliant approach, seeing his role more as Johnson's floor leader in the Senate than as leader of the Senate Democrats. Partly, too, the reticence resulted from the certainty among the majority of Democrats that the president would not look kindly on public opposition to his actions: Johnson left little doubt that he expected party members to fall in line, and he ordered top advisors to apply pressure on wavering law makers. And partly it resulted from the administration's repeated vows that it was keeping all options open, that it genuinely sought a political solution, that it saw real reasons for optimism in the Saigon government's prospects; these claims caused many doubters to swallow their concerns and profess support for U.S. policy. At the same time, however, there was on Capitol Hill a certain willingness to be deceived, a willingness to be strong-armed by the president. Many legislators were quite content to escape responsibility from a policy issue that seemed to be growing more complex each day and for which few of them had a clear prescription.

Then, after the ground troops began arriving in March and April, a different dynamic took hold, one that would retain its power for the next half-dozen years: legislators now confronted the choice of supporting the policy or facing the political consequences of "abandoning the troops" in the field. Richard Russell, for one, promptly became a hawk, telling friends that supporting the troops meant supporting the war. Going against Johnson on the Vietnam issue, Rhode Island Democratic senator Claiborne Pell remarked, henceforth would be "like voting against motherhood."[22]

All of this suggests that it would be a mistake to reduce Vietnam simply to "Johnson's war." Many were responsible. The president chose war, but he was urged on by both civilian and military advisors. Especially important were the big three of McNamara, Bundy, and Rusk, the former two of whom warned LBJ, in late January 1965, of a "disastrous defeat" if the United States chose not to use its military power in Vietnam. Like Johnson, all three men—and especially McNamara—on occasion expressed doubts about the chances of success in the war; like him, they nevertheless pressed forward. Congressional leaders went along, and so did a general public that until mid-1965 remained largely ignorant and apathetic regarding Vietnam (notwithstanding the beginnings of campus dissent in the spring). The public could have forced a debate on the issue in the winter and spring of 1964–1965; enough information existed, notwithstanding the administration's efforts to withhold information concerning the problems in South Vietnam and its plans to rectify them. Whatever the outcome of such a debate, there can be no denying that having it would have served the nation—and ultimately the president himself—well.

In the end, we come back to Lyndon Johnson—and are left with a mystery. At one point in *Path to War*, the gripping 2001 HBO dramatization of the decision for war, the character portraying White House aide Richard Goodwin says of LBJ and Vietnam, "He's the best politician this country has ever seen. He'll find a way out of this." Why, if the first statement is true, did the second not come to pass? The filmmakers do not pause long over this conundrum. In their sympathetic interpretation, which follows closely that presented in much of the literature over the past quarter-century, the president is indeed a master politician who on Vietnam is trapped by forces beyond his control. The better explanation is that Johnson, though he inherited a difficult Vietnam problem from his predecessors, stepped into a trap substantially of his own making, which in turn raises doubts about the extent of his political acumen. No doubt, he was unsurpassed in his knowledge of

the workings of official Washington, in his ability to get contentious legislation through Congress, in his skill at arm twisting; it is far less clear that
he understood the broader political forces in the country at large. He was a
political virtuoso, but inside the Beltway. Here, one can draw a contrast with
the oft-maligned Humphrey, who, as we have seen, did more than simply
assure LBJ that he had the political freedom to maneuver on Vietnam; he
also warned him that a stepped-up war carried a much greater political risk
than did reducing U.S. involvement. Johnson, annoyed by the advice, barred
Humphrey from Vietnam meetings for the better part of a year and went on
to make Vietnam an American war.

NOTES

1. Fredrik Logevall, *Choosing War: The Lost Chance for Peace and the Escalation of War in Vietnam* (Berkeley: University of California Press, 1999). This chapter
recapitulates some of the findings and arguments in *Choosing War*, but also builds
on them in various ways. I wish to thank Daniel Ellsberg for several conversations
and e-mails regarding points raised in this essay.

2. William P. Bundy, unpublished book ms, chap. 18, p. 20, William P. Bundy
Papers, Lyndon Baines Johnson Library, Austin, TX (hereafter cited as LBJL). See
also James C. Thomson, Jr, "How Could Vietnam Happen? An Autopsy," *Atlantic*
(April 1968): 52.

3. Fredrik Logevall, "America Isolated: The European Powers and the Escalation of the War," in Andreas Daum, Lloyd C. Gardner, and Wilfried Mausbach,
eds., *America, the Vietnam War, and the World: Comparative and International
Perspectives* (New York: Cambridge University Press, 2003).

4. On their weakness as compared to the United States, and their awareness of
the fact, see Gareth Porter, *Perils of Dominance: Imbalance of Power and the Road
to War in Vietnam* (Berkeley: University of California Press, 2005).

5. Robert McNamara, James G. Blight, and Robert K. Brigham, *Argument without End: In Search of Answers to the Vietnam Tragedy* (New York: Public Affairs,
1999); and Logevall, *Choosing War.*

6. On the More Flags program, see Robert M. Blackburn, *Mercenaries and Lyndon Johnson's "More Flags": The Hiring of Korean, Filipino, and Thai Soldiers in
the Vietnam War* (Jefferson, N.C.: McFarland, 1994). The "free world" countries
that ultimately sent ground troops to South Vietnam were the Republic of (South)
Korea, the Philippines, Thailand, Australia, and New Zealand.

7. Robert McNamara, *In Retrospect: The Tragedy and Lessons of Vietnam* (New
York: Times Books, 1995); McNamara et al., *Argument without End.*

8. Gordon Walker summary of talks in Washington, 30 June 1965, FO 371/180540,
Public Record Office, Kew, England.

9. McNaughton's 24 March 1965 memorandum outlining this argument can be found in George C. Herring, ed., *The Pentagon Papers: Abridged Edition* (New York: McGraw-Hill, 1993), 115–18.

10. Bundy to LBJ, 20 April 1965, Box 16, NSF (National Security File) VN (Vietnam), LBJL; INR (Hughes) to Rusk, 28 July 1965, Box 31, NSF VN, LBJL. For more internal commentary on Pham Van Dong's Four Points, see Chester Cooper/ James Thomson to McGeorge Bundy (hereafter MB), 24 April 1965, Box 11, Thomson Papers, JFKL (John F. Kennedy Library, Boston, MA); Cooper/Thomson to MB, 29 June 1965, Box 19, NSF VN, LBJL; Cooper to LBJ, 25 May 1965, Box 41, NSF National Security Council Histories—Deployment of Forces, LBJL; Thomson to MB, 24 July 1965, Box 20, NSF VN, LBJL; Richard Goodwin to LBJ, 27 April 1965, Box 2, NSF MPB, LBJL. See also McNamara et al., *Argument without End.*

11. McGeorge Bundy, interview with the author, New York City, 15 March 1994.

12. The memorandum is reprinted in full in Hubert H. Humphrey, *The Education of a Public Man: My Life and Politics* (Garden City, N.Y.: Doubleday, 1976), 320–24. For Johnson's response, see Carl Solberg, *Hubert Humphrey: A Biography* (New York: Norton, 1984), 287–88; and Humphrey, *Education of a Public Man*, 327.

13. Notes of Meeting, 22 July 1965, U.S. Department of State, *Foreign Relations of the United States, 1964–1968: Vietnam*, vol. 3 (Washington, D.C.: U.S. Government Printing Office, 1995), 214.

14. George C. Herring, *LBJ and Vietnam: A Different Kind of War* (Austin: University of Texas Press, 1994), 131.

15. A more detailed articulation of this argument can be found in Logevall, *Choosing War*, chapter 12.

16. Quoted in Charles E. Neu, *America's Lost War: Vietnam: 1945–1975* (Wheeling, Ill.: Harlan Davidson, 2005), 86.

17. LBJ and Bundy telephone conversation, 8 September 1964, in Michael Beschloss, ed., *Reaching for Glory: Lyndon Johnson's Secret White House Tapes, 1964–1965* (New York: Simon and Schuster, 2001), 35–36; Johnson and Richard Russell telephone conversation, 6 March 1965, in ibid., 210–13.

18. Chester L. Cooper, *In the Shadows of History: Fifty Years behind the Scenes of Cold War Diplomacy* (Amherst, N.Y.: Prometheus, 2006), 224.

19. George W. Ball, *The Past Has Another Pattern: Memoirs* (New York: Norton, 1982), 405; Cooper, *Shadows*, 228.

20. De Gaulle's "absurd" comment, made in a cabinet meeting on 22 January 1964, is in Alain Peyrefitte, *C'était de Gaulle: La France reprend sa place dans le monde* (Paris: Fayard, 1997), 494.

21. Mike Mansfield to LBJ, 24 March 1965, quoted in Robert Mann, *A Grand Delusion: America's Descent into Vietnam* (New York: Basic, 2001), 419.

22. Quoted in Mann, *A Grand Delusion*, 436–37.

PART II

The Coming of War in Vietnam

THROUGH A GLASS DARKLY

Reading the History of the Vietnamese Communist Party, 1945–1975

SOPHIE QUINN-JUDGE

During its three decades of war, North Vietnam was a complex, evolving organism, subjected to extreme internal and external pressures. But the further away we get from the war, the more the complexities of Vietnamese politics are likely to be forgotten. The biggest pitfall in our writing about wartime Vietnam is still our eagerness to generalize about "the enemy." This may be a consequence of our lack of documentation on decision-making processes in the Democratic Republic of Vietnam (DRV). We see only small glimpses of the daily debates and accommodations that would go on in any political movement, in contrast to the vast amount of documentation that we possess on U.S. policy development. We can follow month by month Robert McNamara's or Lyndon Johnson's agonizing over their choices, but still have to speculate about much that occurred in Hanoi. Our tendency to generalize also grows out of oversimplified views of communist systems as brutally efficient and monolithic, lacking the subtle grays of Western politics. The Stalinist model has led to an assumption that communist leaders are invariably all-powerful. It is striking, for example, how many writers allow Vo Nguyen Giap to personify the DRV's military leadership or who use Ho Chi Minh as shorthand to represent the North Vietnamese politburo. Lyndon Johnson's habit of describing policy in terms of how "Old Ho" would react is not atypical. These conventions betray real ignorance of the day-to-day workings of the DRV political system—as there appear to have been significant periods when neither man played a leading decision-making role. The contested side of major decisions and the acrimony surrounding them, however, are not things that communist parties like to publicize. Party historians in Hanoi have been content to let Ho Chi Minh's image stand as the iconic representation of communist power.

If we look at our knowledge of Chinese communist politics for a comparable period, it is striking how much more historians have documented about major turning points, such as the Great Leap Forward and its after-math. Roderick MacFarquhar writes in a preface to his third volume on the *Origins of the Cultural Revolution* that, by then, the availability of Chinese sources had increased from a "rushing mountain torrent" to "the broad Yangtze River."[1] There are clear reasons that the Chinese should be more forthcoming about their recent past, the main one being that the Cultural Revolution policies of Mao Zedong have been completely discredited, and many of his victims have been rehabilitated. Scholars do not need to worry about taking the wrong line on these issues.

For Vietnamese communist history, there have been few moments when the party let down its guard or clearly repudiated past mistakes. Both were fairly brief: the months following the apology for the excesses of the land reform in 1956 and the early stages of the economic reform from 1986 to 1989. Thus, there is no comparable flood of documents, just a trickle. The number of volumes of *Van Kien Dang* (*Party Documents*) has continued to increase in recent years, and this series now covers events up to and including the 1970s. But the documents are carefully selected and edited. Today, for example, overly negative references to the United States or China get edited out of historical documents, because these countries are now friends of Vietnam, as an editor at a publishing house explained to me. The documentation on decisions leading to the 1968 Tet Offensive is notably spotty. In the volumes of party documents published for 1967 and 1968, there is no document referring to the offensive from October 1967, when the date of the Tet attacks was decided in a politburo meeting. There is only one statement by an individual leader, which directly touches on the planning of the offensive, published in the 1968 volume: this is Le Duan's intervention at the Fourteenth Plenum in January, taken from an unedited recording.[2] We do not hear other voices nor get to see the politburo in action as a deliberative body. Without knowing what precisely was decided at the October meeting, we have no context in which to interpret Le Duan's argument. A rare example of a personal account that fills in the contours of a higher-level debate is the memoir of southern general Tran Van Tra on the final offensive of the Vietnam War. In his book, he describes debates between southern commanders and politburo member General Van Tien Dung, whose own heroic account of the final communist victory in 1975 glosses over the decision-making process and his own initial reluctance to call for an offensive.[3]

Admittedly, there are many new biographies and memoirs of deceased leaders available in Hanoi's bookstores. Some recent biographies of the leadership from the popular history magazine *Xua va Nay* (*Past and Present*) resurrect the memories of those who lost out in party power struggles, such as General Nguyen Son, an early Communist Party member who spent most of his career in China, where he became a disciple of Mao Zedong. These mainly appeared at a time when the party was restoring its ties with China, and they reflect a change in political fashion rather than a new *glasnost* in historical writing. On the whole, political biographies since the 1990s have been written in the festschrift tradition, celebrating achievements without delving into critical analysis or providing a real chronology. Two examples of this style are the 2001 collection of remembrances about the general secretary from 1986 to 1991, Nguyen Van Linh (*Dong Chi Nguyen Van Linh va Cach Mang Viet Nam*), and a 2004 book about long-time Prime Minister Pham Van Dong (*Dong Chi Pham Van Dong: Nha Lanh Dao Xuat Sac, Nha Van Hoa Lon cua Dan Toc*). One can conclude that the Vietnamese Communist Party (VCP) prefers to depoliticize its past. This allows it to avoid any real accounting for mistakes and, with the exception of one scapegoat, former General Secretary Le Duan, to create an image of all-around comradely unity and perspicacity.[4]

Ways of Reading the Past

The latest research on DRV history is strongly influenced by anthropology and looks at events beyond the traditional focus on the top leadership.[5] Scholars such as Benedict Kerkvliet have assembled fresh accounts of domestic developments at the central, provincial, and village levels in the DRV by using the available archives and supplementing them with newspaper and journal articles and oral histories. Kerkvliet's *The Power of Everyday Politics: How Peasants Transformed National Policy* is a ground-breaking study of the collectivization of agriculture and the subsequent collapse of the cooperatives in the 1980s. He looks at the local level for explanations of these processes.

This sort of research is a much-needed antidote to the political science of the Cold War, which turned to classic paradigms of communist systems as the key to understanding events behind the bamboo curtain. The ways that peasants coped with unreasonable decrees and demands and were sometimes encouraged by local officials are essential parts of the picture of DRV life. As Kerkvliet says, "Everyday politics matters....It can have a huge impact on national policy."[6] Compromises were worked out far from the seat of power, and there were not enough eager young ideologues, of the sort who implemented decrees on collectivization in the Soviet Union and China or who organized the Vietnamese land reform in the early 1950s, to prevent them.

This attention to local politics reminds us that what happened in Vietnam in the DRV years cannot be explained by a simple template; we need to look more closely at concrete historical circumstances (the drain of manpower to the South, for example). Kerkvliet's approach follows the trend in peasant studies, developed by James C. Scott, among others, of using anthropology as a historical tool. Yet there is a danger inherent in this approach, that we will get carried away by a new version of the view of village autonomy expressed by the Vietnamese popular saying: "the emperor's writ stops at the bamboo hedge of the village." Without Communist Party sources, records of province and district party committee meetings, and more knowledge of the discussions in the Central Committee and politburo, we do not have a clear idea of the intensity of debates on agricultural policy nor the party's role in transforming the system.

A history of the ideological forces at work in the DRV would have to ask how closely the debate over production contracts in cooperatives (the three-*khoan* system) was connected to the struggle over contracts that occurred in China in 1962. Who, aside from the party secretary, Kim Ngoc, supported the continuing experiments with contracts in Vinh Phuc province? If we don't ask these questions, we may construct an overly simple dichotomy between the people and the party. Kerkvliet, for example, sees the Communist Party as somewhat distant and stable, with no major splits which might have encouraged popular opposition to government policy.[7] This view of resistance to official agricultural policy as coming uniquely from the bottom up may lead to the mystification of the peasant farmer as the incarnation of virtue and wisdom, a view inherent in much writing about the traditional values of the peasant commune. It minimizes the role of change agents or of the more educated cadres in leading the social revolution. It also, in the long run, lets the Communist Party off the hook, as there are no heroes or villains in this historiography, only party bureaucrats with the wisdom to follow where the people led.

For other historians, the examination of high-level Communist Party policies and the search for supporting documents to explain the past are still preoccupations. A useful contrast to the view of local Vietnamese political life offered by Kerkvliet is provided by an examination of village life in the liberated zones of South Vietnam in the early 1960s. David Elliott undertakes this task in his two-volume study on My Tho province: *The Vietnamese War: Revolution and Social Change in the Mekong Delta, 1930–1975*. Basing his account on interviews with defectors and prisoners, as well as on captured communist documents, Elliott concludes that political education or indoctrination played a large role in the success of the communist struggle. He is struck by the fact that "views from the inner circle reached the grass roots as a result of the systematic and intricately organized system of indoctrination" and that local cadres in My Tho "were extremely well informed about the big picture."[8]

He gives some clear examples of the rapidity with which policy changes could be communicated to the delta. One instance is the changes that occurred after the decisions of the party's Ninth Plenum in December 1963. These included "a rise in revolutionary coercion, increased taxation of the peasants, and a general hardening of the class line in My Tho."[9] This seems to demonstrate that local cadres were ready to implement directives from the upper levels of the party in the early 1960s, as they had done during the early collectivization in North Vietnam. Elliott goes on to explain, however, "in the end this harder class line was abandoned, because it created more problems than it solved."[10] So, clearly, popular unhappiness could help to change policy, but at the same time the party did have the organizational means to implement policy at the grassroots when it really wanted to. It would be useful to know more about the degree to which lower and midlevel cadres resisted central government policies that they disliked.

These two pictures, of North and South, may represent some significant differences between the level of revolutionary zeal in southern and northern Vietnam in the 1960s. They may also reflect the different sorts of responses that come from interviewing actors in the thick of the action or decades after the events being studied. But I believe that another element that affects the picture is Elliott's use of captured party documents. His microstudy of one province in the Vietnam War and the works of international historians who have used communist archives in Eastern Europe, Russia, and China to study the war have this point in common: they emphasize the impact of higher-level policy.

Since the 1990s, it has been outside of Vietnam that most of the documentary discoveries connected to the history of the war have been made. (I will mention only communist sources here.) The first wave of new work on the Vietnam War was part of the post-Soviet effort to use newly available communist archives to document the Cold War. It focused on international relations and was undertaken by non-Vietnamese-speaking international historians. Chinese scholars (now, Chinese American) Chen Jian and Qiang Zhai used provincial archives in China to document the transport of Chinese aid and troops to Vietnam.[11] Although the central Chinese Communist Party (CCP) archives remain mostly closed, these researchers were able to study CCP Central Committee documents and circulars sent to the provinces, in particular for the years 1949–1966. The Russian historian Ilya Gaiduk was given access to a range of Soviet Foreign Ministry and Central Committee archives, which allowed him to document Soviet decision making with far more precision and subtlety than had hitherto been possible. Norwegian scholar Mari Olsen has also been publishing on her extensive research in the Soviet Foreign Ministry archives on Soviet-Vietnamese relations. The work of these historians has created a new depth of understanding of the respective roles and interests of the Soviet Union and the People's Republic of China (PRC) in the Vietnam conflict. One thing we have learned from their studies is that there were only brief periods when a stable balance in this triangular relationship existed. For the Soviet Union, moreover, Vietnam was not a central geopolitical problem until the Sino-Soviet split was well advanced.

More recent research carried out in the newly opened archives of Hungary and the former East Germany has focused on internal DRV politics. In my work, I have also made use of some declassified documents from the Soviet Central Committee archives on the internal affairs of the DRV. These discoveries produce a vision of decision making in wartime North Vietnam that is characterized by internal party conflict and wide-ranging ideological debate. A number of unofficial Vietnamese memoirs, such as those by the Hanoi writer and former political prisoner Vu Thu Hien and by Nguyen Van Tran, an early party member trained in Moscow, also reinforce the importance of leadership politics and ideology.[12]

Although Vietnamese sources uncovered in Hanoi are believed by some scholars of Vietnam to be more trustworthy or authentic, other communist bloc sources can at this juncture make a unique contribution to our knowledge of Vietnam and the Vietnam War. Admittedly, using diplomatic and intelligence reports poses numerous difficulties, and one is obliged to read a large volume of such reports before evaluating the knowledge and perspicacity of the reporter. Yet used in conjunction with the government sources now available in Vietnam, these sources from other formerly socialist countries can provide a more balanced picture of decision making. They show that on its own, the "everyday politics" model is inadequate as a full explanation of key events and policy changes. I will cite some examples here of new information, which can be found in the East German and Hungarian archives, as a way of demonstrating how these sources challenge received views.

Research in former East German archives by Martin Grossheim, a fluent speaker of Vietnamese, shows how in 1963–1964 the DRV was affected by an "antirevisionist" campaign. The main message of this campaign was the rejection of Soviet policies of "peaceful coexistence" and a call for self-sufficient economic development.[13] (East German diplomats and press correspondents in the DRV followed political developments closely and tried to support those Vietnamese who held pro-Kremlin positions.) This campaign, which called for the rapid collectivization of agriculture, seems to have reflected an upswing of Mao Zedong's influence, following his temporary retreat at the end of the Great Leap Forward. But this policy did not seem to have universal support in the Vietnamese party.

By late 1963, East German diplomats were also reporting criticisms of Ho Chi Minh, the DRV's president and the incarnation of its anticolonial movement. The so-called theory of two mistakes was gaining ground among Vietnamese party members. According to this theory, Ho Chi Minh had twice made fatal political mistakes: once in 1945, when he "allowed" the French back into Vietnam, and again in 1954, when he agreed to the partition of Vietnam at the 17th Parallel. Memoirs by Vietnamese dissidents have claimed that Ho's voice was in fact overruled at the Ninth Plenum at the end of 1963, when the military struggle in the South was made a high priority and Hanoi moved closer to the Chinese orbit. To add weight to the view that Ho Chi Minh lost influence at that time, one can cite Mari Olsen's research in the Soviet Foreign Ministry archives. She found a report from the Soviet ambassador in Moscow, which relates that Ho visited him on Christmas day in 1963 and informed him that he was withdrawing from his role in day-to-day political life.[14] This was not the first time in his political career that Ho had come in for criticism within his party—he was a political nonperson during his stay in Moscow in the late 1930s; he had also been heavily criticized in 1948–1949 for dissolving the Indochinese Communist Party.

The Hungarian archives are also providing vital information on the political life of the DRV. Among the documents unearthed in Budapest by Hungarian historian and expert on comparative communism Balazs Szalontai are several that discuss the visit of Vo Nguyen Giap to Hungary in October 1967, ostensibly for medical treatment.[15] Through these sources, we learn that the man who is sometimes described as the architect of the Tet Offensive was out of Vietnam when the vital decisions were made on the timing and execution of the surprise attack on South Vietnam's towns and cities. This supports the revelation in Vu Thu Hien's memoir of his 1967 arrest and interrogation in Hanoi: that General Giap was one of the targets of the arrests carried out in the second half of 1967, in what has come to be known as the Anti-Party Affair. Hien describes his interrogation in detail, including the questioning he was subjected to regarding General Giap's plans and actions.[16] This crackdown on party "dissidents" had an impact on agricultural policy in 1968.

These pieces of information on DRV leadership politics should be enough to demonstrate that, in order to gain a deeper historical understanding of this country, we need to work toward a synthesis of the grassroots, anthropological method with a closer examination of the development of the Communist Party at the central level. Until such time as the VCP opens its archives to researchers, documentation on the latter will have to come from the archives of other communist parties in the former socialist bloc. Such a synthesis is vital to our understanding, not just of domestic policies, but also of the Vietnam-American War. As it now seems clear that there were moderates and extremists within the DRV's Communist Party (known during the war as the Lao Dong or Vietnam Workers Party, VWP), we need to look more closely at intraparty dynamics and how U.S. policy affected these relationships.

Rethinking Party History

There are a number of turning points in the development of Vietnamese communism and of the DRV that need to be elucidated before we can produce a comprehensive history of modern Vietnam. I will discuss three of these here, in conjunction with some of the new sources which shed light on these events. My goal is to show that, while a much deeper historical understanding of the DRV can be gained by studying the sociology, political culture, and anthropology of this state, we still have a long way to go before we can say that we really understand the old-fashioned subject of leadership politics. The three turning points examined below are the dissolution of the Communist Party (1945–1951), the 1963 adoption of Resolution 9, and the 1967 Anti-Party Affair.[17]

The Vietnamese communist movement grew out of a fractious collection of groups that somehow thrived on adversity. Although official histories do not make this explicit, they do make clear that this movement was less than united in the days before its formal founding in February 1930, and that at other points in its history, there were strong differences of opinion. The party's double origin, both as a Comintern-linked movement with strong ties to the French party and as part of the Chinese CP's sphere of influence, gave it an ambiguous status in communist circles. Even before its official foundation, as early as 1928, there was confusion within the Comintern and in the field, as to who had the final word on guiding the Vietnamese communists. From the date of its founding in 1930, the party was an amalgam of nationalist communists recruited by Ho Chi Minh and

more radical anarchist elements, at first mainly from northern Vietnam, who
had no personal links to Ho. Ho Chi Minh's role as the unifier of Vietnam's
communist groups in February 1930 was controversial at the time: there
were other young trainees who had been sent out from Moscow in late 1929
who expected to play that role themselves. In fact, it was soon afterward,
in October 1930, that Ho first was accused of being a bourgeois nationalist, whose short program for the unified party paid too little attention to
class struggle. This was the first time that he had to cede his leadership to a
younger man, Tran Phu, with a more orthodox approach to ideology. This
was also the moment when the Vietnamese Communist Party changed its
name to the Indochinese Communist Party (ICP) and, on the Comintern's
orders, assumed the internationalist task of spreading communism in all of
the French colonial territories of Indochina.

The early history of Vietnamese communism is, from 1930 on, the story
of how Ho Chi Minh returned to a position of importance and reoriented the
party toward nationalist revolution. In 1938, following his imprisonment in
Hong Kong and four years in eclipse in Moscow, he was finally sent back
to Asia by the disintegrating Comintern, after Stalin had been persuaded to
adopt the policy of united fronts with socialist parties. Ho's style of nationalist leadership, his advocacy of a broad coalition of antifascist forces in
Vietnam, was by his 1938 return the approved orthodoxy in the communist
world. He finally persuaded the ICP to change its program in 1941, when
he gathered a small handful of party leaders on the Chinese border to form
the Viet Minh alliance. National independence would take precedence over
agrarian reform and class struggle. Both the Vichy French government and
the occupying Japanese forces became the main enemies of the revolution,
no longer the small and large landowners who supported the anticolonial
movement. Antifascist French socialists could also be potential allies.

Not all party members greeted this change of emphasis with complete
enthusiasm. When word first got back to Vietnam about the Comintern's
united front policy in 1936–1937, the de facto leader, Ha Huy Tap, had done
his best to ignore the change. And even in 1941, the Vietnamese party's
patriarch could not convince everyone that the antifeudal revolution could
be delayed, and some Vietnamese communists stayed aloof from the Viet
Minh.[18] At the time of the August Revolution in 1945, the southern leader
of the alliance that declared independence in Saigon, Tran Van Giau, was
not officially affiliated with the Viet Minh, but was part of a rival regional
committee for the South, known as the Vanguard Regional Committee.[19]

At the decisive moment of his career in August–September 1945, Ho Chi
Minh relied on his contacts with the Americans in the Office of Strategic

Services (OSS) to give his leadership of the nationalist movement the stamp of inevitability. Without the members of the Deer Team (the OSS military trainers who parachuted into the Vietnamese highlands in the summer of 1945) with him in Hanoi and without the OSS envoys from Kunming to give him legitimacy, Ho would have had a more difficult time imposing his leadership on his compatriots and his fellow Communist Party members. This is not to say that his leadership, once he appeared in Ba Dinh Square on 2 September to declare Vietnamese independence, was ineffective or unpopular—the people responded with unfeigned enthusiasm to his gentle determination. If television had existed in 1945, his appeal might have been even more universal. But there were other leaders, including within his own party, who soon began to criticize his policies. What is significant about these critics is that they mainly thought him too compromising, too ready to make a deal with the French or other enemies of the revolution. This is an interesting contrast to the idea, which appears frequently in Western writing about the August Revolution, that Ho Chi Minh showed his true colors in these months by eliminating political opponents. Once one becomes aware of the fragmented nature of power in Vietnam in the fall of 1945, it becomes clear that we can't make assumptions about Ho's ability to command assassinations in Saigon or Quang Ngai from Hanoi. The circumstances in which different Trotskyist and noncommunist opponents were eliminated were different in each instance, and some of these were clearly beyond Ho Chi Minh's reach, in particular the elimination of the Constitutionalist Party members who had collaborated with Japan. In the case of the disappearance of Vietnam Nationalist Party (VNQDD) members in the summer of 1946, this would seem to have been part of a mutual struggle for power, initiated by the VNQDD, in which each side had its own armed assassins and thugs.

Among those who wanted a harder line against France were the leaders of the VNQDD, whose closest allies were the Nationalist Chinese, the occupiers of North Vietnam after the Japanese surrender. Their patrons returned to China after coming to terms with France in March 1946; after that, their resistance to Ho's continued efforts to negotiate a peace settlement that would leave Vietnam united, was their undoing. But another critic was the formal leader of the ICP, First Secretary Truong Chinh. In his September 1946 essay, "The August Revolution,"[20] he singled out a "lack of firmness in the repression of counter-revolutionary elements" as one of the weaknesses of the August 1945 uprising that brought the Viet Minh to power. He also mentioned the need for the government to move quickly to the antifeudal task of agrarian reform, along with the construction of socialism.

This critique came at the point when Ho's failure to extract some kind of face-saving settlement with France during the Fontainebleau negotiations was becoming clear. These discussions had dragged on from early July to 14 September 1946 and resulted in only a provisional modus vivendi, with most important issues unresolved.

Truong Chinh's essay may have also reflected his views of the dissolution of the ICP the previous year. Officially, from November 1945, the ICP had become a Marxist study group. This gave those activists whose power derived mainly from their party positions less prominent roles to play in national politics and in the coalition government established in 1946 than the Viet Minh leadership. This disbanding was generally accepted as cosmetic by Western observers, but there is ample evidence that it caused real dissension among Vietnamese communists and was looked on with suspicion by the foreign patrons of the Vietnamese party. As late as May 1950, this issue was still being discussed in Moscow: a Hungarian diplomat reported to his Foreign Ministry about a lecture he had attended by a Soviet official, Comrade Podkopaev, who defended the correctness of the dissolution of the ICP in 1945. The lecture was followed by a lively debate, which seemed to reflect some Soviet doubts about the political stance of the Viet Minh.[21] But there were earlier signs that this move on Ho Chi Minh's part was a source of disagreement. The defense of the decision to disband the party forms a major part of a report delivered by a secret Viet Minh emissary to the Soviet consulate in Bern in September 1947. It is clear from the tone of this report that the Vietnamese president was aware of the criticism being made of his decision and was trying to make his side of the story known.

The envoy who turned up unannounced at the Bern consulate had just made an undercover journey to Paris to meet with French party leaders Maurice Thorez and Jacques Duclos. He was traveling on a false passport in the name of Lin-tay, under cover as a Chinese businessman who had come to Switzerland to treat his tuberculosis. His Russian interlocutor recorded his name as Pham No Mach, but most likely he was Dr. Pham Ngoc Thach, a specialist in the treatment of tuberculosis who had become an important figure in Saigon's nationalist politics in 1945. In April and May 1947, Thach had made contact with U.S. diplomats in Thailand, including an assistant military attaché. The Americans had cautiously refrained from offering any direct support to the DRV.[22] The Soviet consul's report sent back to Moscow records that the Vietnamese emissary had stopped in Bangkok and Singapore, before traveling on to Europe. We can assume that he was a direct messenger of Ho Chi Minh, since he is identified as a representative of the secretariat of the "President of the Council of Ministers of the Republic of

Vietnam."[23] One of his requests was for permission to travel to Moscow, where he could personally report on the situation in Southeast Asia. Part of his assignment appears to have been to convince the Soviets that the Vietnamese communists were a significant force, worthy of support.

Appended to the Russian consul's report is a document titled "Situation within the Party," which is noted as "translated from the French." It is striking for its defensive tone. It lists nine reasons for the dissolution of the party, which it says "was dissolved on 11 November 1945, to our great regret." Among these were:

> [t]he Party's role during the years of the World War for national liberation had been so dominant that this had provoked suspicion and distrust on the international level; the Party was completely isolated and was not able to maintain any systematic relations with any fraternal party in other countries; the concession to the Chinese reactionaries, who directly or indirectly demanded this; and on the internal level, in order to bring about authentic national unity.

Some of the points were reassurances of the continued influence of communism within the government, e.g.: "The position of the Viet Minh is so secure within Vietnam, while its policies are fully controlled, from top to bottom, by the Party, that the Party's political line can in no way be compromised by its dissolution"; and the final point: "The dissolution of the Party is purely formal, and has only been registered officially, while all sections and cells have been given precise instructions to continue Party activities."

At this juncture in international events, Ho Chi Minh's earlier conciliatory attitude toward France had become fodder for criticism by his rivals within the party. This was the year that the World War II alliance disintegrated; by September 1947, former allies were becoming fierce enemies, as the two camps declared their positions. By early 1947, the Viet Minh had been driven back into the Maquis by the French. Their only outlet to the outside world was now through Thailand, and that would soon be closed by the November 1947 coup that brought Phibul Songkhram back to power. If the Viet Minh could not get support from the United States, it would have to turn to its former patrons in the French Communist Party and the USSR for aid and recognition—hence the secret journey to Bern. But in the end, the Viet Minh would have to wait until 1950 for the Soviet Union to finally follow the Chinese in recognizing its government.

Vietnamese relations with other communist parties had also been complicated by the crisis in the Malayan Communist Party (MCP) in early 1947. Until early in the year, the Malay communists had maintained good relations with the British and had carried out a united front policy to work nonviolently for national independence. But in March, the MCP leader Loi Tek (also spelled Lai Teck) disappeared before a special party meeting to examine suspicions that he had been working for the British. He took with him the party's funds and a detailed knowledge of its structures, probably including much information about contacts with regional parties. (Japanese sources later revealed that he had not only served as a double agent for the British—he had also cooperated with their secret services during their occupation of Malaya and Singapore.) One result of Loi Tek's unmasking was that the new MCP leader, Chin Peng, came under pressure to repudiate his predecessor's more moderate policies, and the party moved toward a phase of violent confrontation with the British.[24]

The end of Loi Tek's undercover career almost certainly had larger repercussions for Southeast Asia. His collaboration with the British could now be portrayed as a betrayal of the party's interests and used to cast doubt on other Southeast Asian communists who had attempted to maintain peaceful relations with the West from 1945 to 1947. This guilt by association could in itself have been damaging for Ho Chi Minh, but to complicate matters, there were two members of his government who had been trained by the British Inter-Services Liaison Department (ISLD), a cover name for MI6, in India before being parachuted back to the Maquis in 1944. They had been imprisoned by the French on Madagascar (Réunion), before being liberated and recruited by the British.[25] A final difficulty for Ho Chi Minh, and perhaps not the least important, was that Loi Tek had come to Malaya around 1934 as a member of the ICP and could claim to have known Ho in China. Judging by a number of overlaps in the biography of Loi Tek provided by British sources and the biography of a Vietnamese communist arrested by the French in 1933 in China, we can guess that the French first knew Loi Tek as the Vietnamese Truong Phuoc Dat.[26] He had been assigned by Ho Chi Minh to propaganda work among Vietnamese sailors in Shanghai in 1930, after he escaped from a military prison in Saigon. In 1933, he had already been responsible for sowing suspicion between the Chinese Communist Party in Shanghai and Vietnamese activists trying to reestablish their own party. He was suspected of having betrayed two of them to the French. One of these was Tran Ngoc Danh, who from 1945 to 1948 became the DRV representative in Paris. Danh was one of those Vietnamese communists who was most vociferous in criticizing in 1948–1950 what he called Ho's "opportunist and nationalist line,"[27] including the dissolution of the ICP.

Although Pham Ngoc Thach never made it to Moscow in 1947, Ho Chi Minh himself finally got there in the winter of 1950, as part of the entourage of Mao Zedong. He made his case for Soviet support successfully this time, even though he really had few strong cards to play. By this time, one of the communications from Tran Ngoc Danh must have also arrived in the Soviet capital. This criticized Ho's "opportunist and nationalist line."[28] Whatever negative feelings about Ho that Stalin may have possessed, based on his involvement in Comintern affairs, they were probably compounded by the harsh criticism emanating from the ICP itself. As we know from Khrushchev's memoirs, Stalin gave Ho a very cool reception. According to Chinese historian Yang Kuisong, it was Mao who gave Ho the endorsement he needed to retain his prestige as the paramount leader of the DRV. Mao cabled Liu Shaoqi from Moscow to instruct him to adopt a "cooperative attitude toward the Vietnamese communists, to encourage their struggle, and not to criticize them." Mao made a clear, but not particularly strong, defense of Ho's past policies: "Ho once disguised his party and declared that the DRV remained neutral. It is too early to say that these two policies were mistakes in principle because the Vietnamese struggle did not suffer as a result of their implementation."[29] The price of Mao's support for Ho Chi Minh and Vietnam was that, for much of the 1950s, the Vietnamese communists became the ideological apprentices of the CCP, in particular in the implementation of land reform. But ignorant of the nuances of Vietnamese communist politics, the U.S. State Department regarded this Vietnamese alliance with the USSR and China as inevitable. A State Department press officer declared, "Ho had been revealed as an 'agent of world communism' and a pseudo-nationalist who wanted 'Indochina for the Kremlin and not Indochina for the Indochinese.' "[30]

This background on Ho's early difficulties in establishing his leadership within his own party should make it clear that he was unable to wield absolute power. During the early 1950s, until the "correction of errors" campaign to repair the damage done by overzealous land reform cadres, the CCP provided the main ideological and technical guidance to the Vietnamese communists, acting as what Mari Olsen has called "subcontractors" for the Soviet Union. In these years, party members who shared the Maoist vision of radical social transformation and class struggle rose to powerful positions in the VWP (Lao Dong), the party's new name after it resurfaced officially at the Second Party Congress in 1952. Le Van Luong, a former teacher and political prisoner, headed a campaign to rectify or purify the party from 1952 to 1956. Before his removal in late 1956, his party organization commission began to target middle-class Viet Minh veterans and to eliminate them from leadership positions. Some party veterans viewed this as an early campaign against Ho Chi Minh's right-hand man, Vo Nguyen

Giap, who was enjoying a high degree of personal prestige following the victory at Dien Bien Phu.[31]

By late 1956, following the momentous changes in the communist world brought about by Khrushchev's Twentieth Congress denunciation of Stalin, Ho Chi Minh was able to regain the initiative within his party for a short time. But this brief window of moderation closed quickly, as the Twentieth Congress led to uprisings in Eastern Europe and Sino-Soviet relations deteriorated. The Chinese leadership was shocked by the criticism of Stalin and fairly quickly distanced themselves from some of Khrushchev's other initiatives, which they termed "modern revisionism." Khrushchev's promotion of "peaceful coexistence," including peaceful competition between the capitalist and communist worlds, was a policy with which the DRV tried to live, but it ended up dividing the leadership. Another aspect of Khrushchev's policies that disturbed the Chinese leadership was the idea that class contradictions no longer played a major role in Soviet society. This was an outright rejection of class struggle, as Yang Kuisong explains it, and as such was unacceptable to Mao. The Vietnamese attempted to maintain a stance of equidistance between their two communist patrons, but in 1960 they signed a communiqué endorsing Soviet policies along with most of the world's communist parties. Yet Khrushchev's call for the admission of the two Vietnamese governments to the United Nations in 1957 and Soviet reluctance to provide significant diplomatic or military support for Vietnam's struggle for reunification caused much unhappiness in Hanoi.

By early 1963, when Czech president Antonin Novotny visited Hanoi and signed a joint communiqué with Ho Chi Minh, which praised peaceful coexistence as "the most correct policy," the conflict between pro-Chinese elements and pro-Soviet elements in the DRV was intensifying. Ung Van Khiem, the foreign minister and a southern party veteran, was later blamed for signing the communiqué and replaced in his post by Nguyen Duy Trinh. Martin Grossheim writes that, at this time, many other Hanoi cadres who had taken pro-Soviet positions since 1956 were also replaced, especially those working in the press and reporting on foreign policy. The East German embassy reported that "all key positions in the press department of the Lao Dong Central Committee and the Ministry of Foreign Affairs, the Vietnam News Agency and radio were occupied by cadres 'who closely followed the Chinese course.' "[32] Following consultations with Chinese theoreticians and Chairman Mao in Wuhan in the summer of 1963, at its Ninth Plenum at the end of the year, the VWP passed a resolution condemning "modern revisionism" and aligning its internal and foreign policies with those of China.

Known to historians of the Vietnam War as the resolution that announced the determination to reunite Vietnam by force, Resolution 9 also made sweeping changes in the Hanoi political scene. Hoang Minh Chinh, until the end of 1963 head of the Institute of Philosophy in Hanoi, who would in 1967 be imprisoned for his "revisionist" views, described the announcement of the Ninth Plenum decisions in an open letter to the Vietnamese National Assembly written in 1993. He explained that at a meeting of 400 top cadres in January 1964, Truong Chinh (at that time, head of the Nguyen Ai Quoc Party School and chair of the national assembly) made the following announcement:

> [D]ue to the complicated situation within the international communist movement, we cannot write out all the points included in Resolution 9. You must pay attention to the fact that the real nature of Resolution 9 must be made known only by word of mouth, that is: the external and internal policy of our Party and government is in fundamental agreement with the policies of the Party and government of China.[33]

Soviet-style revisionism became a political crime within the DRV at this time, and ideas of peaceful coexistence went out of style.

Hoang Minh Chinh credited Le Duc Tho, head of the powerful Party Control Commission, and Truong Chinh with spearheading this realignment of the DRV's policy. Party first secretary Le Duan is also assumed to have supported it, in part because he led a delegation to Moscow in January 1964, where he delivered a long-winded speech detailing all of the points on which the Vietnamese were in disagreement with their Soviet comrades.[34] But whether or not he was the primary booster of this political change is unclear. What is clear is that the passage of Resolution 9 brought even cooler relations between the USSR and the DRV, which resulted in the recall of all Vietnamese students in the Soviet Union and requests for asylum from some of the military officers studying in Moscow. Intellectuals who had studied in Europe were the primary victims of the ideological offensive launched early in 1964, following the plenum's close. They were accused of being influenced by "modern revisionism," a disease which led to bourgeois thinking and pessimism, of lacking an understanding of proletarian dictatorship, and of relying on foreign aid instead of supporting the idea of a self-sufficient economy. Ho Chi Minh's political position clearly changed as a result of this plenum. On Christmas day 1963, on a visit to the Soviet embassy in Hanoi, he announced his retirement from day-to-day political affairs. After this, his role increasingly became that of an icon of the revolution.

The cooling of relations with the Soviet Union was not permanent, of course. Following the ouster of Khrushchev in October 1964, the new premier, Alexei Kosygin, made a visit to North Vietnam in February 1965. This visit, during which Kosygin experienced an American bombing raid, marked a new phase in the relations between the Soviet Union and Vietnam. Although the Russians failed to win the Chinese over to a program of united aid to Vietnam, the new Soviet leadership began to provide a steady supply of heavy weapons and advisors to instruct in their use. The Chinese continued as major suppliers of food, consumer goods, light military equipment, anti-aircraft troops, and even foreign currency, but by the end of 1968 they had been overtaken by the USSR as the major suppliers of aid to the DRV.

This seemingly smooth relationship between the USSR and the DRV in 1966 and early 1967 makes the events that occurred in the late summer and fall of 1967 all the stranger. At the end of August, as planning for a major offensive was intensifying in Hanoi, a number of VWP members with ties to the Soviet Union began to be arrested. One of the victims was Hoang Minh Chinh, the Moscow-trained, former head of the Institute of Philosophy, who had been removed from his post at the end of 1963, in the earlier wave of anti-Soviet measures. Along with him, Vu Dinh Huynh, a former personal secretary to Ho Chi Minh and the father of Vu Thu Hien, was arrested. Other groups of middle-ranking cadres, including generals, professors, writers, and television journalists, all with ties to Eastern Europe, were picked up in successive waves of arrests in October and December. These arrests and the subsequent accusation that the victims were involved in a pro-Soviet plot against the ruling politburo of the VWP became known as the Hoang Minh Chinh Affair, or the Anti-Party Affair. Recently declassified reports from the British consul in Hanoi, John Colvin, show that the Russians had "forecast for some time [a] shake up in [the] Lao Dong Party adverse to their interests." Colvin wrote that on 21 August 1967 a Soviet colonel had told the Indonesian chargé d'affaires that arrests of "several leading Party members had taken place that morning."[35] Other sources on this affair include the memoirs of Vu Dinh Huynh's son, Vu Thu Hien. These were published in Germany in 1997 as *Dem giua ban ngay* (*Darkness in the Daytime*). The letters and petitions for the restitution of the civil rights of Hoang Minh Chinh himself, who is still alive in Hanoi after many years in prison, solitary confinement, and house arrest, corroborate the broad outlines of Hien's account of his arrest and interrogation.

Given the lack of comment from any official representative of the Hanoi regime over the years, it has been very difficult to determine the significance of these events in late 1967 and 1968. The obvious conclusion is that party members considered to be hostile to the escalation of the war were being imprisoned to quell dissent within the government. The improvement of U.S.–Soviet relations that summer, resulting from the summit meeting in Glassboro, New Jersey, between President Johnson and Premier Kosygin, had raised alarm in Beijing and possibly in Hanoi as well. During this meeting Kosygin had received assurance directly from Pham Van Dong in Hanoi that, if the United States stopped the bombing of North Vietnam unconditionally, the North Vietnamese would immediately go to the conference table.

The British consulate in Hanoi was picking up indications of a struggle within the leadership over the issue of negotiations. In March 1968, an analyst at the consulate reported on a *Nhan Dan* editorial on the revival of "Law 63," which he described as a "vehicle for the legal disposal of any dissident members or factions in the Party." His analysis came from a "senior Eastern bloc diplomat," who told him that "there might be a split in the Party at the moment, probably between the doves and the eagles, but he [the Eastern bloc diplomat] thought that the decree would be sufficient warning to all members to toe the line."[36] Don Oberdorfer notes in his recounting of the Tet Offensive that this decree was issued in November 1967 by the Standing Committee of the Vietnamese National Assembly, but was not made public until March 1968. It prescribed "death sentences, life prison terms, and lesser penalties for a long list of 'counterrevolutionary crimes,' including espionage, sabotage, security violations and the crime of opposing or hindering the execution of national defense plans."[37]

The fact that those arrested in 1967 were held until 1972 and then rearrested if they made an effort to gain redress, leads one to believe that they were considered to be long-term threats by some faction of the leadership. Vu Thu Hien believes that the ultimate target of this affair was Vo Nguyen Giap. While in prison, Hien was closely interrogated about his father's relations with General Giap and his own knowledge of Giap's affairs. He concludes that Le Duc Tho and Le Duan viewed Giap as a rival for power, and thus concocted the coup plot to discredit him, along with other influential, second-tier cadres believed to be pro-Soviet.[38] The only formal accusation against the "modern revisionists" came four years later, at a Central Committee plenum in January 1972, when Le Duc Tho announced that there had been a conspiracy to overthrow the party leadership.[39] Soviet ambassador Ilia Shcherbakov and his second secretary, Rashid Khamidulin, were accused of links with the plotters.

Giap himself was never arrested, but in October 1967 he flew to Hungary, ostensibly to garner more support for Hanoi's war effort. However, documents in the Hungarian archives show that Giap was in Hungary as early as 14 October, where he was receiving medical treatment, along with the son of former foreign minister Ung Van Khiem, who was known to have revisionist sympathies. By 19 October, the Vietnamese ambassador reported to the Hungarians that Giap's health was already improving. Ambassador Hoang Luong said that Giap had exhausted himself while writing a long essay on the tactics and strategy of the Vietnamese struggle.[40]

The arrests of 1967 did not touch the top layer of the DRV leadership, but they clearly weakened any support for General Giap as a contender for a top post after Ho Chi Minh's death. Among the arrested were a number of cadres who had been close aides to Giap at the time of the Dien Bien Phu campaign. The real threat that Giap may have represented was his personal popularity, which stemmed from his victory in 1954, but also from his apology for the excesses of the land reform, a unique event in party history.

The ideological fallout from the Anti-Party Affair did have long-term effects on the DRV's domestic and international policies. Speeches by Le Duc Tho and Truong Chinh in late 1967 and 1968 laid out the policies about which they felt strongly. There are a number of overlaps with Mao's policy concerns of the Cultural Revolution years. In a late 1967 speech, Le Duc Tho focused on what he called "rightist deviations" in the construction of the party. He claimed that, since the correction of the errors of the land reform and party rectification, "we made the rightist error of restoring the membership of a number of people who should not have been readmitted." He singled out the upper levels of the party, where he said the majority of members are "petty bourgeois intellectuals."[41] One of the concerns voiced by Truong Chinh in a long speech (or series of lectures) to commemorate the 150th anniversary of Karl Marx's birth was the nature of the revolution in South Vietnam. He emphasized that the party must remain in undisputed control of the united front at all stages of the national democratic revolution and on no account let it fall into the hands of the bourgeoisie.[42] Truong Nhu Tang's eyewitness account of life in the liberated zones of the South confirms that the party's attitude toward the bourgeois members of the provisional revolutionary government grew less welcoming in the 1970s, a fact which he links to Ho Chi Minh's death in 1969.[43] But the groundwork for the hardening of class attitudes was laid in 1967–1968.

Another result of the hardening of the ideological line in the DRV was the ending of production contracts on cooperative farms, which again was one of Truong Chinh's fixations. In the speech cited above, he singled out "the reform of the relations of production and the system of property" as the immediate goal of the communist revolution in the North. In June 1968, a decree from the party's Central Committee secretariat, signed by Le Van Luong, called for the unification of the administration and distribution of food products and movement toward the elimination of the free market in foodstuffs.[44] Truong Chinh's speech calling for the end of the family contract system was delivered to the cadres of Vinh Phu province on 6 November 1968. He explained that the experiments with contracts were the equivalent of a return to individual farming, that they "went against the party's path of cooperativization."[45]

Ho Chi Minh was a fading presence in these years. He spent most of 1967 in China for medical treatment, although this was not made public at the time. Foreign diplomats noted that he was not spotted in Hanoi after 13 April 1967 until late July, when he flew back to receive two French peace envoys, Raymond Aubrac and Herbert Marcovitch. In September, he returned for medical reasons to Beijing, where he stayed until late December.[46] It must have been clear to the members of the politburo that he would not be around much longer to mediate disputes between the party factions nor to serve as a moderating force. (However, there is an enduring story in Hanoi, attributed to Ho's private secretary, Vu Ky, that Ho believed he had narrowly escaped an assassination attempt in December 1967, when his plane had been guided onto the wrong runway on his return from Beijing. His pilot had known the airport well enough to make his own decision about where to land.)

A political consequence of the Anti-Party Affair was that a group of leaders who had built their careers on a close relationship with China and support of Chinese policy saved themselves from irrelevance as the Vietnamese relationship with China weakened. This weakening first occurred because of the Cultural Revolution and the chaos it caused in the country which had for so long been a secure rear base for the Vietnamese revolution. But with the election of Richard Nixon to the U.S. presidency, it was the U.S.–Chinese rapprochement that caused a serious chill in Sino-Vietnamese relations.

Conclusion

This quick survey of some of the turning points in North Vietnamese communist history only scratches the surface. This kind of political history is of necessity dependent on the accumulation of a large amount of detailed information, which is often difficult to parse. Communist politics were convoluted and opaque, because there was no room for a loyal opposition;

those who wanted to change the dominant policies at any moment in time could not afford to make their goals too public or even clear. But we cannot afford to ignore the problem of politics at the higher levels of the party and government.

The VWP and its role within the DRV evolved from 1945 to 1975, as the violent assault on its right to rule a unified Vietnam continued. The nationalist coalition that Ho Chi Minh had constructed by early 1946 was always dependent on its communist core. And Ho's control over this core group was tenuous, despite his great moral influence. What ate away at his power over the years was his inability to win recognition for his new state from his World War II allies.

One reasonable hypothesis remains the idea that U.S. policy strengthened the hand of the radicals who saw revolutionary violence (combined with class war) as the only way to end the conflict in Vietnam. This analysis is not original—observers from Robert Shaplen to Mark Bradley have drawn this conclusion about the early U.S.–Hanoi relationship in the late 1940s. But in view of more recent evidence on the political life of the DRV, we may be justified in extending it to at least 1967.

It is evident that Ho Chi Minh's efforts at compromise in 1945–1946 had weakened him politically, while those party members such as Ung Van Khiem, the former foreign minister, who had supported peaceful coexistence in the 1958–1963 period found their careers in ruins soon after the policy changed. A similar conflict over peace negotiations seems to have occurred in 1967. From the failure to encourage elections in 1956 to the failure to declare a bombing halt in the late summer of 1967, when negotiations were clearly the aim of some of the Vietnamese leadership, U.S. policy could be seen as undermining the forces of moderation. The DRV was a state shaped by war, and its political culture as of 1975 was a reflection of that fact.

NOTES

1. Roderick MacFarquhar, *The Origins of the Cultural Revolution*, vol. 3: *The Coming of the Cataclysm 1961–1966* (Oxford: Oxford University Press, 1997), vii.

2. As the current scapegoat for the party's errors in past decades, Le Duan and his speeches are treated with unusual candor. He is held responsible for the mistakes of the post-1975 period, when Vietnam moved into a full-blown alliance with the Soviet Union. He is often portrayed as the most bellicose member of the politburo during the war with the United States, while the nuances of his views on the role of the nationalist bourgeoisie and political struggle are forgotten. His moderate views on economic and social policies are also rarely mentioned in Hanoi.

3. Tran Van Tra, *Ket thuc cuoc chien tranh 30 nam* [*The Conclusion of the Thirty Year War*] (Ho Chi Minh City: NXB Van Nghe, 1982).

4. Tran Quynh's "Hoi ky ve Le Duan [Memoirs of Le Duan], 1960–1986," an unpublished draft manuscript which has circulated in Hanoi since 1997, refers to a "smear campaign" against Le Duan.

5. The current Western research being carried out on the DRV is naturally determined by the available documentation. There is a division between scholars who are specialists on Vietnam and know the language, and international historians, most of whom, with some important exceptions, do not. Those Vietnamists who work in Hanoi or Saigon archives do not as a rule have access to unedited Communist Party documents, but can use archives created by various government departments. Hanoi's Archive Number III for Contemporary History houses the archives of the National Assembly, selected government departments, committees such as the Government Committee on Reunification (Uy Ban Chinh Phu Thong Nhat), and some of the ministries. These archives do not include the records of the Foreign Ministry or the Ministries of Defense or Interior. These key ministries keep their records closed to foreign researchers, although Vietnamese scholars have some access.

6. Benedict Kerkvliet, *The Power of Everyday Politics: How Peasants Transformed National Policy* (Ithaca, N.Y.: Cornell University Press, 2005), 234.

7. Ibid., 27.

8. David W. P. Elliott, *The Vietnamese War: Revolution and Social Change in the Mekong Delta, 1930–1975* (Armonk, N.Y.: Sharpe, 2001), 2:737–38.

9. Ibid., 1:620–21.

10. Ibid, p. 621.

11. See, for example, Chen Jian, *Mao's China and the Cold War* (Chapel Hill: University of North Carolina Press, 2001), and Qiang Zhai, *China and the Vietnam Wars, 1950–1975* (Chapel Hill: University of North Carolina Press, 2000).

12. Vu Thu Hien, *Dem giua ban ngay* [*Darkness in the Daytime*] (Germany: NXB Thien Chi, 1997); Nguyen Van Tran, *Viet Cho Me va Quoc Hoi* [*Writing for Mother and the National Assembly*] (California: NXB Van Nghe, 1995).

13. Martin Grossheim, " 'Revisionism' in the Democratic Republic of Vietnam: New Evidence from the East German Archives," *Cold War History* 5.4 (November 2005), 451–77.

14. Mari Olsen, "Changing Alliances: Moscow's Relations with Hanoi and the Role of China, 1949–1964," Ph.D. diss., University of Oslo, 2005, p. 224.

15. See Balazs Szalontai, "Political and Economic Crisis in North Vietnam, 1955–1956," *Cold War History* 5.4 (November 2005): 397.

16. Vu Thu Hien, *Dem giua ban ngay*, 271–79.

17. The glaring omission here is land reform and the collectivization of agriculture (1952–1962). Although these topics are usually viewed as domestic issues, a history of the international ideological influences on these campaigns, as well as of their leadership, would be a valuable addition to the accounts of Edwin Moise, *Land Reform in China and Vietnam: Consolidating the Revolution at the Village Level* (Chapel Hill: University of North Carolina Press,1983), of land reform and Benedict Kerkvliet,

Power of Everyday Politics, of collectivization. But these topics would require documentation from the Chinese side and a Chinese-speaking researcher to examine them.

18. David Marr, *Vietnam 1945: The Quest for Power* (Berkeley: University of California Press, 1995), 184–94.

19. Ho Son Dai and Tran Phan Chan, eds., *Lich su Saigon, Cho Lon, Gia Dinh Khang Chien (1945–1975)* [*The History of the Resistance in Saigon, Cholon and Gia Dinh (1945–1975)*] (Ho Chi Minh City: NXB T. P. Ho Chi Minh, 1994), 67.

20. Truong Chinh, *Primer for Revolt: The Communist Takeover in Vietnam* (New York: Frederick A. Praeger, 1963). Includes facsimile edition of "The August Revolution."

21. Szalontai, "Political and Economic Crisis in North Vietnam," 397.

22. Mark Philip Bradley, *Imagining Vietnam and America: The Making of Postcolonial Vietnam, 1919–1950* (Chapel Hill: University of North Carolina Press, 2000), 149.

23. References to this report are from the Russian State Archive for Social and Political History (RGASPI), collection 17 (Central Committee), inventory 128, item 404. This copy of the report was sent to the Central Committee by the First European Section of the Ministry of Foreign Affairs on 20 September 1947, "Report of Pham No Mach to the Soviet Envoy in Switzerland, A. G. Kulazhenkov."

24. See, for example, Phillip Deery, "Malaya, 1948: Britain's Asian Cold War?" Working Paper 3, The Cold War as Global Conflict, International Center of Advanced Studies, New York University, April 2002.

25. These were Phan Boi (aka Hoang Huu Nam) from Quang Nam and Le Gian from Hanoi.

26. Descriptions of Loi Tek's early career from British sources come from Yoki Akashi, "Lai Teck: Secretary General of the Malayan Communist Party, 1939–1947," *Journal of the South Seas Society* 49 (1994): 57–103. This article says that after working in Shanghai, Loi Tek had been designated for study in Moscow, but had been arrested on the Manchurian border and was unable to continue his travels (63). The statement to the French Sûreté of a Truong Phuoc Dat matches many elements of this biography, although a number of dates in the British version appear to be off by a few years. The pseudonym Ly Minh Son is also given in both of these biographies as one used by Loi Tek and by Truong Phuoc Dat in China. The cynical attitude shown by Loi Tek, as described by Akashi, is also uncannily like that expressed by Truong Phuoc Dat toward his erstwhile comrades in his statement to the French police.

27. Christopher Goscha, "Le Contexte asiatique de la Guerre Franco-vietnamienne. Réseaux, relations, et économie, d'aout 1945 à mai 1954," dissertation, Ecole Pratique des Hautes Etudes, Paris, 2000, pp. 678–9, citing Archives of Czech CP CC, collection 100/3, vol. 207.

28. Sophie Quinn-Judge, *Ho Chi Minh: The Missing Years* (Berkeley: University of California Press, 2003), 254.

29. Yang Kuisong, "Mao Zedong and the Indochina Wars," unpublished paper delivered at the Cold War International History Project meeting, New Evidence on China, Southeast Asia and the Vietnam War, Hong Kong, 11–12 January 2000, pp. 4–5, n. 9.

30. Andrew Rotter, *The Path to Vietnam: Origins of the American Commitment to Southeast Asia* (Ithaca, N.Y.: Cornell University Press, 1987), 172, quoting the *New York Times*, 1 February 1950.

31. By this time, the two British-trained intelligence specialists, who had retained the confidence of Ho Chi Minh and Giap, were out of the picture. Phan Boi had drowned in a freak accident in 1947, and Le Gian had been removed from his position as chief of the Ministry of Public Security sometime in 1952.

32. Martin Grossheim, "'Revisionism' in the Democratic Republic of Vietnam," 453.

33. Hoang Minh Chinh's "Open Letter" of 27 August 1993, reprinted in a number of Vietnamese émigré publications, including *Dien Dan* [*Forum*].

34. Ilya Gaiduk, *The Soviet Union and the Vietnam War* (Chicago: Dee, 1996), 6–7.

35. Public Record Office (hereafter PRO; now known as British National Archives), FCO 15/481, Hanoi to Foreign Office, unnumbered, 22 August 1967, signed by Mr. Colvin.

36. PRO, FCO 15/481, 1 January 1968, Conf. Brit. Congen, Hanoi, 30 March 1968, to SEAD, F[oreign] O[ffice], signed by G. S. Hirst.

37. Don Oberdorfer, *Tet!* (Garden City, N.Y.: Doubleday, 1971), 66.

38. Vu Thu Hien, *Dem giua ban ngay*, 271–79.

39. Ibid., 297.

40. My thanks to Balazs Szalontai for providing me with a translation of this document. Memorandum: The Visit of Vietnamese Ambassador Hoang Luong to Dep[uty] Foreign Minister Erdelyi (Hungarian Foreign Ministry Archives, VTS 1967.93.doboz, 146,001025/19/1967).

41. Le Duc Tho, "Xay dung dang kieu moi mac-xit-le-nin-it vung manh," *Hoc Tap* 2 (1968): 32–34.

42. From a U.S. analysis of Truong Chinh's speech, circulated by the French embassy in London. Archives of French Foreign Ministry (Ministère des Affaires Étrangères), Série Conflit Vietnam, 11 (Front National de Liberation), Extraits d'un rapport de Truong Chinh, diffuse par Radio Hanoi, 16–20 September 1968.

43. Truong Nhu Tang, *Journal of a Vietcong* (London: Jonathan Cape, 1986).

44. "Nghi quyet cua ban Bi Thu," so 179, ngay 8, thang 6, 1968 ["Resolution of the Secretariat," no. 179, 8 June 1968], in *Van Kien Dang Toan Tap* [*Collected Party Documents*], vol. 29 (Hanoi: Nha Xuat Ban Chinh Tri Quoc Gia [National Politics Publishing House],1968), 278–302.

45. *Nhan Dan*, 29 January 1968, 2.

46. PRO, FCO 15/535, Secret, Immediate Hanoi to Foreign Office, telegram no. 421, 3 July 1967; William Duiker, *Ho Chi Minh: A Life* (New York: Hyperion, 2000), 556.

VISION, POWER, AND AGENCY

The Ascent of Ngo Dinh Diem, 1945–1954

EDWARD MILLER

Who was Ngo Dinh Diem? In the decades since his 1963 assassination, historians and other writers have offered diverse interpretations of his life and career. That Diem was an important figure in the history of the Indochina wars is not in dispute—after all, the conflict that became the "American war" in Vietnam began as a revolt against Diem's South Vietnamese regime—but there is no consensus about why and how he came to play such a key role. During Diem's tenure in power (1954–1963), many in Vietnam and elsewhere described him as an American puppet who had been installed and supported by Washington to serve U.S. objectives in the Cold War. Accounts written since the 1960s, in contrast, have emphasized his notorious unwillingness to accept American advice and the fact that his alliance with the United States eventually fell apart. Many scholars have thus come to reject the notion that Diem was merely a creature of U.S. foreign policy and have instead portrayed him as a product of premodern "traditions," such as Catholicism or Confucianism. Among these scholars, however, there is no consensus about the meaning and consequences of these "traditional" qualities. In some recent histories, Diem appears as a sage-like national hero who was thwarted by fickle allies; in others, he is portrayed as an inflexible autocrat who was doomed by his adherence to outdated ideas about rulership.[1]

These seemingly disparate representations of Diem—as U.S. stooge, virtuous patriot, or reactionary despot—are more alike than they first appear. By rendering Diem in flat and simplistic terms, they all fail to acknowledge the particular and contingent aspects of Diem's ideas and actions. Whether Diem is alleged to have been merely executing American designs or to have been manifesting traditional cultural or social characteristics, the result is the same: in each case, Diem's capacity to control his own thoughts and deeds is denied. In short, the existing representations of Diem have refused him his due as a historical agent. The effect, as one historian has pointed out, has been to reduce Diem to the historiographical equivalent of a "cardboard cutout."[2]

This chapter proposes to restore a modicum of agency to Diem by examining an understudied part of his career: the decade prior to his 1954 appointment as premier of the state that would become known as South Vietnam. My study challenges the received view of Diem in two ways. First, it disputes the assertion that Diem spent the duration of the Franco–Viet Minh war of 1945–1954 in self-imposed political isolation, quietly awaiting the arrival of his destiny.[3] In fact, Diem did not remain aloof from the struggles which wracked Indochina in these years, and he had dealings with almost all of the key players in Indochinese politics. Thus, instead of portraying Diem as a passive figure entirely or mostly dependent on the support of one or another faction or patron, this chapter shows that he played an active and important role in engineering his own rise to power.

Second, my analysis takes issue with the notion that Diem's ideas and actions during 1945–1954 can be taken as evidence of traditional ways of thinking. As postcolonial scholars such as Ronald Inden have demonstrated, invocations of "tradition" often betray the essentializing tendencies which infuse much of the Western scholarship on Asia and Asians.[4] The examples which Inden critiques are drawn from Indology, but his arguments are applicable to writings about Vietnam generally and to writings about Diem in particular. Just as scholars of India have tended to displace the agency of Indians onto Europeans or onto allegedly essential qualities of Indian life, such as caste or divine kingship, so too have scholars of the Vietnam War displaced Diem's agency onto Americans or onto essences, such as Confucianism or Catholicism. By reducing Diem's words and actions to the lingering effects of premodern patterns of thinking, many authors have overlooked Diem's efforts to refashion old ideas into new forms, as well as his determination to promote a distinctive vision of how Vietnam could become a modern nation.[5] To be sure, Diem's vision of Vietnam's modernization emerged only gradually, and it was far from fully formed in 1954. It was, moreover, a highly idiosyncratic vision, and Diem's efforts to persuade South Vietnamese of its utility and merit would fail miserably in the long run. But failure does not necessarily imply insignificance or inconsequence. In order to arrive at a more historical and less caricatured understanding of Diem's role in the history of the Indochina wars, we must come to grips with the contingent and contemporary nature of his ideas and examine the specific historical context—late colonial Indochina—in which he formulated them.

Diem and the Quest for a "Third Force," 1945–1950

For many Vietnamese nationalists, the onset of all-out war between France and the Viet Minh in December 1946 presented a stark and difficult choice. The thought of rallying to support the colonial regime was distasteful to anticolonial activists who advocated independence for Vietnam, yet many nationalists also recoiled at the thought of lending support to Ho Chi Minh and the communist-dominated Viet Minh. Some refused to cooperate with the Viet Minh on ideological grounds; others were wary of the communists based on experience.[6] Faced with such unpalatable options, these nationalists often declined to choose either side and decided instead to wait for the emergence of a "Third Force"—that is, an independent party or coalition which would be both anticolonialist and anticommunist. From the mid-1940s, there were many attempts to create a Third Force in Indochina, but all of them foundered on the ideological and political fissures which divided Vietnam's myriad noncommunist parties, sects, and factions. As a result, many activists resigned themselves to maintaining a stance of uneasy neutrality in the conflict. The French chided such would-be Third Forcers as "fence sitters" (*attentistes*), while the Viet Minh derided them for "hiding under a blanket" (*trum chan*).

A well-known Catholic leader and nationalist, Diem was counted among the most prominent of the *attentistes*. This was a misleading characterization, however, insofar as it implied that he was reluctant to take political risks. Diem was born in 1901 into a highly accomplished Catholic family: his father, Ngo Dinh Kha, was grand chamberlain of the Vietnamese imperial court; his eldest brother, Ngo Dinh Khoi, served as a colonial provincial governor; and another brother, Ngo Dinh Thuc, became one of the first Vietnamese Catholic bishops. Diem upheld family tradition by becoming an official in the imperial administration, and he rose to the post of province chief while still in his late twenties. His success was due not only to his talents as an administrator but also to the patronage of Nguyen Huu Bai, a Catholic who headed the Council of Ministers in Hue. Though he had long collaborated with the French colonial regime, Bai had become frustrated in the 1920s with French encroachments on the imperial court's prerogatives, and he enlisted Diem and his older brothers in efforts to pressure the French for reforms which would have restored a measure of Vietnamese sovereignty. In 1933, the French tried to mollify Bai by elevating Diem to the post of interior minister; however, the move backfired when Bai counseled Diem to step down in protest of French intransigence on the reform issue. Diem's resignation established his reputation as an uncompromising nationalist, even as it also confirmed his status as a militant and ambitious Catholic leader.[7]

Despite later assertions to the contrary, Diem did not lapse into political obscurity after 1933, but remained active in court politics in Hue throughout the 1930s, even though he no longer held office and was under police surveillance.[8] After 1940, he intensified his activism in order to exploit new political opportunities created by the Japanese occupation of Indochina. The occupation of 1940–1945 was peculiar because Japan allowed the pro-Vichy colonial government of Indochina to remain in place in exchange for garrison privileges and access to provisions. Such a policy contrasted sharply with Japanese practices elsewhere in Southeast Asia during World War II, and it did not sit well with those Japanese officials who considered themselves "idealists" on the issue of liberating their fellow Asians from European colonial rule. The discontent of these Japanese idealists provided an opening for Diem, and by 1942 he had became embroiled in a variety of anti-French intrigues. In 1943, he dispatched an envoy to make contact with Prince Cuong De, a long-time anticolonialist activist and pretender to the Nguyen throne, who had lived in exile in Japan for more than two decades and who had ties to idealist officers and diplomats in both Tokyo and Indochina. Around the same time, Diem established a secret political party known as the Association for the Restoration of Greater Vietnam (Dai Viet Phuc Hung Hoi). This party seems to have operated primarily in Diem's native region of Central Vietnam, and its ranks were filled overwhelmingly—perhaps even exclusively—by Catholics. In the summer of 1944, the French Sûreté learned of the existence of Diem's party and began to arrest its members. Diem escaped the dragnet thanks to the help of the Japanese consul in Hue, who smuggled Diem out of the city by disguising him as an officer of the Imperial Army. Diem was flown to Saigon, where he lived for several months under the protection of the Japanese military.[9]

For a brief moment in early 1945, it appeared that Diem's Japanese stratagems were going to pay off. By late 1944, Japanese leaders had decided that the time had come finally to depose the French colonial regime in Indochina. As plans for a coup were being drafted, idealist Japanese officers proposed to place Cuong De on the Vietnamese throne and to install Diem as premier of a new Vietnamese government. Unfortunately for Cuong De, the senior Japanese commander in Indochina was unimpressed with the idealists' arguments, and he gutted their plans to grant "independence" to the Vietnamese. As a result, when the coup took place on 9 March 1945, the old prince remained in Japan, and the sitting Nguyen emperor, Bao Dai, was allowed to retain his crown. Bao Dai probably knew that Diem had earlier aligned himself with Cuong De; nonetheless, the emperor still considered Diem to be the best candidate to head the new Vietnamese government that would replace the colonial regime, and he therefore summoned Diem to return to Hue from Saigon. In what turned out to be a colossal miscalculation, Diem rebuffed the emperor's offer. Diem came to regret his decision almost immediately and tried to reverse it, but it was too late: Bao Dai had already tapped the scholar and cultural critic Tran Trong Kim to become premier in Diem's place. Diem had missed a golden opportunity, though not for disinterest or for lack of trying.[10]

The August Revolution of 1945 and the stunning rise of Ho and the Viet Minh did not reduce Diem's determination to pursue his political ambitions. Instead of withdrawing from the fray as the French and the Viet Minh fought over the future of Indochina, he pondered how he might exploit the current situation to build a new movement that could eventually eclipse both of these powerful rivals. Diem knew that building a viable Third Force would take time, and in the interim he could not afford to directly challenge either the French or the Viet Minh. He therefore adopted a stance of ostensible neutrality in the war, while at the same time taking care to establish and maintain contacts with both of the warring parties. In this way, Diem hoped both to buy time and to expand the ranks of his supporters at the expense of his rivals.

Diem's efforts to use his position as a fence sitter for maximum political advantage are apparent in his relations with the Viet Minh during the late 1940s. Despite his later claims to the contrary, Diem's dealings with Ho Chi Minh and other Viet Minh leaders were characterized much more by flirtation than rejection. Shortly after the August Revolution, Diem was detained by Viet Minh fighters in Central Vietnam. After being held for a time in a remote mountain location, he was brought to Hanoi in early 1946 to meet with Ho, who offered Diem a position in a Viet Minh unity government.[11] In later years, Diem insisted that he had spurned this offer out of hand; he also claimed that he persuaded Ho to release him simply by fixing the Viet Minh chief with his gaze and asking rhetorically, "Am I a man who fears oppression or death?"[12]

There is no reason to doubt Diem's claim that he spoke sharply and bitterly during the meeting, because he knew that Viet Minh agents had captured and executed his eldest brother, Khoi, a few months earlier. On the other hand, the descriptions of the meeting which Diem related after 1954 omitted the fact that he would have been willing to join a Viet Minh government if Ho had only agreed to his demand for control over certain aspects of policy.[13] Similarly, he never publicly acknowledged that he remained in touch with Viet Minh leaders for at least two years after Ho released him. French intelligence reports of the period suggest that Diem maintained these contacts in the hopes that he might eventually persuade some Viet Minh commanders to abandon Ho and to throw in with him. According to French informants, these exchanges stirred considerable interest within Viet Minh ranks in Nam Bo (Cochinchina) during 1947–1948. Many Viet Minh officials expressed admiration both for Diem and also for his brother Thuc, and there were even whispers that Diem might secure the defection of Nguyen Binh, the top Viet Minh military commander in Nam Bo.[14]

At the same time that Diem was engaged in a pas de deux with the Viet Minh, he was also seeking alliances with anticommunist leaders and groups. Diem's efforts in this regard seem to have been inspired by the example of a short-lived Third Force coalition known as the National Union Front (Mat Tran Thong Nhut Quoc Gia). The Front was formed in early 1947 at a conference of anticommunist political parties and sectarian groups meeting in Nanking, China. After a brief surge of activity in the spring and summer of 1947, the Front abruptly collapsed due to the assassinations of certain key leaders and infighting among its members.[15] Diem seems not to have been involved in the formation of the Front, but as it imploded he moved quickly to take up the Third Force cause. In mid-1947, he aligned himself with Nguyen Ton Hoan, a Catholic leader from Southern Vietnam and a founding member of the Greater Vietnam Nationalist Party (Dai Viet Quoc Dan Dang, usually referred to as the Dai Viet). Throughout the fall of that year, Diem and Hoan worked in tandem to persuade anticommunists to join a new nationalist organization known as the Vietnam National Alliance (Viet Nam Quoc Gia Lien Hiep, VNA). Though they would later become bitter enemies, Diem and Hoan were drawn together in 1947 by their shared ambition to build a viable Third Force movement. Hoan's Dai Viet connections and Diem's network of Catholic supporters made a formidable combination, and for a brief moment it seemed as if the VNA might succeed where the National Union Front had failed.[16]

According to Diem and Hoan, the purpose of the VNA was to mobilize support for a new political movement under the aegis of Bao Dai. After a brief reign as titular head of the Japanese-sponsored "Empire of Vietnam" in 1945, the emperor had been forced to abdicate during the August Revolution. He briefly served as an advisor to Ho's DRV (Democratic Republic of Vietnam) government, but opted after a few months to go into exile abroad. In 1947, Bao Dai set up residence in Hong Kong and began to entertain overtures from Diem, Hoan, and other Vietnamese who hoped that he could preside over a union of Vietnam's fractious noncommunist factions and sects. At the same time, however, the ex-emperor was also meeting with French officials, who flattered him with proposals that he serve as a "mediator" between French colonialism and Vietnamese nationalism. By late 1947, the French blandishments seemed to be having their intended effect: in December, Bao Dai briefly returned to Indochina and agreed in principle to the establishment of a new Vietnamese government within the French union. He then repaired to Hong Kong to consider his next move and to hear advice from various Vietnamese leaders.[17]

Diem was among those who traveled to Hong Kong to offer his counsel to the ex-emperor. Bao Dai had not forgotten Diem's previous refusals to serve under him; still, the former emperor listened carefully as Diem urged him to hold out for more concessions from Paris. Diem was especially strident in warning that Vietnamese nationalists would accept nothing less from France than the dominion status which Britain had recently conceded to India and Pakistan. Bao Dai seemed receptive to these arguments; still, Diem feared that the ex-emperor remained susceptible to French overtures.[18] In February 1948, Diem and other nationalist leaders met in Saigon to define a framework for negotiations with the French on the matter of Vietnamese independence. Diem subsequently went back to Hong Kong in March to try to persuade Bao Dai to support this scheme; he also lobbied French officials for additional concessions on the scope of Vietnamese sovereignty. Significantly, the plan which Diem advocated in these meetings reflected his republican convictions: it called for the establishment of a new Vietnamese assembly which would appoint Bao Dai as its representative in negotiations with the French, and it also stipulated that the ex-emperor would be obliged to consult with the assembly before making any agreements on the independence issue.[19]

Unfortunately for Diem, all of his efforts were in vain. At a "minicongress" in Hong Kong in late March 1948, Bao Dai informed Diem and other Vietnamese leaders that he intended to move ahead with the establishment of a new government according to the terms offered by Paris. In June, the ex-emperor signed a second agreement with colonial officials, which purported to grant Vietnam its independence as an "associated state" within the French union. After more negotiations, the details of the new Franco-Vietnamese relationship were eventually spelled out in the Elysée accords of 8 March 1949. The accords established limited administrative autonomy for Vietnam, but allowed France to retain overall control of diplomatic, economic, and military policy. Shortly after signing the accords, Bao Dai returned to Indochina and declared himself head of the new and ostensibly independent state of Vietnam (SVN).

The implementation of the "Bao Dai solution" during 1948–1949 was deeply disappointing for Diem. Many anticommunist nationalist leaders and groups—including Nguyen Ton Hoan and the Dai Viet Party—opted to back Bao Dai and the SVN in the hope that the new state might serve as a vehicle for the gradual realization of Vietnamese independence. Diem, however, was disgusted with what he viewed as the ex-emperor's capitulation to French demands, and he decided that the time had come for him to voice his dissatisfaction publicly. On 16 June 1949, Diem published a statement in which he implicitly rejected the Elysée accords by repeating his demand for dominion status for Vietnam. At the same time, Diem also served notice that he had no intention of collaborating with the Viet Minh. In sharp contrast to his earlier willingness to consider an accommodation with Ho, Diem now called for a new anticolonial movement led by "those elements who have rendered meritorious service to the Fatherland" and especially "resistance fighters"—an unequivocal signal that Diem intended to challenge the Viet Minh by luring away those of its supporters who were willing to defect to his side.[20]

Diem's statement of June 1949 signaled a major shift in his strategy. By breaking publicly with both Bao Dai and the Viet Minh, Diem was not simply removing them from his list of potential allies. He was also declaring that he possessed what amounted to an alternative vision for the transformation of Vietnamese life and society. Later suggestions to the contrary notwithstanding, this vision was not a reactionary plan to restore traditional values and institutions. Indeed, Diem made it clear that he considered his views to be at least as revolutionary as the proposals offered by his rivals:

> It should be known that the present struggle is not only a battle for the political independence of the Fatherland, but also a social revolution [*cach mang xa hoi*] to restore independence to the peasants and workers of Vietnam. In order that each and every person in Vietnam can have sufficient means to live in a matter befitting the dignity of a man who is truly free, I advocate social reforms that are sweeping and bold, with the condition that the dignity of man will always be respected and will be free to flourish.[21]

For the moment, the details of Diem's "social revolution"—including those pertaining to the crucial problem of its realization in policy and practice—remained obscure. He also neglected to offer any explanation of the origins of his vision or to indicate what had inspired it. Nonetheless, he had taken an important step toward the elucidation of a distinctive program of political action and social transformation. This vision of Vietnam's future, though still protean and vague in 1949, would become steadily more elaborate and detailed in the coming years, and in various ways it would inform all of Diem's important decisions and policies until the end of his life.[22]

Diem had hoped that the publication of his 16 June statement would serve to rally public opinion in his favor. In this regard, however, the move was a failure. The statement was widely read and noted within Vietnam, but it did not produce a new upsurge of popularity for Diem nor derail the Bao Dai solution. In fact, the most immediate effect of the statement was to exhaust the patience of both the French and the Viet Minh for any further intrigues with Diem. As a result, Diem would soon be obliged to consider alternative strategies and to go in search of new allies.

Diem's American Exile, 1950–1953

By early 1950, Diem's room for political maneuvering had been drastically reduced by developments within Indochina and abroad. In February of that year, the Viet Minh achieved a diplomatic breakthrough when both China and the Soviet Union extended official recognition and support to Ho and the DRV. Meanwhile, the ratification of the Elysée accords after a long delay led to formal American and British backing for the state of Vietnam and Bao Dai. These international shifts presaged a general hardening of political positions within Indochina. With the DRV now tilting toward the communist bloc, Ho and his colleagues were less willing to make concessions to secure the cooperation of the noncommunist nationalists. At the same time, Bao Dai and the French turned their attention to Washington and its promised military aid in hopes of gaining the upper hand on the battlefield. The effect of these developments was to diminish the leverage which Diem had previously enjoyed as an ostensibly neutral party in the conflict. This reduction in leverage became frighteningly apparent to Diem in early 1950, when he learned that the Viet Minh had issued orders for his assassination.[23] For Diem, it was time to consider alternative strategies and to seek support from other quarters. In August 1950, he departed Indochina on a trip which he expected would last a few months; as it happened, he would be abroad for nearly four years.

Diem probably departed Vietnam without a single strategy or master plan. Instead, he seems to have been exploring a number of different ways of garnering support from various foreign groups and governments. Accompanied by Bishop Thuc, who was as energetic as ever in support of his younger brother's political goals, Diem set out first for Japan. With the help of one of his old idealist supporters from the occupation years, Diem had his first face-to-face meeting with his old ally, Prince Cuong De, who was still living in Tokyo. Diem later recalled his encounter with Cuong De as a pleasant affair, and presumably there was a good deal of reminiscing about the events of 1945, but there was also talk of a new collaboration between the two men.[24] Before departing Vietnam, Diem and Thuc had expressed interest in a scheme in which Bao Dai would be persuaded to abdicate in favor of his teenage son Bao Long, thus paving the way for Cuong De to return to Indochina as the royal regent for the young prince.[25] Cuong De might well have been interested in such a plan. A few weeks prior to his meeting with Diem, the prince had attempted to travel by ship to Indochina, only to be denied entry by French authorities. As it turned out, this would be Cuong De's last attempt to return to his homeland; he died in Tokyo on 6 April 1951, having spent the last thirty-six years of his life in exile. Years later, after he became leader of South Vietnam, Diem arranged for Cuong De's remains to be brought back to Vietnam for burial in his native Hue.[26]

In retrospect, the most important event of Diem's stay in Japan was not his meeting with Cuong De, but his introduction to an American political scientist named Wesley Fishel. Only thirty-one years old, Fishel was already establishing himself as an expert on East Asian politics. Like many political scientists of his generation, Fishel took a top-down approach to his discipline; this approach was reflected in the interest he took in Asian political elites, who were the subjects of much of his research. But if Fishel wanted to study elites, he also aspired to influence and advise them. As one of his colleagues later recalled, Fishel made a habit from early in his career of cultivating personal connections with Asian leaders whom he deemed likely to acquire power in the future.[27] Fishel found Diem to be an "extremely keen person"; Diem was apparently also impressed with Fishel, and the two men agreed to correspond with each other.[28] Fishel subsequently became one of Diem's most enthusiastic American supporters, and Diem would make good use of Fishel's government and academic connections during and after the period of his exile.

Even before meeting Fishel, Diem and Thuc had already determined that the next stop on their itinerary would be the United States. Just as Diem had tried to exploit Japanese idealist sympathies to win Tokyo's support during the early 1940s, so he now hoped to turn American anticolonial sentiments to his advantage. In early September 1950, the brothers crossed the Pacific to the United States and arrived eventually in Washington, D.C., where they were received at the State Department. The officials who met with Diem and Thuc were intrigued by their proposal to use Catholic militia fighters as the core of a new Vietnamese National Army. However, the Americans were mostly unimpressed with Diem and his potential as a leader. One official declared afterward that Diem was "concerned equally if not more...with furthering his own personal ambitions than solving [the] complex problems facing his country today."[29]

Having failed to win any promises of U.S. support, Diem and Thuc continued on to Europe in October 1950. Diem later reported that he had an audience with the pope at the Vatican; he also traveled briefly to Paris where he met with French and Vietnamese officials and arranged for a message to be delivered to Bao Dai. The message tendered an offer by Diem to serve as prime minister of the SVN, qualified by the stipulation that he receive a grant of authority sufficient to rein in the power of the regional administrations within Vietnam. This proposal seemed to be a climb-down for Diem because it omitted his earlier demand that Vietnam receive dominion status before he would consent to serve in an SVN government. Bao Dai, however, was unimpressed by Diem's newfound flexibility and replied noncommittally.[30]

By December 1950, Diem's fortunes had reached their nadir. His ventures to Japan, the United States, and Europe had all failed to produce the immediate political boost that he needed to rally support for a Third Force. But if he returned to Vietnam, he faced political isolation and possible assassination. Diem therefore decided to change course, both strategically and geographically. Taking his leave of Thuc, who was due to return to Vietnam, Diem recrossed the Atlantic back to the United States. For the next two and a half years, he worked quietly to build support among sympathetic Americans and waited for the political winds in Indochina to shift in his favor.[31] As was the case during his initial visit, not all of the Americans who met Diem during his exile were impressed with him. Truman administration officials were generally underwhelmed by Diem, in part because they tended to believe that the Bao Dai solution was the best arrangement possible under the circumstances. From their perspective, Diem's anti-French attitude was naïve and even dangerous. Though Diem had several meetings at the State Department during 1950 and 1951, the officials there showed scant interest in his proposals. Instead, they seemed rather more concerned about persuading him to moderate his critical view of French policies.[32]

Fortunately for Diem, there were other Americans who were more sympathetic to his anti-French stance and his Third Force convictions, and he proved to be remarkably successful in seeking them out. The list of prominent Americans who met and professed their admiration for Diem during the early 1950s included a Roman Catholic cardinal, a justice of the U.S. Supreme Court, at least a half-dozen members of Congress, numerous journalists, several important academics, and even William J. Donovan, the founder and former head of the famous Office of Strategic Services (OSS).[33] As a group, Diem's American admirers defied easy categorization. Though many were Catholic, a significant number were not; Wesley Fishel, for example, was Jewish. Similarly, Diem's appeal was not confined either to conservatives or to liberals. In addition to attracting the attention of prominent conservatives like Donovan, Diem also impressed liberals such as Senator Mike Mansfield and the journalist Gouverneur Paulding. Indeed, the roster of American boosters which Diem assembled during the early 1950s is notable for its inclusion of liberals and conservatives alike, as well as for its ecumenical and bipartisan qualities.

What accounts for Diem's ability to garner the support of such a diverse collection of American notables? As virtually every report of Diem's career has noted, part of his appeal to Americans lay in his staunch anticommunism. Diem's stint in the United States coincided with the high-water mark of McCarthyism, a period when anticommunist credentials were de rigueur for any foreign leader who hoped to win American support for a cause. And yet, if anticommunism were necessary to Diem's campaign to attract American support during the early 1950s, it was hardly sufficient to ensure the success of that campaign. By itself, anticommunism did not distinguish Diem from the French and Bao Dai, who retained their statuses as official U.S. allies.

Instead of anticommunism, some writers have fingered Diem's identity as a Catholic as the key factor that helped him to attract American supporters. Diem certainly relied heavily on the Vatican connections of Thuc and other Vietnamese prelates during his exile; among other things, he used these connections to arrange introductions to prominent Americans and lodging at Catholic seminaries. Moreover, Diem was not averse to using his status as a leader of Vietnamese Catholics in order to win support from his American coreligionists.[34] However, the claim that Diem's Catholicism was the key element which explained his ability to garner American support is at best an exaggeration.[35] Though he discussed religious matters in his private correspondence and in conversations with his fellow Catholics, he does not seem to have envisioned U.S.–Vietnamese collaboration as a prospective Christian alliance. On the contrary, in his conversations with non-Catholic Americans and especially in public remarks delivered during his exile, Diem invariably eschewed religious statements and language in favor of secular arguments about shared commitments to the twin causes of anticommunism and anticolonialism.[36]

Rather than emphasizing religion, Diem seemed more interested in appealing to American beliefs about development, modernization, and the transformative capacity of U.S. technology. In particular, Diem sought to exploit the new official American interest in "technical assistance" for foreign nations. In 1949, U.S. president Harry Truman announced the "Point Four" program, which dramatically increased levels of nonmilitary U.S. foreign aid. Though Point Four was a direct descendant of the 1947 Marshall Plan for the reconstruction of Western Europe, it was global in scale and included a broader variety of types of aid. In addition to grants and subsidies, the technical assistance to be provided also included equipment, training, and expert knowledge. As many scholars have pointed out, Point Four heralded a new American confidence in the capacity of U.S. aid and expertise to shape economic, political, and social change around the world. As a key Cold War battleground, Vietnam appeared to many American officials to be in desperate need of the help that Point Four was designed to provide. By the time that Diem arrived in the United States in 1950, a small American technical assistance program was already operating in Indochina, and U.S. technical aid to the associated states steadily increased thereafter.[37]

In his efforts to shape the form and content of U.S. technical assistance to Vietnam, Diem received the invaluable help of his friend Wesley Fishel. Fishel was well positioned to assist Diem in this regard because in 1951 he joined the faculty at Michigan State College (soon to be renamed Michigan State University). During the 1950s, under the energetic leadership of President John Hannah, Michigan State administered government-sponsored technical assistance projects in countries such as Brazil, Colombia, and Japan.[38] Soon after arriving at Michigan State, Fishel arranged for Diem to work there as a consultant, which afforded the two men the chance to collaborate on a proposal for a technical assistance project for Vietnam. The 1952 letter in which Fishel presented the proposal to the U.S. Mutual Security Administration clearly bore his influence, because it envisioned a project that was similar to other Michigan State ventures. However, the letter also included ideas that were obviously contributed by Diem, such as the stipulation that the program be based in Diem's hometown of Hue. The scope of the proposed project—which would have been much broader than the existing Michigan State programs—also seems to have been defined largely by Diem. He declared that Vietnam needed help in areas as diverse as "police science," "foreign trade problems," and even "studies for the adoption of democratic institutions."[39] In retrospect, the proposal demonstrates Diem's remarkable prescience in seeking to shape the form and content of what would later become a huge flow of U.S. assistance to his government.[40]

Diem's ability to win over influential American supporters was apparent at a luncheon held in his honor in Washington on 8 May 1953. The event was hosted by Supreme Court justice William O. Douglas, who had become convinced of the need for a Third Force in Indochina during a visit there the year before. Douglas arranged the lunch to introduce Diem to other like-minded Americans; the guests included U.S. Senators Mike Mansfield and John F. Kennedy, both of whom were destined to play key roles in Diem's future relations with the United States.[41] The senators and their fellow diners were all impressed with Diem, who spoke forcefully against Bao Dai and the prospects for independence within the French union and who also regaled his listeners with an account of his 1946 encounter with Ho Chi Minh. As Mansfield later recalled, he left the lunch "with the feeling that if anyone could hold South Vietnam, it was somebody like Ngo Dinh Diem."[42]

As many historians have pointed out, Diem's ability to connect with Americans such as Fishel, Mansfield, and Kennedy would eventually pay off. Especially after 1954, the personal relationships that Diem had established during his exile helped to ratify and reinforce Washington's official support for him and his government. But in May 1953, Diem was not yet in a position to reap these political dividends, and his American friends had so far offered him little more than encouragement and moral support. He therefore made ready to seek his objectives by other means. During the lunch in Washington, Diem announced that he intended to leave soon for France and that he hoped eventually to return to Vietnam.[43] Of course, neither Diem nor anyone else at the lunch that day could have foreseen the events that would take place over the next twelve months and that would culminate, almost exactly a year to the day later, in the surrender of the French garrison at Dien Bien Phu to the Viet Minh. Nonetheless, even if he did not anticipate these events, Diem would be well positioned to exploit them. Already in the spring of 1953, Diem was laying plans for his political comeback. The critical impetus for this comeback would be provided not by his new admirers in the United States, but by the loyal supporters whom he had left behind in Vietnam.

Brother's Keeper: The Emergence of Ngo Dinh Nhu, 1950–1953

It has long been assumed that Diem was out of touch with events and sentiments in Vietnam during the period of his exile. His residences at Catholic seminaries and monasteries in both the United States and Europe have often been taken as indicative of a desire to retreat from world affairs in general, and from politics in particular. Even before Diem's exile had ended, some U.S. officials were already deriding him as "a Yogi-like mystic" who had "just emerged from a religious retreat into the cold world" and who was therefore ill prepared for the daunting political tasks that were ahead of him.[44] Those who have written about Diem's life and career have generally agreed that he was isolated during his exile, and they therefore usually portray him as floating helplessly on a sea of intrigue when he finally returned to Saigon in the early summer of 1954.

Such a representation of Diem is open to challenge on at least two points. First, this interpretation overlooks the possibility that Diem's monastic retreats during the period of his exile might have been less isolating and more strategic than they appeared at the time. Very little is known about Diem's activities during the months he spent at Catholic monasteries and seminaries in the United States and Belgium during 1951–1954, and the assumption that he was cut off from the outside world while he lived in these cloisters is at best an unproven hypothesis. In fact, these institutions likely provided him with a relatively secure means for communicating with his allies in Indochina, because they provided him access to international networks of Catholics who could safely carry messages that might otherwise have been intercepted by the French police. For example, Diem received the Vietnamese Catholic activist Tran Chánh Thanh during his stay at a monastery in Belgium in early 1954. Since Thanh had been a close associate of Ngo Dinh Nhu's since at least 1952 and since he subsequently became one of the most powerful figures in the Diem government, it seems reasonable to conclude that he was serving as a courier for Diem as he traveled between Europe and Indochina during this critical time.[45]

Second, the claims that Diem was isolated are undermined by evidence which suggests that he was coordinating his activities during his exile with the efforts of his supporters in Indochina, who were working to prepare the way for his return. One of the most glaring omissions in the existing accounts of Diem's rise to power in 1953–1954 concerns the important assistance rendered by his brothers. In addition to the aforementioned support of his older brother, Bishop Thuc, Diem would also benefit during his exile from help provided by his three younger brothers: Ngo Dinh Nhu, Ngo Dinh Can, and Ngo Dinh Luyen. While Can and Luyen played important roles in Diem's eventual success, the most crucial contributions of all were provided by Nhu.

Can and Luyen were the youngest of the Ngo brothers, and they could not have been more different from each other. Can was reclusive, cantankerous, and the least educated of the brothers; he reportedly never once traveled outside of Vietnam, and he spent most of his time in Hue. In contrast, Luyen was a cosmopolitan and personable engineer who had studied in Europe and spoke several languages. Not surprisingly, Can and Luyen lent support to Diem in different ways. Can began in the early 1950s to build a clandestine network of supporters in Central Vietnam; he used this organization to build and consolidate support for Diem in that part of the country, while also expanding his personal influence there. Meanwhile, Luyen was working on Diem's behalf in Europe. After Diem moved from the United States to France in May 1953, Luyen became his main advisor and his personal representative in negotiations with Bao Dai and other Vietnamese leaders.[46]

The Ngo family had no shortage of unusual and enigmatic personalities; nonetheless, Nhu was arguably the most unusual and enigmatic of them all. The fourth of the six brothers, Nhu was said to be studious, thoughtful, and reserved. He was neither provincial like Can nor polished like Luyen, and he displayed little interest in the imperial court politics which so preoccupied his older brothers Khoi, Thuc, and Diem. Indeed, as a young man, Nhu seemed to prefer bookish pursuits to politics. He spent much of the 1930s in Paris, first taking a degree in literature and then studying paleography and librarianship at the famous École de Chartres. In the late 1930s, Nhu returned to Vietnam and embarked on a career as an archivist; by 1945, he had attained a senior post at the National Library in Hanoi.[47] After the August Revolution, Nhu became more involved in politics and especially in his brothers' efforts to mobilize support among Vietnamese Catholics. Still, he maintained a relatively low profile until the time that Diem departed into exile. With his young wife, Tran Le Xuan—later to gain international fame and infamy as "Madame Nhu"—Nhu in 1950 was still living in relative obscurity in the town of Dalat in the southern highlands, where he indulged in his hobby of raising orchids.[48]

Like his brothers, Nhu was both a devout Catholic and a staunch Confucian. However, just as his education and early career were different from those of the other Ngo brothers, so too did the evolution of his ideas and his politics follow a distinctive course. In France, Nhu had been profoundly influenced by the lay Catholic philosopher Emmanuel Mounier. In his books and in the pages of his journal, *Esprit*, Mounier responded to the Great Depression and the suffering it caused by developing a critique of liberal capitalism. Mounier particularly decried the liberal preoccupation with individualism and argued that it led inevitably to isolation, alienation, and exploitation. Yet, as a conservative Catholic, Mounier was unwilling to embrace Marxism because its materialist precepts gave short shrift to what he called the "spiritual" dimensions of human nature. Instead of capitalism or communism, Mounier looked forward to a postcapitalist social order in which both individual material needs and communal prosperity would receive their due—but without either one becoming the exclusive focus of social policy. Instead, Mounier proposed to focus attention on the development of the total person (*la personne*), which he defined as inclusive of spiritual needs and material concerns. Mounier's emphasis on the person as an antidote to the individual was a key theme in his writings, and he therefore came to describe his ideas as "personalism."[49]

By the time he returned to Indochina from France, Nhu had become an enthusiastic personalist who was convinced that Mounier's doctrine—which he translated into Vietnamese as *nhan vi*—could be applied in Vietnam.[50] Especially after 1945, the possibility that personalism might represent a "third path" to social development seems to have become particularly attractive to Nhu. For Nhu, Mounier's rejection of both liberalism and communism became congruent with the Third Force politics which Diem was promoting. That Nhu found his older brother to be receptive to his ideas is reflected in the fact that Diem's remarks and writings from this period contain references to terms adopted from the personalist lexicon.

After 1950, Nhu became a leading figure in the efforts to mobilize support for Diem among noncommunist Vietnamese. At the same time, Nhu also became more ardent in promoting personalism as a guide for Vietnam's social and political development. In April 1952, Nhu outlined his views about personalism in a talk at the newly established Vietnamese military academy in Dalat. Nhu acknowledged that the concept of *nhan vi* was a Catholic idea, but insisted that it had a universal relevance and utility, especially in war-torn Vietnam. Addressing the non-Catholics who made up the majority of his audience, Nhu declared, "the anxieties of Catholics are like an echo answering the worries that are roiling your own hearts and souls." All Vietnamese of all political and religious backgrounds, Nhu argued, had to join together in "a sudden and fierce unanimity" in order to "preserve the person" (*bao ve nhan vi*) against the forces which threatened to crush it. These forces included liberalism and communism, both of which offered only "false liberation" and perpetual war.[51]

Though his audience did not know it at the time, Nhu's speech was a harbinger of things to come. Besides being long, dense, and abstract—qualities of Nhu's which many Vietnamese would come to know and resent over the ensuing decade—the speech featured many of the key themes which would characterize Diem's and Nhu's later speeches and pronouncements about the utility and value of personalism. These themes included not only the dangers posed by liberalism and communism but also the importance of spiritual concerns as opposed to mere material considerations. In addition, the speech also highlighted Nhu's conviction that what Vietnam needed was nothing less than a thoroughgoing revolution:

> These are great undertakings, and they can be summarized as a politico-economic revolution [*mot cuoc cach mang chinh-tri kinh-te*], aimed at making the Person the focus of concern. I say "revolution" because it will be a great waste if we try to patch over the fissures in a creaky house, when what is needed is to transform the entire internal structure of the house.[52]

Like Diem, Nhu clearly understood by the early 1950s that the creation of a Third Force in Vietnam would depend on more than mere promises to return to ancient traditions, values, and practices. In order to succeed, such a movement would have to promote transformation and revolution—albeit along noncommunist lines. Nhu believed that personalism could form the basis of a new universal ideology that would appeal to all Vietnamese, non-Catholics as well as Catholics.

If Nhu fancied himself as a philosopher, he also knew that the movement he envisioned would also require a great deal of organizing; as it turned out, his true talents lay more with the latter than the former. Perhaps as early as 1950, Nhu had formed the nucleus of a new political party, which eventually became known as the Dang Can Lao Nhan Vi; this name would later be officially translated as the Personalist Labor Party or as the Labor Party for Human Dignity, but it was colloquially referred to both by Vietnamese and Americans simply as the Can Lao.[53] At its inception, the Can Lao organization seems to have operated entirely in secret, and little is known about the early years of its existence. The party functioned as a network of cells, and most recruits generally knew the identities of only a handful of their fellow members. After 1954, the existence of the Can Lao was officially acknowledged, but its activities still remained mostly confined to the shadows. Eventually, the Can Lao would become the most important and most infamous component of Diem's and Nhu's security apparatus. In its early years, though, Nhu's key objective was the mobilization of support for a new nationalist political movement headed by Diem.

The name which Nhu selected for his political party was revealing. Specifically, the use of *can lao* (meaning "labor" or "hard work") reflected Nhu's intense interest in the latent political potential of the Vietnamese working masses. Contrary to what some observers supposed, this interest in labor organizing (where "labor" was understood to include both industrial workers and poor tenant farmers) stemmed less from Nhu's admiration of Marxist-Leninist strategies than it did from his embrace of certain ideas associated with French syndicalism. In particular, Nhu embraced the syndicalist notion that workers should be organized into groups such as unions or cooperatives to ensure that their interests would not be subordinated to the interests of capital. Though Nhu tended in his public and private discourse to place the accent on the personalist elements of his philosophy, the style and substance of his organizing efforts also bore the imprint of these syndicalist principles.[54]

Besides the secret activities of the Can Lao, Nhu also undertook more overt kinds of organizing. These initiatives included establishing an alliance with a labor activist named Tran Quoc Buu, a veteran organizer who had been affiliated at various times with the Cao Dai religious sect and the Viet Minh. In the late 1940s, after becoming disillusioned with communism, Buu fell in with a French labor organizer who educated him in the ideas and tactics of the Christian Democratic trade union movement. After a brief stint in Europe, Buu returned to Vietnam in 1949 and began illegally unionizing urban and rural workers. In 1952, changes in the SVN's labor laws permitted Buu to legalize his confederation of unions under the moniker of the Vietnamese Confederation of Christian Workers and to affiliate with the Brussels-based International Federation of Christian Trade Unions.[55] It is not clear when or how Buu and Nhu began to collaborate with each other, but Nhu had become closely associated with Buu's confederation by 1953. In February of that year, Nhu and his allies began publishing a journal in Saigon entitled *Xa Hoi (Society)*, which strongly backed Buu and the confederation. Besides coming out in support of unionism, *Xa Hoi* also staunchly supported the creation of workers' and farmers' cooperatives— a stance which prefigured the policies that Diem and Nhu would implement later as leaders of South Vietnam.[56]

As events in the later 1950s and early 1960s demonstrated, Nhu's efforts to build broad support among Vietnamese workers and peasants for his revolutionary objectives would fail in the long run. But eventual defeat does not preclude the possibility of interim victories; the fact that the Ngo brothers were later overthrown does not prove that their ideas and plans were always ineffective, nor that they were doomed from the outset. Indeed, in the factionalized and fragmented world of Indochinese politics during the 1950s, Nhu's ability to wield power through both mass organizations and clandestine networks was a potent tool. Diem seemed to understand this, and during his exile he counted heavily on Nhu to lay the political groundwork for his return. As it turned out, Diem's faith in his younger brother was well placed. By the summer of 1953, Nhu was already plotting the tactics and strategies which would carry Diem to power.

Diem's Campaign for the Premiership, 1953–1954

Diem's decision to depart the United States for Europe in May 1953 was the opening move in a new political gambit. Though the war in Indochina still appeared stalemated, Diem and his allies had detected a political shift which they hoped to use to Diem's benefit. From his vantage point in Saigon, Nhu noted that many noncommunist nationalists were becoming impatient with Bao Dai and his strategy of seeking independence within the French union. In the four years since the signing of the Elysée accords, France had made few concessions to Vietnamese nationalism, and the state of Vietnam remained at best only nominally independent from Paris. Most nationalists were also frustrated with SVN premier Nguyen Van Tam, who was widely regarded as a Francophile and an autocrat. Finally, nationalist sentiment had been piqued by Paris's unilateral decision in early May 1953 to devalue the Indochinese piaster, a move which both contravened earlier agreements with the associated states and exacerbated inflation and hardship within Indochina.[57] As dissatisfaction with France and Bao Dai swelled, the Ngo brothers sensed that the time had come to make a new bid for power.

As they made their plans, Diem and Nhu knew that they would have to tread carefully. They needed to discredit Bao Dai and his strategy of seeking independence via piecemeal concessions; however, they would also have to refrain from direct criticism of the ex-emperor, lest he become so annoyed that he would reject Diem's candidacy out of hand. Fortunately for the brothers, events in the summer of 1953 provided exactly the kind of opportunity they needed. In early July, the French government proposed a new round of talks with the associated states aimed at "perfecting" their independence within the French union. Had the French made such an offer in 1949 or 1950, it might have been viewed as a validation of Bao Dai's gradualist stance. But by 1953, the prospect of more negotiations only fueled the nationalists' anxieties about French sincerity.

In a series of meetings with other nationalist leaders during July and August, Nhu adroitly exploited these anxieties. Working in tandem with Nguyen Ton Hoan of the Dai Viet—who, as noted above, had worked briefly with Diem in 1947–1948 before rallying to support the SVN—Nhu floated the idea of convening an unofficial Unity Congress (Dai Hoi Doan Ket) in Saigon in early September, after Bao Dai had departed for France. The idea of a congress was quickly embraced by many of the nationalists who had been counted among Bao Dai's most prominent supporters; besides Hoan of the Dai Viet, these included the Cao Dai leader Pham Cong Tac, General Tran Van Soai of the Hoa Hao sect, General Le Van Vien of the Saigon-based Binh Xuyen syndicate, and several key Catholic figures. In addition, several groups that had previously withheld support from Bao Dai and the SVN (such as the Dong Minh Hoi and VNQDD parties and certain Buddhist organizations) also agreed to attend the congress. General Vien consented to let the event take place at Binh Xuyen headquarters in Saigon.[58]

The Unity Congress on 5–6 September 1953 was a chaotic affair. The fifty-five delegates in attendance endorsed a statement which fiercely denounced Bao Dai's gradualist policies. As soon as the statement was signed, however, the participants began to bicker about its implications. General Vien became concerned that the congress was becoming uncontrollable, and he brought the event to a premature end by closing the conference hall after just two days. The Cao Dai's Tac, who had been harshly critical of Bao Dai in remarks issued before the conference, now joined with the chiefs of the Binh Xuyen and Hoa Hao in sending a telegram to the emperor that reaffirmed the loyalty of all three groups to the SVN. Nhu, meanwhile, announced that the congress had produced a new political organization known as the Movement for National Union and Peace (Phong Trao Dai Doan Ket va Hoa Binh); however, he also was careful to distance himself from some of the harshest of the anti–Bao Dai statements by denying that the congress had adopted an official political stance.[59]

As an exercise in coalition building, the Unity Congress was a failure. For Nhu and Diem, however, the congress was intended mainly to force the hand of Bao Dai, and in this regard the event turned out to be a brilliant success. From France, Bao Dai sought to regain the political high ground by announcing that an official National Congress would take place in Saigon in October. The senior leaders of the Cao Dai, Hoa Hao, and Binh Xuyen immediately agreed to participate, along with representatives of most of the other nationalist groups. Nhu and his allies, however, were conspicuously absent when the National Congress convened on 12 October 1953. At first, the congress seemed likely to deliver the expected affirmation of support for Bao Dai and his policies. But on 16 October, the delegates suddenly approved a resolution that rejected participation in the French union in favor of "total independence." Bao Dai loyalists subsequently managed to qualify the offending statement with an amendment that an independent Vietnam would not remain in the union "in its present form," but the political damage had been done. Intended as a show of nationalist support for Bao Dai, the National Congress had instead confirmed the extent of the nationalist dissatisfaction with him and his policies.[60]

Diem and Nhu had disassociated themselves from the October congress, no doubt because they feared that it would serve to shore up support for Bao Dai.[61] They soon discovered, however, that the unanticipated outcome of the event had prompted Bao Dai to take a friendlier approach to Diem and to reconsider the possibility of appointing him to the premiership. In early October, before the National Congress had even opened, Bao Dai consented to meet privately with Diem in Paris; it was their first face-to-face meeting in four years.[62] After the congress debacle, the ex-emperor became even more conciliatory. In a second meeting with Diem in Cannes on 26 October, Bao Dai broached the possibility of Diem's appointment to the premiership with a "hypothetical" inquiry about his willingness to serve.[63] The former monarch would put off making a decision about Diem for some months after this meeting; nonetheless, it was clear by the end of 1953 that the Ngo brothers' gamble was already paying big dividends. Bao Dai's prestige and standing among his subjects had been shown to be miserably low. Diem's strong anti-French stance, in contrast, appeared to be very much in keeping with the general tenor of nationalist sentiment in Saigon, and therefore he seemed suddenly to be someone that the emperor could ill afford to do without.

In the months following the October congress, the pressure on Bao Dai continued to increase, and Diem and Nhu continued to push their advantage. In December 1953, Bao Dai bowed to nationalist complaints and dismissed the autocratic SVN premier, Nguyen Van Tam. By replacing Tam's government with a caretaker cabinet headed by Prince Buu Loc, a member of the royal household, Bao Dai hoped to buy time to look for a way to shore up his faltering support among his subjects. But time was now at a premium, and the Ngo brothers were unrelenting. In early March 1954, after Bao Dai assented in principle to the creation of a new National Assembly, Nhu and his allies published an article in Saigon in which they claimed victory and also pressed for further concessions. This move provoked schisms within the ranks of several nationalist groups; while some leaders rallied to support Bao Dai, factions within the Cao Dai, Hoa Hao, and Dai Viet publicly backed Nhu and his "revolutionary nationalist" demands.[64]

As the political infighting in Saigon intensified, word arrived from the North in mid-March that the Viet Minh had laid siege to the French garrison at Dien Bien Phu. This news, in tandem with the French government's agreement to hold talks on Indochina at an upcoming great-power conference in Geneva, suddenly made the possibility of a French withdrawal from

Vietnam appear imminent. In Paris, Bao Dai sensed that he was running out of options. As the French position at Dien Bien Phu became more precarious, the ex-emperor sent word to Diem via his youngest brother, Ngo Dinh Luyen. Dien Bien Phu fell to the Viet Minh on 7 May 1954; a few days later, Diem arrived in Paris for another audience with Bao Dai. According to the latter's account of the meeting, Diem was so coy that he initially pretended to have no interest in the premiership. Bao Dai was obliged to ask him a second time to take the job, imploring him to see that "le salut du Vietnam l'exige" (the salvation of Vietnam depends on it).[65]

The events which took place in Saigon and France during 1953–1954—and Diem and Nhu's involvement in them—have important implications for our understanding of Diem's rise to power and the alleged involvement of the United States in securing his appointment. It has long been asserted that American officials secretly pressured Bao Dai to select Diem.[66] Historian David L. Anderson, however, has pointed out that senior officials in the Eisenhower administration were only "vaguely aware" of Diem in early 1954 and that available American official documents do not support the allegations of a covert U.S. campaign on Diem's behalf. Instead, Anderson argues that Bao Dai's decision was shaped primarily by the emperor's convictions that the SVN would need U.S. support in order to continue to exist and that Diem was the leader who was best able to secure this support. While Anderson's claim might appear at first to be of relatively minor significance, it looms large in the continuing debate over the origins and evolution of the U.S. involvement in Vietnam during the 1950s.[67]

The evidence presented here suggests that Anderson's explanation is correct but incomplete. In addition to international considerations, Bao Dai's decision was crucially shaped by political developments in Vietnam. By the spring of 1954, events had validated Diem's decision to hold out for "true" independence from France. Even before the French defeat at Dien Bien Phu, the popularity of Diem's stance on the independence issue as compared to Bao Dai's had been apparent. Moreover, Nhu and his allies had demonstrated convincingly that Diem retained considerable political clout within Vietnam. As Bao Dai himself later acknowledged in his memoirs, the esteem in which Diem and Nhu were held by their fellow nationalists was a crucial part of his political calculus:

> From my earlier experience with him, I knew that Diem had a difficult character. I was also aware of his fanaticism and his messianic tendencies. But, in the present situation, there was no better choice. He was well-known to the Americans, who appreciated his intransigence. In their eyes, he was the

man best suited for the job, and Washington would not be sparing in its support of him. Because of [Diem's] past and because of the presence of his brother at the head of the "Movement for National Union," he would have the cooperation of the fiercest nationalists, those who had brought down Tam and then Buu-Loc. Finally, because of his intransigence and his fanaticism, he could be counted on to resist communism. Yes, he was truly the right man for the situation.[68]

Historians have so far failed to turn up any documentary evidence of a secret U.S. plot to install Diem as SVN premier in the spring of 1954. But even if such a plot had been hatched and executed, it would not have had much of an effect on Bao Dai's decision. By May 1954, Bao Dai had been overtaken by events and outmaneuvered by Diem and Nhu. He was left with little choice but to offer Diem the premiership on the terms that Diem had long demanded: "full powers" over all aspects of the SVN government, military, and economy.

On 16 June 1954—exactly five years to the day after he had issued his manifesto for an alternative approach to "social revolution"—Diem formally agreed to form a cabinet and thus returned to political office for the first time since 1933. For Diem, who had endured a decade of political frustration, the moment was replete with vindication. Of course, Diem was too experienced in the vicissitudes of Indochinese politics to believe that his triumph was complete or that his long-term success was assured. On the contrary, he knew that his appointment granted him nothing more than the opportunity to grapple with the daunting and enormous tasks confronting the SVN government. Nonetheless, Diem now had the political opening which he had sought with such determination for so long, and he relished the accomplishment. "The hour of decision has arrived," he declared immediately after his appointment was announced.[69] As events would demonstrate, the decisions made in 1954–1955 did indeed have profound consequences for Vietnam and for all of the foreign powers who sought influence there. By dint of patience, perseverance, planning, opportunism, and no small amount of luck, Diem had secured a chance to shape many of those decisions. For Diem, it was the role of a lifetime, and he would play it to the hilt.

Conclusion

When Diem arrived in Saigon on 25 June 1954 as prime minister–designate of the SVN, many in Vietnam and elsewhere expected that his tenure in office would be brief. The SVN state which Diem took over still functioned mostly at the behest of French colonial officials, whose reactions to Diem's appointment ranged from resigned acceptance to untrammeled hostility. American officials, meanwhile, were sharply divided over whether or not to support Diem. If Diem could not count on foreign support to maintain him in office, neither could he expect to preserve his rule simply by manipulating the levers of state power. The Vietnamese National Army was commanded by Francophile generals who were deeply suspicious of Diem. SVN authority was mostly limited to Vietnam's large cities and towns, and the countryside was a patchwork of de facto independent satrapies. Even in Saigon, Diem's power was circumscribed by the fact that the local police force was under the control of the Binh Xuyen. Within weeks of taking office, the scope of Diem's control was further reduced by the announcement that the French and the DRV had reached an agreement at Geneva to divide Vietnam into northern and southern zones in advance of nationwide elections in 1956—elections which were widely expected to result in communist victory.

Despite all of this, Diem's position was not as hopeless as it appeared to be. Over the next eighteen months, Diem would rally the army, rout his sectarian rivals, oust Bao Dai, and proclaim the formation of a new South Vietnamese state with himself as president. A thorough discussion of how Diem managed to defy expectations and consolidate his authority during 1954–1955 is beyond the scope of this essay; nonetheless, the arguments presented here suggest that the received wisdom about Diem and the means by which he sustained himself in power after 1954 may need to be revised. Three points in particular stand out.

First, at the time of his elevation to the premiership, Diem was not as lacking in Vietnamese allies as he is often supposed to have been. Besides his Catholic backers, Diem was able to count on support from certain key non-Catholic leaders and groups, thanks in large part to the efforts of his brothers during the period of his exile. The activities undertaken by Ngo Dinh Nhu during the early 1950s (such as the creation of the Can Lao Party and the recruitment of Tran Quoc Buu's labor unions) were especially significant, because they would provide the means by which Diem was able to mobilize support during the tumultuous first months of his rule.

Second, Diem in 1954 was neither beholden to the United States nor particularly inclined to follow U.S. advice. No reliable evidence exists to support the claim that Diem owed his appointment to a pressure campaign conducted by U.S. officials on his behalf. Instead, Diem secured the premiership through a combination of good fortune and careful coordination of his activities with those of his supporters in Indochina. Since Diem was neither dependent on U.S. support nor following U.S. directives prior to June 1954, there is no reason to assume that he suddenly became highly reliant on American officials for guidance after that date. Having come to power mainly through his own efforts and those of his brothers, Diem was not inclined to defer to Americans on matters of policy and political strategy. On the contrary, he returned to Saigon more determined than ever to follow his instincts and to pursue his plans for consolidating and expanding his power. Diem's tendency to keep his own counsel should be kept in mind when analyzing events which took place after 1954 and especially when evaluating his relations with American officials.

Finally, Diem's words and deeds during the period 1945–1954 demonstrate the inadequacy of the existing representations of him as a "traditional" figure who was uninterested in modernization and development. Despite his penchant for intrigue, Diem sensed that the ultimate success or failure of his new regime would hinge on more than secret plots and schemes. In his first speech delivered after his return to Saigon, Diem reaffirmed his intent to promote revolutionary change in Vietnam:

> In this critical situation, I will act decisively. I will move with determination to open a path to national salvation. A total revolution [*mot cuoc cach-menh toan dien*] will be implemented in every facet of the organization and life of the nation.[70]

As in his earlier statements on such matters, the vision of revolution that Diem offered in June 1954 was still inchoate and vague. But it was a vision nonetheless, and he had staked the success of his new regime on his ability to realize it. With Nhu's help, Diem's vision would gradually become more detailed and elaborate in the coming months and years. By 1957, the regime had publicly embraced personalism as its official ideology and declared the "personalist revolution" to be the ultimate objective of its policies. As this choice of words suggested, Nhu's notion of *nhan vi* was the conceptual keystone of this new ideology. Until 1963, the Ngo brothers continued to refine this ideology, even as they presented it as the rationale underpinning their nation-building policies in areas such as economic development, agrarian reform, and national security.

In the end, the personalist revolution would not come to pass. As Diem's critics (and even many of his admirers) noted, the Diemist brand of personalism was not only intricate but also incredibly abstract and often so dense as to be impenetrable. Though it informed and shaped the regime's policies, it had little utility as a means of generating support for those policies. But to say that Diem's vision was unrealized is not to say that it was inconsequential, nor that it should be dismissed as merely the delusion of a hopelessly backward tyrant. As many Vietnamese and more than a few Americans discovered, Ngo Dinh Diem possessed a formidable capacity to inspire those who met and heard him. That he could also be boring, imperious, and even cruel should not obscure this capacity. Like many other leaders, Diem wrapped his ambitions for power together with his vision of the future in complicated and sometimes contradictory ways. Unraveling the complexity of Diem's politics and his ideas is therefore a crucial step toward a revised and richer understanding of his role in the long and tangled struggle to shape the modern destiny of Vietnam.

NOTES

This chapter is reprinted from the *Journal of Southeast Asian Studies* 35.3 (October 2004): 433–58, with permission from the Department of History, National University of Singapore.

1. Both Diem's admirers and his critics have portrayed him as an exponent of "traditional" ideas and practices. During the 1960s, authors in both camps treated Diem's devotion to Confucianism as proof of a premodern cast of mind; compare, for example, journalist Denis Warner's scathing account of Diem's rule, *The Last Confucian* (New York: Macmillan, 1963), with Anthony Bouscaren's hagiography, *The Last of the Mandarins: Diem of Vietnam* (Pittsburgh, Pa.: Duquesne University Press, 1965). According to some authors, Diem's traditional Confucian habits were reinforced by a Catholic identity which inclined him to favor ancient forms of government; see Bernard Fall, *The Two Viet-Nams: A Political and Military Analysis*, 2nd ed. (New York: Praeger, 1967), 236. Scholars who have written about Diem since the end of the Vietnam War in 1975 have been more sophisticated in their analyses of him and his ideas, but their conclusions about the traditional nature of his Confucian and Catholic convictions are strikingly similar to those proffered earlier. For recent critiques of Diem in this vein, see Neil Jamieson, *Understanding Vietnam* (Berkeley: University of California Press, 1993), 235; William Turley, *The Second Indochina War: A Short Political and Military History, 1954–1975* (Boulder, Colo.: Westview, 1986), 13; George Kahin, *Intervention: How America Became Involved in Vietnam* (Garden City, N.Y.: Anchor, 1987), 93; and Stanley Karnow, *Vietnam: A History*, 2nd ed. (New York: Penguin, 1997), 229. For examples of post-1975 accounts which portray Diem's affinity for tradition in a more sympathetic light, see Ellen J. Hammer, *A Death in November: America in Vietnam, 1963* (New York: Dutton, 1987), 52; and Pham Van Luu, "The Buddhist Crises in Vietnam, 1963–1966," Ph.D. diss., Monash University, 1991, 102–3.

2. Philip E. Catton, *Diem's Final Failure: Prelude to America's War in Vietnam* (Lawrence: University of Kansas Press, 2002), 2.

3. For claims that Diem was politically isolated during the 1940s and 1950s, see John Mecklin, *Mission in Torment: An Intimate Account of the U.S. Role in Vietnam* (Garden City, N.Y.: Doubleday, 1965), 31; Robert Shaplen, *The Lost Revolution* (New York: Harper & Row, 1965), 111; Frances Fitzgerald, *Fire in the Lake: The Vietnamese and the Americans in Vietnam* (Boston: Little, Brown, 1972), 82; George Herring, *America's Longest War: The United States and Vietnam, 1950–1975*, 4th ed. (Boston: McGraw-Hill, 2002), 59; and Ross Marlay and Clark Neher, *Patriots and Tyrants: Ten Asian Leaders* (Lanham, Md.: Rowman & Littlefield, 1999), 119.

4. Ronald Inden, *Imagining India* (Oxford: Basil Blackwell, 1990), especially 1–48.

5. Consider the following statement by the author of a bestselling textbook on the Vietnam War: "Not perceiving the extent to which the French and Vietminh had destroyed traditional political processes and values, [Diem] looked backward to an imperial Vietnam that no longer existed. He had no blueprint for building a modern nation or mobilizing his people" (Herring, *America's Longest War*, 59).

6. In the spring of 1946, a short-lived alliance of convenience between the Viet Minh and noncommunist parties in northern Vietnam broke down, sparking a wave of fighting and a brutal Viet Minh elimination campaign. See François Guillemot, "Au cœur de la fracture Vietnamienne: L'élimination de l'opposition nationaliste et anticolonialiste dans le Nord du Viet-nam (1945–1946)," in Christopher E. Goscha and Benoît de Tréglodé, eds., *Le Viet Nam depuis 1945* (Paris: Les Indes Savantes, 2004), 175–216.

7. For Bai's maneuvers and Diem's 1933 appointment and resignation, see Bruce Lockhart, *The End of the Vietnamese Monarchy* (New Haven, Conn.: Council on Southeast Asian Studies, 1993), 60–86.

8. Ibid., 87–92.

9. For the Japanese intrigues involving Vietnamese nationalists during 1940–1945, see Ralph Smith, "The Japanese Period in Indochina and the Coup of 9 March 1945," *Journal of Southeast Asian Studies* (hereafter *JSEAS*) 9.2 (1978): 268–301; Kiyoko Kurusu Nitz, "Independence without Nationalists? The Japanese and Vietnamese Nationalism during the Japanese Period, 1940–45," *JSEAS* 15.1 (1984): 108–33; Tran My-Van, "Japan and Vietnam's Caodaists: A Wartime Relationship (1939–1945)," *JSEAS* 27.1 (1996): 179–93. Diem's involvement with the Japanese during 1943–1944 is discussed in Vu Ngu Chieu, "The Other Side of the 1945 Vietnamese Revolution," *JAS* 45.2 (1986): 299, 306. On Diem's dispatch of an envoy to Cuong De, see Cuong De, *Cuoc Doi Cach Mang [A Revolutionary Life]* (Saigon: Nha in Ton That Le, 1957), 137–38. For the founding and subsequent repression of the Dai Viet Phuc Hung Hoi, see François Guillemot, "Révolution Nationale et Lutte pour L'Indépendance au Viet-Nam: L'Échec de la Troisieme Voie 'Dai Viet,' 1938–1955," Doctoral thesis, École Practiques des Hautes Études, 2003, 206–7. Diem's escape from Hue in the summer of 1944 is in Nitz, "Independence without Nationalists?" 117.

10. For the planning and aftermath of the Japanese coup of March 1945, see Masaya Shiraishi, "The Background to the Formation of the Tran Trong Kim Cabinet in April 1945: Japanese Plans for Governing Vietnam," in Takashi Shiraishi and Motoo Furuta, eds., *Indochina in the 1940s and 1950s*, vol. 2 (Ithaca, N.Y.: S[outh] E[east] A[sian] P[rogram], 1992), 113–41. Shiraishi proves conclusively that Diem received the second of two telegrams which Bao Dai sent to him after the coup, and also demonstrates that Diem turned down the emperor's request of his own volition. However, the reasoning behind Diem's decision remains unclear. Shiraishi cites Japanese sources which suggest that Diem was counseled by his idealist allies to reject the premiership on the grounds that the original independence plan had been diluted. But Stein Tønnesson uses French documents to argue that Diem's refusal was a ploy to increase his leverage, and he shows that Diem became angry when he realized that the offer would not be made again; see Stein Tønnesson, *The Vietnamese Revolution of 1945: Roosevelt, Ho Chi Minh and de Gaulle in a World at War* (Oslo: International Peace Research Institute, 1991), 285.

11. The specific date and circumstances of Diem's detention in 1945 are unclear. According to French intelligence, Diem was seized in the city of Phan Thiet while traveling to Hanoi as a member of a delegation appointed to represent a coalition of southern Vietnamese nationalist groups. See "M. Ngo Dinh Diem, Nouveau Président du Conseil Vietnamien," June 1954, dossier 157, Sous-sèrie Indochine, Sèrie Asie-Oceanie, 1944–1955, Archives de la Ministére des Affaires Étrangères, Paris (hereafter MAE).

12. Karnow, *Vietnam*, 232–33. See also Marguerite Higgins, *Our Vietnam Nightmare* (New York: Harper & Row, 1965), 157–58; and Shaplen, *Lost Revolution*, 110. One of Ho's aides later claimed that the Viet Minh leader feared that keeping Diem in detention might alienate nationalists in Diem's native Central Vietnam; see George Boudarel and Nguyen Van Ky, *Hanoi: City of the Rising Dragon*, trans. Claire Duiker (Lanham, Md.: Rowman & Littlefield, 2002), 90–91. For the claim that Diem's release was secured by Catholic bishop Le Huu Tu, see Doan Doc Thu and Xuan Huy, *Giam Muc Le Huu Tu va Phat Diem, 1945–1954: Nhung nam tranh Dau hao-hung* (Houston, Tex.: Xuan Thu, 1984), 117.

13. For Diem's earlier acknowledgment that he would have joined Ho's government in exchange for a measure of control over Viet Minh security policy, see Ellen J. Hammer, *The Struggle for Indochina, 1940–1955* (Stanford, Calif.: Stanford University Press, 1966), 149–50; and Memorandum of Conversation, Edmund S. Gullion, 8 May 1953, printed in *Foreign Relations of the United States* (hereafter *FRUS*), 1952–1954, vol. 13 (Washington, D.C.: U.S. Government Printing Office, 1982), 553–54.

14. The relevant French sources are described in Tran Thi Lien, "Les Catholiques et la République Démocratique du Viet-Nam (1945–1954): Une approche biographique," in Goscha and de Tréglodé, eds., *Naissance d'un État-Parti*, 253–76.

15. On the establishment of the Front, see Guillemot, "Révolution Nationale," 474–78. For the Front's collapse, see Jamieson, *Understanding Vietnam*, 210–13.

16. Guillemot, "Révolution Nationale," 488–91.

17. Lockhart, *End of the Vietnamese Monarchy*, 165–71; Hammer, *Struggle for Indochina*, 208–16.

18. Philippe Devillers, *Histoire du Viet-Nam de 1940 a 1952* (Paris: Seuil, 1952), 420. For Bao Dai's account of the meeting, see Bao Dai, *Le Dragon D'Annam* (Paris: Plon, 1980), 190. For Diem's views of the French proposals and his concern about Bao Dai's attitude at the time of this meeting, see Telegram, Hopper to Sec[retary of] State, 20 December 1947, printed in *FRUS*, 1947, vol. 6 (Washington, D.C.: U.S. Government Printing Office, 1972), 152–55.

19. Devillers, *Histoire du Viet-Nam*, 425–29.

20. Ngo Dinh Diem, "Loi tuyen bo cua Chi-si Ngo-Dinh-Diem ngay 16 thang 6 nam 1949," reprinted in *Con Duong Chinh nghia: Doc lap dan chu: Hieu trieu va dien van quan trong cua Tong Thong Ngo Dinh Diem*, vol. 1 (Saigon: So Bao Chi Thong Tin, Phu Tong Thong, 1956), 221–22.

21. Ibid.

22. Significantly, the 16 June 1949 statement seems to have been the only document authored by Diem prior to 1954 which was republished by his government after he became the leader of South Vietnam.

23. The assassination orders were intercepted by the French, who then informed Diem that they would be unable to protect him. See Telegram, Donald Heath to [Dean] Acheson, 28 July 1950, State Department Decimal File 751G.00/7-2850, Record Group 59, U.S. National Archives II (hereafter USNA2), College Park, Maryland. All references to USNAA materials are from this record group and will be cited by their decimal file number only.

24. Translation of letter, Ngo Dinh Diem to Wesley Fishel, 3 June 1951, Folder 33, Box 1184, Wesley R. Fishel Papers, Michigan State University Archives, East Lansing, Michigan. Fishel is not specifically identified as the recipient of the letter, but the contents and date strongly suggest that Diem wrote it to him.

25. Telegram, [Edmund] Gullion to Sec[retary of] State, 24 January 1951, *FRUS*, 1951, vol. 6 (Washington, D.C.: U.S. Government Printing Office, 1977), 359–61. See also Telegram, Heath to Sec[retary of] State, 28 July 1950, State Department Decimal File 751G.00/7-2850, RG 59, USNA2. According to Gullion, who was the chargé d'affaires at the U.S. embassy in Saigon in 1950 and who knew Diem and Thuc, the Bao Long scheme envisioned a joint regency shared by Cuong De and Empress Nam Phuong. The empress, unlike her husband, was Catholic.

26. Cuong De's final effort to end his exile is described in Hammer, *Struggle for Indochina*, 275. For his acknowledgment that he and Diem had discussed how the prince might play a political role in Indochina, see Memorandum of Conversation, Dallas Coors, 8 January 1951, State Department Decimal File 794.00/1-851, RG 59, USNA2. On the repatriation of Cuong De's remains in 1956, see the *Times of Vietnam Weekly*, 21 April 1956, 8.

27. Author interview with Professor Ralph Smuckler, Washington, D.C., June 2001.

28. For Fishel's account of his Tokyo meeting with Diem and Thuc, see Memorandum on Ngo Dinh Diem, 28 August 1950, included as an enclosure to Report, Charles Spinks to Dep[artment] of State, 2 September 1950, 751G.00/9-250, USNA2. (Thanks to Joseph Morgan for providing a copy of this document.) This memorandum is unsigned, but other State Department records make it clear that Fishel was in fact the author; see the January 1951 memorandum cited in note 26. The Japanese contact who arranged all of the meetings in Tokyo involving Diem, Cuong De, and Fishel during the summer of 1950 was the liberal writer and adventurer Komatsu Kiyoshi; see Fishel's memorandum and also Demaree Bess, "Bright Spot in Asia," *Saturday Evening Post*, 15 September 1956, 130.

29. Telegram, Acting Secretary of State to Saigon Embassy, 28 September 1950, printed in *FRUS*, 1950, vol. 6 (Washington, D.C.: U.S. Government Printing Office, 1976), 884–86.

30. Telegram, [Dean] Acheson to Saigon, 16 January 1951, printed in *FRUS*, 1951, *vol. 6*, 348. A slightly different version of the exchange between Diem and Bao Dai's representatives is recounted in Memorandum of Conversation, William O'Sullivan, 15 January 1951, 751G.00/1-1551, USNA2.

31. Diem's explanation of why he decided to return to the United States in late 1950 is in D. M. Coors, "Conversation with Mr. Ngo Dinh Diem, Prominent Vietnamese Catholic Leader," 26 July 1951, 751G.00/7-2651, USNA2.

32. Ibid.; see also the telegram of 28 September 1950, cited in note 29.

33. Joseph Morgan, *The Vietnam Lobby: The American Friends of Vietnam, 1955–1975* (Chapel Hill: University of North Carolina Press, 1997), 1–14.

34. For example, in a 1951 memorandum he wrote to a Catholic member of Congress, Diem described the Catholic districts of Phat Diem and Bui Chu in northern Vietnam as a "Third Force zone" populated by people who "understand true Western values" and who "are not anti-West but anticolonialist." Ngo Dinh Diem, "Indo China" memorandum of July 1951, enclosed in letter, Representative Edna Kelly (D-NY) to Senator Mike Mansfield (D-MT), 20 July 1951, Mike Mansfield Papers, Series IV, Box 221, folder 14, Mansfield Library, University of Montana-Missoula. (I am grateful to Mr. Don Oberdorfer for providing me with a copy of this memorandum.)

35. In the 1960s, it was often alleged that U.S. support for Diem had been orchestrated primarily by Cardinal Francis Spellman, the powerful Catholic cardinal of New York; see Robert Scheer, *How the United States Got Involved in Vietnam* (Santa Barbara, Calif.: Center for the Study of Democratic Institutions, 1965), 20–25. More recent arguments along these lines have been less conspiratorially minded, but they still maintain that religion was the core of Diem's appeal to Americans; see Seth Jacobs, " 'Sink or Swim with Ngo Dinh Diem': Religion, Orientalism and United States Intervention in Vietnam, 1950–1957," Ph.D. diss., Northwestern University, 2000.

36. For example, in two speeches delivered toward the end of his stay in the United States, Diem made only one passing reference to Christianity; Ngo Dinh

Diem, "Recent Developments in Indochina," address delivered at the Fifth Annual Meeting of the Far Eastern Association, Cleveland, Ohio, 1 April 1953; and "Talk by Mr. Ngo Dinh Diem before Southeast Asia Seminar, Cornell University," 20 February 1953. Copies of both of these speeches are available in Cornell University's Kroch Library, Ithaca, N.Y.

37. For an overview of the U.S. technical assistance program to the associated states, see the Mutual Security Agency pamphlet entitled "US Technical and Economic Assistance to the Far East: A Part of the Mutual Security Program for 1952–1953" (Washington, D.C.: MSA, March 1952). (A copy of this pamphlet is contained in USNAA, RG 59, U.S. State Department Lot Files, Box 1, Entry 1393.) The classic account of Point Four and its consequences is Robert Packenham, *Liberal America and the Third World: Political Development Ideas in Foreign Aid and Social Science* (Princeton, N.J.: Princeton University Press, 1973).

38. Paul L. Dressel, *College to University: The Hannah Years at Michigan State, 1935–1969* (East Lansing: Michigan State University Press, 1987), 276–77.

39. Letter, Wesley Fishel to MacDonald Salter, 14 March 1952, Box 1184, folder 14, Fishel Papers, MSUA.

40. Fishel's letter describing the proposal seems not to have generated much interest at the MSA in 1952. However, the ideas that Diem and Fishel outlined were eventually realized in the technical assistance program that Michigan State set up in South Vietnam after Diem came to power in 1954. See John Ernst, *Forging a Fateful Alliance: Michigan State University and the Vietnam War* (East Lansing: Michigan State University Press, 1998).

41. William O. Douglas, *North from Malaya: Adventure on Five Fronts* (Garden City, N.Y.: Doubleday, 1953), 147–210. See 180–81 for Douglas's sympathetic representation of Diem as an "honest and independent" alternative to the French. Like Douglas, Mansfield and Kennedy had also traveled to Indochina and become converts to the Third Force cause. Other Americans present at the lunch meeting included Bill Costello, a reporter for CBS News; Ray Newton, an official of the American Friends Service Committee; Edmund S. Gullion of the State Department's policy planning staff, who had met Diem during his earlier stint as chargé d'affaires at the U.S. mission in Saigon; and Gene Gregory, who had also served in the embassy in Saigon and had arranged to introduce Diem to Douglas after the latter's return from Indochina. The luncheon was also attended by Hoang Van Doan, bishop of Bac Ninh in northern Vietnam. Author interview with Gene Gregory, Ho Chi Minh City, March 2002; Letter, Douglas to Diem, 8 May 1953, William O. Douglas Papers, Box 1716, Library of Congress.

42. Don Oberdorfer interview with Mike Mansfield, 28 August 1998. (I am grateful to Mr. Oberdorfer for permission to use this quotation here.) Mansfield likely meant to say "Vietnam" rather than "South Vietnam," since the latter did not exist as a distinct political entity in May 1953. On the luncheon, see Memorandum of Conversation, Edmund S. Gullion, 8 May 1953, *FRUS*, 1952–1954, vol. 13, 553–54. The date on this document (both the published version and the original in the U.S. National Archives) is 7 May 1953; however, based on other documents produced

at the time, I believe that the luncheon actually took place on 8 May. See the letter from Douglas to Diem, cited above, which dates the meeting on the eighth. See also the enclosures in Letter, Kennedy to [John Foster] Dulles, 7 May 1953, State Department Decimal File 751G.00/5-753, RG 59, USNA2, which show that Kennedy's office made an urgent request to the State Department on the morning of 8 May for immediate answers to questions about the current U.S. policy on Indochina.

43. See the Memorandum of Conversation cited in the previous note.

44. Telegram, [Douglas] Dillon to State Dep[artment], 24 May 1954, printed in *FRUS*, 1952–1954, vol. 13, 1608–9.

45. The *Times of Vietnam Weekly*, 17 March 1956, 7; Georges Chaffard, *Indochine: Dix ans d'independence* (Paris: Calmann-Lévy, 1964), 30.

46. Ibid., 27–30; and "Ngo Dinh Luyen," undated biographical summary, dossier 22, sous-série Sud-Vietnam, série V[ietnam] L[ao] C[ambodge], M[inistère des] A[ffaires] E[trangères]. On Can, see Cao Van Luan, *Ben Giòng Lich Su, 1940–1965* (Saigon: Trí Dung, 1972), 180–89.

47. "Ngo Dinh Nhu," in *Souverains et Notabilités D'Indochine* (Hanoi: Gouvernement Général de l'Indochine, IDEO, 1943), 62; "Curriculum Vitae of Mr. Ngo Dinh Nhu," n.d., folder 22, Box 2, John Donnell Collection, Vietnam Archive, Texas Tech University (hereafter Donnell Papers, VA, TTU). Nhu seems to have retained his job at the National Library during the period in which Hanoi was under the control of the Viet Minh; see "Lich-su Day Du ve gia-Dinh cu Ngo-D.-Diem," *Saigon Moi*, 23 June 1954.

48. Author interview with Gene Gregory, Ho Chi Minh City, March 2002. One of Nhu's associates later recalled accompanying him on a visit undertaken on Diem's behalf to a Catholic region near the Laos border in 1946. See A. J. Langguth, *Our Vietnam: The War, 1954–1975* (New York: Simon & Schuster, 2000), 87. Another Catholic source reported that Nhu was forced to flee by sea from Hanoi to the diocese of Phát Diem upon the outbreak of war in December 1946, and from there managed to travel overland to Hue. Doan Doc Thu and Xuan Huy, *Giam Muc Le Huu Từ*;, 116.

49. Emmanuel Mounier, *Personalism*, trans. Philip Mairet (London: Routledge & Paul, 1952), 17–19 and 103–5. The views of Mounier and other French personalists can be distinguished from American personalism, which flourished in Boston in the late nineteenth and early twentieth centuries under the intellectual leadership of Borden Parker Bowne. Although the French and American brands of personalism both drew inspiration from Roman Catholic theology, American personalists tended to be more staunchly idealist than their French counterparts, who acknowledged the independent existence of material reality even as they argued that it should not be overemphasized. See "Personalism" in Paul Edwards, ed., *The Encyclopedia of Philosophy*, vol. 6 (New York: Macmillan, 1967), 106–9; also "Personalism" in Robert Audi, ed., *The Cambridge Dictionary of Philosophy* (Cambridge: Cambridge University Press, 1995), 575.

50. In translating personalism as *nhan vi*, Nhu was following the lead of Father Buu Duong, a Catholic priest and scholar who coined the term in lectures he delivered during the 1940s. See Nguyen Trai, "The Government of Men in the Republic of

Vietnam" (unpublished manuscript, 1962), 139. A copy of this document is available in Widener Library at Harvard University. It is not clear whether or not Nhu actually studied with Mounier in France. Some of his Vietnamese associates claimed he had, but Nhu denied it on at least one occasion. See "Nhu and Personalism," undated notes, folder 14, Box 3, Donnell Papers, VA, TTU.

51. Ngo Dinh Nhu, "Su gop cuc cua nguoi Cong-giao vao Hoa-Binh o Viet-Nam," speech delivered on 18 April 1952 at Dalat Military Academy. Reprinted in *Xa Hoi* magazine (hereafter *XH*) (February 1953): 5, 14, 18–22.

52. Ibid., 21.

53. The precise date and circumstances of the formation of the Can Lao Party remains mysterious, but it seems certain that the party was established prior to Diem's return from his exile in 1954. Diem told Wesley Fishel in 1955 that the party had been formed sometime around 1952. See Memorandum, Fishel to Collins, 7 March 1955, reprinted in *FRUS*, 1955–1957, vol. 1 (Washington, D.C.: U.S. Government Printing Office, 1985), 111.

54. The syndicalist inclinations of the Can Lao Party and its founder were later explicitly acknowledged by party officials:

The program of the Can Lao Nhan Vi follows syndicalist lines, advocating co-management of national industries by representatives of capital and labor and workers' participation in the profits and technical development of industries. The party has taken a strong position of support for agrarian reform for the same reason, namely that possession is a right of the worker. (*Times of Vietnam Weekly*, 25 February 1956, 9)

55. Edmund S. Wehrle, " 'No More Pressing Task than Organization in Southeast Asia': The AFL-CIO Approaches the Vietnam War, 1947–1964," *Labor History* 42.3 (August 2001): 277–95; *Times of Vietnam Magazine*, 4 March 1962, 18–19. Significantly, the confederation's Vietnamese name (Tong Lien Doan Lao Dong Viet Nam) did not indicate the group's Christian affiliation; this undoubtedly reflected Buu's determination to attract non-Christian workers as well as Christians, and also his own identity as a Buddhist.

56. "Tong Lien-Doan Lao-Dong V.N.," *XH* (February 1953): 31, 34; "Ban kien-nghi cua Lien-Hiep nghiep Doan Trung-Viet goi Tong-Lien Doan Lao Dong V.N.," *XH* (July 1953): 16; Dan Sinh, "Tim hieu to-chuc hop-tac-xa," *XH* (15 September 1953): 23; Dan Sinh, "Muc-Dích va Phuong-phap huan-luyen," *XH* (10 November 1953): 33–34; Dan Sinh, "Mau sac to-chuc hop-tac-xa cac nuoc," ibid., 28–29.

57. Hammer, *Struggle for Indochina*, 281–86, 300–301.

58. For the planning of the September congress, see Guillemot, "Révolution Nationale," 628–32.

59. A detailed account of the Unity Congress is contained in Telegram, [Randolph] Kidder to Dep[artment of] State, 22 September 1953, 751G.00/9-2253, USNA2. For published accounts, see *Tieng Doi*, 8 September 1953, 1, 4; *Le Monde*, 8 September 1953; Donald Lancaster, *The Emancipation of French Indochina* (Oxford: Oxford University Press, 1961), 275–77. Bao Dai did not mention the September conference

in his memoirs, but he did acknowledge rebuffing a request for a congress made by Nhu and others during the summer of 1953; Bao Dai, *Dragon D'Annam*, 312–13. For the announcement of the creation of the Movement for National Union and Peace, see Phong Thuy, "Y-nghia va Gia-tri cuoc Dai-Hoi Doan-Ket Ngay 6-9-53," *XH* (15 September 1953): 2.

60. For details on the October congress proceedings, see *Vietnam Presse* 31–36 (12–17 October 1953). See also *Le Monde*, 17–20 October 1953.

61. See Diem's letter published in *Le Monde*, 25–26 October 1953. The efforts of Nhu and his allies to stake out a distinct political position in advance of the October conference are detailed in [Paul] Sturm to Dep[artmen]t of State, "Press Conference Held by Protagonists of 'National Congress' of Early September 1953," 16 October 1953, 751G.00/10-1653, USNA2.

62. Telegram, Dillion to [John Foster] Dulles, 14 October 1953, 751G.00/10-1453, USNA2; the meeting took place on 12 October. As early as September, Diem was described by an American source as confident that he and Bao Dai were about to reconcile ([Walter Bedell] Smith to Saigon and Paris, 14 September 1953, 751G.00/9-1453, USNA2).

63. The circumstances of the second meeting were reported in *Vietnam Presse* 45 (27 October 1953); see also *Le Monde*, 28 October 1953. Bao Dai's query about Diem's willingness to serve was reported to U.S. officials by a member of the imperial entourage (Telegram, Dillion to Dulles, 28 October 1953, 751G.00/10-2853, USNA2).

64. Guillemot, "Révolution Nationale," 627–34.

65. Bao Dai, *Dragon D'Annam*, 328. Bao Dai implied that this exchange with Diem took place in June 1954; however, contemporary sources show that Diem had accepted Bao Dai's offer during an earlier meeting in mid-May. See Telegram, Dillion to Dep[artment of] State, 24 May 1954, printed in *FRUS*, 1952–1954, vol. 13, 1608.

66. Early formulations of this theory are found in Chaffard, *Indochine*, 19–20, 26–29; and in Robert Scheer and Warren Hinkle, "The 'Vietnam Lobby,'" *Ramparts* (July 1965): 16–24. In his memoir on Vietnam, U.S. official Chester Cooper noted that some Americans had concluded that the CIA was backing Diem as early as the spring of 1953; see Chester Cooper, *The Lost Crusade: America in Vietnam* (New York: Dodd, Mead, 1970), 120. Allegations of U.S. influence also appear in Townsend Hoopes, *The Devil and John Foster Dulles* (Boston: Little, Brown, 1973), 251; Marilyn Young, *The Vietnam Wars, 1945–1990* (New York: HarperCollins, 1991), 44; Kahin, *Intervention*, 78; and Jacobs, "Sink or Swim with Ngo Dinh Diem," 100–116.

67. David Anderson, *Trapped by Success: The Eisenhower Administration and Vietnam, 1953–1961* (New York: Columbia University Press, 1991), 41–64, especially 52–55.

68. Bao Dai, *Dragon D'Annam*, 329.

69. Ngo Dinh Diem, "Tuyen bo khi nhan lap Chanh-phu (Ba-Le, 16-6-1954)," printed in *Con Duong Chính nghia*, vol. 1, 13.

70. Ngo Dinh Diem, "Hieu-trieu quoc-dan khi ve toi Saigon, ngay 25-6-1954," printed in ibid., 16.

TAKING NOTICE OF THE EVERYDAY

DAVID HUNT

While it has long been obvious that Vietnam was caught up in the international politics of the Cold War, the place of the Vietnamese in the social history of the period has received less attention. Summing up the global significance of the moment, Eric Hobsbawm declares that the mid-twentieth century witnessed "the greatest and most dramatic, rapid, and universal social transformation in human history." Literacy spread, advances in communication technology overcame constraints in time and space, and commodities generated by "a single, increasingly integrated and universal world economy" found buyers everywhere. The "disintegration of the old patterns of social relationships" opened new possibilities and created new dangers for women and young people. In many regions, shifts in agricultural practice and outmigration from the countryside led to the "death of the peasantry." "For 80% of humanity," Hobsbawm concludes, "the Middle Ages ended suddenly in the 1950s."[1]

Signs of this "social transformation" were plentiful in the Mekong Delta of southern Vietnam. In an economy increasingly driven by outside forces, monetization spread, and customary forms of exchange lost traction. Printed texts found new readers, and radio broadcasts called attention to distant actors whose schemes affected even the most isolated hamlet. Village atheists demanded the floor, while recently formed cults such as the Cao Dai and Hoa Hao took on an established air only because upstart prophets followed closely on their heels. Household arrangements broke down, as one or the other parent got sick or died, took off in search of work, or found a new partner. Gossips jeered at "concubines" even when the targets of their barbs were restless women looking for ways to live that did not involve being kept by any man. Elders muttered about youthful "cowboys," in an echo of the uneasiness occasioned at the same moment by "juvenile delinquents" in the United States. Indeed, all of this turmoil was part of a worldwide rupture in time and space and behavior.

Beginning with the concerted uprising of 1959–1960, southern revolutionaries declared themselves sponsors and organizers of this unrest, which they hoped to appropriate and speed up according to their vision of a new society. Disoriented by seismic changes in the villages and in the world, they valued the "boon of continuity" with the past. But of equal importance was the longing within the movement for an end to feudal backwardness and for an unprecedented future happiness. In the war that followed, two armed camps and two visions of progress were battling for supremacy. Policy makers in Washington and their allies in Saigon called for "modernization," a reference to reforms they wished to bestow on the population. By contrast, I reserve the term "modernism" for the efforts of a popular movement to block externally sponsored projects and to chart its own route forward. Marshall Berman draws this distinction by calling attention to the men and women who have worked to make themselves "the subjects as well as the objects of modernization," who have sought "to change the world that is changing them, to make their way through the maelstrom and to make it their own." Their "visions and values," he declares, "have come to be loosely grouped together under the name of 'modernism.'" The American war sucked Vietnam deeper into the maelstrom and imposed all the dilemmas of modernism upon those Vietnamese who aspired to change the world.[2]

In this chapter, I hope to show how peasant journeys between village and town prepared the way for change in the Vietnamese countryside. While scholars have portrayed the city, with its grand boulevards and back alleys, its pleasures and estrangements, as the privileged locus of modernity, my purpose is to launch discussion from the perspective of what lay outside the city and, for many, stood as its antithesis. The object is not just to identify who was left out or left behind in an increasingly urbanized society, but to study how peasants interrogated what it means to be modern. Exposure to urban life shaped the consciousness of the population in the Mekong Delta, but village-based militants were not content merely to absorb an enlightenment disseminated from metropolitan sources. What follows might be understood as the first chapter in a larger study of their revolutionary modernism.[3]

Taking Notice of the Everyday

To pursue the question, I have been obliged to read and reread the evidence in new ways, to descend from the domain of history writ large to the mundane details of the everyday. In the course of interviewing prisoners and defectors from the National Liberation Front in My Tho province, the Rand Corporation asked a nineteen-year-old female defector, "Were you afraid that you would be arrested or shot on your way to rally?" "No," she replied:

I had lived for four years in My Tho [city] when I was going to school, so I knew how to get there. I took the bus to My Tho and when I arrived here I asked the people how to get to the Chieu Hoi Center. Then I went to the Chieu Hoi Center and called to the guard who took me inside. I was on the same bus as four Popular Force soldiers from Long Binh Dien Village when I went to My Tho, but none of them knew that I was a VC cadre.

Engrossed in her escape narrative, I at first did not notice that this poor peasant had lived and studied in the city for four years. Her older sister resided in My Tho and must have provided a home away from home while she attended school.[4]

In summing up the session with interviewee 206, a poor peasant from Long Hung village, a Rand staffer wrote: "He never had any opportunity to make contact with the people in the GVN-controlled zone and to understand the conditions there." The staffer did not notice that the speaker had mentioned serving in the French army and then working in Saigon for three years as a pedicab driver, in the heart of "the GVN-controlled zone." Informants themselves sometimes failed to notice. Interviewee 193 began by saying, "I have never left my village," then, a moment later, declared, "In 1957, I left my village for one year. I was then drafted by the GVN." He was sent to the Quang Trung Training Center near Saigon and later transferred to an ammunition depot at an unnamed place outside of his home province. "I have been living in…Long Dinh Village from my childhood to the day I was arrested," remarked interviewee 178, who elsewhere in the session recalled his participation in a 1959 rural youth training course run by the government and a year and a half stint as a laborer, both in Saigon. Perhaps these two informants did not wish to remind the interviewer that their experience was wider than he might have assumed. Or maybe they, too, failed to notice, failed to assign any larger significance to, the displacements that had interrupted their village lives.

Fernand Braudel warns us not to be mesmerized by the *event*, not to lose sight of quotidian realities that form the bedrock of human experience. "Everyday life consists of the little things one hardly notices in time and space," he affirms. "Sometimes a few anecdotes are enough to set up a signal which points to a way of life."[5] In studying the revolution in My Tho province, I am trying to notice "the little things" that Rand staffers and interviewees neglected as they carried on their dialogue about the event we call the Vietnam War. Asides and afterthoughts in the transcripts have the power to illuminate the way Vietnamese lived their lives in the middle of the twentieth century. Dilemmas of modernity were posed with the greatest urgency in the sphere of the everyday, and the experience of everyday life generated the resentments and the yearnings and the creative energy that enabled country people to join together and become a revolutionary force. In what follows, I offer the beginning of a social history of the southern revolution in My Tho from 1959 to 1968, a dimension underlying and also shaping the political and military events that up to now have been taken as the crux of the Vietnam War.

A thirty-three-year-old man I will call the "Platoon Leader" spoke more freely than many of the other defectors questioned by Rand. When the interviewer asked what had put him at ease, he laughed and replied:

> Because I saw that you were sincerely moved by my story when I told you of all the painful experiences I had had when I was a child. If you were a cadre planted here, you would certainly not be affected like that. Out there (in the Viet Cong area) amidst all the denunciations there were countless stories that were more heart wrenching than mine.

Unlike the Vietnamese who worked for Rand and who belonged to a different "social class," he explained, NLF cadres would view the informant's life "as just one of a thousand other stories of misery" and not at all unusual.

So, then, what was this everyday "story of misery"? The Platoon Leader began by saying:

> Because he was so poor, my father did not get married until later in his life, and only had one child—myself. As I was growing up, I couldn't go to school, although I wanted to very much. Because my family was extremely poor and didn't have enough to eat, my father kept insisting that I go to work and become a buffalo herder for a landlord in the village when I was only 11 years old.

The boy's inability to prevent buffalo from foraging in the rice fields brought down the wrath of his master ("the beatings and cursings were as regular as rain"). After a few months, the family moved to Ca Mau and lived as wood cutters until four years later, when the father was arrested by the French, accused of affiliation with the Viet Minh, and imprisoned on Poulo Condore Island. His son "never saw him again." An uncle then volunteered to take him to Phnom Penh, where he might have a chance for a better life, but once in Cambodia, he was treated like an indentured servant and put to work selling papers and shining shoes. In 1950, he escaped and returned home, only to be "crushed" by the news that his mother had decamped to Saigon (neighbors said she hoped to find a job selling soup). Since he "didn't know the way to Saigon, and because of the war," this seventeen-year-old, now effectively an orphan, had to stay in the village with his grandfather. Recruitment by the Viet Minh soon followed. In line with the cease fire provisions in the Geneva Accords of 1954, he regrouped to the North, then returned to the delta in 1960 and rose to the position of platoon leader in the People's Liberation Armed Forces (PLAF). His first wife had remarried while he was in the Democratic Republic of Vietnam, and when he married again, to the widow of an ARVN soldier, comrades objected. Irked by their criticisms, persuaded by U.S. escalation that the Front could not win the war, and with the prospect of an affluent life in the Saigon zone (his new father-in-law was a wealthy man), the Platoon Leader defected to the GVN.

At the end of the session, the Rand interviewer commented, "The subject's abilities and comprehension showed how much training courses given to him have changed him. From an ignorant buffalo tender, he has become a very good platoon leader whose comprehension on political matters is really astonishing." After rallying, the Platoon Leader at first tried to masquerade as a simple peasant. But the ruse did not fool a soldier assigned to escort him to the Chieu Hoi Center. "I have met many ordinary citizens here," the soldier declared,

> and I have noticed that when they get to the district, everything is a surprise for them. Moreover, they are reluctant and afraid. Your attitude was completely different. You took it very matter of factly and gave the impression that you were very familiar with life in the towns. That's what made me think that you were a ranking cadre in there.

Here one finds the assumption, common in the urban milieu, that peasants were mere bumpkins who could be transformed into self-confident human beings only by the alchemy of the NLF and the Communist Party.

I prefer to see a larger meaning in this story, with its emphasis on movement in space, awareness, and comportment. No doubt, service in the Viet Minh and the Front helped to develop in the Platoon Leader an uncommon sophistication. But his trials and wanderings must also be counted among the forces that changed him. He was already a resilient survivor, toughened by family tragedy, political repression, and years away from home when he found the Viet Minh and the Viet Minh found him.

Rural Estrangements

Displacements of this sort and the difficulties that prompted them were common in the lives of peasants in the delta. Often supporting dependent children and elders too old to work, the household economy in My Tho was fragile. Most units engaged in subsistence farming, while some family members also worked for a wage in the village or elsewhere or traded agricultural goods in marketplaces near and far. When one of the producers disappeared, the security of everyone else could be called into question.

As the Platoon Leader's story illustrates, children were especially vulnerable. Interviewee 189 was orphaned at four, interviewees 175 and 208 were both orphaned at six, interviewee 186 was orphaned at eight. Interviewee 231, a Khmer, was orphaned at thirteen, and he and his brother survived by working as servants. Interviewee 180 was orphaned at fourteen, then followed his older brother to Saigon and became a pedicab driver in Cholon. Another orphan, interviewee 230, joined the Viet Minh as a teenager. When the First Indochina War was over, he recalled, "As I didn't have to support anyone because my parents were dead, I decided to regroup in the North."

Other informants grew up in single-parent families. The father of interviewee 77 died when he was three, and his mother "had to slave" to raise him and his brothers and sisters. Though "very young," interviewee 243 was required to work in support of his brothers and aged mother after the disappearance of his father. The father of interviewee 203 was killed in battle against the Viet Minh, but the government refused to pay his mother the "death allowance" to which she was entitled. "This is why I hated the GVN even when I was young," he explained. The father of interviewee 198 died when he was two, and he and his many siblings were raised in penury by their mother. He was forced to tend ducks and buffaloes for others, spent only one year in school, and was too poor to marry. "I feel very sad whenever I am reminded of my miserable childhood," he declared. Interviewee 278, whose father died when he was thirteen, asserted that "my family has never been prosperous at all." The mother of interviewee 184 died when he was seven, and, after an unstable childhood and adolescence, he found work as a GVN spy and informer. The mother of interviewee 153 died when he was thirteen. His father insisted that he leave school and work as a buffalo boy, then arranged his marriage and refused to let him make his own decisions until he was twenty-five. The father of interviewee 252 died when he was a child, and he earned a pittance as a buffalo boy while his mother tried to support a family of nine on the income from a tiny parcel of land.

The father of interviewee 290 was killed by the Viet Minh when he was twelve, and "with great courage" his mother worked as a day laborer to raise him and his siblings through "a series of hardships and misfortunes."

Arrangements that poverty or illness or imprisonment or accidents of war did not disrupt were often undone by deteriorating relations between husbands and wives. Polygamy had not disappeared from the countryside, and promiscuous men, like interviewee 26, who kept "two wives" and "courted" village women, destabilized more than one household. Responsibility for children was unclear in the case of interviewee 41, who shared a residence with his father and his father's "concubine" in Saigon while also periodically visiting his mother in My Thuan village. Interviewee 188 was raised by his grandmother. "When I was still living at home," he reported, "I found life very hard. My father had some money but he didn't pay any attention to me. He only thought of the well being of his second wife and her children." In a world where the stability of domestic arrangements was crucial for survival, many country people, and especially the very young, were at risk when households fell apart.

In other cases, women took the initiative. Interviewee 160 was born into a very poor family, and when his mother left his father, he was put in a grandmother's care. "I had to suffer a lot from the rumors still circulating about my mother's behavior," he declared, "and I felt very bitter about my family situation during my younger years." In July 1964, interviewee 1 reported, "my wife suddenly left me to go elsewhere and live with another man," leaving no one "to take care of my three little ones." A few months later, he defected from the Front, leaving two of his children with a grandparent and taking the third along, because he "thought the soldiers would never fire on a man accompanied by a child." When the wife of interviewee 89 insisted on going to the NLF zone in order to take care of her mother, he refused to follow and passed his two children on to their grandmother. Here and elsewhere, unstable family arrangements left children hanging.

Tensions between parents and children were no less acute than those between husbands and wives. Interviewee 76 was beaten by his father after failing school examinations and "longed to get away" in order to "lead a new life." He agreed to follow a cadre because "I couldn't stand my father's treatment any longer." Interviewee 100, a buffalo boy "frequently beaten" by his stepfather, was recruited by the NLF at thirteen. A poor and illiterate orphan, interviewee 138 was mistreated by an aunt, who refused to let him attend school, and became a village guerrilla when he was twenty. "I didn't dare let my father know about my decision" to join the PLAF, reported interviewee 102, who enlisted at sixteen. Interviewee 22 reported that his father disowned him when he opted for the Front at the age of eighteen. Interviewee 225 ran away from home in 1965, when he was fourteen, to join the 514th Battalion. One almost has the impression that the NLF adopted rather than recruited these village youth.

Peasant Encounters with the City

Rand interviewer 130 assumed that peasants never ventured out of their hamlets and were therefore like "a frog at the bottom of a well seeing only a piece of the sky," while interviewer 19 thought that those who were exposed to city life would not "be bluffed by VC propaganda." But stories told by the Platoon Leader and others indicate that villagers had often been to town and had developed critical perspectives on what they had seen. Many were drawn to Saigon to attend school; to sell fruit, cabbage, pigs, sugar cane, bananas, and coconuts; to drive pedicabs, trucks, and buses; to work as domestics, haulers, chauffeurs, dishwashers, coconut pickers, bricklayers, silversmiths, carpenters, seamstresses, masons, stevedores, and mechanics, and in a brewery, a textile mill, a rice noodle plant, an import-export firm, a coconut warehouse, a recording studio, and a fish sauce container factory. In addition to these cases, one might note informants with relatives in Saigon: a sister working as a maid or a seamstress, a brother driving a cab or a cyclo, an aunt whose husband was a journalist, a mother who was a fruit dealer, a father who was a construction worker, a husband employed by "a firm," a wife who had lived in the capital city (and picked up a smattering of English) before marriage, a son employed in a post office. Others ventured even farther afield: a bus driver's assistant in Dalat, a trucker in Bien Hoa, a carpenter in the Highlands, a man seeking medical treatment in Cao Tho. Still others had been drafted and trained in Quang Trung, then assigned to posts in Kontum, Hue, and elsewhere.

My Tho was no Saigon, but it was unmistakably a city, with a population of 40,000; schools that attracted village children; medical services patronized by people of all ages; and markets for fruit, sugar, ducks, and other farm products. Some itinerants found jobs there: an apprentice tailor, a bricklayer and bicycle repairman, a cook, a seamstress, and a worker in a dredging company. District capitals were even more modest agglomerations, but encouraged a division of labor beyond what might be found in villages, so that the transcripts refer to a poor peasant who attended primary and secondary school, a gas station attendant, an apprentice tailor, a tri-wheel Lambretta driver, a servant in Cai Be, an ice cream vendor in Cho

Gao, an apprentice watchmaker and two high-school students in Cai Lay, and a man who worked in his cousin's Chinese soup shop in Giao Duc.

A few of the mobile villagers interviewed by Rand were from well-off households that could afford to send children to urban schools. Typical in this regard was interviewee 136, born into a landlord family in 1907. As a teenager, he studied in the *école normale de pedagogie* in Saigon, taught elementary school in Ben Tre province, then took a job as a principal in Binh Duc village. This educated and traveled man was well qualified to help the Front establish an intelligence presence in Saigon. But most itinerants were more like interviewee 178, who worked as a Saigon bricklayer and whose circumstances were so dire that he was "the only man in the village who did not raise any pigs."

Some urban sojourns were temporary, as in the case of the teenager from My Thanh village, who got a job as a gas station attendant at the Cai Be intersection for one lonely month, then went back home; or the poor peasant from Tan Binh village, who, as a twenty-four-year-old, was briefly employed in a Saigon brewery. Others developed a taste for movement. A precocious young man from An Thanh Thuy village, interviewee 30 made a living taking coconuts by boat from his home through Long An to Saigon, Bien Hoa, and Phuoc Tuy and also had worked for a year and a half in Saigon as a domestic servant. Interviewee 57 joined an entertainment group at the age of seventeen and performed all over Saigon, then periodically returned to sell fruit from his family orchard in Phu An. "Sometimes I spent a whole month in Saigon," he declared. Classified as a very poor sharecropper, interviewee 10 was at home in the marketplace selling sugar cane and stayed in touch with relatives and friends outside of his native village of Xuan Son. His wanderings seemed as much for pleasure as material gain. "I went out of my village at least once every two months," he remarked, "to the GVN-controlled areas to learn about the general situation and to see my friends living there." Curiosity also drove the man who enlisted in the Imperial Guard in Dalat because he "wanted to know more about the country."

As these accounts suggest, some itinerants were drawn to the city. A poor peasant born in 1906, interviewee 269 went to Saigon in 1933 and got a job with Denis Frères, an import-export company. "Life was then easy," he recalled. Interviewee 66, who worked as a hired hand in the capital city, reported that this sojourn "was very pleasant and one could do what he pleased." Interviewee 96 envied his mother-in-law, a fruit dealer in Saigon. "She was free and happy," he reported, "she had to work only half a day and still had a comfortable life." Interviewee 148 noted that if a man were strong enough to carry up to 100 kilograms, he could make a lot of money as a stevedore at the Saigon docks, so that after working only three days a week, he could send 2,000–3,000 piasters a month to his family. My Tho city made a positive impression on interviewee 73, a deserter from the PLAF, who enjoyed "taking a stroll in the public garden near the river" and marveled at the marketplace displays of meat and fish not seen in his native village. "Going to the theater is great!" he exclaimed. Interviewee 59 was also charmed by urban styles, as represented by "town girls." "I noticed that they are more attractive than peasant girls. I knew that because some of the town-girls often came back to Tam Hiep during the Tet festivities or to attend the ancestor worship rites." He added, "Every bachelor in the Front's ranks longed to live in the towns and to marry a town-girl."

Others were not so taken with urban life. Interviewee 82, a very poor twenty-four-year-old from My Duc Dong village, moved to Saigon with his father, worked as an ARVN truck driver in Bien Hoa, then deserted and made a living painting wooden shoes in the capital city. When it became apparent that the police were hunting AWOL (absent without leave) personnel, he returned home, only to find that the NLF had instituted a draft of its own, a step that once more drove him to Saigon. Employed as a bricklayer for seven months unable to pay his bills, he again faced military duty in ARVN ranks. Once more, he decamped to My Duc Dong, only to be conscripted by the NLF. He twice deserted and was forcibly reintegrated, deserted a third time, then hosted a banquet for friends to celebrate his return to civilian life. "You defected from your unit," local cadres fumed, "and you dare to kill a duck to celebrate your desertion?" Sensing that their patience was running out, he headed yet again for Saigon, and, "because life is very hard in town," decided to rally and to enlist in an ARVN unit. That this chronic draft evader was unable to find an alternative to military service underscores the difficulties for peasants trying to make a place for themselves in the city.

Rand transcripts suggest that a gulf remained between urban and rural comportment. Interviewee 8 "often came to My Tho," yet still felt uneasy because "I was a peasant in town and my behavior was not normal." Interviewee 159 complained, "In the cities, people wear revealing clothes and form fitting] pants," and objected to government resettlement camps ("strategic hamlets") because their inhabitants "had to live in close quarters like in the cities." Interviewee 19, a twenty-eight-year-old defector, did not want to venture out of the Saigon Chieu Hoi Center because he was "afraid of being kidnapped by the 'cowboys.'" District capitals are better understood as villages with a smattering of administrative offices, but even there peasants acted "reluctant and afraid," as noted in the interview with the Platoon Leader, cited earlier.

Material difficulties often reinforced this sense of alienation. Interviewee 57, from Phu An village, frequently traded fruit and visited his sisters in Saigon, but thought "it was impossible" to earn a livelihood there. "Living on my garden," he noted, "I had enough to eat." Due to Diemist repression in the late 1950s, interviewee 69 found life "unhappy" in Cam Son village. "I went to Saigon many times," he reported, "but didn't succeed in getting a job and settling in town." Interviewee 80, a twenty-eight-year-old from Dau Thanh village, recalled, "At first, I made my living by repairing bicycles in My Tho. I worked thereafter as a bricklayer for a contractor. I led a very hard life." A poor peasant from Vinh Kim village, who was in his mid-twenties at the time of the Rand interview, had already worked for a dredging company in My Tho, a sugar mill in Cap Saint Jacques, a fish sauce plant in Ca Mau, and a rice noodle firm and a construction crew in Saigon. He reported that employers "liked me a great deal and never spoke harsh words to me. But the thing was that I didn't earn enough money to live on. I kept changing jobs, hoping to make more money, but it was always the same." When he was thirteen, interviewee 128 was sent from Long Khanh village to Saigon, where he resided with his uncle. He became an apprentice silversmith, but could not survive on a "meager salary of 800 piasters a month." Fleeing "miserable conditions," he and his wife came back to Long Khanh. "Saigon is certainly very heavily populated," he observed, "but you live with strangers and therefore you feel more lonely than living with your family and friends in the countryside."

Some commentators called attention to the injustice of the urban social order. Interviewee 107, from My Phong village, went to Saigon at seventeen to study, while rooming with his eldest brother, a military policeman. He recalled, "My parents were poor so they could only help us from time to time by bringing us rice from the countryside." After he had earned a "baccalaureate first degree," his brother and sister-in-law "scorned" his lack of "connections" and made light of his prospects for gainful employment. Disgusted with "the division and sectarianism prevailing in the society at that time," he went back to My Phong. A twenty-seven-year-old from a poor family in Binh Xuan village, interviewee 258 was raised in Saigon, where his father worked as a janitor. He dropped out of school when his parents moved to the countryside, "where the cost of living was lower than in the city. I went on living in Saigon and tried to find a job to support myself so that I could go on studying. I soon found out that life in the city was full of injustice," especially manifest in "the misfortunes and miserable life of the labor class." A possible alternative arose when "during vacation, I returned to my native village and heard the people whisper about the activities of the Front." Soon after, he reestablished himself in Binh Xuan and joined the NLF. Interviewee 224, a twenty-six-year-old poor peasant from Tan Ly Tay village, went to Saigon with his two younger brothers and worked as an apprentice to a practitioner of Oriental medicine. He returned to the village in 1962 and volunteered as a guerrilla, "because at that time the Government was drafting young people of the working class into the military while most youths of rich families were exempted from military service."

To sum up, peasants were on the move, prompted by a desire to see the world or to avail themselves of jobs and services not found at home or to get away from a countryside where poverty was endemic and domestic arrangements proved unable to secure the livelihood of the inhabitants or to meet their demands for happiness. Some adjusted more readily than others, but all had to be alert observers if they hoped to survive in the metropolis. The heightened contrasts of urban life, the mix of wealth and poverty, of cultural effervescence and workplace drudgery, the unpredictable rhythms in the labor market—all honed critical awareness. The effort to make sense of this alien terrain had the added benefit of sharpening an appreciation for resources and possibilities in the countryside that the town could not match. Exposure to an urbanity that stood in marked contrast to rural folkways also drove home the point that hamlet arrangements did not represent the only possible forms of social organization. Every person of a certain age in My Tho had lived through more than one revolution, and only the most blinkered rustic could have been insensitive to the currents reworking everyday life. Exposure to the different costumes and gestures, sights and smells, work regimes and leisure patterns in the city served as additional reminders that other ways of living were possible. Schooling in the contingency of social arrangements did not make revolution inevitable, but it did help to enlarge the consciousness of a nomadic peasantry.

Odyssey of the Ethnographer

These themes are well illustrated in the extraordinary story told by interviewee 233, a witness I call the "Ethnographer." He was born in 1936 in Tan Ly Dong village. Both his mother and his father, a Cao Daist teacher and tobacco trader, were dead by the time he was nine, and two siblings died soon after. He grew up with a grandmother, then with an uncle, who had him tend buffalo, and in 1949 he ran away to join the Viet Minh. After a year of service as a liaison agent, he returned to Tan Ly Dong, was employed by another uncle as a buffalo boy, and managed to save 1,000 piasters catching fish and breeding chickens. A relative who worked as a nurse in My Tho brought him to the city, where he rented an ice box and sold ice cream. In 1956, he apprenticed as a silversmith, only to be treated more as a servant than as an aspiring craftsman, so he quit and went back to the village. "I'm very poor," his uncle told him, "it is up to you to go and look for yourself the type of job you can do." Now twenty, he returned to My Tho and "bought some pieces of musical songs for resale," but was not successful. He next tried working for "a hat-washing firm" and had "almost mastered the trade when the proprietor went bankrupt as a result of his large gambling losses." He switched to a glassware shop run by a Chinese retailer, but that enterprise also collapsed, so he moved over to another shop across the street.

At this point, the uncle, who "was afraid that I might live a loose life in the city," called the Ethnographer back to the village, arranged his marriage to a local woman, and gave him a parcel of land and 500 piasters. A baby was born soon after. "But since my childhood I had known nothing of farming, and I did not know what to do. So I gave the rice and money to my wife to live on, while I went to Saigon to look for a job." He worked installing traffic lights for the Railway Service (40 piasters a day), then wrapped medicine and collected money in an Oriental medicine shop (600 piasters a month, plus meals and extra for overtime). Meanwhile, back in Tan Ly Dong, his wife was spending extravagantly and having an affair with a bus driver. In 1961, the child died, and the Ethnographer was fired from his job at the medicine shop after spending too much time studying for night-school classes. "I wanted to have my elementary school certificate because we have to have a degree in any type of work," he explained, "and because I wanted to enlist in the Navy or in the Police." Having failed repeatedly to escape from poverty and loneliness, he had reached an impasse. "I reluctantly returned to Tan Ly Dong, completely heart broken," he recalled. "My wife had left me, my child had died, and I only had 1,000 piasters left at that time."

This orphan and drifter was rescued by the NLF. Adept at resolving disputes and tempering the excesses of his comrades, he functioned effectively in a variety of roles within the movement. Security cadres were instructed to watch the everyday behaviors of the villagers, an assignment that enabled the Ethnographer to employ his skills as an observer and commentator on rural social relations. At the same time, possibly as a consequence of his long experience of disappointment and hardship, one senses in his account a chronic restlessness, a taste for what he called "modern and strange things." Twice expelled from the party for illicit love affairs, he periodically retreated into a kind of escapism, meeting every day with other disaffected cadres for an "eating and drinking party." But until the moment of his rally and perhaps beyond (we cannot say what happened to him after the Rand interview), he could not let go of the revolution. "We are Bolsheviks," comrades said to him,

> and we are not afraid of shortcomings. Therefore, you should not feel embarrassed. You should think it over and try to contribute your efforts in the Front activities in your area in order to promote the revolutionary movement and contribute to the struggle against the Americans and the traitors to liberate our people and reunify our country.

This appeal had the desired effect, but then, in August 1967, after almost getting killed in a commando raid (not his only brush with death), he rallied to the GVN.

In his village and in My Tho and Saigon, the Ethnographer had twice lost his family and had been a buffalo boy and cultivator, fisherman and chicken breeder, ice cream vendor and apprentice silversmith, sheet-music peddler and hat washer and glassware salesman and traffic light installer and medicine shop clerk. Habits formed during a lifetime of wandering did not readily bend to party discipline. "I was not a member of any organization," he reported:

> I could go anywhere I pleased. When I came to an area where I had friends or acquaintances, I would stay with them for a while. If I felt like it, I would cooperate with the local village security cadres and work with them. Otherwise, I would join some friends for a drinking party.

The NLF appealed to, depended on, and then had to find ways to live with restive country people who refused to stay in place.

I call 233 the Ethnographer because of the keenness and penetration of his extended commentary on village life. In a sample filled with individual displacements, he was perhaps the most nomadic of the informants and was also the most astute observer of everyday life, and I cannot help thinking that there is a connection between these two aspects. In his extended dialogue with Rand (the interview transcript runs to 397 pages), he offered both a history of the NLF in My Tho and a commentary on the advent of a certain kind of modernity in the countryside, and in the telling, he drew out the interplay between these two developments. Highly attuned to movement politics, he also had much to say about changes in farming techniques, the fraying of relations between old and young, a new fascination with consumer items such as radios and sewing machines, and a general acceleration and dislocation in the rhythms of work and leisure. "In short," he summed up, with reference to both the political and the social, "the life of the people changed completely in every respect as compared to the previous six years of peacetime."

Among town dwellers, there was no counterpart to the peasant meditation on the urban-rural divide. According to Philip Taylor, they regarded the countryside as "a symbol of tradition, yet one in which they would not like to spend too much time." The delta, they marveled, was a place where "you can just stick something in the ground...and it will grow." This was an expression of self-serving blindness among

> creditors, process factory owners, and tax agents who benefit from the agricultural wealth of the delta without having to undertake the manual labor or suffer the loss of livelihood and well-being in the economically and environmentally unstable conditions of agricultural commodity production. The wealth of the land is imagined not as a human product for which a substantial debt of gratitude might be owed, but as a natural blessing to the Vietnamese people.

At best patronizing, urbanites did not always succeed in masking the disdain that informed their view of the agrarian population. In one moment, country life was seen as "quaint," and villagers were portrayed as "simple, forthright and full of charmingly archaic turns of phrase." In the next, they were ridiculed as superstitious boors. While itinerancy gave peasants at least a modicum of experience on which they might base a claim to speak for the nation, the ignorance and bigotry of privileged city dwellers helps to explain their paralysis when rebellion broke out in the countryside.[6]

The *Rassemblement*

The trends reviewed above underscore the danger of assuming that the village community and the peasant class were static entities. A snapshot view of the agrarian social order reveals differences between the rural poor and prosperous truck farmers, between the illiterate and the handful who attended secondary school, between devout and agnostic, old and young, men and women. Pictured over time and with attention to patterns of movement, the social formation appears even more ambiguous. Individuals who left their hamlets often could not predict when or if they might return. Many city-dwelling migrants continued to think of the village as home, but as time passed, occasional visits, as for Tet celebrations, became no more than ritual pauses in a new, urbane way of living. Modernization everywhere, and not just in Vietnam, constantly makes and unmakes communities and class solidarities, obliging those caught up in its rhythms to ask again and again who they are and where they fit in society.

Living in unsettled times may also sharpen a sense of need and open the imagination to commonly shared hopes. That is what happened in 1959–1960, when southern militants launched the concerted uprising. As they broke the grip of the regime, drove landlords from the countryside, and challenged hierarchies of every kind, thousands of peasants came to think of themselves as revolutionaries. Their uprising ushered in what one informant called a "golden period," filled with debates over the organization of material life, the relationship between religion and politics, the function and control of print communication, the proper use of entertainment and leisure, the roles of youth and elders and of, women and men. It also sponsored a remapping of space in the delta. As cities lost their earlier power of attraction, the wanderers turned back to the countryside; the outflow of migrants trying to get away from the penury and frustration of rural life gave way to an inflow of villagers coming home as a disinherited rural population rediscovered its peasant identity.

Born in 1914, interviewee 111 came from a wealthy family and attended primary school in My Tho. In 1933, his father set him up as a tradesman, moving fruit from Ca Mau to Saigon, his livelihood until 1960, when he joined the NLF. His son joined, too, and was killed in 1964 while attending a medic training course. This affluent villager quit the Front in 1962, was called back, quit again, was inactive for three years, then rallied in order to acquire GVN identity papers. That a man so well situated, from an entrepreneurial rich-peasant family, could have been swept into the movement, even if only for a couple of years, is eloquent testimony to the power of the *rassemblement*, the gathering of the people, set in motion by the concerted uprising.

It was less surprising when poor people came home. After being evicted by his landlord, interviewee 142 went to Saigon in 1957 and found employment as a carpenter with Johnson, Drake, and Piper, the U.S. construction company building the Saigon–Bien Hoa highway. With savings from a salary of 152 piasters a day, he moved with his two children to Bien Hoa and built a house that cost 2,000 piasters. When the highway project ended, the informant had to take a sequence of odd jobs. Frequently unemployed, he sold his house for 1,000 piasters, moved back to Saigon, and lived with a brother, whose income as a cyclo driver "was barely sufficient for him and his family of six children." It was during this time that he "got wind of the uprising of the Viet Cong." Return to the countryside was "the direct result of my inability to find a job in the capital city of Saigon and my assumption that I would make an easier living in my own native village now that the Front had given back the lands to me for farming."

A similar impression emerges from the testimony of interviewee 137, who was classified as a poor peasant, but who declared that he did not "know anything about farming and worked in the market place" as a barber and tailor. At first portraying himself to Rand as a reluctant recruit, he later indicated that his mother had received a parcel during the NLF land reform. When asked to name the good deeds of the Front, he responded:

> I liked most of all the distribution of wealth to the poor people. I saw that the
> poor people were the slaves of the rich, they had to work as servants and hired
> laborers for the rich. I loved the poor people and was convinced that the rich
> class was exploiting the poor class.

The revolution was drawing this seemingly deracinated peasant back to the land in his native village. Other returning poor peasants included interviewee 178, who was frightened by the concerted uprising and fled to Saigon, where he worked as a bricklayer, then returned to Long Dinh village in 1962, in the middle of the golden period because, in his own words, he was "homesick"; and interviewee 167, who found a job in a Saigon textile factory, then retraced his steps "in order to add to the number of dependent exemptions in my family for the (VC) land reform program."

The *rassemblement* constituted a development of extraordinary interest and originality in the history of southern Vietnam. Peasants of My Tho lived and worked within an orbit dominated by the Saigon metropolis, with its concentration of administrative and political power, its seductive commodities and styles, its insatiable appetite for the produce of the delta, its huge labor market, which employed and dismissed working people according to a logic that no one could anticipate or control. By creating a sense of novelty and progress more gripping than any urban fashion, the revolution shifted the locus of modernity to the villages. A Rand informant noted:

> [I]n 1962, 1963, and 1964, the Front was absolutely supported by the people.
> Even the people who lived in the city were with the Front. Students left school
> to ask to be Liberation soldiers. We didn't push the enlisting movement, but
> even so, many people volunteered to be soldiers. People who lived in the
> GVN zone, when they reached the age of military service, would run away

with the Front. There wasn't much difference between life in the city and in the Liberation zone, especially in clothing and in material needs. Coffee shops were filled with people. People came in great numbers to do business. Whenever there was a festival, a lot of people were present.

The attempt to end the age-old subordination of rural to urban space counts among the most ambitious goals of what was a many-sided cultural revolution.

As in all revolutions, attempts to assign spatial and institutional forms to utopian dreams collided with the desires of activists avid for novelty. Land reform is often cited in the literature on the Front program, and many Rand informants spoke of it as a goal and ideal. But whereas some wanted a countryside filled with household parcels because that innovation promised to stop the erosion of custom and give to everyday life a more fixed and stable character, fixity was just what many activists did not want. The restlessness among those country people, especially the young who "loved new and strange things," was therefore a source both of energy and of tension within the NLF. According to the Ethnographer, people in the movement

> have always taken dialectical materialism as a guideline for the settlement of their problems. They think that everything in this world never stood at one place but always changed. A human being or a thing experiences the same change of conditions. If a party cadre or member does not think so, he is a backward person.

This was a demanding—a modernist—credo among revolutionaries who were suspicious of blueprints for society drawn up in advance and who refused to be pigeonholed as individuals.[7]

"All men want to go around and get to know more and learn more things," affirmed a PLAF soldier. "I knew I might get killed if I kept fooling around with weapons. But each day I remained alive meant that my knowledge was furthered by what I saw on that day." Initially assigned roles as privates in the People's Liberation Armed Forces or as hamlet-level cadres in the NLF's civilian sector, many activists hoped for promotion to higher levels in the PLAF or to village, district, or province echelons in the Front's quasi-government. More diffuse, but just as powerful, was the hunger for education, for travel, for challenges and self-realizations that were no less keenly desired for being difficult to anticipate in any concrete way.

The surge of energy these rural revolutionaries brought into the movement was tinged with apprehension. Impatient when promotions did not come as swiftly as he would have preferred, the Platoon Leader expressed a common fear when he said, "No matter how much a buffalo tries to wear down his horns, he will always remain a buffalo." Interviewee 203 cited that same maxim, while also insisting, "I wasn't struggling and making sacrifices to stay forever in the village." "I was in the guerrilla unit for a year," reported a twenty-three-year-old from My Duc Tay:

> I got a little bored because, for the whole year, we didn't do anything of any importance—we stood guard on the roads, or stood guard during meetings to maintain order, or we planted grenades and mines—so I volunteered to join the Front['s] big units when the Front launched an intensive campaign to make the youths enlist in its forces. My ambition in enlisting in the big units was to get promoted and to progress in my work, because I thought that if I stayed in the guerrilla unit, I would work like a buffalo for the Front all my life without any hope in the future.

Village militants would not be content with monotonous toil in the fields and knew from experience or from the reports of neighbors what it was like to work as a maid or chauffeur in Saigon. They counted on the revolution to provide something better.

Women on the Edge

Rand's fourteen female informants lived on the fault lines of rural society and felt its estrangements with a particular urgency. Three of the fourteen were orphans, and at least five others were raised in single-parent households. Three fled from arranged marriages and one from a tyrannical mother-in-law, and eight others ran away from home to join the Front. Although very young (at the time they were interviewed by Rand, seven were teenagers and four others were twenty-four years old or less), five had already spent time in cities prior to joining the Front, two as maids in Saigon, plus one at school, one trading fruit, and another baby sitting, all in My Tho. Two female informants went to town after quitting the movement and before rallying, one to My Tho, where she worked as a cook, and another to Cai Lay.

Once in the Front, the women were channeled into a number of niches, which did not always live up to their expectations. Five of the fourteen served as liaison agents carrying documents and letters and escorting cadres from one zone to another (the ability of women to "pass" was useful here). For some, this assignment devolved into a tedious back-and-forth along the same path delivering the mail (interviewee 78 characterized it as boring), while others were energized by a sense that they were maintaining the communication system on which the movement depended. Medical sectors also incorporated five women, an assignment promising to impart a complex, interesting, and socially valued skill. On the other hand, it required studious application, which may have been beyond the capacity of someone like interviewee 213, who was expelled from a medical course after getting in a fist fight with another student and who was perhaps better suited to "demolitions training," the slot she was occupying when captured. Two of the informants ended up with clerical jobs in NLF base areas, which they did not like, and two served in entertainment troupes. Another was assigned to a Front textile factory where labor discipline was strict. The regimen in a Saigon mill might have been even more draconian, but on the other hand, a worker there would have been living in a bustling city rather than in a sparsely populated and heavily bombarded base area. The one teacher in the group seemed to have enjoyed her work.

Leadership roles within the Women's Association were the most likely to lead toward positions of prestige and authority, and in the early years of the Front, when contributions rather than systematically assigned taxes financed the movement and there were more volunteers than the PLAF could absorb, the association's political work was both gratifying and likely to earn promotion. Interviewees 65, who joined the Front in 1961, and 133, who joined in 1963, were both able to flourish and to gain entry into the Communist Party. Indeed, the golden period was identified in several interviews as the high-water mark of the Women's Association, when propaganda was a movement priority and female militants were among the most active of the propagandists.

Options for women (and men) closed down with escalation in 1965. As the terrain was increasingly militarized, liaison work became almost as hazardous as service in the PLAF, villagers no longer dared to attend Front shows or to send their children to NLF schools, and propaganda efforts could do nothing to prevent panic-stricken villagers from evacuating to the GVN zone. Still, intrepid women were drawn toward the revolution. Ambitious, confident, and unfazed by mounting violence, interviewee 253 joined in 1965. She had turned down several marriage proposals and, from her days trading fruit in My Tho, had developed a skeptical attitude toward the urban milieu. "If I then live in a city," she anticipated:

> I could not have a sufficient level of education to earn a relatively adequate material living, as those who have lived there long before. I am able to earn

my living only as a worker or a servant in a rich family. Thus, my wages can be used only to support myself. I am unable to support my family and to build up my own future. Do you think that I can be a servant until I get old and die? It was also due to my hope of living a better life that I participated in the revolution.

Her engagement with the Front was no less critical than with the town, and she grew just as impatient with her initial "mediocre" hamlet-level assignment as with the thought of being "a worker or a servant" in the city. Outcomes were more promising after she was invited into the Executive Committee of the village Women's Association. "I carefully examined all reports submitted by hamlet cadres," she recalled, and "studied all directives day and night in order to produce good results in my activities." But when a hard-won promotion to district level was not accompanied by an invitation to join the Communist Party (on the grounds that her brother had ties to the GVN), she felt herself to be "in the condition consistent with the saying that goes, 'You'll remain a buffalo although you have tried to sharpen your horns.'"

In this story and in others, one can see the promise and the limits of the *rassemblement*. The village was the home base and launching pad for the movement, carried forward by a peasantry of high class consciousness. But the persisting symbolism of the buffalo suggests that some country people were haunted by a fear that they would not be able to escape what they took to be the drudgery of rural life. Overthrowing the GVN and expelling the Americans could only be counted a part of the Front mandate. Delivering on the promise of personal liberation loomed just as large.

Saigon's Ellis Island

As the war escalated in 1965, bombing and shelling, troop sweeps, and chemical warfare turned the countryside into a killing zone and drove many inhabitants to urban areas controlled by the GVN. As was the case with prerevolutionary ferment, the consequences of U.S. intervention should be placed in a wider context. Eric Hobsbawm was thinking globally and not just about South Vietnam when he said that "the 1960s will probably go down as the most disastrous decade in the history of human urbanization." The American tactic of "generating refugees" was, after all, "forced draft urbanization and modernization," as conceived by U.S. war makers (and given a name by Samuel Huntington). It formed part of a larger strategy for remaking "underdeveloped countries," to employ the language of the day, and for thwarting communist insurgencies in Vietnam and elsewhere.[8]

For most ex-Front members, defecting was not just, indeed not primarily, a political choice, but functioned instead as a mechanism for rural dwellers trying to find their way to the relative safety of the towns. Interviewee 12 heard through the grapevine that the Chieu Hoi Centers offered "500 piasters for home coming travel expenses," and "200 piasters for miscellaneous expenses," plus board and lodging. "Everyone is greedy for this," he noted, and recommended that defectors "should be asked to stay at the Chieu Hoi Center for only a month" and "should be given a six-month or one-year deferment from military service." Then, reminding himself that he was supposed to be "rallying" and that his tone might sound crass, he promised to join the ARVN at an unspecified later date and added, "Who can neglect national affairs?" He was not the only defector to bargain with Chieu Hoi authorities. Interviewee 172 stated:

> My wishes remain the same, to live peacefully in the GVN zone, so that I can work to support my wife and my 5 children, and be reunited with them. If I plant rice, I will need at least 8 cong of land; and if I go to work, 3,000 piasters a month will be enough for us to live on.

The interviewer remarked that this informant promised to help in getting others to rally, then noted, "However, he also wants to get a reward from the Government."

Rand and Chieu Hoi personnel must have been disappointed to find that most defectors "wanted to get a free, and non government job rather than work for the GVN." Many of the individuals interviewed in 1965 were raw recruits, drafted by the NLF into main-force units at a moment when it seemed that a big push might bring the war to a triumphant conclusion. Taken away from their homes and families and marched toward distant battlefields, frightened by bombing raids and corpses along the road, they deserted and rallied, often within days of induction. Tales of carnage in the Tay-Ninh Eastern Zone made military service seem even more terrifying than the rapidly deteriorating situation in My Tho, so that rumors of impending NLF call-ups provoked new waves of desertion. Individuals who rallied in order to avoid the NLF draft were not eager to plunge again into the war, this time on the side of the GVN.

The demoralization of more seasoned fighters added to the ranks of defectors. Homesickness, quarrels with superiors, and battlefield trauma persuaded some to leave the PLAF. Wounded soldiers in dispensaries refused to return to their units, as did combatants on home leave. Front cadres often bargained with AWOL soldiers by offering them postings as village guerrillas or hamlet militia men. But deserters might be subject to surveillance as "bad elements" and in any case would be hectored to resume their places in main-force units. Afraid of being reconscripted, a number chose to rally instead.

On the civilian side, a number of defectors were in the middle of adulterous love affairs, with attendant difficulties at home and disparaging gossip among villagers, and saw in the Chieu Hoi program an escape route and opportunity to start over with a new partner. Others resented being passed over for promotion or took offense after drawing criticism for dereliction of duty, or they feared punishment for licentiousness, embezzlement, assault, or even homicide. A few of these individuals were angry to the point of wanting to revenge themselves on former comrades, but most simply wished to get away from the war. For them, six-month deferments from military service were an important part of the package of benefits offered to ralliers.

To reenter the labor market, defectors needed identification cards, which the NLF had confiscated in the early years of the revolution or which had been lost or destroyed by accidents of war. Many who had left the Front months or even years before turned themselves in to the Chieu Hoi Centers because they had been unable to get a job without a card. The Center also provided vocational training for peasants now destined for the urban sector of the economy. In all of these respects, the Chieu Hoi program functioned as a kind of Ellis Island, mediating the passage of rural dwellers from their villages to the cities. It was a displacement from the liberated zone of the NLF to the zone of government control, from the modernism of the rural revolution to the modernization of the Saigon milieu.

Defectors who had lived in cities were in better shape than those who had no contacts or past experience in the GVN zone. But even seasoned itinerants may have felt that taking to the road once again amounted to a retreat into a world of uncertainty, hardship, and corruption. Interviewer 211, a defector who wished to resume his "former profession" as a mechanic and bus driver, reported that when he asked for help in securing the necessary documents, "someone at the Chieu Hoi Center told him that if he gave him 20,000 piasters, he would help obtain them. Otherwise, the person would cause him trouble when he tried to go through the administrative channel." At a deeper level, officials could not undo the reality that many of the restless individuals they were trying to resituate in the GVN zone had previously lived outside of their villages and had not been satisfied with the outcomes.

Testimony from interviewee 180 illustrate the problem. Having followed his older brother to Saigon in 1947 at the age of fourteen, he became a pedicab driver in Cholon, then in 1960 returned to Binh Trung village, where the concerted uprising was already under way (Binh Trung was one of the first locales to join the revolt). "I was young," he stated. "I had no serious thoughts, I just wished I could live a better life"—an aspiration that seemed within reach, given that, when the NLF "came out of its underground activities and set up its infrastructure in the village, it paid special attention to and took special care of the poor peasants, who then gave strong support to it." After defecting, the informant hoped he would be allowed to "go to Cholon to become a tricycle pedicab driver and build a new life." But this "new life" was not new at all. Before 1960, he had worked as a pedicab driver in Saigon, then, in search of a "better life," he had joined a movement that promised to take "special care" of him and other poor peasants. When the NLF was on the defensive in 1967, he made a decision that involved going back to what he had been doing seven years before. For him and other defectors, the revolution was over.

Villagers Who Refused to Move

The pattern outlined above conveys an impression of symmetry, with itinerant habits temporarily suspended during the revolution, only to be resumed when war intensified. But if this sketch were the whole story, if the villagers had migrated to the towns and cadres and if the fighters had gone with them, then the Front would have collapsed, and the GVN and the Americans would have won the war. The final phase of my inquiry centers on what happened to those who remained in place after 1965 and to the modernist spirit that had driven their movement from the days of the concerted uprising. Bombs and shells destroyed much of what had been created during the golden period, pulverized the means of life on which everyone depended, overthrew habitual conceptions of time and space so that people feared they were losing their minds. To stay at home was a political and military necessity, and at another level it amounted to a test of will for activists who in more hopeful days had been energized by a love of movement. Now, circumstances obliged them to grit their teeth and hunker down—and not to move.

As at other junctures, my intent here is to rethink, to "normalize," what was imposed on the Vietnamese. Their experience in a war zone constitutes an extreme case of what David Harvey describes as "the deep chaos of modern life and its intractability before rational thought." Harvey's notion of a "time-space compression" speaks to the horrors of guerrilla war, its rhythms determined by people traveling on foot and information spread by word of mouth, against an adversary capable of lightning-fast deployments. But fighting and dying amounted to only half of the story. Combatants and others who remained in the countryside had to secure food and shelter in a chaotic version of the "perfect market" so much anticipated by modernization theorists, a terrain without custom or law, inhabited by individuals who could draw on their capital and their labor and nothing else. "Because of the war, the ways of life of the population have completely changed," declared a poor peasant from Nhi Binh:

> Everybody is afraid of thinking of tomorrow and of the future. Trade and farming in the village have actually undergone a lot of changes to fit the new ways of life, a life in which everything seems to be just temporary and risky. Many families, having settled in their new houses along the highway, sold all their valuable objects to get a capital (amounting to about two or three thousand piasters) to start some kind of trade to live from hand to mouth. They usually buy fruit, chickens, and ducks and resell them at government-controlled market-towns making a daily profit of about 100 piasters, while other people try to earn some extra money by working as hired laborers to contribute to the daily expenses of a family of five or six people.

Disoriented in every aspect of their existence, the Vietnamese had been plunged into the epicenter of the maelstrom.[9]

One might wonder how cadres and soldiers were able to win the war, but what concerns me here is the fate of the adjoining project: to create an alternative to a Saigon-based modernization. I want to know what happened to village militants when utopian dreams absorbed a heartbreaking blow and when shattered their everyday could no longer provide inspiration for revolutionary modernism. The drama, the grandeur, lies in their refusal to relinquish hope that, when human will is tested to the limit, "the deep chaos of modern life" can be mastered.

NOTES

My thanks to Peter Weiler and Marilyn Young for many helpful criticisms of earlier drafts. As with all students of events in My Tho and in Vietnam more generally, I have had the luxury of building on the comprehensive work of David

Elliott, *The Vietnamese War: Revolution and Social Change in the Mekong Delta, 1930–1975* (New York: Sharpe, 2003).

1. Eric Hobsbawm, *Age of Extremes: A History of the World, 1914–1991* (New York: Pantheon, 1994), 15, 288, 289. Among objections to Hobsbawm's template, one might note that French colonialism and the Japanese occupation in Indochina are not well characterized as "medieval" phenomena and that the peasantry of the delta had not "died." With respect to the peasant issue, Hobsbawm adds, "Only three regions of the globe remained essentially dominated by their villages and fields: sub-saharan Africa, South and continental South-east Asia, and China" (ibid., 291).

2. On the "boon of continuity," see Eric Wolf, *Peasant Wars of the Twentieth Century* (New York: Harper & Row, 1968), 276; on "modernization" and "modernism," see Marshall Berman, *All That Is Solid Melts into Air: The Experience of Modernity* (1982; reprint, New York: Penguin, 1988), 16.

3. I am thinking here of Berman, *All That Is Solid*, and David Harvey, *The Condition of Postmodernity* (Cambridge, Mass.: Blackwell, 1989), 25, which have been important in pushing me to think in a more global way about the Vietnamese revolution.

4. As part of its study of "Viet Cong Motivation and Morale," commissioned by the Pentagon, the Rand Corporation interviewed 286 prisoners and defectors from the National Liberation Front (NLF) in My Tho province. My Tho province was located between fifty-five and sixty-five kilometers south of Saigon and was valued by the government as a link between the capital city and the Mekong Delta. Bordering on the Plain of Reeds, which served as a guerrilla base area, and inhabited by a population with a history of political activism, the province was a stronghold for both the Viet Minh and the National Liberation Front. Interviews were conducted from 1965 to January 1968, translated, typed, copied onto microfilm, then released to the public in 1971. The Saigon government renamed My Tho province "Dinh Tuong," and the My Tho interviews are identified in the Rand collection as the DT series. Readers who would like the pages and question numbers for the citations should contact me at david.hunt@umb.edu, and I will be happy to send them along. For more on this source, see Phillips Davison, *Users Guide to the Rand Interviews in Vietnam* (Santa Monica, Calif.: Rand, 1972). The Republic of South Vietnam, referred to in the interviews as the government of Vietnam (GVN), set up Chieu Hoi Centers to receive and process "ralliers" (defectors). Chieu Hoi means "call back" in Vietnamese and was translated as "open arms" by the Americans.

5. Fernand Braudel, *The Structures of Everyday Life*, trans. Sian Reynolds (Berkeley: University of California Press, 1992; first published in French in 1979), 29.

6. This passage is based on the work of anthropologist Philip Taylor, *Goddess on the Rise: Pilgrimage and Popular Religion in Vietnam* (Honolulu: University of Hawaii Press, 2004), 121–22; and Taylor, *Fragments of the Present: Searching for Modernity in Vietnam's South* (Honolulu: University of Hawaii Press, 2001), 160–61.

7. On "blueprint utopias," see Russell Jacoby, *Picture Imperfect: Utopian Thought for an Anti-Utopian Age* (New York: Columbia University Press, 2005),

xivff.; and on how "[u]topias of spatial form are typically meant to stabilize and control the processes that must be mobilized to build them," see David Harvey, *Spaces of Hope* (Berkeley: University of California Press, 2000), 173; see also Berman, *All That Is Solid*, 6.

8. Hobsbawm, *Age of Extremes*, 262; Samuel Huntington, "The Bases of Accommodation," *Foreign Affairs* 46.4 (July 1968): 652. See also Michael Latham, *Modernization as Ideology: American Social Science and "Nation Building" in the Kennedy Era* (Chapel Hill: University of North Carolina Press, 2000); and, for Ngo Dinh Diem's attempt to craft a modernization strategy distinct from the designs of both the United States and the Communist Party, see Philip Catton, *Diem's Final Failure: Prelude to America's War in Vietnam* (Lawrence: University Press of Kansas, 2002); and Edward Miller's essay in this volume.

9. Harvey, *Condition of Postmodernity*, 44.

CO SO CACH MANG AND THE SOCIAL
NETWORK OF WAR

HEONIK KWON

The Vietnam War was a complex reality for the Vietnamese. One way to explore this complexity is to consider a set of organizational and social networks that proliferated during the war, particularly in the urban areas of the southern region. This chapter continues David Hunt's "history from below" approach to the subject and investigates further the movement and displacement of the people highlighted in Hunt's essay. My discussion will focus on two analytically distinct types of network: the purposeful, political organizational network and the crosscutting, informal social network of human actors existing within and across defined political groups. These two different types of human network were both integral to the grassroots experience of the Vietnam War and were interconnected in a myriad of ways. This chapter will describe their historical connectedness and the contemporary meanings of this history based on my research in a peripheral urban neighborhood near Danang, the wartime commercial and strategic center of Central Vietnam. I call this neighborhood the community of Tiger Temple, taking note of the central symbolic importance of this animist temple for the identity of the place.

The Infrastructure of Revolution

For many people in southern and Central Vietnam, the idea of a network is not merely a technical concept from the hypermodern information age. Young people, skilled in navigating the Internet, call their virtual network *mang luoi*. Yet, their parents, who spent their youth during the war years, used to call the prolific revolutionary network of covert actions *mang luoi* (network) or *mang luoi gian diep* (covert network). The lucrative circles of the informal economy from the postwar years, such as the popular lottery organizational network of *so de*, also call their operations *mang luoi* or

mang luoi chu de. The Vietnamese idea of network is rooted in their historical experience of war and their everyday encounters with the informal economy. Their experience of the Vietnam War, at the grassroots level, was very
much a network-type phenomenon, especially in the urban areas. Moreover, these political organizational networks must be considered within the
broader context of multivariate, informal social networks.[1]

In the urban zones of southern and Central Vietnam under the control
of South Vietnamese and U.S. military forces, a single wartime revolutionary cell, called *to* (or *to ba nguoi*, meaning "three-member cell"), typically
consisted of three to five men and women belonging to the "revolutionary
infrastructure," or *co so cach mang*, which refers to the covert civilian activists loyal to the revolutionary cause. Each cell was connected to a wider
circle—a network of networks in today's jargon—but its members usually
had no knowledge of the expanse of the circle.[2]

Under the hostile conditions in towns, the cell itself often took the form
of a network in which the infrastructure workers were largely unknown to
one another. Each had contacts with the cell operator via various means of
communication. The workers met their superiors and network operators in
the graveyard or the temple (unless they were already neighbors, kinfolk, or
workmates); alternatively, they were sent coded messages via messengers.
The workers often mistook the messenger for their superior. Two neighbors
could be doing similar activities without knowing each other's identity or
activity since they belonged to different niches of the *mang luoi*. The exposure of one worker rarely led to collateral damage in the network, for the
workers themselves were unaware of the terrain beyond their immediate
chain of work. The relationship between the operator and the workers was
both hierarchical and horizontal. The workers received orders and directives
from the operator and in turn supplied information and practical support
back to the operator. The activities of individual workers were conducted,
nevertheless, largely within their existing social networks, in accordance
with their own judgment and in terms of their own capacities for action. The
operator's influence on the workers' technical operations remained marginal and fluctuated depending on the wider political situation. The network
operator was more vulnerable to the failure or disloyalty of the workers than
vice versa. Morally, however, the workers and their superior maintained
a horizontal relationship, calling and perceiving each other as *dong chi*,
partners, who shared the same purpose.

The nature of this cell organization was such that it could expand
infinitely without losing its practical autonomy. It is best to discuss this
aspect of wartime Vietnamese political organizational network through case

studies of its actual operation. Among the cases I investigated is one that took place in 1969 in the municipal hospital of Danang.

In the hospital, one nurse had a long-established network. She gathered information from the wounded soldiers and smuggled out medicine, and she was connected to a network of covert action through the daughter of a local pharmacist. A wounded ARVN (Army of the Republic of [South] Vietnam) officer also had a highly covert network with officers and soldiers. He was also connected to a small network of friends and relatives outside his army life. This had been created by the officer's elder brother and was run, after his death, by a childhood friend, who managed a bicycle repair shop. The patient in the bed next to the officer belonged to his own counterinsurgency network. He was an informant hired by the South Vietnamese military intelligence, which was suspicious of the wounded officer's loyalty. The children who sold toothbrushes and towels to the patients had their own extremely mobile and effective network. Their group belonged to the more complex network of street children that incorporated orphans, children of prison inmates, old gangs of playmates, and children of refugee families.

All of these networks, unknown to one another, were fused into the single event of the ARVN officer's escape from the hospital in May 1969. The nurse was instructed to make contact with the wounded officer. She took his neighbor, the informant for ARVN military intelligence, to the examination room at the appointed hour late one afternoon. The officer escaped to a Buddhist pagoda and there met the children he had seen in the hospital. The children showed him the tunnel dug underneath a tomb. In the early hours, one of the workers in the officer's own network turned up and escorted him out to the riverside. There, he was handed over to an unknown National Liberation Front liaison, and both men swam to the opposite side of the river and disappeared in the direction of the mountains.

A myriad of organizational networks existed in the wider milieu of social and civil networks. The officer's elder brother was a known Viet Cong operative. Their mother's house was under surveillance not only by the South Vietnamese police but also by a neighbor, who was a police informant. This neighbor was relatively new to the area, and the officer's mother had much wider and closer relationships with the other neighbors. In one season, the woman's aging husband contracted dysentery and was gravely ill. The officer's elder brother was brave enough to visit his dying father. On the day of his visit, a few women in the neighborhood organized an evening of gambling and invited the mother and the wife of the informant. Two boys took the dogs out of the neighborhood, and their elder sister brought all of the street-playing children to the school playground. There was a lot of noise in the house across the street while the father and son were exchanging farewells. What these women did that evening and on numerous other occasions, however, had nothing to do with the son's political network. None of these women, including the officer's mother, was part of any organized network, and none of them acted on that evening based on a political commitment. The neighborhood simply took sides with a member it trusted and with whom it had a long relationship.

The nurse became a *co so* (infrastructure) worker through a childhood friend, who was a pharmacist's daughter. The pharmacist found her the relatively secure and well-paid job in the hospital. Her two brothers were in combat units of the ARVN. Her parents knew about her clandestine work, as did the wife of her eldest brother. When the nurse was arrested, her sister-in-law put together her savings and her mother-in-law's gold leaf and brought them to a colleague of her husband's army superior. The pharmacist, after her release, supported the nurse's family with medication for the young woman's multiple wounds from interrogation. The toothbrush-selling boys and girls had orphan friends who worked as domestic servants for the families of ARVN officers or had close friendship with foreign officers. They met regularly, traded toys for food, and exchanged gossip. When one of the street children was arrested, her act of playing "mad and stupid" failed. She was relatively new to the group, and the other members concluded later that she was overacting. A servant boy persuaded his patron/friend, an officer in the U.S. Army, to intervene; the kind officer not only saved her but also found her a job. As a grown man, the former houseboy said that he had never been a *co so*. Rather, he was simply lonely and bored, he said, and liked playing with the *co so* boys and girls.

Tiger Temple

The wartime episodes described above were drawn from a crowded residential area in the outskirts of Danang that surrounds an old community temple (Mieu Ong Cop) dedicated to the spirit of the tiger. The community of Tiger Temple is typical of the peripheral urban communities that were invented by war. The area, once a stronghold of the anticolonial Viet Minh resistance, is now booming with tourist and industrial activities. The Tiger Temple is carefully hidden from the bustling town, at the end of a deceptive cul de sac that leads, along a narrow bicycle path, to a large wartime cemetery. The temple faces a narrow strip of austere lower-middle-class houses to the west. These houses border either the old prison to the north or the army base to the south. During the war, from the army camp, one could hear the soldiers singing patriotic songs during their early morning runs. The neighborhood's children learned these songs and used some of them to accompany and coordinate their street play. The adults also benefited from the army camp. They listened to the army's loudspeakers that disseminated information about the nation's political and military affairs. To have the People's Army as an immediate neighbor had the additional benefit of helping the residents to feel secure from criminals.

The prison building on the northern side of the neighborhood is now abandoned and waiting for demolition. This used to be the single most dreaded site for many locals during the war. The South Vietnamese police force used the building for interrogating prisoners and selectively executing them. Before it became a prison, it had served as the army barracks of the Third Infantry Division of the ARVN. The Tiger Temple originally stood in the middle of the site until the ARVN soldiers relocated it to its current position in 1965. The elders of Tiger Temple recalled that the ARVN soldiers, teenage peasants from the Mekong Delta, had been frightened by the idea of touching a sacred communal building. The elders compared these innocent ARVN soldiers to the triumphant officers of the People's Army after the liberation, who, in their memory, were not careful with communal shrines and Buddhist pagodas. When they said this in my presence, their grown-up children looked uncomfortable and told me in whispers that their views on the issue were not the same as those of their parents.

The residents who lived next to the prison building used to keep their wooden shutters permanently closed to block out the prisoners' screams. In stark contrast to the residents on the side of the army camp, some of those on the prison side still observe the custom of having their shutters firmly locked at night. They still feel unsafe despite this measure. There are no prisoners any more, yet some residents fear that their ghosts might crawl, as they had done many times in the neighborhood's oral history, into their rear gardens and kitchens. Local custom has it that there is nothing more frightening in life than an encounter with the ghost of a prisoner. This type of ghost has a mutilated body and an elongated tongue, like the infamous Mau Ma—the long-haired, bare-breasted, female spirit of water who is believed to seduce people into death. Three young women from the neighborhood have experienced this horrible vision, and one of them never entirely recovered from the shock.

Most people in the Tiger Temple neighborhood have a relatively shallow history of urban life. They were incorporated into this marginal urban space through the rapid spread of distorted city life during the time of war.

Before the war, coconut trees and rice paddies surrounded the area, and people made their living primarily on the land. Like other urban peripheries in South Vietnam, this neighborhood was deeply, if invisibly, divided between the secret supporters of the revolutionary forces and those who were incorporated into the South Vietnamese economy and administration. Because of its marginal status, there were no important officials of the South Vietnamese administration or officers of the ARVN living in the neighborhood. A few took employment as low-ranking administrators or laborers in the foreign military installations, and others managed market stalls or small tailor shops. Several households had links, of varying strength, with the revolutionary authorities. Some families supported the revolutionary side as soldiers, some with labor, and some with money, information, or simply in spirit.

In historical terms, therefore, this neighborhood was a mixture of "collaborators" and "patriots." During the war, this mixture often resulted in critical situations. The South Vietnamese police ran an elaborate, if not particularly effective, network of neighborhood surveillance. Arrests of mobile Viet Cong activists and their residential patriotic supporters as the result of a next-door neighbor's informing did occur, although much less often in reality than in rumor, and this strategy had some success in provoking mutual distrust and isolation in urban communities. The "collaborator" families were rarely in a safe haven, either. Periodically, they received hand-delivered letters of appeal or warning from the revolutionary authorities. The first letter would urge the recipient in polite language to make a material contribution to the revolutionary cause. If this failed to be answered, the subsequent letters would deliver vividly threatening messages about the consequences of their failure to cooperate. The recipients of such communiqués were, officially, obliged to report the incidents to the South Vietnamese authorities. Failure to do so was a crime, and such a crime could invite disproportionate punishment. However, people wisely rarely reported such incidents.

The result of these divisive psychological strategies was, in people's recollection, constant fear and isolation. Rumors that a close neighbor or friend had betrayed someone traveled widely throughout the town and reinforced secrecy and mutual distrust. Ironically, this divide-and-rule strategy of the war administrators contributed to the expansion of the covert revolutionary support network among civilians. In addition to the political and moral motivations of the civilian activists, there was a strong realization that the *cach mang* (revolutionary) network was the only stable and trustworthy social organization in the wartime situation. Hopelessly isolated, materially and psychologically, many desperate Vietnamese, particularly women, were drawn to the revolutionary circles to recover a sense of human solidarity. As a former *co so* activist recalled, "Life without a husband was possible. Life without relatives was possible. But life without a neighbor was not. I had to find one."

One of the important activities of the women *co so* activists was to relate to the young conscript ARVN soldiers as substitute mothers, which was part of the general *binh van* activity, or the "proselyt[iz]ing program."[3] A woman living in the environs of the Tiger Temple ran a makeshift noodle bar in the late 1960s. She smuggled seventeen South Vietnamese soldiers back to their hometowns in the My Tho and Can Tho areas of the Mekong Delta in 1971 alone. Desertion of this type was frequent, especially during the early phase of the war.[4] It was a tightly organized activity based on the collaboration of various network organizations. Different niches of the network prepared railway tickets, civilian clothing, false identification cards, and food for the AWOL. Some of these young soldiers knew about the political identities of their adoptive mothers, but the bond was often too strong to surrender to the pressure from the opposite political force against treason. For the *co so* mothers too, their adoptive kinship with the enemy soldiers often went far beyond the strategic parameters of their covert activities. They were keen on obtaining information from their adopted children about the enemy's military movements. But they also knew how to censor part of this information before it reached the revolutionary headquarters in order not to jeopardize the safety of their children. When the soldiers went to battle, the mother activists prayed for the safety of their adopted children at the Tiger Temple or the coastal Whale Temple on the opposite side of the community.

When they did so, their prayer offerings were often on behalf of their children fighting on "this side," the revolutionary side, as well as their other children working on "that side," the American side. It was common among these mothers to have their birth children fighting on both sides. The revolutionary side generally refrained from recruiting all of a family's male children in order to allow the family unit a minimal genealogical continuity, whereas the recruitment strategy of the U.S.–Saigon administration did not have such an affirmative policy for "the family seeds." As a result, many mothers in this area have elder children who were martyred for the revolutionary war and younger sons who were killed in action on the opposite side of the battlefield. The *co so* mothers prayed to their ancestors for the safe return of their birth children and went to the animist temples, and some to the Buddhist pagoda farther away, to pray for the safety of all their children, including the adopted ones. As a result, the old record book kept in the Tiger

Temple, which lists donations and the names for whom the donations were made, shows the names of young people killed on both sides of the war as well as the names of those who people remember were from distant places.

An interesting aspect of wartime desertion is that a relatively smaller number of Saigon soldiers deserted than the number who deserted from the other side. Desertions to the revolutionary side did take place, sometimes in a group, and with or without assistance from mother activists. Desertions by foreign soldiers especially, although many alleged cases remain dubious, generated immense publicity along the front. In most cases, however, the desertions were made in the hope of returning to their hometowns and reuniting with their families.[5] The adoptive *co so* mothers contributed to this process of exodus in psychological and practical terms. The idea of persuading their son-like young men to change sides and continue fighting was not enthusiastically pursued by these mother activists, although this was one of the main objectives of their activity and was a priority in the communiqués they received from the cadre leaders. Although loyal to each urban revolutionary cell, the *co so* mother activists also created a loyalty of their own across the cells and beyond. If she pushed her "children" to the other side of the front too hard, the mother activist risked her own life by weakening the invisible moral shield provided by other village women who otherwise would have ignored and concealed her identity. Their maternal feelings were a powerful weapon against the enemy forces; yet, this weapon, being fundamentally constructive, not destructive, was not entirely under the control of the revolutionary forces either.[6] As the former mother activist introduced earlier put it, she lived through solitary wartime hardship with the singular joy of watching the young Saigon soldiers eating her noodles, imagining with every soup bowl they emptied that someone in the wide world was feeding her own hungry children.

In practical life, therefore, the rigid classification of patriots versus collaborators was unrealistic when applied to ordinary people. Even in the worst situation of 1968–1969, when the region suffered its fiercest battles on every corner, much evidence suggests that the neighborhood played a vital role in survival. A *co so* woman could not complete her nightly obligation of delivering information and money to her contacts if she did not have the support of her unquestioning neighbor, who took care of her children. In return, the same woman might save her neighbor's daughter, who was working as a secretarial clerk in a U.S. Army base. One day, for example, a woman tried to persuade her neighbor's daughter to help her bring goods from the Danang central market. The daughter was unwilling, so she promised her a pair of handsome shoes. That afternoon, a National

Liberation Front platoon launched a surprise attack against the daughter's workplace, which caused many casualties. In this type of artful exchange for survival, usually no question was posed and no information extracted. To do so would have jeopardized both parties. People simply found ways of saving the lives of others by acting on and in the others' lives. The daughter's mother told me that she had known that her neighbor was a *co so*. She had prepared a letter to denounce her. In case her neighbor was arrested, she meant to show this letter to the police. In the letter, which she still kept, she informed the neighbor's absent husband of her suspicion that his wife must have taken a lover since she often went out late at night. She prepared this letter, hoping that it might help to save her neighbor's life in case the police found her. In this complex, artful, mutual support, the patriots and the collaborators were interpenetrative. In the end, both groups had to collaborate with each other to survive. Each administration discouraged its people from collaborating with the opposite side. However, in the streets of a violent bipolar conflict under crossfire, only those who collaborated well across the drawn boundary of political loyalty survived, both physically and morally.

The classification system of "patriots" versus "collaborators" is still a formative element in the contemporary social life of many Vietnamese. Of many instruments of political control, the family record system (*ho so*) has been one of the most explicit and routine sources of shame and agony for former collaborators. A handwritten summary of one's personal biography and family history must be handed to the administration before the bureaucracy can initiate any administrative procedures for civil affairs. Whether the procedures concern purchasing a plot of land from the government, marriage or divorce, registration of death, entry into school, or a job application, a detailed and comprehensive report of the family's background is mandatory. The report includes the individual's profession, religion and educational history, date and place of birth, and current residence. Most notably, the report requires a detailed description of the "work history" of the individual's kinfolk. The boundary of the kinship varies, depending on the purpose of the record. It can be the immediate family of three patrilineal generations or a wider relationship that includes collateral kin. In the past, the official report form contained specific sections on the individual's wartime activity, namely, whether the person worked for "our side" or "their side." The applicant at one time was also obliged to classify his or her parents and grandparents, siblings, and sometimes more distant relatives, such as father's brothers. Nowadays, there are no such explicit entries to fill in. All applicants know, however, that they must introduce clear indications of their family's political identification if they want the report to be accepted by the administration. A history of wartime military service makes the identification straightforward, a record of a revolutionary honor or time in a reeducation camp has the same effect, while the entry of overseas relatives is used to make the family look impure. The trajectory of previous residences and a graduation record from a particular school in a particular area during a particular period can also determine, although much more subtly, the general picture of the individual's place in the political spectrum.

The net result of the use, and the abuse, of the family record system is that an individual's wartime collaboration goes far beyond a biographical episode and becomes an organizing element of collective identity. Grandfather's wartime service to the ARVN shapes the identity of his school-attending descendants in the view of the school administration. These children are much less likely to be acknowledged as "model students" than their peers whose family backgrounds demonstrate an untainted history of revolutionary activity. In order to be a model student, the school children must obtain proof of good behavior and good academic performance; yet, the genealogical factor of healthy origins counts as an equally important source for judgment. Most children are acutely aware of the implications, if not the details, of their family records.

In the Tiger Temple community, there are as many former collaborator families as families with a history of revolutionary struggle. The difference between the two groups is evidenced through the household ancestral altar, which displays not only the ancestors' paraphernalia but also the certificates, if any, of their revolutionary activities offered by the government, such as the heroic death certificates from the time of the American War. When we look more closely at the informal economy of war memory, however, most families turn out to have had a much more complex, ambiguous genealogy.

Same Same

The community's complex experience of the war can be explored through the biography of a man whom I will call Lap. Everyone knows Lap in the environs of the Tiger Temple. He is a long-time resident of the small neighborhood that surrounds the animist temple and the oldest among the community's several amputees. Lap is unemployed and earns pocket money by doing all sorts of odd jobs within the community. He is in charge of the

Tiger Temple's prayer gongs and has earned the status of a member of the informal council that manages the communal temple.

I met Lap many times, including at his favorite hideout from the heat, the old underground military bunker near his home. One evening during the annual opening ceremony days of the temple, when he kept vigil for the shrine, I saw him at a house adjacent to the temple, where he rested from time to time. Two other familiar faces in the neighborhood of Tiger Temple followed the sixty-year-old amputee. One of them was the host's next-door neighbor, the driver of the commuter bus to Danang's central market, whom I had the privilege to know was at one time a first-class sergeant in the ARVN. The other man was from the neighborhood at the back of the temple. Everyone in the area knew that he had been awarded a certificate of honor for his wartime work as a local partisan and a small pension for the injury he suffered.

While Lap was settling into his chair, there was an anticipatory, light-hearted atmosphere. He was seriously studying the host's incomplete ancestor altar, and the host's daughter had already succumbed to stomach cramps because of her excessive laughing. Encouraged, Lap said, "America boom-boom, Viet Cong boom-boom," pointing to his amputated leg with his index finger. Then, the familiar feast of laughter started:

VC (the former partisan fighter): Did the Americans do this to your leg?
Lap: Yes, yes, Americans. They shot me because I was bad.
ARVN (the former first-class sergeant): Who shot your leg? Were they VC?
Lap: Yes, yes, the VC. They fired [at] my leg because I was bad.

Everyone was in fits of laughter. At his turn, the host asked, touching Lap's leg, "Uncle, who did this terrible thing to you? Americans or VC?" Lap said, looking confused, "Yes, yes, you're right. Yes, Americans. Yes, the VC. Yes, yes, America boom-boom, Viet Cong boom-boom." Then, the interrogation started again:

VC: You told me the Americans shot your leg. Now you say it's the VC who did this to you. You lied to me. Tell me, did the VC shoot you?
Lap: Yes, yes, the VC. You're right. It's the VC who shot my leg. VC boom-boom, America boom-boom.
ARVN: You said the VC shot your leg. Now you say it's the Americans who fired at you. You don't make sense. You lie to me. Tell me, did the Americans shoot you?

Lap: Yes, yes, the Americans. You're right, of course. America boom-boom, Viet Cong boom-boom.

The host took a deep breath and pointed at Lap's leg with his index finger, "Uncle, I'm shooting this bullet at your leg right now. Tell me, am I VC or American?" Then, Lap folded back his trouser to show his artificial leg and said, "You're right, of course. America and Vietnam, same same. You are right. America boom-boom, Viet Cong boom-boom. Same same."

Lap was born in 1945 in Chu Lai, the place that later held one of the largest U.S. military installations in Central Vietnam. He grew up as an orphan, having been handed over to a distant relative by the will of his late parents. He attended primary school and worked as a village buffalo boy. At the age of seventeen, Lap was recruited into the revolutionary *mang luoi* by an absent village elder called Le Tan Cuong. His main work was to gather information about the villagers' social lives and political opinions and to report them to the cell operator. He was also asked occasionally to lay mines. At the time, his village area was being transformed into a major fortification for the South Vietnamese armed forces, and this resulted in an intense invigoration of the local revolutionary organizational network. The South Vietnamese counterinsurgency activity also became intensive, introducing more people into their village and neighborhood surveillance web. This web of watchful eyes and sharp ears caught Lap only three months into his work. He was sent to the Danang prison in 1963 and was released in 1970. He survived the prison, unlike many other young and old prisoners, partly thanks to the art of survival that a sympathetic inmate had taught him:

If the interrogators are all Vietnamese, rub your hands fast and pray for mercy, scream hard if they kick you, cry and defecate as much as you like if they put electrical wires on you, and say you know nothing and be yourself who knows nothing. They will think you are just a simple, silly peasant boy, which you are. If you see an American adviser in the room, grab his leg, if you can, and remember to repeat one word in his language—*same same*. Point your finger to the other Vietnamese and yourself and say, "Same same"; point to the American and yourself and say, "Same same." Hopefully, the American will think you are mad, not recognizing the most fundamental differences in the reality he knows.

On his release, Lap immediately returned to Chu Lai. By this time, his village area had become a gigantic military base. His old revolutionary network contact was dead, and he could not enter another network easily with his credentials as a former inmate in the South Vietnamese prison. He could not disprove the invisible tag on his body that made him a possible agent of South Vietnamese intelligence. Starving, dispirited, and suffering from his prison experiences, he took up manual work in the American base like the other villagers. The base was the only place where people, especially landless agricultural laborers, could earn a living at this time. For the first time in his life, Lap was not hungry, and he could offer food to others instead of begging for it. However, he was soon drafted into the South Vietnamese army and sent to the Hoa Cam military base for six months of training. In 1971, Lap came back to the Tiger Temple community, not as a political prisoner but as an ARVN soldier. He was assigned to the security force of the prison. He married the same year and settled in the community. He built a small bamboo house next to the much taller brick prison guard tower. He worked and earned a small amount; his wife worked in the marketplace and brought food to him.

While in prison in 1963–1970, Lap had participated in the Ong Cop (the spirit of tiger worshiped in Tiger Temple) ceremony from his cell. He had saved food and obtained incense from the prison guards. He had held a private ceremony for every gate-opening ceremony of the temple. He had prayed that if he survived the prison with the strength of Ong Cop, he would serve the shrine for the rest of his life. Lap is not the only one in the community who believes that the people of Tiger Temple, having no traditional ties of place or blood, are nevertheless all fatefully connected. Several neighbors whose origins are in the Central Highlands claim different relationships with the tiger spirit. A man from Tra My, in his childhood, was a child of Ong Cop, whose parents "sold" him to the area's tiger spirit, hoping that the spirit would protect the sickly and bookish boy from the war's greed for death. The Tra My Tiger Temple turned to ashes, leaving no opportunity for the boy to be bought back from the tiger spirit. The man, now in his late forties, believes that he has been led to move to his current address in order to be with his fierce, protective foster parent.

The people of the Tiger Temple neighborhood have other, more secular reasons for becoming part of the community. Most of them have multiple histories of displacement and loss of roots. War brought them together in this community. Some worked for the revolutionary network, and others earned a living in the state institutions that fought the network. Some moved to the community as the families of prison inmates before the liberation, and others moved there after the liberation. The former began their postwar lives as the families of patriots and the latter as the families of collaborators. It is uplifting how this community, built on long years of violent and often lethal confrontation, has managed to keep its spirit.

The presence of Tiger Temple has supported the community's resilience. Virtually all of the neighbors, whether they belong to collaborator or patriot families, participate in the maintenance and ceremonial calendar of the temple just as they did during wartime. Their contributions to temple activities, the yearly opening ceremony in the first lunar month in particular, have been a way of making a community out of people who rarely have regional or blood ties. People like the amputee Lap have also helped the community's strength. He is sympathetic to the demonstrative pride of the patriot families and attentive to the hidden stigma of the collaborator families. People like Lap are aware that there are often untold histories of uncertainty underneath the pride or the stigma and that the wartime biographies of ordinary people are rarely clear-cut.

Lap's biography includes radical displacement from one political sphere of the war to another. He fought a revolutionary network war; he was also driven to fight the opposite war on the side of state hierarchy. His performance of "same same" restores this history and dramatizes it with body language. His missing leg is an emblem of the painful history of survival in a violently bipolarized world, which many people have shared but which is nevertheless missing from the public sphere. Lap's performance crystallizes in his amputated leg the dual structure of bipolar politics that he experienced as a humble actor and tells the absurdity of this structural condition within a feast of laughter. In the end, Lap's amputated leg works magically. His phantom leg inscribes the bipolar political structure and leaves the rest of the body surviving without it.

If I understand this man's one-legged body as an antistructure of bipolar history or perhaps as a symbolic weapon against its forceful dualism,[7] the political identity of his body is perhaps extendable to the entire community of Tiger Temple. There is not a single family in the community that has survived the war unharmed and intact. Every family has suffered a wound of amputation of varying depth as a social body. Moreover, the family's multiple wounds of war are seldom attributable to a single side of the war. An individual loss in a family may be specific and structured. The entire loss of a family, on the contrary, is seldom reducible to either this or that side of the bipolar political structure. If we extend the idea of family to a larger kinship circle or to an entity that is inclusive of friendship and neighborhood, the losses and the wounds become more politically unclassifiable. Political identity can fluctuate depending on how we define the width and breadth of the holder of the identity.

The history of sociality such as that discussed in this essay is an important dimension of the lived history of the bipolar politics in Vietnam.

It complements a traditionally dominant approach to the social history of the Vietnamese revolution which tends to privilege the political mobilization and moral solidarity of rural villages for nationalist and revolutionary causes, by showing how the politics of war, in the context of a total war, involved the radical dislocation of the population and how those politics continued in their displaced lives.[8] It also shows the relevance of a network perspective to social and political conflicts in grasping the grassroots experience in the urban zones of the Vietnam-American War.

The idea of network is becoming an overly belligerent concept in certain contemporary analytical trends. This is particularly evident in the speculations about the so-called network war or the paradigm of "netwar" as a countermeasure against the menace of international terrorism. Some specialists in contemporary security studies advocate that the old geopolitical perspective of global conflict from the Cold War era should give way to a new network-centric view of warfare and preparations in tune with the broader context of globalization and the advancement of information technology.[9] Network is a double-edged concept when applied to a condition of war; it can be an instrument of war or it can turn out to be an instrument against the politics of war. In my view, the analysis that privileges exclusively only one domain of instrumentality fails to appropriate the full theoretical capacity of the concept.[10]

The nonpartisan subjectivity of the Tiger Temple community may resemble the mature tolerance of a liberal society. This subjectivity, however, is primarily a manifestation of maturity as a result of a long history of life under siege. The British historian E. P. Thompson, who is known for his antinuclear activism as well as his monumental studies of the English working class, once described the Cold War in the language of an industrial corporation. In line with his approach to history, which emphasized normative orientations at the popular level, Thompson sought to distinguish the interests of "executives" in the Cold War political structure from the labor and aspirations of ordinary citizens, whom these executives systematically exploited.[11] We may say in a similar light that Cold War history consists of two separate discourses. One is prominent in the literature and describes the global conflict in terms of balance of power, interstate alliances, containment and the domino theory, or nuclear deterrence and game theory.[12] The other is scarcely recorded, and it is mainly about split communities and neighborhoods, bifurcated families and kinship, and divided consciousness and identities. The laborers' experience of bipolar history was primarily about their suffering through the unbearable pain of dismemberment, and this is at odds with the very idea of a "cold war" or "imaginary war" with which we are accustomed to grasping at the political history of the second half of the twentieth century.[13]

In the historical field, the doctrinal, ideological, hierarchical state institutions and organizational networks were inflated; yet, the antidoctrinal, non-ideological, collateral social networks also proliferated. People's history of the violent bipolar conflict was, in significant measure, about networking—pooling resources and sharing risks, and thereby connecting individuals and social units within and against the escalating hostilities of geopolitics. In this historical milieu, the network-centric war coexisted and fought with the geopolitical war. In the battlefields between these two forms of war, furthermore, people built extensive social networks to counter both the mechanized, geopolitical Vietnam War and the organizational, networked, "people's" American War. Here, the ultimate winner of a particular war is neither the manufacturer of the Vietnam War nor necessarily the maker of the American War. Many Vietnamese fought the Vietnam War and many more fought the American War, and all of them have been struggling to undo the violent legacy of these two wars. One of the popular ways to demobilize the legacy has been to build concrete social relationships upon the hidden history of survival—the civil network of collaboration across the fronts. Winning the war on the streets of the violent Cold War is not the same as winning it in the strategic administration of the war. The bipolar political history, for the residents of Tiger Temple, consists of the countless everyday actions required for survival. Their very ordinary actions of exchanging information and sharing resources with neighbors turned out to be a powerful weapon against the geopolitics of the Cold War. The most basic and mundane requirements of a neighborhood founded the technical and moral basis of what turned out to be extraordinary social networks of survival.

To conclude, something more has to be said about the history of Lap's missing leg. In 1974, Lap left his position as a prison guard. He became a driver of an army vehicle and was happy with his new job despite the risk of being behind the wheel during that turbulent time. At the end of that year, he had the opportunity to visit his hometown of Chu Lai with an officer on tour. He knew the way by heart and knew the names and stories of the important rocks and trees. After all, this was where he had worked for Le Tan Cuong before he joined the army. He parked the jeep and walked ahead of the others, proud of being in his hometown. It was just past noon when Lap stepped on an antipersonnel mine that was later found to be the work of a local Viet Cong network. He experienced the liberation of Danang on 29 March 1975 in the city's military hospital. Discharged from the hospital shortly thereafter, he eventually returned with his family to the Tiger Temple neighborhood, the only community to which, he told me, he ever knew he could belong.

NOTES

1. See Mary Kaldor, *New and Old Wars: Organized Violence in a Global Era* (Stanford, Calif.: Stanford University Press, 2001), 29–30.
2. Douglas E. Pike, *Viet Cong: The Organization and Techniques of the National Liberation Front of South Vietnam* (Cambridge, Mass.: MIT Press, 1966), 229–30.
3. Ibid., 253–68.
4. Robert K. Brigham, *ARVN: Life and Death in the South Vietnamese Army* (Lawrence: University Press of Kansas), 48–50, 113–14.
5. Ibid., 109–22.
6. See Sara Ruddick, *Maternal Thinking: Towards a Politics of Peace* (London: Women's Press, 1990).
7. On the idea of antistructure as a positive, generative notion, see Victor Turner, *Dramas, Fields, and Metaphors: Symbolic Action in Human Society* (Ithaca, N.Y.: Cornell University Press, 1974), 272–73. About the idea of a symbolic weapon, see Roy Wagner, *Symbols That Stand for Themselves* (Chicago: University of Chicago Press, 1986), 50–51.
8. See Alexander B. Woodside, *Community and Revolution in Modern Vietnam* (Boston: Houghton Mifflin, 1976); Hy Van Luong, *Revolution in the Village: Tradition and Transformation in North Vietnam, 1925–1988* (Honolulu: University of Hawaii Press, 1992); James W. Trullinger, *Village at War: An Account of Conflict in Vietnam* (Stanford, Calif.: Stanford University Press, 1994); George Condominas, "La guerilla viet: Trait culturel majeur et pérenne de l'espace social vietnamien," *L'Homme* 164 (2000): 17–36; Heonik Kwon, *After the Massacre: Commemoration and Consolation in Ha My and My Lai* (Berkeley: University of California Press, 2006), 33–50.
9. John Arquilla and David Ronfeldt, *Networks and Netwars: The Future of Terror, Crime, and Militancy* (Santa Monica, Calif.: Rand, 2001). Arquilla and Ronfeldt present the "network war" as a novel paradigm, distinct from the old Cold War era territorial warfare and competition for spheres of influence. Most Vietnamese of the war generation will find the idea of network war hardly an innovative concept or view it as merely self-evident. If the concept appears new to some, it is partly because they understand the "old" war primarily in a state-centric view as a contest of power along clear borders, not considering the fact that the old war was very much a network-type phenomenon at the grassroots level.
10. The term *network* has been an important concept in anthropological research, particularly in studies of tribal politics and tribal warfare. In so-called kinship-based societies, the solidarity of the culturally prominent group is often based on the

principle of descent and is crosscut with other, less-pronounced relationships, such as ties through marriage. It is argued that this network of close affinal and other ties that exist in and across the descent-based groups, although ideologically less prominent compared to the ties of descent, may develop into an important political force in general social crises, such as tribal war, and can contribute to countering the escalation of hostilities between the contending descent groups. See Max Gluckman, *Custom and Conflict in Africa* (Oxford: Blackwell, 1973), and Simon Harrison, *The Mask of War: Violence, Ritual, and the Self in Melanesia* (Manchester, England: Manchester University Press, 1993).

11. E. P. Thompson, "Ends and Histories," in M. Kaldor, ed., *Europe from Below: An East-West Dialogue* (New York: Verso, 1991), 7–25.

12. See Townsend Hoopes's excellent description of how all of these elements actually worked together in the formulation of policies. *The Limits of Intervention* (New York: McKay, 1969), 7–32.

13. The expression "imaginary war" is from Mary Kaldor, *The Imaginary War: Interpretation of East-West Conflict in Europe* (Oxford: Blackwell, 1990).

PART III

War's End and Endless Wars

COLD WAR CONTRADICTIONS

Toward an International History of the Second
Indochina War, 1969–1973

LIEN-HANG T. NGUYEN

Although the latter half of the Second Indochina War has begun to attract more attention from scholars, compared with the prodigious literature on the first half of the war, the studies concentrating on the period of negotiations from 1969 to 1973 appear relatively meager. The main reason for the imbalance is the dearth of primary sources available on the latter half of the war as opposed to the plethora of documentation on the early period. For historians of American decision making, there are no Pentagon Papers; the *Foreign Relations of the United States* volumes on this period have only begun to appear; and until recently, Richard M. Nixon's presidential materials have been tied up in litigation. For scholars interested in the foreign policy of the Democratic Republic of Vietnam (DRV) or North Vietnam, particularly regarding its relations with the Soviet Union and China, the latter half of the war will remain shrouded in mystery so long as Hanoi's present-day relations with the two countries remain ambiguous. Finally, for the small academic community focused on the Republic of Vietnam (RVN) or South Vietnam, not only is there less interest, but the entire period of direct American military involvement has also been conveniently ignored.[1] However, as archives worldwide open their doors and declassifications occur in (somewhat) regular fashion, the materials are now becoming available for historians interested in writing international histories of the latter half of the war. Since the 1990s, there has been an encouraging trend of a global archival *glasnost*: the declassification of top-level documents in U.S. archives; the releases of materials from China, Eastern Europe, and Russia; and the opening of Vietnamese archives in Hanoi and Ho Chi Minh City.

Moreover, a history of the latter half of the war must be transnational in scope, for the war itself transcended the borders of Vietnam, particularly after the Tet Offensive. Prior to Tet 1968, third-party nations and international pressure as a whole exerted little influence on the manner in which the leading combatants, namely, Washington and Hanoi, waged war in Vietnam. The United States rejected international calls for neutralization of the Vietnamese situation prior to 1965 and later rejected European and UN attempts to initiate contact between the United States and the DRV after war broke out.[2] The North Vietnamese managed to prevent foreign interference by playing the Chinese and Soviets off against one another without relinquishing control of the war effort to either communist ally.[3] Instead, the United States and the DRV each wanted to gain victory through military and political means rather than to settle for a negotiated peace through diplomatic compromise. Hence, the two sides more or less fought each other with minimum external distraction and obstruction by thwarting international pressures to engage in any discussions.[4]

In the aftermath of the Tet Offensive, however, the nature of the war changed dramatically. The military stalemate in South Vietnam, the political fallout in the United States, and the foreign policy developments in North Vietnam ensured that the post-Tet war would be markedly different as it unfolded on the international arena. Militarily, the stalemate in South Vietnam opened the way for the regionalization of the conflict as the air and ground wars engulfed neighboring Laos and Cambodia. Politically, transnational social movements acted as a constraint as well as a goad to great-power diplomacy and collusion.[5] But the most dramatic change occurred in the diplomatic sphere of the war. With the initiation of peace talks at Paris in May 1968, a new theater of war emerged that forced the parties involved in the conflict to redefine victory from military conquest to a negotiated settlement at Paris that would give them political or military advantages neither had won on the battlefield. Although the U.S./RVN and DRV/Provisional Revolutionary Government (PRG) entered into negotiations ostensibly to end the war and bring peace to the region, the initiation of negotiations instead signaled the advancement of the diplomatic struggle. In turn, the Paris forum enabled third-party nations and international opinion as a whole to assume more active roles in the conflict. Indeed, "talking while fighting" was the strategy employed by all of the parties involved in the war.

In response to the post-Tet developments, the capital cities at war, namely, Hanoi, Saigon, and Washington, had to construct integrated "international" strategies that took into account the interplay among the military, political, and diplomatic spheres of the fighting and the intersections of the local, regional, and international levels of the war.[6] The centerpiece of the Nixon administration's diplomatic strategy included exploiting the contradictions in the Cold War to aid America's cause in the Vietnam War. Through détente with the Soviet Union and rapprochement with the People's Republic of China (PRC), the United States hoped to bring Russian and Chinese pressure to bear upon the North Vietnamese to settle on American terms at the negotiating table. Meanwhile, the Hanoi polit- buro accelerated its already-successful world relations campaign focused on balancing the tricky Sino-Soviet split and neutralizing superpower obstruction by promoting small-power diplomacy aimed at winning over support from the nations of the Third World and the Non-Alignment Movement.[7] With the help of the PRG, the DRV was able to mobilize revolutionary forces north and south of the 17th Parallel to minimize great-power manipulation. Finally, with the divergence of aims between the United States and the RVN after Tet, the Saigon government under Nguyen Van Thieu had to exert more control over its destiny and take on a more proactive role in the war against the Vietnamese communists. The Thieu administration manipulated and cajoled its American ally in order to extract aid, neutralize pressure, and retard withdrawal. Moreover, the Saigon government also looked to a future without a major American military presence in South Vietnam by bolstering the RVN's position in the region.

A history of the latter half of the Second Indochina War that takes into account the internationalization of the post-Tet war will shed fur- ther light on key questions that have eluded historians in the field. What effect did the emergence of U.S. détente with the Soviet Union and rap- prochement with the PRC have on the diplomacy of the Vietnam War? How did the relationships between the great powers and their Viet- namese clients—the United States and the RVN, on the one hand, the Soviet Union, China, and the DRV, on the other—evolve as a result of the negotiation process? Did the Sino-American rapprochement, and the improvement in Soviet-American relations that paralleled it, have the effect of accelerating or retarding the peace talks? And most important, why did peace fail?

This chapter is divided into two sections, the first of which briefly sur- veys the literature on the latter half of the Second Indochina War, with a focus on interpretations that address the diplomatic sphere of the war from 1969 to 1973. The second and more substantive section is an effort to inte- grate the literature and move toward an international history of the post-Tet war by focusing on North and South Vietnamese responses to American diplomacy from 1969 to 1973.

Post-Tet War Historiography

On 27 January 1973, the parties involved in the Vietnamese conflict, including the United States, the RVN, the DRV, and the PRG, signed the Paris Agreement on Ending the War and Restoring Peace. Although the ceremonial event on the Avenue Kléber trumpeted peace, the war in Vietnam did not end with the signatures in Paris but only concluded two years later with the fall of Saigon. The ambitiously titled treaty and ceasefire failed to ensure the Vietnamese even a momentary respite from fighting.[8] After 202 plenary sessions and 24 private meetings that took place over four years and nine months, the Paris agreement did not mark the end of the war but only heralded a new stage of fighting in Indochina. What were the causes of this broken peace?

Although international or transnational histories, defined as studies that examine more than one country's experience with an event, are beginning to appear with more frequency, on the whole, the scholarship on the latter half of this war remains divided by region. The studies attempting to answer the question can be categorized according to perspective: the latter half of the war in American history and in Vietnamese history.

America's Vietnam War

Because Tet coincided with the defeat of the Democratic Party in U.S. elections, any study of the latter half of the Vietnam War in U.S. history inevitably focuses on Richard M. Nixon's handling of America's post-Tet conflict. Although the Nixon administration inherited a losing war in 1969, American intervention did not end until 1973. Campaigning on a platform of "peace with honor," Nixon and his national security advisor, Henry A. Kissinger, constructed an international strategy, which included exploiting the Sino-Soviet split, to preserve the government of the RVN. However, due to the secretive and controversial nature of the Nixon administration's policy toward Vietnam, historians remain deeply divided over Nixon and Kissinger's war aims and strategy from 1969 to 1973.

In particular, the debate revolves around the failed nature of the 1973 Paris peace agreement, which ended America's involvement in the war but gave only temporary relief to the Vietnamese. Three schools of interpretation have emerged, which can be summarized as the "stab in the back," "decent interval," and "permanent war" theses. The stab-in-the-back thesis was first articulated by the historical actors themselves, who blamed North Vietnamese intransigence for the prolongation of the talks and, more important, congressional obstruction for rendering the United States unable to enforce the peace. Nixon and Kissinger claimed that the 1973 agreement was not perfect but that it did provide for a political solution had North Vietnam not violated it and had Congress not engaged the president in a constitutional battle over executive privilege and abuses of power in 1973. This view has more or less been rejected by most scholars in the field though, as current debates over the Iraq War indicate, it is alive and well.

The second interpretation, best represented in Jeffrey Kimball's *Nixon's Vietnam War*, posits that Nixon and Kissinger aimed only for a "decent interval" between American withdrawal and the fall of South Vietnam. Kimball argues that Nixon and Kissinger needlessly prolonged the war by implementing a strategy that they thought could win the war initially but instead, the strategy ended up losing the peace.[9] He argues that the "Nix-inger" strategy, a combination of superpower diplomacy, aimed at cajoling and coercing Beijing and Moscow to put pressure on Hanoi, and "mad-man" bombing, targeted at intimidating and punishing Hanoi militarily, did not garner any substantive concessions for the United States at the nego-tiation table nor did it destroy the enemy's military capabilities. Far from negotiating a peace that would be sustainable, Washington knew by at least December 1970 that its ally would inevitably lose to the communists on the battlefield.[10] In other words, the agreement constituted a "fig leaf" which the United States used to exit Vietnam.[11]

The most recent interpretation, that of "permanent war," suggests that Nixon and Kissinger knew full well that they had negotiated a ceasefire that would immediately be violated. By negotiating a faulty peace, Nixon had hoped to return with B-52s to punish Hanoi for its transgression, but Watergate squashed Nixon's chances to indefinitely prolong America's air war in Indochina.[12] Larry Berman's persuasive argument, supported by newly declassified documents from the Nixon Project as well as from first-hand interviews with former South Vietnamese officials, presents a more nefarious picture of Nixon's intentions regarding Vietnam and the price that he was willing to pay to prevent North Vietnamese victory. Aiming for an indefinite stalemate, Nixon was willing to use American airpower to prop up the Saigon government.

Vietnamese War: *Cuoc Khang Chien Chong Can Thiep My/Chien Tranh Viet Nam*

The monoglottalism of most U.S.–based scholars has resulted in the neglect of North and South Vietnam's war efforts while scholars in area studies have opted not to devote much attention to the Second Indochina War.[13] Thus, the post-Tet war in Vietnamese histories that analyze the diplomatic sphere of the war in any depth is dominated by official histories, memoirs, and studies written by former participants in the war. Regarding the DRV/PRG war effort, state control over historical scholarship has resulted in studies that concentrate on the unilaterally successful and farsighted nature of communist diplomacy during the American War. The Vietnam Workers' Party (VWP) led the revolutionary forces and the people to victory over a neoimperialist power and its puppet regime. On the other side, the diasporic studies of the vanquished Republic of Vietnam emphasize American betrayal in the peace process. South Vietnamese leaders rarely take credit—or responsibility—for the war, the peace, and ultimately, the country. Agency, then, is a key issue in Vietnamese diplomatic histories, although the treatment of the issue differs greatly depending on which side of the 17th Parallel the author locates her- or himself.

Vietnamese communist foreign policy during the conflict remains an understudied aspect of the war, since the Ministry of Foreign Affairs (MOFA) archives are closed to virtually all foreign scholars and to the vast majority of native historians.[14] Luu Van Loi and Nguyen Vu Anh's *Le Duc Tho–Kissinger Negotiations in Paris* stands as an exception: the Hanoi publication includes transcripts of the secret talks between the United States and North Vietnam from the Vietnamese MOFA archives since the authors were participants in the negotiations and are now official historians.[15] Although the communist strategy of " 'simultaneous talk and fight' led eventually to the signing of the 1973 Paris agreement on the cessation of war and restoration of peace in Vietnam," Luu and Nguyen claim that "how Vietnam did it in fact was unknown."[16] By advancing the diplomatic struggle to the same level as the military and political struggles following the failure of the Tet Offensive to incite a general uprising, the authors assert that the North Vietnamese undertook a flexible position during the secret peace talks because they viewed the negotiated settlement as only a step toward the ultimate goal: reunification.[17] Regarding southern communist diplomacy, the former chief delegate for the PRG at the Paris negotiations and later vice president of Vietnam, Nguyen Thi Binh, contributed an essay along with other participants from the PRG who were present in Paris. Entitled *The NLF-PRG at the Paris Conference on Vietnam (Recollections)*, the volume commemorated the fortieth anniversary of the founding of the National Liberation Front (NLF) in December 2000.[18] All of the essays, especially Madame Binh's, address the success of Ho Chi Minh, the party, and southern revolutionaries in mobilizing the powerful force of world opinion for their cause at Paris. In pushing forward the diplomatic struggle, the essays present a seamless alliance between northern and southern revolutionaries, who were working together for the common cause of defeating the United States/RVN forces and liberating the country.[19]

Although materials on the Republic of Vietnam are easier to access for Western scholars, there have not been many studies devoted solely to the RVN under the Nguyen Van Thieu administration.[20] As a result, Saigon's diplomatic struggle is left to the purview of former officials who have written memoirs based on their lives and careers. The dominant theme that runs through these memoirs revolves around U.S. betrayal of South Vietnam.[21] Saigon leaders felt completely shut out of the negotiation process since first, they were not privy to the secret talks between Kissinger and Le Duc Tho, and second, Kissinger purposely failed to submit Saigon's objections during his private meetings.[22] The resultant Paris agreement that ended American involvement in the war and provided for a ceasefire for the Indochinese was largely crafted without South Vietnamese input. After the 1973 peace agreement, first Nixon and later Gerald Ford failed to deliver on private commitments made to South Vietnamese leaders, which included continuing high levels of military and economic aid and possible reintervention in the Vietnamese conflict. Nguyen Tien Hung and Jerrold Schecter's *The Palace File* includes personal letters from Nixon and Ford to Thieu that contained these secret promises and assurances of American commitments, which were unknown to Congress and were ultimately never carried out.[23] Another common thread that runs through the vast majority of memoirs from former South Vietnamese officials is the bitter rivalries and contentious nature of Saigon politics during the war.[24] At the time, the internal divisions within the ruling elite of South Vietnam crippled the war effort and, after the conflict, has resulted in shifting blame and finger pointing.[25]

International Histories

Finally, there are a few studies that focus solely on the peace process during the Second Indochina War and do so by incorporating the perspectives of at least two major parties, the United States and the DRV.[26] Gareth Porter's *A Peace Denied: The United States, Vietnam and the Paris Agreement* appeared a few months after the fall of Saigon.[27] In his study, Porter argues that the Vietnamese communist strategy of talking while fighting (*dam va danh*) was more successful than the U.S. strategy during negotiations. Porter challenges the belief held at the time that Linebacker II, the bombing campaign leading up to the final round of negotiations, was successful, arguing that international and domestic outcry over the Christmas bombings forced Nixon to end the campaign and did not win him any concessions in Paris. Allen Goodman, in his work *The Lost Peace: America's Search for a Negotiated Settlement of the Vietnam War*, argues that Hanoi viewed America's offer to negotiate as a sign of weakness. According to Goodman, the United States and the DRV approached the negotiation process differently: the United States saw the negotiations as a process of compromise leading to a settlement, whereas the DRV saw negotiations as a process of war, a means to an end that had never fluctuated since the outset of hostilities. However, Goodman also argues that Hanoi's agreement to enter into peace talks in 1968 was detrimental to its overall war effort since it allowed the United States to drag the conflict out for another four years.[28] Finally, Pierre Asselin's study *A Bitter Peace* is really the first generation of new international histories that integrates American and North Vietnamese strategies in the negotiation process.[29] Using declassified documents in Washington and Hanoi, Asselin argues for the primacy of the diplomatic sphere of the war. In this view, the 1973 agreement was decided at the negotiating table rather than on the battlefield. In the end, Asselin argues that it was due to a "combination of domestic constraints and military difficulties that caused the White House and the VWP politburo to accept a negotiated settlement in January 1973 and to do so against the misgivings of the GVN [Government of Vietnam] and the PRG."[30]

There is now a critical mass of studies on the Second Indochina War from 1969 to 1973 that would make writing an international history of the period feasible. The studies on the war in American and Vietnamese histories provide a sturdy foundation for scholars with the necessary languages. Presently, there is little dialogue between Americanists and Vietnam studies scholars regarding the war. However, with the opening of archives and the availability of documents pertaining to the war from all sides, it is imperative that scholars tear down the historiographical barriers in order to produce grand syntheses that take into account the perspectives of all sides in the conflict.

Toward an International History

Although much work has been done on Sino-Soviet-American triangular relations in the Cold War, until recently little was known about Vietnamese responses to great-power politics during the Vietnam War. As small powers in the Cold War, Hanoi and Saigon were at the mercy of their larger allies and thus had to employ similar tactics and weapons to maintain autonomy and to extract maximum aid for their respective war efforts under the client-patron relationship. During the latter half of the Second Indochina War, North and South Vietnam faced the nadir of their relationships with their larger allies as a result of Nixon's triangular diplomacy. Neither Hanoi nor Saigon welcomed Washington's internationalization of the diplomatic sphere of the war through détente with the Soviet Union and rapprochement with China and the effect that both developments were perceived to have on their respective war efforts. Based on archival materials from Vietnam, newly declassified materials from the Nixon Project, and secondary literature in America and Vietnam, this section explores the DRV's and the RVN's responses to Sino-Soviet-U.S. relations from 1969 to 1973.

Nixon's War: Sowing the Seeds for Internationalization

Prior to 1969, Nixon and Kissinger separately arrived at the conclusion that great-power diplomacy afforded the United States bargaining leverage in Vietnam. Furthermore, they believed that once they were in office nothing would prevent them from implementing such an international strategy. Vowing to end America's war through peace with honor by preserving the Saigon government and a noncommunist South Vietnam, the two men employed realist tactics toward ostensibly idealist ends. Although much debate exists surrounding the actual intentions of the president and his national security advisor, the two men were undeniably effective in creating more room to maneuver, given what they inherited from the Johnson administration.[31] In particular, the cornerstone of their strategy included bringing Soviet and Chinese pressure to bear upon Hanoi at the negotiating table in Paris.

After Nixon's inauguration, one of Kissinger's first tasks included an order to key national security agencies to respond to a series of questions regarding the negotiating environment, the military and political effectiveness of the South Vietnamese military and government, enemy capabilities, and U.S. military operations. In addition, the study directive also included questions regarding the role of Moscow and Beijing in Hanoi's war effort. The final result, the National Security Studies Memorandum (NSSM) 1, compiled in March 1969, revealed general agreement among the different agencies.[32] Regarding Hanoi's allies, NSSM 1 found that neither Beijing nor Moscow had attempted to exert heavy pressure on Hanoi and were unlikely to do so for various reasons. For instance, the Central Intelligence Agency

(CIA) noted that, "in competing for influence, Peking and Moscow tend to cancel out each other."[33] Despite the conclusions reached in NSSM 1, Nixon and Kissinger proceeded to devise a strategy that ultimately aimed at fostering a competition of sorts between the communist countries for America's favor. Essentially, Moscow and Beijing were to demonstrate their desire for bettering relations with Washington by selling out Hanoi.[34]

In early 1969, Nixon and Kissinger resolved to concentrate on one leg of the triangle. Washington hoped to link U.S.–Soviet talks on strategic armaments limitations with progress toward an acceptable settlement of the Vietnamese conflict.[35] The events that allowed Nixon and Kissinger to use diplomatic linkage took place not in Southeast Asia but at the Sino-Soviet border on 2 March 1969. Chinese and Soviet troops clashed on the island of Zhenbao (Damansky), a territory in the Ussuri River claimed by both sides. Although China and the Soviet Union had been at odds for nearly ten years, the skirmishes on the border constituted the first military clash between the two nations.[36] By no means would they be the last. Over the remainder of the year, in fact, no fewer than 400 clashes occurred between border troops on both sides of the Sino-Soviet divide.

According to Kissinger's memoirs, the Soviet Union approached the United States following the exchange of hostilities. Kissinger wrote, "[A]n emotional Ambassador Dobrynin raised the Ussuri incident with me.... When I tried to change the subject by suggesting it was a Sino-Soviet problem, Dobrynin insisted passionately that China was everybody's problem."[37] In June, Kissinger met with the Soviet ambassador again in order to convey America's position on a variety of issues, including U.S.–Soviet relations, U.S.–Chinese relations, and the Vietnam War.[38] During the meeting, Kissinger acknowledged the positive role that the Soviets had thus far played in the negotiations at Paris but expressed concern that the Soviets had not utilized their maximum leverage over the North Vietnamese, especially since Moscow was, at that point, the main supplier of military and economic aid to Hanoi. Although Kissinger did not take full advantage of the outbreak of hostilities between the communist countries by reiterating Washington's noninterference, he continued to dangle a threat by insisting that the United States would still seek relations with China. Referring to the continuing deterioration in Sino-Soviet relations and to the improvement in Soviet-Vietnamese relations, Kissinger suggested that it would be in Soviet interests to help the United States in Vietnam because ending the war ran contrary to Chinese interests. According to Anatoly Dobrynin, Kissinger added in an "ironical" manner that the Soviet Union had taken over America's position as China's "main object of attacks."[39] By invoking commonalities between the United States and the Soviet Union as super-power realists and portraying Mao's China as a nonrational lesser actor, Kissinger asserted that Nixon would prefer to deal with Moscow.[40]

Nixon and Kissinger's China card, however, was more slow to develop. According to Jeffrey Kimball, Nixon originally aimed to use the threat of aligning with the Chinese against the Soviets in order to force Moscow to cooperate on international issues.[41] Although Nixon had broached the idea of normalizing relations with China prior to his presidency, once in office, Nixon moved slowly toward rapprochement given the possible negative domestic and strategic repercussions of dealing with the radical Asian power. According to Kissinger's memoirs, the Nixon administration used antagonistic rhetoric toward China up to March 1969.[42] With the Sino-Soviet clashes on the Ussuri River, however, the opportunity arose for a shift in U.S. policy toward the PRC. By July, the United States began lifting travel and trade restrictions, ending patrols of the Seventh Fleet in the Taiwan Straits, and sending, via third parties, diplomatic messages stating that the United States would not support Moscow's proposal for a collective security system in Asia. Concurrently, Beijing's leaders began to see the Soviet Union, rather than the United States, as China's major security threat. In a 17 September report, the four marshals, Chen Yi, Ye Jianying, Xu Xiangqian, and Nie Rongzhen, proposed that the PRC resume Sino-American ambassadorial talks in an effort to capitalize on the U.S.–China contention against Moscow.[43]

A Funeral and a Reunion

In 1969, then, the international picture was bleak for the Vietnamese communists. On 22 March, as the North Vietnamese and the Americans first met privately to try to find a diplomatic settlement to the war, Xuan Thuy, the DRV's chief delegate at Paris, stated that the United States would gain nothing from the divisions between the Soviet Union and China and that, despite the clashes, Moscow and Beijing would continue to aid Hanoi.[44] Internally, Hanoi was not as confident. According to Hanoi's foremost diplomatic historian, Luu Van Loi, the North Vietnamese realized early on that the border skirmishes would lead both Moscow and Beijing, particularly the latter due to the failure of the Cultural Revolution, to entertain thoughts of reconciling with the United States to counterbalance the other side.[45]

In early September 1969, an event brought both despair and hope to the Vietnamese communists: the death of Ho Chi Minh. On 2 September,

Ho Chi Minh passed away in the early morning of National Day, the twenty-fourth anniversary of the founding of the DRV and the August Revolution of 1945.[46] Although by the time of his death, Ho Chi Minh was more or less a figurehead as president of North Vietnam, Bac Ho (Uncle Ho) still commanded international respect as a revolutionary who had devoted his life to liberating his country from the Japanese, French, and later the Americans. In addition, he had played a crucial diplomatic role that helped North Vietnam to manage a policy of equilibrium between China and the Soviet Union. Following Ho's death and the subsequent publication of his testament, Hanoi leaders pressured Moscow and Beijing to suppress their own interests to honor the wishes of their legendary comrade:

> Being a man who had devoted his whole life to the revolution, the more proud I am of the growth of [the] international communist and workers' movement, the more pained I am by the current discord among the fraternal Parties. I hope that our Party will do its best to contribute effectively to the restoration of unity among the fraternal Parties on the basis of Marxism-Leninism and proletarian internationalism, in a way which conforms to both reason and sentiment. I am firmly confident that the fraternal Parties and countries will have to unite again.[47]

Ho Chi Minh's posthumous appeal ensured that Moscow and Beijing would need to avoid any allegation of collaboration with the United States. The Soviet Union appeared to do a *volte-face* while China stopped even its timid steps toward Washington.[48]

Not only did Ho's death bring an abrupt halt to the improvement of relations between Hanoi's major allies and the United States, the Vietnamese leader's death also brought about an attempt at reconciliation between the Chinese and Soviets. At his funeral in Hanoi, the North Vietnamese used the occasion to pressure their allies to reconcile their differences. Consequently, the Soviets sent a message to the Chinese leaders requesting an end to the hostilities on the Sino-Soviet border. When he did not receive a response, Alexei Kosygin returned to Moscow via Calcutta. While en route, the Soviet leader received a message from the Chinese proposing a meeting and on 11 September, Zhou Enlai and Kosygin met in the Beijing airport for the first time since February 1965. The meeting did not result in "the restoration of unity" that Ho Chi Minh had wanted, but it nonetheless revealed the ongoing political power of the Lao Dong (Vietnam Workers' Party) in the communist world.[49]

The Ugly Mistress

Meanwhile in Saigon, where Sino-Soviet relations mattered little, RVN president Nguyen Van Thieu was dealing with his own alliance issues. After very directly helping Nixon to get elected in 1968, Thieu had bought some time for Saigon by ensuring a Republican administration in Washington, but it soon became apparent that de-Americanization was a (bipartisan) fait accompli.[50] In the summer of 1969, when the South Vietnamese president stopped in Taipei following his Midway meeting with Nixon, Thieu confided in his good friend Chiang Kai-shek: "You know when Nixon decides to withdraw, there is nothing I can do about it. Just as when Eisenhower, Kennedy, and Johnson decided to go in, there was very little my predecessors had to say about it."[51] In commiseration, as a fellow junior ally of the United States, Chiang recalled his own inability to resist American pressure to compromise with Mao Zedong. Two years later, Chiang's words reverberated in Saigon as Thieu believed that Sino-American rapprochement would soon force South Vietnam to compromise its own chances for survival.

Although Nixon's international strategy to bring the contradictions of the Cold War to bear upon Vietnam resulted in tentative steps in 1969, the complicated courtship between Washington and Moscow, and to a lesser extent Beijing, suffered even more setbacks with the regionalization of the Vietnam War.[52] On 18 March 1970, while Norodom Sihanouk was in Moscow, there was a coup d'état in Cambodia. Under the more pro-American Lon Nol regime, the U.S.–ARVN forces were able to launch an invasion in May. As a result, the PRC could not appear interested in improving relations with the United States at the risk of offending the Indochinese revolutionary leaders.[53] However, developments in Cambodia only succeeded in slowing down rapprochement, not reversing it. In October, Beijing began to send signals to the Americans that it was willing to explore diplomatic possibilities once again.[54] As a result, when ARVN forces launched Operation Lam Son 719 in early 1971, Nixon took measures to protect the tentative steps Beijing and Washington had made by announcing in a news conference that the offensive in Laos was not directed against communist China.[55] The PRC responded accordingly with criticism that was muted compared to Beijing's passionate indignation over Cambodia a year before. By spring, Mao's invitation to the U.S. table tennis team permanently cleared the path for Sino-American rapprochement.

As the gulf between Beijing and Washington narrowed, the rift between Washington and Saigon deepened. Following Nixon's 15 July announcement of Kissinger's secret trip to China, Thieu began to doubt his allies.[56] According to Nguyen Tien Hung, Thieu was highly suspicious of Nixon and Kissinger's diplomatic strategy to end the Vietnam War: "had Kissinger made a secret deal with Zhou Enlai? Did he stop in Hanoi before Beijing? What role would South Vietnam play in America's new strategy after the normalization of relations with Beijing?"[57] Thieu even told his advisors, "America has been looking for a better mistress and now Nixon has discovered China. He does not want to have the old mistress hanging around. Vietnam has become ugly and old."[58] In other words, since U.S. policy toward Vietnam had been predicated at least in part on stopping Chinese expansionism, what would happen to South Vietnam now that China no longer was believed to be a threat?

In the six months leading up to Nixon's visit, Saigon leaders tried to prevent the United States from offering the RVN as a sacrificial lamb to Sino-American rapprochement. Thieu dispatched his special advisor for foreign affairs, Nguyen Phu Duc, to meet with various American officials in order to ascertain a clearer picture of U.S. intentions. According to Duc, the officials he met insisted that Beijing did not desire increased North Vietnamese influence in Indochina, yet his report to Thieu still advised caution.[59] Duc's warning reaffirmed Thieu's belief that the communist side of Indochina, which in his estimation included not only the North Vietnamese but also the Chinese and Soviet parties, regarded any settlement short of total conquest as only a "strategic pause."[60] Eliciting the opinions of South Vietnamese elected officials, Thieu's foreign minister, Tran Van Lam, met with the Senate Foreign Relations Committee on 26 August 1971 to discuss Nixon's upcoming trip to Beijing and its impact on the RVN.[61] The Vietnamese officials raised concerns regarding the lack of a coherent policy toward Sino-American rapprochement. Compared with the other Asian nations, including South Korea, Taiwan, the Philippines, and Thailand, which responded quickly with new policies, South Vietnam's lack of direction, the U.S. senators warned, placed the RVN in danger of being left behind in isolation. Particularly since issues between the United States and the RVN had not been settled regarding a peace initiative, the senators advised Thieu to address those issues with Nixon before his visit to Beijing.[62]

By late 1971, it was too late for Thieu to incorporate the input of his advisors and the Senate Foreign Relations Committee. Thieu's default strategy in dealing with the Americans had been based on extorting as much aid from Nixon as possible before Kissinger sold him out.[63] According to the RVN's ambassador to the United States, Bui Diem, Thieu consistently sent him detailed instructions on how to negotiate with the Americans to get more aid under Vietnamization but only gave him vague orders on how to evade American intrusion on South Vietnamese politics.[64] In his memoirs, Bui Diem characterized Thieu's modus operandi in deflecting American pressure to curb South Vietnamese corruption and to institute political reforms:

> For his part, Thieu never refused anything. His usual way was to agree, acquiesce and make promises, then to wait and see what would happen. As long as he sensed that the American position was not being pressed with great force or energy, which was the case most of the time, he would procrastinate, waiting for issues to disappear by themselves or to lose their urgency as other, more demanding matters piled up.[65]

But by late 1971, Thieu feared that Kissinger's second trip to China had already paved the way for the United States to strike a secret deal behind South Vietnam's back, making it ever more urgent to procure sufficient funds and equipment for the Republic of Vietnam Armed Forces (RVNAF).[66] More important for Thieu, his own personal power, which had been reaffirmed after his victory in the questionable 1971 presidential elections, was in jeopardy.[67] During General Alexander Haig's visit to Saigon in the fall, Kissinger's deputy presented America's new negotiating position, which contained a provision for a new presidential election within six months of signing a peace treaty and called for Thieu's resignation one month before the internationally supervised election.[68] To Thieu, South Vietnam and Thieu himself had become a tiresome old hag that needed to be eliminated in order to ensure the success of Nixon's trip to visit his new mistress in Beijing.

The Fine Line between Friend and Foe

The year 1972 was one of betrayal, battles, bullying, and bombing in the Vietnam War. For the United States, the year began with historic summits that marked the triumph of Nixon's triangular diplomacy in the Cold War and ended with the infamous bombing campaign that revealed the failure of Nixon's international strategy in the Vietnam War. Throughout the year, the Vietnamese parties found themselves fighting not only each other on the battlefield but also their allies behind closed doors. Like an international relations soap opera, the line between ally and enemy became completely and irreversibly blurred.

Betrayal

As the world rejoiced over the ostensible ratcheting down of Cold War tensions embodied in the upcoming Beijing and Moscow summits, the two Vietnams braced themselves for betrayal. Although the great powers promised that they would not "sell out" their allies nor "deal over the heads of their friends," neither North or South Vietnam put much stock in American, Chinese, and Soviet promises.[69] On 25 January 1972, in preparation for his visit to Beijing, Nixon announced a comprehensive political and military peace proposal that furtively dropped the formal demand for the mutual withdrawal of forces. Thieu had to outwardly support Nixon's proposal but was "deeply disturbed" by the shift from mutual to unilateral withdrawal in a manner described by Thieu's private secretary and cousin, Hoang Duc Nhã, as "cavalier."[70] Resolving to go along with the United States as long as Nixon increased the amount of aid to South Vietnam, Thieu sent Nixon a letter on the eve of the president's trip to China that, regardless of Thieu's resignation or any signed peace agreement, the ability of the RVN to defend itself was the key to lasting peace in the area. When RVN foreign minister Tran Van Lam ironically declared, "[W]e fully approve of Mr. Nixon's trip. No one can deny that it helped create an atmosphere of eased tensions," he did not mean the atmosphere of U.S.–RVN relations.[71]

For North Vietnam, Chinese and Soviet treachery was equally if not more problematic than U.S. betrayal of South Vietnam. Throughout 1971, the VWP politburo tried in vain to dissuade its allies from bettering relations with the United States and ultimately meeting with the U.S. president.[72] In October, Chairman Nikolai Podgorny visited Hanoi before the official announcement of Nixon's visit to Moscow. After Kissinger's second visit to Beijing, Pham Van Dong consented to visit China in November even though he had rejected an earlier Chinese invitation after Kissinger's first visit in July. From 20 to 25 November 1971, the Vietnamese prime minister failed to persuade Mao Zedong and Zhou Enlai, just as he had failed to persuade Soviet leaders, to cancel Nixon's upcoming visit in 1972.[73] Both the Chinese and the Soviets refused North Vietnamese requests by claiming that bettering relations with the United States would ultimately help the Vietnamese cause.[74] The U.S. support of Thieu (including supporting the sham October elections) and vague statements regarding troop withdrawal (maintaining a residual force)—the very issues that caused Saigon to doubt Washington—forced Hanoi to conclude that Beijing's and Moscow's activities had not helped Vietnam's position at all.[75] In fact, since Chinese and Soviet policies toward the Vietnamese revolution were dictated by their own geostrategic calculations under the veneer of ideological solidarity, the allies were once again poised to sell out Vietnam's struggle for their own ends as they had in 1954 at the Geneva Conference.[76]

In response to "big power chauvinism," Hanoi extorted as much military and economic aid as possible before socialist funds ran out for the Vietnamese cause. Although both communist allies increased weapons shipments, promised greater economic support and cooperation in technical fields, and signed more protocols and supplementary aid packages, Hanoi read these measures as palliatives for détente and rapprochement.[77] And with good reason. Until 1972, Beijing and Moscow had struggled for influence with Hanoi not just out of desire to be at the vanguard of international proletarianism but, more important, as a way to gain leverage with the Americans.[78] Now, in essence, Moscow and Beijing were doing Nixon's bidding, at least from Hanoi's perspective. Chinese leaders invoked Beijing's tolerance of Chiang Kai-shek in Taiwan in order to persuade Hanoi to relent on demanding Thieu's ouster in Saigon. At the same time, Soviet leaders urged Hanoi to refrain from launching an offensive in 1972 and, instead, to concentrate on the diplomatic arena.[79]

Battles

In addition to demanding more aid and resisting Beijing's and Moscow's advice, VWP leaders resolved to launch what they would call the Nguyen Hue Offensive in the spring of 1972.[80] On 30 March 1972, an estimated 15,000 People's Army of Vietnam (PAVN) troops armed with Soviet tanks and weaponry crossed the Demilitarized Zone (DMZ) in a large-scale offensive that swept along Route 9 from Khe Sanh to Dong Ha.[81] Although the official Vietnamese statement at the time (and after) claimed that the offensive was launched strictly to alter the military balance of power on the ground, Hanoi timed the offensive to take place between the Beijing summit (21–28 February) and the Moscow summit (22–30 May).[82]

Although détente was at risk, Nixon ordered the bombing of the Hanoi area and the mining of North Vietnamese ports in early May as retaliation against the communist offensive. However, Linebacker I sent a message not only to the North Vietnamese to cease its attacks on South Vietnam but also to the Soviets and Chinese that they needed to place more pressure on the North Vietnamese to return to the negotiating table rather than supply Hanoi with more tanks.[83] Moscow's leaders were divided on whether or not to hold the summit but ultimately, Leonid Brezhnev and Kosygin chose bettering Soviet-American relations over demonstrating ideological solidarity. In the

236 Of War's End and Endless Wars

end, both the Chinese and Soviets issued only diplomatic protests over the bombing of their ships as a result of Linebacker I and indicated that American attacks should not derail rapprochement or détente.[84]

Bullying

On 19 May 1972, the Hanoi politburo sent a message to Le Duc Tho in Paris that "the Soviets desired the upcoming [21 May] meeting so that they could further pressure us to come to a settlement by using the results of the meeting to haggle with the US."[85] As a result, North Vietnamese leaders decided to cancel the meeting with Kissinger. In mid-June, however, Soviet president Podgorny traveled to Hanoi in order to convince the North Vietnamese to return to the negotiating table.[86] From a letter sent by DRV foreign minister Nguyen Duy Trinh to Le Duc Tho on 13 June, we know that Podgorny's appeal fell on deaf ears.[87] It was only at Washington's insistence that talks resumed in July.[88] Although Washington "blinked" first, Nixon's triangulation continued to pay dividends.[89] On 12 July, Zhou Enlai engaged Le Duc Tho in a long discussion aimed once again at persuading Hanoi to drop its insistence on Thieu's ouster. Although Zhou Enlai resorted to softening Hanoi's position with flattery, Le Duc Tho rejected the Chinese leader's attempts to make Thieu more palatable as only one of three representatives in a coalition government.[90] However, as the negotiating record reveals, throughout the summer and fall of 1972, Le Duc Tho was willing not only to accept Thieu's participation in a coalition government alongside the PRG and third parties, but when Kissinger resisted the idea of a coalition government, the North Vietnamese leader conceded and accepted a looser body called the Committee of National Reconciliation. By October 1972, when Kissinger overreached and thought he could produce a settlement before the elections, it can be argued that the North Vietnamese succumbed more to Soviet and Chinese diplomatic weight than to American military pressure.

Bombing

Although it is hard to discern which Vietnamese party held Kissinger in greater contempt and disdain, Thieu's handwritten notes from his 22 October meeting with Nixon's ambitious "errand boy" tentatively point toward South Vietnam.[91] One week before the U.S. presidential elections, Kissinger, who wanted to secure his place with Nixon and in history, flew to Saigon from Paris in order to seal the deal. However, Thieu used the remaining weapon in his arsenal: he refused to go along with U.S. demands. After delaying Kissinger for two days in order to study the draft agreement, Thieu began their meeting by saying, "I have a right to expect that the U.S. has connived with the Soviets and China to sell out South Vietnam."[92] Kissinger, who did not possess a high regard for the South Vietnamese president, responded:

> I admire the courage and heroism which have characterized your speech. However, as an American I can only deeply resent your suggestion that we have connived with the Soviets and Chinese. How can you conceive this [to be] possible when the President on May 8 [Linebacker I] risked his whole political future to come to your assistance?[93]

Looking at Thieu's frantically scribbled notes, we can see that the South Vietnamese leader was furious over America's "surrender or humiliation" tactic, which was satisfying the "invader" by withdrawing troops and giving the NLF a position in the coalition. During the course of the meeting, it became apparent to Thieu that the RVN's concerns were never raised by Kissinger during the secret talks. Thieu listed three main issues: the continued presence of North Vietnamese troops in the South, the National Council for Reconciliation and Concord (NCRC) as a decoy for a coalition government, and the impossibility of establishing the DMZ as a secure border. In a rare glimpse of small-power subversion in the making, the final section of Thieu's notes includes detailed plans on how to outmaneuver Kissinger and kill his draft agreement through a major press campaign.[94] In other words, South Vietnam would use the public media and target international opinion in order to wage a battle of wills against its ally, the United States.

When the October draft agreement failed to pass through both South Vietnamese parties and the peace talks broke down again in November, a reelected Nixon threatened the North Vietnamese with "disastrous consequences" if they did not negotiate and threatened the South Vietnamese with a unilateral deal with Hanoi if they did not cooperate.[95] Neither Vietnamese party capitulated.[96] On 14 December, Nixon ordered a resumption of the bombing, and on 18 December, Linebacker II, otherwise known as the Christmas bombings, began. During the twelve-day campaign, 3,420 sorties carpet-bombed mainly the Hanoi–Hai Phong area, inflicting severe damage to North Vietnam both in physical and psychological terms. Although the Chinese and Soviets issued strong condemnations of the fiercest bombing campaign in the Second Indochina War, both allies again exerted pressure on Hanoi to settle with the Americans.[97] The VWP, however, did not have to be coerced into showing "flexibility" and approaching negotiations "seriously." On 8 January 1973, talks between Le Duc Tho and Kissinger resumed. Thieu, on the other hand, encouraged by Nixon's bombing, continued to hold out for PAVN withdrawals and other significant changes to the agreement. But, upon the very real threat of the immediate cutoff of U.S. aid, the South Vietnamese president finally relented on 21 January. On 23 January 1973, after a tumultuous year, the Paris Agreement on Ending the War and Restoring Peace managed to end the American phase of the war but gave little respite for the Vietnamese.

Conclusion

Although the Vietnam War stayed within the military demarcations of Indochina, the diplomatic theater of the war transcended local and regional boundaries to occupy the international level. As a result, a history of the war during the period of peace negotiations must take into account the global dimensions of the conflict, particularly the diplomatic struggles of the major parties involved in the war and their perspectives on the international battleground. In turn, an international history such as the one above may provide some tentative answers to the questions posed at the outset of this essay.

The internationalization of the war in the aftermath of the Tet Offensive and the initiation of negotiations had three major consequences: it pitted small-power diplomacy against great-power politics; it radically changed the nature of the alliances in the Cold War; and it ultimately doomed a viable peace. First, the emergence of détente with the Soviet Union and rapprochement with the PRC affected the diplomacy of the Vietnam War by carving a niche for small-power diplomacy to influence Cold War balance-of-power politics. Although Nixon intended to use great-power diplomacy for American ends in the Vietnam War, Hanoi and Saigon were able to obstruct and thwart superpower manipulation. Nonetheless, Nixon's triangular diplomacy radically changed the relationships between the great powers and their Vietnamese clients—the United States and the RVN, on the one hand, and the Soviet Union, China, and the DRV, on the other. The line between friend and foe became irrevocably blurred. The North Vietnamese feared the results of Nixon's triangular offensive on their war effort and rightly so: Beijing and Moscow did place pressure on Hanoi to come to a negotiated settlement, albeit not enough to content Nixon. The South Vietnamese, once they realized that Sino-American rapprochement sounded the final death knell of the U.S.–RVN alliance, dug in their heels and waged a battle of wills against the United States. Surprisingly, then, the DRV and the RVN faced similar predicaments in the post-Tet war as a result of Nixon's triangular diplomacy. Finally, Sino-American rapprochement and the improvement in Soviet-American relations that paralleled it accelerated the negotiations process but ultimately doomed a viable peace. A real and sustainable agreement had no chance when viewed from the perspectives of the junior partners in the Cold War: neither the North nor the South Vietnamese wanted to see a peace defined by their larger allies.

NOTES

1. Although American involvement spanned the entire existence of the RVN, the Americanization of the war after 1965 has received less attention from scholars of South Vietnam. For excellent studies of the earlier period of South Vietnamese history under the Ngo Dinh Diem administration, see Edward G. Miller, "Grand Designs: Vision, Power and Nation Building in America's Alliance with Ngo Dinh Diem, 1954–1960," Ph.D. diss., Harvard University, 2004; Jessica M. Chapman, "Staging Democracy: South Vietnam's 1955 Referendum to Depose Bao Dai," *Diplomatic History* 30.4 (September 2006): 671–703; and Philip Catton, *Diem's Final Failure: Prelude to America's War in Vietnam* (Lawrence: University Press of Kansas, 2003).

2. See Frederik Logevall, *Choosing War: The Lost Chance for Peace and the Escalation of the War in Vietnam* (Berkeley: University of California Press, 1999), who argues that America's European and Canadian allies were against growing U.S. involvement in Vietnam, refusing to join the war effort during President Johnson's "More Flags" campaign.

3. See Lien-Hang T. Nguyen, "The War Politburo: North Vietnam's Diplomatic and Political Road to the Tet Offensive," *Journal of Vietnamese Studies* 1.1–2 (February–August 2006): 4–58.

4. See James G. Hershberg, "Who Murdered 'Marigold'?—New Evidence on the Mysterious Failure of Poland's Secret Initiative to Start US–North Vietnamese Peace Talks, 1966," Working Paper No. 27 (Washington, D.C.: Cold War International History Project [hereafter CWIHP], Woodrow Wilson Center). See also George Herring, ed., *The Secret Diplomacy of the Vietnam War* (Austin: University of Texas Press, 1983).

5. See Jeremi Suri, *Power and Protest: Global Revolution and the Age of Détente* (Cambridge, Mass.: Harvard University Press, 2003).

6. The governments in Phnom Penh and Vientiane as well as the revolutionary parties in Cambodia and Laos were key players in the internationalization of the Second Indochina War though their roles are even more vastly understudied.

7. The Non-Alignment Movement grew out of the Bandung Conference in 1955 of postcolonial states, particularly in Asia and Africa. The nations present at Bandung declared "nonalignment" in the East-West struggle and opposed colonialism and neoimperialism of any kind.

8. See Luu Van Loi and Nguyen Vu Anh, *Cac cuoc thuong luong Le Duc Tho–Kissinger tai Paris [Le Duc Tho–Kissinger Negotiations in Paris]*, 1st ed. (Hanoi: Cong An Nhan Dan Press, 1996), 453; and Gareth Porter, *A Peace Denied: The United States, Vietnam and the Paris Agreement* (Bloomington: Indiana University Press, 1975), 179–88, for discussion of Nguyen Van Thieu's flagrant disregard for and violation of the ceasefire and terms of the peace agreement. See also Lewis Sorley, *A Better War: The Unexamined Victories and Final Tragedy of America's Last Years in Vietnam* (New York, 1999), 363, which cites U.S. intelligence reports that the North Vietnamese were the first party to violate the Paris agreement.

9. Jeffrey Kimball, *Nixon's Vietnam War* (Lawrence: University Press of Kansas, 1998). Kimball also suggests that the record shows Nixon to be the strategist and Kissinger the tactician. For an interpretation which views Kissinger as the chief visionary not just for Indochina but globally, see Richard Thornton, *The Nixon-Kissinger Years: The Reshaping of American Foreign Policy* (New York, 1989).

10. Kimball, *Nixon's Vietnam War*, 240.

11. See William Bundy, *A Tangled Web: The Making of a Foreign Policy in the Nixon Presidency* (New York: Hill and Wang, 1998). Bundy, who served as assistant secretary of defense and state under JFK and LBJ, argues that a clear-cut withdrawal would have been far less damaging than the policy the Nixon administration pursued and that Hanoi had essentially already won the war in 1968. See also Frank Snepp, *Decent Interval: An Insider's Account of Saigon's Indecent End Told By the CIA's Chief Strategy Analyst in Vietnam* (New York: Vintage Books, 1977).

12. See Larry Berman, *No Peace, No Honor: Nixon, Kissinger, and Betrayal in Vietnam* (New York: Simon and Schuster, 2002).

13. There are a growing number of area studies specialists who are devoting attention to the Second Indochina War, but on the whole, the period has been overlooked in Vietnam studies in efforts to move beyond the war. For the communist war effort, see David Elliott, *The Vietnamese War: Revolution and Social Change in the Mekong Delta, 1930–1975*, 2 vols. (Armonk, N.Y.: Sharpe, 2003); Kim Ninh, *A World Transformed: The Politics of Culture in Revolutionary Vietnam, 1945–1965* (Ann Arbor: University of Michigan Press, 2002); Ang Cheng Guan, *Ending the Vietnam War: The Vietnamese Communists' Perspective* (London: RoutledgeCurzon, 2004); Robert Brigham, *Guerrilla Diplomacy: The NLF's Foreign Relations and the Viet Nam War* (Ithaca, N.Y.: Cornell University Press, 1999); and William Duiker, *The Communist Road to Power in Vietnam*, 2nd ed. (Boulder, Colo.: Westview, 1996). For histories of the RVN, particularly under the Ngo Dinh Diem administration, see note 1. See also Neil Jamieson, *Understanding Vietnam* (Berkeley: University of California Press, 1993); and Robert Topmiller, *The Lotus Unleashed: The Buddhist Peace Movement in South Vietnam, 1964–1966* (Lexington: University of Kentucky Press, 2002).

14. The party and military archives are also separate from the national archives controlled by the Ministry of the Interior. To date, I am the only American scholar who has gained entry into the Ministry of Foreign Affairs Archives. For helpful guides to the Vietnamese archives, see David Marr's "The National Archives of Vietnam," *CORMOSEA Bulletin* 19.1 (June 1990): 8–16; Mark Bradley and Robert Brigham, "Vietnamese Archives and Scholarship on the Cold War Period: Two Reports," Working Paper No. 7 (CWIHP, September 1993); David Wolff, "News from Hanoi Archives: Summer 1998," Bulletin 11 (CWIHP, Winter 1995–1996): 275–76; and Matt Masur and Edward Miller, "Saigon Revisited: Researching South Vietnam's Republican Era (1954–1975) at Archives and Libraries in Ho Chi Minh City" (CWIHP, September 2006). For Vietnamese-language publications, see *Luu Tru Viet Nam (Archives Journal)*, edited by Duong Vam Kham, which is published every other month, for both recent releases and administrative and legal issues concerning declassification in the national archives of the Socialist Republic of Vietnam (SRV).

15. Loi and Anh, *Cac cuoc thuong luong Le Duc Tho–Kissinger tai Paris*, 1st ed. See also memoirs written by former Hanoi officials regarding the diplomatic struggle, including Nguyen Duy Trinh, *Mặt tran ngoai giao thoi ky chong My cuu nuoc, 1965–1975 [The Diplomatic Struggle during the Anti-American Struggle for National Salvation]* (Hanoi: Su That Press, 1979); Mai Van Bo, *Tan cong ngoai giao va tiep xuc bi mat [Diplomatic Offensives and Secret Contacts]* (Thanh Pho Ho Chi Minh [hereafter TPHCM]: TPHCM Press, 1985) and *Hanoi–Paris: Hoi ky ngoai giao cua Mai Van Bo [Hanoi–Paris: Diplomatic Memoirs of Mai Van Bo]* (TPHCM: Van Nghe TPHCM Press, 1993).

16. See the authors' English translation published in 1996 by The Gioi Publishers in Hanoi, *Le Duc Tho–Kissinger Negotiations in Paris*, 10.

17. Luu Van Loi also wrote a history of the pre-1968 peace initiatives in *Cuoc tiep xuc bí mat Viet Nam–Hoa Kỳ truóc Hoi nghi Paris [Secret Contacts between Vietnam and the United States before the Paris Conference]* (Hanoi: Vien Quan He Quoc Te Press 1990). In addition, he expands on the theme of the farsighted and correct nature of Vietnamese diplomacy in his two-volume study, *Nam muoi nam ngoai giao Viet Nam, 1945–1975* (Hanoi, 1996).

18. Nguyen Thi Binh et al., *Mat tran Dan toc Giai phong Chinh phu Cach mang lam thoi tai Hoi nghi Paris ve Viet Nam (Hoi uc) [The National Liberation Front–Provisional Revolutionary Government at the Paris Conference on Vietnam (Recollections)]* (Hanoi: Chinh Tri Quoc Gia Press, 2001).

19. For a different viewpoint, see Brigham, *Guerrilla Diplomacy*, xi. Brigham argues, "[The] Front was neither a puppet of Hanoi nor an autonomous organization," and that the NLF viewed the diplomatic struggle as an integral part of the war effort rather than as a means of negotiation. See also Carlyle Thayer, *War by Other Means: National Liberation and Revolution in Viet-Nam, 1954–1960* (Sydney: Allen and Unwin, 1989).

20. Materials on the Republic of Vietnam can be found in the U.S. National Archives and Records Administration (hereafter NARA) in College Park, Maryland,

and in the Vietnam Archives at Texas Tech University in Lubbock. In addition, the National Archives Center II in Ho Chi Minh City is easier to access for Western scholars than its counterpart, the National Archives Center III in Hanoi.

21. For example, see Nguyen Ba Can, *Dat nuoc toi [My Country]* (San Jose, Calif.: Hoa Hao Press, 2003).

22. See Nguyen Phu Duc, *The Viet-Nam Peace Negotiations: Saigon's Side of the Story* (Christiansburg, Va.: Dalley Book Service, 2005).

23. Nguyen Tien Hung and Jerrold L. Schecter, *The Palace File* (New York: Harper & Row, 1989).

24. See Bui Diem, *In the Jaws of History* (Bloomington: Indiana University Press, 1987); Nguyen Xuan Phong, *Hope and Vanquished Reality* (New York, 2001); Cao Van Vien, *Nhung ngay cuoi cua Viet Nam Cong Hoa [The Final Days of the Republic of Vietnam]* (Washington, D.C., 2003).

25. Nguyen Cao Ky, *How We Lost the War in Vietnam* (New York, 1976), and *Buddha's Child: My Fight to Save Vietnam* (New York, 2002).

26. Berman has addressed the South Vietnamese perspective in the peace negotiations in *No Peace, No Honor*. In particular, he argues that the Thieu administration was able to "kill the deal" in the fall of 1972 by refusing to consent to Kissinger's demands to sign the October draft of a peace agreement hammered out between the U.S. and DRV negotiators in their private meetings. See Berman, *No Peace, No Honor*, 160–79.

27. Porter, *A Peace Denied*. See note 8.

28. Allen Goodman, *The Lost Peace: America's Search for a Negotiated Settlement of the Vietnam War* (Stanford, Calif.: Stanford University Press, 1978).

29. Pierre Asselin, *A Bitter Peace: Washington, Hanoi, and the Making of the Paris Agreement* (Chapel Hill: University of North Carolina Press, 2002).

30. Ibid., p. 180.

31. Before departing, the Johnson administration firmly set into place the deescalation of the air war by ending Operation Rolling Thunder and the de-Americanization of the ground war by ensuring troop withdrawal after the Tet Offensive. In addition to great-power diplomacy, Nixon and Kissinger devised a strategy to end the war which included establishing private negotiations with Hanoi while publicly transferring the war over to Saigon and officially deescalating the ground war to diffuse political pressure while secretly expanding the air war over Indochina to gain military leverage. In sum, the Nixon administration succeeded in creating more room for maneuver in promulgating war and negotiating peace by privileging the diplomatic sphere of the conflict and elevating the war to the international level.

32. During the preinaugural period, Kissinger commissioned the Rand Corporation to do a study on America's strategy in Vietnam. The Rand study acted as a guide to Nixon and Kissinger's strategy and as a result, NSSM 1 served more to map the layout of the foreign policy apparatus through which Nixon and Kissinger had to navigate. See "Vietnam Policy Alternatives," Box 3: VN-RAND, HAK [Henry A. Kissinger] Administration and Staff Files, HAK Office Files, National Security

Council Files, Nixon Presidential Materials Staff, NARA. See also Jeffrey Kimball, *The Vietnam War Files: Uncovering the Secret History of the Nixon-Era Strategy* (Lawrence: University Press of Kansas, 2004), 10–11.

33. "Revised Summary of Responses to NSSM 1: The Situation in Vietnam," 22 March 1969, 6–7, Presidential Directives on National Security from Truman to Clinton, National Security Archives.

34. See Kimball, *Nixon's Vietnam War*, 97.

35. See Ilya Gaiduk, *The Soviet Union and the Vietnam War* (Chicago: University of Chicago Press, 1996), 194–222.

36. In late 1967, Soviet and Chinese border guards had engaged in a few squabbles but no deaths resulted from these conflicts. The first loss of life occurred when Soviet vehicles crushed four Chinese fishermen in January 1968.

37. Kissinger, *The White House Years* (hereafter *WHY*) (Boston: Little, Brown, 1979), 172.

38. "Memorandum of Conversation of the Ambassador to the USA A. F. Dobrinyn [*sic*] with Kissinger, Aide to President Nixon to A. Gromyko," 12 July 1969, Communist Party of the Soviet Union Central Committee Archive, reprinted by CWIHP, issue 3 (Fall 1993): 65–66.

39. Ibid., 65.

40. The Soviets reported Kissinger's assertions this way:

Nixon's logic as a realist is very simple: the Soviet Union is much more capable than present-day China to confront the USA in different parts of the world, and that can create dangerous situations, possibly leading to conflicts in which the very existence of the US as a nation may be at stake if the war breaks out. As for its military-economic potential, China for several years won't be able to present such a threat to the USA, but the USSR can. Besides, added Kissinger, Mao Tse-Tung's actions can't be evaluated using rational logic.... Another thing is that the Soviet Union is governed by realistically thinking politicians who are interested in their people's and their country's well-being.... it would be possible to prevent dragging the world into major military conflicts, until China "grows up" and more responsible leaders come to power in Beijing. (Ibid., 66)

41. Kimball, *Nixon's Vietnam War*, 119.

42. Kissinger, *WHY*, 171.

43. Qiang Zhai, *China and the Vietnam Wars, 1950–1975* (Chapel Hill: University of North Carolina Press, 2000), 181–82. There were four reports in total, but only two have surfaced.

44. Kissinger, *WHY*, 173. See also Luu Van Loi, *Cac cuoc thuong luong Le Duc Tho–Kissinger tai Paris*, 2nd ed. (Hanoi: Cong An Nhan Dan Publishers 2002), 311.

45. See Loi and Anh, *Cac cuoc thuong luong Le Duc Tho–Kissinger tai Paris*, 1st ed., 55.

46. According to the preface written in *President Ho Chi Minh's Testament* (Hanoi, 1989) by the general secretary of the Central Committee of the Communist Party of Vietnam, Nguyen Van Linh, the Political Bureau of the Third Party Central Committee in 1969 decided to declare the time of Ho Chi Minh's death to be at 09:47 hours on 3 September so that it would not coincide with the national celebration.

47. The Central Committee of the VWP published President Ho Chi Minh's testament on 10 May 1969.

48. "France et le Vietnam (voyage de M. Alphand a Moscou) [France and Vietnam (Alphand's trip to Moscow)]," 31 December 1969, Box 288, Sud-Vietnam, Cambodge-Lao-Vietnam (hereafter CLV), Asie-Oceanie (hereafter AO), Archives du Ministère des Affaires Étrangères (French Foreign Ministry Archives, hereafter MAE), Paris. The shift in Soviet policies was more noticeable than China's since Moscow's policies were more in line with Washington's. Particularly in the realm of negotiations, Moscow's active participation stopped with the death of Ho Chi Minh.

49. "Rencontre entre Kosygin & Chou En Lai [Meeting between Kosygin and Zhou Enlai]," 12 September 1969, Box 70, Nord-Vietnam (hereafter NV), CLV, AO, MAE.

50. Buoyed by receiving messages from the Nixon camp to "hold out," Thieu defied Johnson's 31 October announcement that talks were imminent by delivering his own speech which stated that he would not send a team to Paris. Democratic candidate Hubert Humphrey, who had been leading in the polls prior to Thieu's announcement, lost to Nixon by a slim margin. Moreover, "de-Americanization" is a more apt description of America's post-Tet policy than "Vietnamization" since the Republic of Vietnam Armed Forces (RVNAF) had played an integral part in the Second Indochina War from the outset.

51. Quoted in Hung and Schecter, *The Palace File*, 34.

52. The Vietnamese war engulfed Cambodia and Laos at the outset but with the cessation of Rolling Thunder and the stalemate in South Vietnam after the Tet Offensive, the air and ground wars intensified in neighboring countries.

53. Initially, the Chinese leadership was ambivalent toward Sihanouk, waiting to issue a condemnation of his overthrow until 5 April, when the CCP eventually decided to support the Cambodian leader to strengthen its positions vis-a-vis not only the Soviets, but the North Vietnamese as well. The Soviets, on the other hand, opted for an international conference that would guarantee against a Chinese- or American-dominated Indochina. In particular, Moscow favored France's 1 April call for a conference involving all interested parties—as opposed to governments, so that Sihanouk's party, the Pathet Lao, and the PRG would be able to attend—to ensure Cambodian neutrality. On 17 April, Moscow joined the clamor of international voices by suggesting reconvening another Geneva conference. On the whole, though, Moscow played it safe by maintaining its diplomatic mission in Phnom Penh. See "Conversations franco-sovietiques sur l'Indochine [French-Soviet Conversations on Indochina]," 22 May 1970, Box 178, CLV, AO, MAE.

54. American journalist Edgar Snow came to Tiananmen for National Day on 1 October 1970, which is when Mao made his first intimation to Washington that he

desired a meeting; this was followed by the American response via Pakistani channels that the United States was prepared to send an envoy.

55. Kissinger, *WHY*, 706–7.

56. During Kissinger's first visit to Beijing in mid-July, he linked Chinese help with an honorable American withdrawal from Vietnam with the Taiwan issue and PRC representation in the United Nations. See Zhai, *China and the Vietnam Wars*, 196.

57. Hung and Schecter, *The Palace File*, 9. At the time, Nguyen Tien Hung was a professor at Howard University. When he returned to Vietnam in 1973, Hung became a special assistant to President Thieu and later, minister of economic development and planning.

58. Ibid., 10.

59. See Nguyen Phu Duc's confidential report entitled "Thai do cua Nga va Trung-Cong doi voi thoi cuoc Dong-Duong [Soviet and Chinese Attitudes regarding Indochina]," 2 June 1971, file 1890, Phu Tong Thong De Nhi Chinh Phu Cong Hoa (Office of the Presidency of the Second Republic; hereafter PTTDeNhi), Trung Tam Luu Tru Quoc Gia II (Vietnam National Archives Center II; hereafter VNA-II), Ho Chi Minh City (TPHCM).

60. Hung and Schecter, *The Palace File*, 49.

61. "Viec Tong Thong Nixon di Bac Kinh va anh huong doi voi Viet Nam Cong Hoa [The Business of President Nixon's Trip to Beijing and the Impact on the RVN]" appeared in a report by Cao Van Tuong, who held the position equivalent to the White House chief of staff. Tuong's role was focused on relations with the National Assembly. See "Phieu trinh cua Tong thong Viet Nam Cong Hoa cua Bo Truong Dac Trach Lien Lac Quoc Hoi v/v y kien cua cac Nghi-Si ve the ngoai giao cua Viet Nam [Report for RVN President from Ministry of National Assembly Relations regarding the Opinions of the Senate Foreign Relations Committee]," file 1773, PTTDeNhi, VNA-II, TPHCM.

62. The exact words were: "Nay o Nixon sap di Beijing thi viec thanh ly cac dien kien giai ket cang can duoc Viet Nam Cong Hoa doi hoi gap cho xong." Ibid. According to Hung, Thieu had invited him back to Saigon in response to his letter that had urged the South Vietnamese president to begin his own peace initiative toward North Vietnam before Nixon's China trip. See Hung and Schecter, *The Palace File*, 10.

63. See Lien-Hang T. Nguyen, "Saigon Diplomacy," paper presented at the Association of Asian Studies annual meeting, San Diego, California, March 2004.

64. Bui Diem, interview by author, 17–18 March 2006, Lubbock, Texas. See also Bui Diem, *In the Jaws of History*, 266–67, for Thieu's handwritten response to Bui Diem's cables regarding U.S. Secretary of State William Rogers's pressure on Thieu to reform his government: "Leave this initiative alone for the time being. Restrict yourself to talking about Vietnamization. I will inform you of the opportune moment to raise this subject.... Do not let Rogers pre-empt me on this either. It annoys me. He should respect me on this."

65. Bui Diem, *In the Jaws of History*, 276.

66. Hung and Schecter, *The Palace File*, 48–49. Thieu was right in not trusting Kissinger: the historical record shows that Thieu was not being fully informed about what transpired at the secret meetings with Le Duc Tho by U.S. ambassador Ellsworth Bunker. Regarding Vietnamization, Thieu wanted to establish two additional reserve divisions since he believed that South Vietnam did not possess enough reserves to counter any thrust by the PAVN across the DMZ. In addition, the pace of U.S. troop withdrawal proceeded much faster than Thieu was led to believe at Midway. From the almost half million U.S. troops in 1969, 65,000 troops were withdrawn by the end of that year, 50,000 in 1970, and 250,000 in 1971, leaving 139,000 troops in 1972. With the upcoming U.S. presidential elections, Thieu knew that 1972 was a pivotal year to get as much for South Vietnam as possible as U.S. ground troops numbers dwindled.

67. In the summer before the South Vietnamese presidential elections, Thieu had forced an electoral law through the National Assembly that required candidates to obtain signatures from either forty National Assembly members or one hundred members of the provincial council. By intimidating and bribing the legislators, only Duong Van Minh (known as "Big Minh" to the Americans) was able to obtain the requisite signatures, and Nguyen Cao Ky, the vice president, could not. In the end, Big Minh dropped out, even though he was bribed by the Americans to stay on, enabling Thieu to run unopposed and thus be reelected in early October 1971.

68. Since Thieu knew that the communists would never agree to a presidential election, he did not oppose the proposal to step down one month before the elections. Communicating directly with Nixon via personal letters, Thieu urged caution against accepting a coalition government with the communists and insisted that, regardless of any formal settlement, the key to peace lay in South Vietnam's ability to defend itself.

69. For Nixon's promise to "make no agreements in Peking at the expense of other countries" and that, during his May 1972 visit to Moscow, he wished "to make it clear that the United States [had] no intention of dealing over the heads of its friends and allies," see his first personal letter to Thieu reprinted in Hung and Schecter, *The Palace File*, 18–19. For Chinese attempts at easing North Vietnamese suspicions, see Zhai, *China and the Vietnam Wars*, 196–201.

70. Hung and Schecter, *The Palace File*, 49. Bunker gave Thieu the contents of Nixon's speech only a few days before but asked for Thieu's immediate acquiescence.

71. Quoted in Hung and Schecter, *The Palace File*, 50.

72. Following Kissinger's first visit to Beijing in July, Zhou Enlai immediately flew to Hanoi in order to quell Vietnamese suspicions by saying that the Americans desired better relations with the PRC following the start of Sino-Soviet negotiations on the border issue on 20 October 1969, and that Taiwan was a less important issue than Indochina. See "Dien den: Noi dung Chu an Lai thong bao dong chi Le Duan va Pham Van Dong ve cuoc trao doi Chu an Lai-Kissinger, 13-07-1971 [Arriving Telegram: Contents of Zhou Enlai's Report to Le Duan and Pham Van Dong on the

COLD WAR CONTRADICTIONS   247

Zhou Enlai–Kissinger Meeting, 13 July 1971]," reprinted in Bo Ngoai Giao [Ministry of Foreign Affairs], *Dai su ky chuyen de: Dau tranh ngoai giao va van dong quoc te trong nhung chien chong My cuu nuoc* [hereafter *Daau tranh ngoai giao*] *[Important Account of a Special Subject: The Diplomatic Struggle and International Activities of the Anti-American Resistance and National Salvation]* (Hanoi: Internal Foreign Ministry Publication, 1987), 291–92. See also Zhai, *China and the Vietnam Wars*, 196–97, for the Chinese version of the 13 July meeting.

73. Zhai, *China and the Vietnam Wars*, 198–99. At the first meeting, Pham Van Dong brought up North Vietnam's contribution to the PRC's reentry into the United Nations, implicitly comparing Hanoi's support of the PRC with Beijing's betrayal of the DRV.

74. The CCP 26 May report concluded that Sino–U.S. discussions would facilitate U.S. troop withdrawal and the Paris peace talks. See Zhai, *China and the Vietnam Wars*, 195.

75. By the end of 1971, the breakdown of talks at Paris and the intensified bombing of the DRV reaffirmed Hanoi's suspicions that Chinese and Soviet activities with the Americans had only resulted in a hardening of the U.S. position.

76. The clearest example to the Vietnamese of the extent to which its allies had shifted positions was Beijing's change in attitude toward negotiations. Beginning in late 1970, Chinese leaders began applauding the DRV's adept diplomacy and negotiating strategies, rather than castigating Hanoi for engaging in talks. On 23 September 1970, Mao said to Pham Van Dong, "I see that you can conduct the diplomatic struggle and you do it well. Negotiations have been going on for two years. At first we were a little worried that you were trapped. We are no longer worried." Quoted in Odd Arne Westad et al., eds.,"77 Conversations between Chinese and Foreign Leaders on the Wars in Indochina, 1964–1977," Working Paper No. 22 (CWIHP, May 1998), 180.

77. See "Aid Agreements for 1971 between North Vietnam and Communist Countries," 1 April 1971, Box 69, NV, CLV, AO, MAE, for the exact details of the increases in aid to Vietnam from China and the Soviet Union.

78. The Chinese and Soviets each feared that the other would strike a deal with the United States on Vietnam. See Gaiduk, *The Soviet Union and the Vietnam War*, 232.

79. Kimball, *Nixon's Vietnam War*, 284.

80. According to the official PAVN history, the politburo issued directions for the 1972 campaign on 14 May 1971. See Institute of Military History of Vietnam, *Victory in Vietnam: The Official History of the People's Army of Vietnam, 1954–1975*, trans. Merle Pribbenow (Lawrence: University Press of Kansas, 2002), 283. However, the history of the Tri Thien region, encompassing the two northernmost provinces of South Vietnam, places the key decision by the politburo, the National Defense Council, and the Ministry of Defense in July 1971. See Bo Quoc Phong, Vien Lich Su Quan Su Viet Nam [Ministry of Defense, Institute of Military History, hereafter BQPVLSQSVN], *Huong tien cong chien luoc Tri-Thien nam 1972: Luu hanh noi bo [The Direction of the 1972 Offensive in Tri-Thien: For Internal*

Distribution] (Hanoi: Vien Lich Su Quan Su Press, 1987), 13–14. This is reaffirmed in the official classified history of the 1972 spring offensive, published a year later in 1988, which states that the communist forces prepared in two stages: from July to December 1971 and then from January to March 1972. See BQPVLSQSVN, *Chien dich tien cong Nguyen Hue: Luu hanh noi bo [The Nguyen Hue Offensive: For Internal Distribution]* (Hanoi, 1988), 21–29. According to comments made by former Foreign Minister Nguyen Co Thach to historian Jeffrey Kimball after the war, the Hanoi Politburo had begun preparation for a 1972 offensive as early as 1970, but the key decisions were made between May and October 1971. With the breakdown of negotiations during the 16 August session, Thieu's reelection in October, the uncompromising U.S. proposal, Kissinger's second visit to Beijing, and the announcement of Nixon's Moscow trip, Hanoi may have "decided finally on the spring offensive." See Kimball, *Nixon's Vietnam War*, 284.

81. See BQPVLSQSVN, *Cac chien dich trong khang chien chong My, cuu nuoc [The Offensives in the Anti-American Struggle for National Salvation], 1954–1975* (Hanoi: Vien Lich Su Quan Su Press, 2003), 274–87.

82. Major-General Nguyen Dinh Uoc claimed that the offensive did not factor in the international scene because the Soviets and Chinese were North Vietnam's allies. He emphasized the military balance of power on the ground, namely, that the Americans had a remaining force of 90,000 with only 30,000 fighting troops. Author's interview, October 2002. However, see David Elliott, *NLF-DRV Strategy and the 1972 Offensive* (Ithaca, N.Y.: Cornell University Press, 1974), which states that Soviet and Chinese considerations also played a part in Vietnamese calculations.

83. See Kimball, *Nixon's Vietnam War*, 304.

84. To add insult to injury, Beijing compounded Hanoi's logistical problems by refusing to redirect Soviet aid through PRC territory, given the dangers of North Vietnamese ports. See "Telegramme l'arrivée, diffusion réservée: Visit de M. Katuchev aHanoi [Arriving Telegram, Reserved Distribution: "Mr. Katuchev's Visit to Hanoi]," May 1972, AO, CLV, NV, Box 69.

85. "Dien di: Bo Chính Tri gui anh Tho, Paris, 19-05-1972 [Departing Telegram: Politburo to Le Duc Tho, Paris, 19 May 1972]," reprinted in BNG, *Dau tranh ngoai giao*, 324–25.

86. Gaiduk, *The Soviet Union and the Vietnam War*, 240–41.

87. "Dien di: Anh Trinh & Xuan Thuy gui anh Tho, 13-06-1972 [Departing Telegram: Nguyen Duy Trinh and Xuan Thuy to Le Duc Tho, 13 June 1972]," reprinted in BNG, *Dau tranh ngoai giao*, 326.

88. Nixon and Kissinger authorized the military attaché in Paris, Colonel Georges Guay, to contact North Vietnam's delegate-general, Vo Van Sung. See "Dien den: Anh Vy gui anh Tho, Trinh, Xuan Thuy, 26-06-1972 [Arriving Telegram: Comrade Vy to Le Duc Tho, Nguyen Duy Trinh, and Xuan Thuy, 26 June 1972]," reprinted in BNG, *Dau tranh ngoai giao*, 326–27.

89. See Kissinger, *WHY*, 1196.

COLD WAR CONTRADICTIONS 249

90. See "Buoi tiep d/c Le Duc Tho tai Bac Kinh, 12-07-1972 [Le Duc Tho's Meeting in Beijing, 12 July 1972]," "Ho so bien ban tiep xuc cua phong LT, Van phong Trung uong Dang [Minutes of Meetings File in the Archives, Office of the Central Committee of the Party]," both reprinted in BNG, *Dau tranh ngoai giao*, 328, and for the translated version, see Meeting between Zhou Enlai and Le Duc Tho on 12 July 1972, in Westad et al., "77 Conversations between Chinese and Foreign Leaders on the Wars in Indochina," 182–84.

91. When Nha told Kissinger that Thieu would be unable to meet him on 20 October, Kissinger was quoted as saying, "I am the Special Envoy of the President of the United States of America. You know I cannot be treated as an errand boy." Hung and Schecter, *The Palace File*, 100.

92. Ibid., 103.

93. Hung and Schecter, *The Palace File*, 104.

94. Although there is no date and Thieu does not include his signature, it is apparent that the handwritten notes are Thieu's. I have compared the handwriting that appears in other archival documents that Thieu signed or initialed to the documents that appear in *The Palace File*. Regarding the date, given the content of the notes, it is obvious that they refer to Kissinger's comments made during his late October 1972 visit to Saigon. Last, and most important, Hoang Duc Nhã confirms that the notes belong to his cousin Nguyen Van Thieu and were taken on 22 October 1972. See no title, n.d., file 458, PTTDeNhi, VNA-II, TPHCM.

95. Berman, *No Peace, No Honor*, 180–97. See also Brigham, *Guerrilla Diplomacy*, 108–10, for how the PRG stalled the peace talks in October 1972.

96. For the South Vietnamese side, see Nguyen Phu Duc, *The Viet-Nam Peace Negotiations*, 340–66. For the North Vietnamese side, see Luu Van Loi, *Cac cuoc thuong luong Le Duc Tho–Kissinger tai Paris*, 2nd ed., 543–83.

97. See Zhai, *China and the Vietnam Wars*, 206; Gaiduk, *The Soviet Union and the Vietnam War*, 244.

"HELP US TELL THE TRUTH
ABOUT VIETNAM"

POW/MIA Politics and the End
of the American War

MICHAEL J. ALLEN

On 27 November 1965, the National Liberation Front (NLF) announced the release of Sergeants George Smith and Claude McClure in "response to the friendly sentiments of the American people against the war in South Vietnam," specifically the March on Washington for Peace in Vietnam to take place later that day. "With [the] sympathy and support of all strata of American people and progressive people the world over," NLF chair Nguyen Huu Tho proclaimed in the radio announcement of their release, "we are sure to realize our just goal and win complete victory." With high hopes for the "brilliant success" of the March for Peace, Tho sent Smith and McClure across the border and into Cambodia, ending their two-year ordeal as prisoners of war. Upon reaching the capital city of Phnom Penh, the returnees were greeted by a cable from the antiwar group Students for a Democratic Society (SDS), telling them that "millions of Americans support you. Help us tell the truth about Vietnam."[1]

"I want to tell people the truth about Vietnam," echoed Smith at the pair's first press conference three days later. Asked, "how will you do that?" he replied, "I will join the peace movement." "I didn't have any idea what the peace movement really was," he later admitted, "but they had somehow influenced my release, so they sure as hell weren't the bad guys." Neither, he and McClure made clear, were their former captors. "The Vietcong treated us very well," McClure insisted, before adding, "[T]he United States has nothing to gain from the war in Vietnam." Smith agreed, "I have known both sides, and the war in Vietnam is of no interest to the United States." Military officials dismissed their words as evidence of "brainwashing" and soon released them with less-than-honorable general discharges. Freed from military censors, Smith continued to speak out against the war until the last Americans left Saigon in 1975.[2]

This episode fits poorly within the existing literature on the Vietnam wars, and not at all within scholarship on American prisoners of war, which has long viewed the "POW/MIA issue" as a propaganda tool of President Richard Nixon. Since H. Bruce Franklin's book, *M.I.A.; or, Mythmaking in America*, initially published in 1992, first argued that "the fate of American prisoners did not become a major public issue until the spring of 1969," when "the incoming Nixon administration" made them "an indispensable device for continuing the war," scholars have placed American POWs and those who cared about them on Nixon's right wing. Neil Sheehan distilled Franklin's thesis to its essence in a 1993 piece for the *New Yorker*. "To buy time and divert attention from the fact that instead of ending the war he was trying to win it," Sheehan wrote, "Nixon launched a campaign to focus public hatred on the Vietnamese for holding American prisoners." In the years since, this analysis has dominated scholarship on POWs and MIAs and been widely adopted by historians of the war's final phase. Gerald Nicosia's adaptation for his 2001 history of the veterans' movement is typical. "For the past two years, Nixon had been exploiting the heart-tugging potential of the POWs and MIAs as a rationale for prolonging the war," Nicosia reported. "As a negotiating strategy," Jeffrey Kimball wrote in his 1998 *Nixon's Vietnam War*, this emphasis on POWs "would ultimately backfire" by giving the enemy a valuable bargaining chip, "but as a public relations strategy, the POW campaign was ultimately successful, for the demand for a quick release of POWs deflected attention from the real purposes of Nixon's strategy while creating 'deep emotional support' for the war." According to the another survey of the war, "Hanoi's treatment of U.S. prisoners of war became Nixon's trump card in the domestic political debate over Vietnam."[3]

This interpretation has predominated because it offers a persuasive answer to the central question of the war's last years: why did Americans keep fighting after the 1968 Tet Offensive, when an ever-growing majority of the public and an impressive array of political and cultural leaders considered the war to be a grievous mistake? They were misled, the received narrative tells us, fooled into fighting for prisoners who could only return when the war ended and for thousands more of the missing dead. Delegitimating the phenomenon it seeks to explain, this analysis has the added benefit of confirming post-Watergate antipathy toward Nixon while relieving the American public and Vietnamese officials of real responsibility for the war's continuation.

So long as the focus is on Nixon and his supporters, this answer works reasonably well. The archives make abundantly clear how hard Nixon and his staff worked to mislead everyone on virtually every matter of public interest, including POWs and MIAs. Yet, however accurately the existing scholarship describes Nixon's machinations, it cannot explain or even accommodate the release of Smith and McClure, nor the fact that Vietnamese communists, American peace activists, and outspoken POWs used American captivity to seek an end to the war, not its continuation, years before Nixon took office. Nor can it account for the dozens of other POWs released by the Vietnamese before the general prisoner exchange in 1973, over half of whom were freed before Nixon's inauguration, often directly into the hands of peace activists.[4] Its disregard for local and international actors with diverse, often competing agendas leads to an unnecessarily cramped view of POW/MIA politics and its contested role in ending the American War.

As the release of Smith and McClure suggests, Nixon was hardly alone in his attempts to use POWs and MIAs to sway public opinion. Vietnamese communists, antiwar activists, POW and MIA families, and POWs themselves publicized the plight of American prisoners before Nixon, and they redoubled their efforts once he entered the fray. Their motives varied and changed over time, but many who engaged in POW/MIA politics did so to end the war and to mitigate its violence. Throughout the conflict, critics of American involvement in Vietnam used the imprisonment of POWs and the uncertainty surrounding MIAs, along with the anguish of their families, to press for the only thing that could end their suffering—American withdrawal. Rather than manufacture public concern for POWs, Nixon sought to thwart an ongoing campaign initiated elsewhere, which was using that concern to end the war. His intervention muddied the politics and diplomacy of the POW/MIA issue, but it did not unite Americans behind his continuation of the war. Quite the contrary, it generated mounting pressure to trade withdrawal for the return of American POWs. Such pressure did not end the war, but it did constrain Nixon's options and revealed deep disillusionment with the war among its presumed supporters.

"The Obvious Solution to the POW Problem Is to End the War"

Twenty-five years before Richard Nixon became president, during the Second World War, the League for the Independence of Vietnam, or the Viet Minh, rescued an American pilot shot down by Japanese forces over North Vietnam and returned him to U.S. authorities in southern China in hopes of winning their support for Vietnamese independence. Pham Van Dong commemorated the event in a special edition of *Vietnam Independence*, which featured an eight-panel illustration with the message "whoever saves American pilots will be generously rewarded by the Viet Minh." The dramatic play *Rescue of American Pilots* spread the news throughout the region, as the Viet Minh "sought to mobilize the population in support of its foreign initiatives."[5] It was the first act of POW/MIA politics in the Vietnam wars.

A decade later, with the United States heavily invested in France's doomed effort to retain possession of Indochina, Privates Doyle Morgan and Leonard Sroveck and Airmen Ciro Salas, Giacomo Appice, and Jerry Schuller became the first American prisoners of Vietnamese communists. Captured in June 1954, the five men spent ten weeks in Viet Minh custody. Upon their release, the Viet Minh broadcast their confession. "Since our capture we slowly came to realize American intervention in the Indochina war was against peoples fighting resolutely for independence," the men professed in language suspiciously florid for American GIs. "Had we realized the truth beforehand, we would not have agreed to come to this country."[6] Their repudiation of the war was the first of many such statements American POWs would make—voluntarily and involuntarily—over the next two decades.

As these episodes make clear, the leaders of the Vietnamese Communist Party practiced POW/MIA politics long before Nixon. Once its victims—Ho Chi Minh, Pham Van Dong, Vo Nguyen Giap, Truong Chinh, and Le Duc Tho were all held in colonial prisons in the 1930s—they became its masters as the escalation of U.S. forces in Vietnam led to a growing number of Americans in Vietnamese hands.[7] Three dozen Americans had been captured in Vietnam and Laos by the end of 1964, 83 more were captured in 1965, 106 in 1966, 189 in 1967, 162 in 1968, and 205 more by war's end.[8] As their numbers grew, their captors gained a potent public relations tool that they put to use quickly, frequently, and in sometimes brutal fashion.

In June 1965, South Vietnamese guerrillas announced the execution of Sergeant Harold Bennett in response to the South Vietnamese government's public execution of the communist saboteur Tran Van Dong. Three months later, NLF radio announced the deaths of Captain Humbert Versace and Sergeant Kenneth Roraback "in retaliation for the murder of three patriots in Danang" by the Saigon regime. Subsequent testimony suggests that these men were killed for insubordination or died from the hardships of war, but by linking their fates to Saigon's executions, the NLF politicized their deaths and pressed the United States to put a stop to its client state's worst excesses.[9] Alarmed, U.S. officials halted Saigon's public killings and called on the International Committee of the Red Cross (ICRC) to condemn such acts, which it did in October 1965, condemning the use of prisoners as "objects of retaliation." Rather than take sides, though, the ICRC urged "all authorities involved in an armed conflict" to abide by the Geneva Convention, which granted prisoners of the Saigon government the same protections against "violence to life and person" that it afforded Americans.[10]

Having halted the public executions, the NLF may have hoped to offset the resultant adverse publicity with the November release of Smith and McClure. Its 1965 vacillation may also reflect uncertainty over how to respond to the rapid influx of American combat forces.[11] Just as likely, the NLF made a virtue of necessity in releasing Smith and McClure. Due to the clandestine nature of its operations and constant American bombardment, the NLF had difficulty keeping prisoners concealed and alive, not to mention preventing their escape. Twenty percent of POWs in the South died, compared to 5 percent in the North, and 10 percent escaped. It is possible that Bennett, Versace, and Roraback were not executed at all, but succumbed after suffering abuse for their vocal support of the American invasion.[12] With Smith and McClure ready to express opposition to the war, it made sense to release them in hopes of achieving a propaganda victory rather than watch them die or escape.

In the North, the Democratic Republic of Vietnam (DRV) similarly used POWs to pressure U.S. policy makers. North Vietnam captured its first American on 5 August 1964 when Lieutenant Everett Alvarez was shot down while participating in Gulf of Tonkin reprisal attacks. From that day forward, the DRV would capture more Americans than the NLF, since the airmen shot down over North Vietnam were harder for U.S. forces to rescue than were lost or wounded foot soldiers in the South. And since its prisoners were aviators engaged in what DRV officials deemed to be an illegal war of aggression, North Vietnamese authorities threatened to prosecute them for war crimes. The DRV had signed the Geneva Convention in 1957 with the express reservation that it did not extend to "prisoners of war prosecuted for and convicted of war crimes." In early 1966, its Ministry of Foreign Affairs made the case against the Americans with a seventy-seven-page dossier entitled *US War Crimes in North Vietnam*.[13]

The State Department was sufficiently concerned by this development that it created the Interdepartmental Prisoner of War Committee and assigned Averell Harriman "supervision of Department actions concerning prisoners held by both sides in the conflict in Viet-Nam."[14] But neither President Lyndon Johnson nor his senior advisors were dissuaded from waging war on North Vietnam, which promised more POWs and further diplomatic wrangling over their fate. When Johnson attacked oil depots near

Hanoi and Haiphong in June 1966, DRV officials retaliated by marching American POWs through the streets of Hanoi, where they were mobbed by crowds chanting "death to you who have massacred our dear ones."[15] Since many of these men later reported that Vietnamese soldiers had saved them from angry mobs when they were shot down, the march seemed intended to threaten Americans in Washington more than those in Hanoi. No doubt, it was also meant to appease an angry population suffering under American bombs. The *Nation* dismissed it as "a standard technique of governments which are impotent to protect their people from air attacks," while the *National Review* concurred that the communists hoped to turn the POWs "into a special psywar weapons system" that could shield Hanoi from bombardment and aid in the "general world campaign to picture the U.S. as the blood-dripping aggressor."[16]

Still, if intelligent observers doubted that North Vietnam would carry out its threats, the performance and subsequent publication of war crimes charges in the Hanoi newspaper *Nhan Dan* rattled Washington. Harriman embarked on "a major diplomatic campaign to warn the DRV of the inadvisability of holding war crimes trials," asking the Soviet Union, Poland, India, Sweden, and the Vatican to intercede. Meanwhile, at the administration's behest, eighteen senators who had criticized the war, including William Fulbright, Eugene McCarthy, and George McGovern, released a statement advising North Vietnam to "refrain from any act of vengeance against American airmen" lest it incite "public demand for retaliation swift and sure, inflicting new levels of suffering and sorrow." The Senate Armed Services Committee chair, Richard Russell, vowed "the application of power that will make a desert of their country" should the Vietnamese execute more POWs. And UN secretary-general U Thant, Pope Paul VI, and Dr. Benjamin Spock spoke out against the plan. Johnson capped off this flurry of activity with a press conference where he promised to "react accordingly" should American prisoners be tried and convicted.[17]

By the time Johnson held his press conference, President Ho Chi Minh had begun to back away from the idea of prosecuting American POWs. On the same day that Johnson held his news conference, Ho replied to expressions of concern from the National Committee for a Sane Nuclear Policy and from socialist Norman Thomas, co-organizers of the November 1965 March for Peace, by cabling them that "the policy of the Government with regard to the enemies captured in war is a humanitarian policy."[18] Four days later, Ho abruptly informed CBS News that there was "no trial in view."[19]

Harriman's special assistant, Frank Sieverts, who would go on to become the only high-ranking official to handle POW matters in both the Johnson and Nixon administrations, cited this crisis as "an earlier example of how it was possible to use what I guess nowadays is called 'public diplomacy' to accomplish a goal" on behalf of POWs.[20] From his unique institutional vantage point, Sieverts saw more continuity than difference between this little-known episode and Nixon's vaunted POW campaign. Much like Nixon, Johnson used the threat to POWs to compel critics and opponents to close ranks behind his leadership without altering the policies that imperiled them in any fundamental way. But unlike Nixon, Johnson sensed the risks of POW politics and diplomacy. For a president unable to win the war and unwilling to end it, the passions that POWs inspired posed problems. Without hope of bringing them home, Johnson had little to gain and much to lose by focusing on POWs, so he avoided discussing them whenever possible and encouraged others to do the same.

But ignoring the POWs proved impossible because they swayed public opinion in such powerful ways. The *Nation* observed this phenomenon when it noted that those like Richard Russell behaved "as if they *wanted* the men to be put to death, so that their hawkish passions would be justified."[21] In the POWs, the war's supporters found a cause that could inspire Americans to pursue victory, or vengeance, at all costs. Conversely, for the antiwar movement, the POWs might dissuade Americans from continuing a war with such unforeseen and unending costs. The war's advocates always minimized the war's costs in favor of the dire consequences they predicted would follow defeat. But the plight of the POWs illustrated the war's toll in ways that Americans found difficult to minimize or ignore. By speaking out against the war that caused their captivity, its opponents could question its value while shielding themselves against charges of being un-American. Above all, though, Vietnamese communists focused attention on American POWs. Unlike Johnson, Nixon, the Congress, or the American people, they controlled the fate of these men. In a kind of good cop/bad cop routine, they alternately threatened and absolved POWs to turn public opinion against U.S. foreign policy.

The early release of cooperative POWs like Smith and McClure to antiwar activists was a key part of that strategy. After Ho rescinded the threat of war crimes trials, the DRV and the NLF regularly released Americans to foster good will and encourage negotiations. In February 1967, the NLF placed Sergeant Sammie Womack and Private Charles Crafts on a civilian bus to freedom.[22] In November, it released Sergeants Edward Johnson, Daniel Pitzer, and James Jackson, Jr., to SDS leader Tom Hayden. And in January 1968, it released Private Luis Ortiz-Rivera and Lance Corporal Jose Agosto-Santos in return for six communist prisoners. At the same time, the DRV invited David Dellinger of the National Mobilization Committee to End the War in Vietnam, popularly known as "the Mobe," to Hanoi to receive the first POWs released from the North. Dellinger asked antiwar activists Daniel Berrigan and Howard Zinn to go in his place, and in the midst of the Tet Offensive, they took custody of Major Norris Overly, Captain Jon Black, and Lieutenant David Matheny. Such rapid-fire releases on the eve of the offensive has invited speculation that they were intended as "diversions or propaganda enhancements" to maximize its effect.[23]

Whether or not this is true, the early releases clearly marked a determination to insert POWs into international debate on the war. The releases only intensified as that debate reached its climax. In August 1968, the DRV released Majors James Low and Fred Thompson and Captain Joe Carpenter to the pacifist American Friends Service Committee.[24] After Nixon's election, the NLF released eleven captives in December and fifteen more in early 1969 to induce the United States to negotiate over POWs as a means of gaining diplomatic recognition. And in August 1969, the DRV released Seaman Douglas Hegdahl, Lieutenant Robert Frishman, and Captain Wesley Rumble to the Mobe's Rennie Davis.[25]

In a 1966 conversation at Hoa Lo prison, the Marxist intellectual Nguyen Khac Vien told Commander James Stockdale that he and his fellow POWs would be used to end the war, leaving Stockdale convinced that "we were a major factor in the strategy of the Vietnamese. We would be, sort of, a branch of the American antiwar movement."[26] Indeed, a small "peace committee" formed among Americans inside North Vietnamese prisons, and a number of those granted early release spoke favorably of their captors.[27] Not all of those released denounced the war, however, and many who did so later recanted, but those who acknowledged U.S. aggression were more likely to be released than those who refused, and enlisted men and racial minorities in the South were favored over the predominately white officers and aviators in the North.[28] In this way, the communists did what they could to reinforce the propaganda that invariably accompanied early releases in party newspapers and radio broadcasts. And by releasing many of these men to antiwar activists, the DRV and the NLF enlisted their support in sending a message to the American people.

Prisoner releases communicated that the enemy could give Americans something they dearly wanted in return for U.S. withdrawal. They implied that the only thing standing in the way of a general prisoner release and an end to the war was U.S. government intransigence. Robert Sheer, who participated in the August 1968 handover, argued that "those who are working for peace have better success in negotiating than the State Department and the Pentagon, and that is obviously because the Government is not willing to make concessions."[29] "The obvious solution to the POW problem is to end the war," the Joe Hill Collective argued in an antiwar pamphlet.[30] Until that happened, Senator McGovern told delegates to the Paris talks in 1971, POW releases "unquestionably strengthened the efforts of those of us in this country who are working for a complete U.S. withdrawal."[31]

As McGovern's crushing electoral defeat in the 1972 presidential election made clear, POW propaganda was not an unalloyed benefit for the antiwar Left. The heavy-handedness of POW propaganda, involving prisoners in coercive press conferences and parades and making them props for visiting peace delegations, outraged many Americans and made pariahs of most who participated in such spectacles. American POWs resulted from combat, and the political and diplomatic purposes that the release of POWs served were more combative and less humanitarian than the peace movement was willing to admit. POW propaganda was meant not just to win friends but to demoralize foes—in Vietnam, the United States, and the wider world. *Nhan Dan* instructed its readers to make every effort to capture American pilots since "to lose one of these 'precious sons'" created "anxiety over losing someone whose worth cannot be calculated in terms of money, such as military secrets which he possesses and the loss of morale by his friends over his disappearance."[32]

But if the effect of POW propaganda on Americans was complicated, what is clear is that the communists were the first to politicize American POWs. Subsequent steps on the part of the U.S. government and POW/MIA activists were *responses* to Vietnamese actions. Americans responded in part because they worried about the well-being of American POWs and deemed it inhumane to enlist them in enemy propaganda. But they also reacted because POW propaganda made clear the enemy's determination to control the war and dictate the peace despite American military might. "We were always working under the assumption that if you just kept hitting the enemy hard enough he would quit," General Douglas Kinnard later confessed, "but the assumption was totally wrong. The enemy was not going to quit, no matter how good our statistics looked.... While we had the power, it turned out they had the will."[33] They also had the prisoners; the capture, coercion, conversion, and politicization of American soldiers and airmen was one clear sign that the enemy was stronger than imagined. In capturing and releasing American prisoners, the Vietnamese demonstrated not just their humanity and generosity but their willpower and determination. Anything that heightened concern for POWs, including early release, strengthened those who alone had the power to release them.

This 1967 North Vietnamese postage stamp illustrates what Tom Engelhardt has called an "iconography of triumph," which made American POWs submitting to Vietnamese guards representative of ultimate Vietnamese victory.

"Help Us with the Anti-Propaganda Campaign against Hanoi's Propaganda Campaign"

Richard Nixon tried to defy this calculus with his "Go Public" campaign, which began in May 1969 when Secretary of Defense Melvin Laird called a press conference to complain that, although "the North Vietnamese have claimed that they are treating our men humanely," there was "clear evidence that this is not the case." "The North Vietnamese and the Viet Cong have never identified the names of all the U.S. prisoners whom they hold," Laird insisted, nor had they complied with other requirements of the Geneva Convention. He concluded with a call for "the prompt release of all American prisoners," which was soon a staple of U.S. rhetoric at the Paris peace talks.[34]

Publicizing the plight of American POWs represented one of many attempts on the part of the incoming administration to seize the initiative in Vietnam and regain the moral high ground from the war's critics. In countless bull sessions with his staff and in compulsive notes to himself, Nixon adopted the word "go" as his mantra in the summer of 1969, ordering himself to "go for broke...get going, take risks, be exciting....Now is the time to go."[35] His obsessive pursuit of the "big play" led him to "go public" on the abuse of American prisoners in order to throw his opponents on the defensive. But, as happened so often in his presidency, Nixon's killer instincts played into his enemies' hands. As an American staffer at the Paris peace talks told the Senate Select Committee on POW/MIA Affairs years later, the Vietnamese fought the war "like jujitsu, where you use the superior power of the enemy to force him to tumble over himself. You let him lunge at you then you just trip him."[36] In that sense, seizing on the POW/

MIA issue was less a shrewd gambit, as some would have it, than another desperate lunge that would, like all of the others, result in a further loss of leverage and control.

Nothing was more important to the Go Public campaign than the emergence of POW and MIA families in public discourse on the war. The attractive, articulate, highly sympathetic wives and mothers of the career officers who made up the bulk of the POW/MIA population became an outspoken presence in the war's final phase, "exerting political influence far out of proportion to [their] small number."[37] Since most of these women—fathers were discouraged from playing an active part—supported Nixon's public relations push, at least at the start, administration critics at the time and since attributed their mobilization to his administration. Laird and his assistant secretary of defense for public affairs, Richard Capen, laid the basis for this view by taking credit for bringing the families "together for the first time" through a series of nationwide briefings in the summer of 1969. "A conscious decision was made by me," Laird boasted, "that we go forward and make the whole question of prisoners of war held by North Vietnam [into] a public matter."[38]

Yet, what became the National League of Families of American Prisoners and Missing in Southeast Asia had begun to take shape in 1966, well before Nixon and Laird, when Sybil Stockdale, wife of James Stockdale, contacted other POW wives in the San Diego area to share information and support. Because many of the war's prisoners were aviators based out of San Diego's naval and marine bases, potential recruits were close at hand. By 1967, she had organized thirty-three women into what one early member called a "sorority."[39]

As the wives of military officers, these women shared social networks that reinforced their geographic proximity. They attended the same functions, served on the same boards, shopped in the same stores, sent their children to the same schools, shared the same news, and were tightly integrated into military life. When their husbands disappeared over North Vietnam, Stockdale and her cohort found themselves isolated and adrift. As walking reminders of war's risks, they soon learned that "other squadron wives don't feel comfortable with us around."[40] Stripped of their place in the military they called home, they sought community in each other. In San Diego, Virginia Beach, Omaha, and other pockets of military aviation across the country, they formed new bonds within but distinct from their old world.[41]

"The last generation of hat-and-glove military wives," these women hardly seemed likely to engage in political activism.[42] Yet most were well educated, well connected, and well versed in military politics. They knew or soon learned how to pressure the Pentagon into providing them with services and information. Here too, Stockdale was extraordinary and instructive. A woman of prodigious talent and energy, she had earned a master's degree from Stanford University in 1959 while having two children (and two more later) and worked as a full-time teacher once her youngest son started school. While working and raising four boys by herself, she also found time to organize the National League of Families, engage in wartime espionage, and lobby national leaders.

In 1966, Stockdale permitted military authorities to transform her correspondence with her husband into a covert communications channel using invisible inks, allowing Jim to report on conditions inside North Vietnamese prisons without drawing the ire of Vietnamese censors. His letters to her, which she shared with defense officials, made her keenly aware of the hardships POWs faced.[43] Until 1969, the prisoners were routinely tortured to extract intelligence and to provide propaganda.[44] Stockdale's awareness of Jim's suffering imparted an urgency to her efforts that government officials seldom shared and gave her leverage to make demands on them, including a private luncheon with Chief of Naval Operations admiral Thomas Moorer in August 1967. "For the first time I had focused the attention of Jim's leaders more clearly on his dire situation," she exulted after their meeting.[45] But when he and others around President Johnson proved less responsive than she hoped, she took steps to have them replaced.

Stockdale's frustration led her to intervene in the 1968 presidential election. Following the prisoner release in August of that year, she complained to Harriman about North Vietnam's use of such acts for propaganda and was outraged when he said that the release was "a gesture of good will" that he hoped would lead to "further releases." Knowing her husband was being tortured to denounce the war, it angered her that the enemy rewarded those who did so. Desirous of a more hard-line approach, she gave an interview to the *San Diego Union* in October in hopes of swaying voters in Nixon's favor. Though ostensibly nonpartisan, she expressed impatience at the war's lack of progress and, in the interview's most striking passage, appealed to U.S. officials to "help us with the anti-propaganda campaign against Hanoi's propaganda campaign."[46]

When Nixon prevailed, Stockdale called on all of her contacts, including assistance from California governor Ronald Reagan, to generate 2,000 telegrams to the new president on his first day in office, urging him to make POWs a top priority. He replied to each one, and so began his bid to turn American POWs to his advantage.[47] Some POW/MIA families later claimed that their early efforts convinced the incoming administration that "they'd best facilitate and try to work with the families lest it get completely out of control."[48] This overstates the case. Instead of fearing the nascent League of Families, Nixon's staff recognized it as a potential ally that could help him to seize control of an issue that had been dominated by his enemies. Joseph Lelyveld's 1971 assessment for the *New York Times Magazine* strikes the right balance: "the Administration did not start—and probably could not have prevented—the campaign by the [POW] wives... but there is no doubt that it helped orchestrate their efforts."[49] As Lelyveld and those who followed him made clear, the Nixon administration did all it could to foster a larger, more militant league, beginning with a twenty-city tour by the State Department and the Department of Defense that briefed 1,400 POW and MIA relatives in the summer of 1969, knitting together Stockdale's San Diego group and a similar Virginia Beach group with POW/MIA families across the country.[50]

Yet despite the league's growth, and the ambitions of its administration allies, the July 1969 announcement that Hanoi would release three more Americans to antiwar activists showed how little Nixon's election had changed things: the war continued unabated and U.S. prisoners remained in Vietnamese hands. "We have no alternative if we want our men back," Undersecretary of State Elliot Richardson told Vice President Spiro Agnew when he complained about the arrangement. To object would cause "fruitless public controversy." Agnew admitted that "humanitarian considerations probably outweigh the obvious propaganda advantages conceded to the enemy," but feared that such acts "undermine confidence in the strength and will of the government and people of the United States."[51]

As the massive Vietnam Moratorium scheduled for mid-October and the Mobilization against the War to follow in mid-November threatened to further undermine that confidence through the largest antiwar demonstrations in American history, Nixon ordered his staff to "*do something.*"[52] Casting about for a counteroffensive, the White House announced that Nixon would address the nation on 3 November. On that evening, he offered no new diplomatic or military initiatives. Instead, he called to life "the great silent majority." Describing a conflict between a "vocal minority" and a "silent majority," Nixon recast the war as a struggle between Americans. "North Vietnam cannot defeat or humiliate the United States," he insisted, "only Americans can do that." By erasing the Vietnamese from his equation and reframing the war in terms of political speech, he encouraged Americans to fight each other. "It was a speech that seemed to be designed not to persuade the opposition but to overwhelm it," James Reston wrote in his analysis for the *New York Times*, "and the chances are that this will merely divide and polarize the debaters in the United States, without bringing the enemy into serious negotiations."[53]

While Nixon applauded taciturn Americans, he knew that "in a war of words, a 'silent majority,' no matter how large, would be ineffective."[54] In the months before the speech, his staff had searched for a way to make it "the occasion for the birth of a movement." They wanted to "give ordinary people who need to expend energy on 'helping to end the war' something to be *for*"; something "simple and reasonable and something everyone can understand"; "something to do," like "join a committee," "sign a petition," "hold a rally," "march in a parade," or "picket the UN."[55] "We need bumper stickers," declared White House aide Lyn Nofziger.[56]

POWs were the obvious choice. An estimated 50 million POW/MIA bumper stickers were sold in the next four years as were 135 million POW/MIA stamps.[57] Unlike the president, the POWs and their families had "the sympathy of just about everybody these days," as an aide put it in October 1969, and Nixon was eager to enlist them in his silent majority.[58] By associating himself with their cause, he would rally voters to his side and marginalize the antiwar movement. "We all know that there is disagreement in this country about the war in Vietnam," he admitted at a White House meeting with POW wives and mothers in December, but "on this issue, the treatment of prisoners of war, there can be and there should be no disagreement."[59]

"Hanoi May Use Prisoners...to Squeeze a Timetable Out of Us"

So long as Go Public was limited to expressions of concern for POWs and their families, Americans were united and eager to take part. The millions of POW/MIA bumper stickers and ID bracelets they purchased, the countless petitions they signed and letters they wrote, the rallies they attended, and the packages and donations they sent in support of POWs showed their concern. Nixon often used these expressions as evidence of the silent majority's size and support. But sympathy for POWs and their families did not translate into universal support for Nixon or the war, as the massive fall demonstrations against the war and its steadily declining support in the polls made clear. When Nixon tried to equate the two, he encountered resistance from the Vietnamese, the antiwar movement, and, eventually, some POW/MIA families.

In word and deed, the Vietnamese were quick to respond to Nixon's Go Public campaign. "The U.S. government is using the 'prisoner of war issue,'" DRV premier Pham Van Dong wrote to Senator William Fulbright in late 1970, "to cover up its odious crimes against the Vietnamese people, its war acts against the Democratic Republic of Viet Nam, and its schemes to prolong and extend the war of aggression."[60] Well before then, Dong and his southern compatriots had sought to counter Nixon's schemes with another round of early releases. To show support for the moratorium and the Mobe, the DRV had freed Hegdahl, Frishman, and Rumble in August, while the NLF released Private Jessie Harris in October, then Private First Class James Strickland, Private Coy Tinsley, and Specialist 4 Willie Watkins in November, and finally Warrant Officer Michael Peterson and Sergeant Vernon Shepard in December.[61] The rapid-fire releases bolstered the fall demonstrations and undermined administration rhetoric, as when Strickland, Tinsley, and Watkins praised their former captors and questioned the war from the front page of the *Chicago Tribune* on the same day that Nixon's ally H. Ross Perot placed a full-page advertisement entitled "United We Stand: The Majority Speaks" inside the newspaper.[62]

Likewise, the antiwar movement frustrated official efforts to equate support for POWs with support for the war. Days after the "silent majority" speech, Rennie Davis and David Dellinger produced the first list of Americans in North Vietnam, courtesy of the North Vietnamese delegation to the Paris talks.[63] Two weeks later, Dellinger provided a more extensive list of 59 prisoners, including 5 men previously listed as MIA. Together with antiwar activist Cora Weiss, he formed the Committee of Liaison with Families of Servicemen Detained in North Vietnam (COLIAFAM) in January 1970, thereby institutionalizing the antiwar presence in POW politics. It soon demonstrated results, including an updated list of 156 POWs in January, followed by a more complete list of 335 names in April, and it tripled the volume of prisoner mail in 1970 over its 1969 level.[64] Until war's end, COLIAFAM traveled to Hanoi on a monthly basis to deliver and retrieve prisoner mail.[65] By acting as a courier, it helped North Vietnam to bypass official channels and direct its POW propaganda directly at the American people. As it passed mail and information to POW families, the press, and the public, COLIAFAM reminded them that "the safe return of U.S. servicemen...can only come with a decision on the part of the U.S. government to completely withdraw from Vietnam."[66]

The logic of this message was readily apparent to most observers, irrespective of their views on the war. Even for Nixon's supporters, it made more sense than the president's plan to "get this issue separated out and progress made on it prior to the time that we reach a complete settlement of the war."[67] When he told POW/MIA wives and mothers that "he would try to separate the prisoner issue from the war" at their December 1969 White House meeting, Sybil Stockdale recalled thinking, "[T]hat didn't make any sense to me. How could you separate one from the other when one was an integral part of the other?"[68] Those less inclined to give him the benefit of the doubt suspected that Nixon was only seeking a diversion to prolong the war. Their suspicions were confirmed in February 1971 when he vowed: "as long as the North Vietnamese have any Americans as prisoners of war, there will be Americans in South Vietnam and enough Americans to give them an incentive to release the prisoners."[69] This Catch-22 was a formula for endless war. "As long as there is one American being held prisoner by North Vietnam," Nixon told the *Los Angeles Times* in April, "we are going to retain that force," adding, "I think it will work in the end."[70]

He was wrong; his attempt to prolong the war indefinitely failed. By making POWs the rationale for war, Nixon only increased their value and raised more pressing questions as to why he did not withdraw in order to win their return. His adversaries capitalized on the faulty logic of his position by offering POWs in exchange for peace. Frank Sieverts at the State Department had warned in June 1970, "Hanoi may use prisoners explicitly to try to squeeze a timetable out of us," but by then the administration was too heavily invested to avoid the trap it had set for itself.[71] The trap was sprung in September when Madame Nguyen Thi Binh of the Provisional Revolutionary Government offered to "engage at once in discussions" concerning the release of POWs in return for complete U.S. withdrawal from Vietnam by 30 June 1971.[72] For the rest of the war, Binh and her DRV counterparts, Le Duc Tho and Xuan Thuy, used the groundswell of support for American POWs to make their case. In a July 1971 interview, Tho told the *New York Times* that "all American prisoners may promptly return to their homes" with the "withdrawal of all American forces from Vietnam."[73] Outplayed, Henry Kissinger seethed "we will not settle the war just for prisoners" at their next secret meeting.[74] But he could hardly say this publicly, nor expose the DRV's private demands that Nixon oust President Nguyen Van Thieu in Saigon, without exposing Nixon's own priorities.[75] Unwilling to admit that they valued Thieu's survival over the return of American prisoners, administration officials could only complain, as Agnew did, that "North Vietnam thinks that by holding our men hostages, they can compel the President to cave in to their demands—demands for a United States pullout, abandonment of the present elected government of South Vietnam, an end to all U.S. military activity."[76]

Most Americans no longer saw an alternative to this outcome. A May 1971 Harris poll found that 60 percent of Americans favored withdrawal from Vietnam even if it meant the collapse of the Saigon government. A growing number of POW/MIA families shared this view. In March, MIA wife Mrs. Tom Beyer told the president that she was "fed up (to say the least) with the way the Missing and Prisoner of War situation is being handled. Anyone in their right mind knows that the only way the prisoners will be released is when there is a *complete* withdrawal of our troops from Southeast Asia."[77] She was not alone. In April, 123 dissidents calling themselves POW/MIA Families for Immediate Release placed an ad in the *Washington Post* demanding a timetable for withdrawal.[78] By October, the group had 350 members, despite the Pentagon's refusal to mail its membership materials to POW/MIA families, something it did routinely for the National League of Families.[79] Shortly thereafter, a larger, more conservative family group called the Ad Hoc Committee for POWs and MIAs placed another ad in the *Post*, which called on Nixon to announce his intention to remove all U.S. forces from Vietnam within 150 days of the communists' agreement to repatriate American POWs.[80] "It shook me up when the administration made it appear we were [in Vietnam] because of the POWs," MIA wife Mrs. Randolph Ford told a reporter. "I resent using the POWs as an excuse to stay in Vietnam."[81] The national coordinator for POW/MIA Families for Immediate Release, POW wife Alice Cronin, urged "all Congressmen to support the POWs by voting to cut off funds for the war, contingent *only* on guarantee of the safety of withdrawing troops and release of the prisoners."[82]

Though the leaders of the National League of Families steadfastly opposed such a plan, dissenting families were a powerful voice for peace in the war's final years. After hearing POW wife Mary Anne Fuller call for "total withdrawal," Representative Charles Bennett, "by conviction a Hawk," told Nixon, "we have now gone so far in the direction of ending our participation in the war that it makes more sense to me to remove ourselves entirely as promptly as we can from South Vietnam in a way in which we can secure the prisoners of war."[83] Such conversions led Republican National Committee chair Bob Dole, himself an early supporter of the Go Public campaign, to reverse himself on the importance of POWs. "We don't want to get out just for the prisoners," he told reporters in 1971. "They're very important, but they represent less than one half of one percent of the Americans who've died in South Vietnam."[84]

Dole's backtracking illustrates how badly the Nixon administration was outmaneuvered on the POW/MIA issue. The plight of the POWs and MIAs it had worked so hard to publicize only added to the list of reasons to end the war. What's more, it strengthened the bargaining position of those who held them captive and highlighted the activities of those in the antiwar movement working to bring them home. If Go Public began a counteroffensive to POW/MIA initiatives already under way from those quarters, enlisting millions of Americans in POW/MIA politics who otherwise might not have participated, there is little evidence to suggest that support for POWs translated into renewed support for the war, aside from the unsubstantiated claims of the Nixon administration.

"All Our Sons in Vietnam Are POWs"

American POWs dominated political discourse and public diplomacy on the war after 1968. "The wounded, the dying, and the dead went virtually unnoticed," Jonathan Schell wrote in his 1975 instant history of the Nixon presidency, "as attention was focused on the prisoners of war." "Following the President's lead," Schell continued, "people began to speak as though the North Vietnamese had kidnapped four hundred Americans and the United States had gone to war to retrieve them." "They became the objects of a virtual cult, and many people were persuaded that the United States was fighting to get its prisoners back."[85]

Such Nixon-centric analysis has long dominated scholarship on the POW/MIA issue, just as Nixon has dominated scholarship on the war's end. But Nixon's was not the only voice in POW/MIA politics. "All kinds of people have been trying to justify their causes in the name of the POW families," one POW wife complained.[86] "Our husbands were used to fight the war, and we have been used as a reason to keep fighting," another echoed. "Now we are being used as a reason to get out of the war, but the men are still there."[87] Captive to a war without end, these men and their families became stand-ins for the countless Americans who had lost faith in the war but could not escape it. "The truth of the matter is that all our sons in Vietnam are POWs," one POW mother wrote to Another Mother for Peace. "We cannot for one moment forget the danger and deprivation which the rest of our 337,900 sons in Vietnam face daily."[88]

The Vietnamese who fought the Americans made sure not to let them forget. Alternately threatening and releasing POWs, they did all they could to keep them in the public eye. They did so well before Nixon got involved and continued to do so until the war's end. Their initiatives have gone largely unrecognized in part because vital evidence was unavailable for research until the Senate Select Committee on POW/MIA Affairs ordered "the most rapid and comprehensive declassification of materials on a single subject in American history" during its 1991–1993 tenure.[89] National security files released at the Gerald Ford Presidential Library in 2000 and from the Nixon Presidential Materials Collection in 2005, along with official histories from the late 1990s shed additional light on the subject, while Vietnamese records from the Paris peace talks appeared in English translation in 1996, giving historians access to evidence of POW diplomacy from the other side.[90]

Yet new evidence has been slow to prompt a reappraisal of POW/MIA politics. Since the late 1990s, Jeffrey Kimball and Larry Berman have penned damning accounts of Nixon's handling of the war that, among other things, detail intense diplomatic wrangling over POWs. Those details suggest greater Vietnamese agency than previously recognized. But neither historian emphasizes this revision nor explores its implications, in part because new evidence of Vietnamese maneuvers pales next to fresh evidence of Nixon's misdeeds, which consume most of their attention. Their books indicate that evidentiary advances may only reinforce scholars' preoccupation with Nixon by offering an inexhaustible record of his abuses of power. Both are so intent on exposing Nixon's plots, tricks, and schemes that they reinforce his reputation as a conniving genius who single-handedly gave rise to POW/MIA politics and used it to dominate his enemies.

Even those who reject the narcissism of the "silent majority" speech— that North Vietnam did not defeat the United States because only Americans could do that—have eagerly engaged in the internecine war of words it inspired. Faced with the national revanchism and historical revisionism that began with Nixon's election and intensified after he left office, scholars have identified the still-ubiquitous POW/MIA issue as an ideological weapon in an ongoing war of ideas. "America's vision of the war was being transformed," Franklin tells us, as real images of the war's horrors were "replaced by simulated images of American POWs in the savage hands of Asian Communists."[91] Such subrogation not only prolonged the war, according to this view, it also gave rise to the narratives of American victimization that now dominate public memory. Those writing in opposition to such trends have been disinclined to revisit an interpretation that neatly reveals the issue's reactionary roots, especially when the archives offer abundant new evidence of Nixon's manipulation with every declassification.

The idea that Vietnamese communists and U.S. antiwar activists played leading parts in POW/MIA politics complicates a received narrative that presents these groups as victims of Nixon's wars. Some may feel that such an analysis ignores power imbalances that make Nixon's actions more significant than those of his opponents. But if we take local and transnational perspectives seriously, we must acknowledge that grassroots and international actors had the power to thwart U.S. policy makers.

"Because his opposition was so fierce and effective and dedicated," Nixon's chief of staff, H. R. Haldeman, later lamented, "Nixon felt that we had to be fiercer, more effective, and more dedicated... Inevitably, this effort became unbalanced itself. We pushed too hard and overplayed our hand. Part of this was due to our ineptitude compared to the skill of the opposition."[92] Historians need not accept the Nixon administration's self-pitying paranoia to take Haldeman's point. Nixon could no more control the fate of American POWs than he could dictate the war's outcome. To understand the vital role the former played in the latter, we must confront a complicated history in which Vietnamese were both victors and victims, and Americans paid a heavy price for their own aggression.

In a sense, the massive outpouring of public concern for POWs and MIAs in the war's last years represented the final repudiation of the war in Vietnam. A war that was entered into, explained, justified, measured, and contested with arguments of Byzantine complexity had been reduced, in the end, to a hostage negotiation, and all that still mattered was getting the prisoners home. The suffering of POWs supplemented rather than supplanted other negative images of the war, dramatizing the way it endangered all it touched. The thought of American POWs and their families suffering so much for so long for so little purpose resonated with war-weary Americans who themselves felt captive to the war. The playing of POW/MIA politics was hardly Nixon's trump card in his bid to prolong the war. If anything, participation in POW/MIA politics convinced the no-longer-silent majority that the war in Vietnam was not worth the price; there were more pressing enemies to fight at home.

NOTES

1. George E. Smith, *P.O.W.: Two Years with the Viet Cong* (Berkeley, Calif.: Ramparts, 1971), 302n16; Seymour Topping, "Asian Communists Sure Public Opinion in U.S. Will Force War's End," *New York Times*, 28 November 1965, 1, 87.

2. Smith, *P.O.W.*, 281, 304n19; "Two Freed G.I.'s Say U.S. Should Quit Vietnam," *New York Times*, 1 December 1965, 1.

3. Quotes, taken in order, from H. Bruce Franklin, *M.I.A.; or, Mythmaking in America*, rev. ed. (New Brunswick, N.J.: Rutgers University Press, 1993), 40, 48; Neil Sheehan, "Prisoners of the Past," *New Yorker*, 24 May 1993, 45; Gerald Nicosia, *Home to War: A History of the Vietnam Veterans' Movement* (New York: Crown, 2001), 155–56; Jeffrey Kimball, *Nixon's Vietnam War* (Lawrence: University Press of Kansas, 1998), 167; Robert Schulzinger, *A Time for War: The United States and Vietnam, 1941–1975* (New York: Oxford University Press, 1997), 293.

4. My research suggests that Vietnamese communist forces freed fifty-seven American captives between 1954 and the general prisoner release in 1973. I arrived at this figure by subtracting foreign nationals and prisoners released by Cambodia and Laos from the comprehensive list of "U.S. Personnel Captured in Southeast Asia, 1961–1973 (and Selected Foreign Nationals)," in Stuart I. Rochester and Frederick Kiley, *Honor Bound: The History of American Prisoners of War in Southeast Asia, 1961–1973* (Annapolis, Md.: Naval Institute Press, 1999), appendix 3, 600–620, using contemporary news reports to confirm the details of early releases and adding the five Americans released by the Viet Minh in 1954.

5. Mark Philip Bradley, *Imagining Vietnam and America: The Making of Postcolonial Vietnam, 1919–1950* (Chapel Hill: University of North Carolina Press, 2000), 122–23; William J. Duiker, *Sacred War: Nationalism and Revolution in a Divided Vietnam* (Boston: McGraw-Hill, 1995), 43–44.

6. Rochester and Kiley, *Honor Bound*, 25–27.

7. Ho Chi Minh was a prisoner of British authorities in Hong Kong, while the others mentioned here were in French colonial prisons. See Peter Zinoman, *The Colonial Bastille: A History of Imprisonment in Vietnam, 1862–1940* (Berkeley: University of California Press, 2001), 300.

8. Rochester and Kiley, *Honor Bound*, appendix 3, 600–620.

9. Ibid., 69–70, 235, 245.

10. Vernon E. Davis, *The Long Road Home: U.S. Prisoner of War Policy and Planning in Southeast Asia* (Washington, D.C.: Office of the Secretary of Defense, 2001), 60–61.

11. Debate over whether to respond to the U.S. escalation with force or diplomacy was raging within the Vietnamese Communist Party throughout the latter half of 1965. See Robert K. Brigham, *Guerrilla Diplomacy: The NLF's Foreign Relations and the Viet Nam War* (Ithaca, N.Y.: Cornell University Press, 1999), chapter 3.

12. Rochester and Kiley, *Honor Bound*, 67, 228–45.

13. Democratic Republic of Vietnam, Ministry of Foreign Affairs, *US War Crimes in North VietNam*, February 1966, discussed in Rochester and Kiley, 192.

14. Davis, *The Long Road Home*, 68–74.

15. "Hanoi's Kind of Escalation," *Time*, 22 July 1966, 12.

16. "An Instructive Episode," *Nation*, 8 August 1966, 108; James Burnham, "Hanoi's Special Weapons System," *National Review*, 9 August 1966, 765.

17. Davis, *The Long Road Home*, 79–80; "18 Senate 'Doves' Urge Hanoi Spare Captured Pilots," *New York Times*, 16 July 1966, 1, 3; "Thant Bids Hanoi Spare U.S. Fliers," *New York Times*, 17 July 1966, 1, 8; "An Instructive Episode," *Nation*, 108.

18. "Trial and Error?" *Newsweek*, 1 August 1966, 36.

19. "An Instructive Episode," *Nation*, 108; Davis, *The Long Road Home*, 83–84.

20. Deposition of Frank Sieverts, 1 May 1992, Transcripts of Depositions, Records of the Senate Select Committee on POW/MIA Affairs, 102nd Congress, 1991–1993, Records of the U.S. Senate, RG 46, National Archives, Washington, D.C., 30–31.

272 Was's End and Endless Wars

21. "An Instructive Episode," *Nation*, 108 (italics in original); see also "The Endangered Prisoners," *New York Times*, 17 July 1966, 10E.

22. Rochester and Kiley, *Honor Bound*, 260.

23. Davis, *The Long Road Home*, 101–7; Rochester and Kiley, *Honor Bound*, 449.

24. Davis, *The Long Road Home*, 110–12.

25. Rochester and Kiley, *Honor Bound*, 373–74, 477.

26. Freida Lee Mock and Terry Sanders, *Return with Honor* (American Film Foundation, 1998); Jim Stockdale and Sybil Stockdale, *In Love and War: The Story of a Family's Ordeal and Sacrifice during the Vietnam Years* (New York: Harper & Row, 1984), 179–82.

27. Craig Howes, *Voices of the Vietnam POWs: Witnesses to Their Fight* (New York: Oxford University Press, 1993), 205–31.

28. Rochester and Kiley, *Honor Bound*, 173–75, 239.

29. Quoted in "Three U.S. Pilots Arrive in Laos From Hanoi," *New York Times*, 3 August 1968, 1, 7.

30. Joe Hill Collective, "POWs—The Big Lie," n.d. [1971], unmarked folder, Box 25, VIVA Collection, Kent State Archives, Kent, Ohio.

31. Larry Berman, *No Peace, No Honor: Nixon, Kissinger and Betrayal in Vietnam* (New York: Free Press, 2001), 101.

32. Translated text of "Practical Military Matters" column titled "Capturing Parachuting Pilots," in *Quan Doi Nhan Dan*, 5 December 1970, folder 1, Box 2, Records Received: State Department, Selected Records of Frank A. Sieverts, Records of the Senate Select Committee on POW/MIA Affairs, 102nd Congress, 1991–1993, Records of the U.S. Senate, RG 46, National Archives, Washington, D.C.

33. Quoted in Christian Appy, *Patriots: The Vietnam War Remembered from All Sides* (New York: Penguin, 2003), 322.

34. Quoted in Davis, *The Long Road Home*, 202.

35. Kimball, *Nixon's Vietnam War*, 160–61.

36. Berman, *No Peace, No Honor*, 44.

37. Franklin, *M.I.A.*, 49–50.

38. Joseph Lelyveld, "Dear President Nixon—the P.O.W. Families," *New York Times Magazine*, 3 October 1971, 56; Davis, *The Long Road Home*, 242; George C. Wilson, "POWs Caught in Swirl of U.S. Politics," *Washington Post*, 10 September 1972, A2.

39. House Subcommittee on National Security Policy and Scientific Developments of the Committee on Foreign Affairs, *American Prisoners of War in Southeast Asia, 1970: Hearings before the Subcommittee on National Security Policy and Scientific Developments of the Committee on Foreign Affairs*, 91st Cong., 2nd sess., 29 April, 1 May, 6 May 1970 (Washington, D.C.: U.S. Government Printing Office), 60–61; Douglas L. Clarke, *The Missing Man: Politics and the MIA* (Washington, D.C.: National Defense University Press, 1979), 31.

40. Judy Klemesrud, "Navy Wives Who Find Comfort in Sharing a Common Anguish," *New York Times*, 25 August 1970, 36M.

41. Louise Mulligan formed a similar group in Virginia Beach in 1966. Stockdale's and Mulligan's groups merged with other, smaller cells when the league was formally incorporated in 1970. Barbara Mullen Keenan, *Every Effort: A True Story* (New York: St. Martin's, 1986), 44.

42. Donna Moreau, *Waiting Wives: The Story of Schilling Manor, Home Front to the Vietnam War* (New York: Atria, 2005), xv; Mullen Keenan, *Every Effort*, 88–89.

43. Stockdale and Stockdale, *In Love and War*, 131–48, 194–98.

44. For a balanced treatment of the explosive subject of torture, see Howes, *Voices of the Vietnam POWs*, chapter 3.

45. Stockdale and Stockdale, *In Love and War*, 52, 203, 222.

46. Beverly Beyette, "Navy Wife Keeps Vigil for Captive Pilot," *San Diego Union*, 27 October 1968, 1, 8.

47. Memo from William Rogers to Richard Nixon, 27 January 1969, folder ND 18-3, Prisoners [1969–1970], Box 1, White House Central Files, Nixon Presidential Materials Staff, National Archives at College Park, Maryland; Stockdale and Stockdale, *In Love and War*, 303–4.

48. Ann Mills Griffiths, interview with the author, tape recording, Washington, D.C., 8 November 2000.

49. Lelyveld, "Dear President Nixon—the P.O.W. Families," 56.

50. Davis, *The Long Road Home*, 242.

51. Quoted in ibid., 231–33.

52. Stephen E. Ambrose, *Nixon: The Triumph of a Politician, 1961–1972*, vol. 2 (New York: Simon and Schuster, 1989), 303; Kimball, *Nixon's Vietnam War*, 161 (italics in original).

53. James Reston, "Nixon Makes His Stand," *New York Times*, 4 November 1969, 1, 17.

54. Peter N. Carroll, *It Seemed like Nothing Happened: America in the 1970s* (New Brunswick, N.J.: Rutgers University Press, 1990), 6.

55. Memo from William Safire to H. R. Haldeman, 22 October 1969, folder: Memoranda Received October–December 1969, Box 8, White House Special Files, Alexander P. Butterfield Correspondence File, Nixon Presidential Materials Staff, National Archives at College Park, Maryland.

56. Memo from Lyn Nofziger to Alex Butterfield, 9 October 1969, folder: Memoranda Received October–December 1969, Box 8, White House Special Files, Alexander P. Butterfield Correspondence File, Nixon Presidential Materials Staff, National Archives at College Park, Maryland.

57. Franklin, *M.I.A.*, 49; Fred Turner, *Echoes of Combat: The Vietnam War in American Memory* (New York: Anchor, 1996), 101.

58. Memo from Harry S. Dent to H. R. Haldeman, 20 October 1969, folder: Ex ND 18-3/CO 165 Beginning 31 December 1969 [2 of 2], Box 1, White House Central Files, Nixon Presidential Materials Staff, National Archives at College Park, Maryland.

59. Davis, *The Long Road Home*, 244.

60. Letter from Pham Van Dong to William Fulbright, 14 December 1970, folder 203, Box 1, Records Received: Department of Defense, Office of Secretary of Defense, Policy Files, Records of the Senate Select Committee on POW/MIA Affairs, 102nd Congress, 1991–1993, Records of the U.S. Senate, RG 46, National Archives, Washington, D.C.

61. Rochester and Kiley, *Honor Bound*, 477.

62. "Freed POW Lauds Treatment by Cong," *Chicago Tribune*, 10 November 1969, 1, 7.

63. Ben A. Franklin, "Two Civilian Groups Release Purported POW Lists," *New York Times*, 13 November 1969, 4.

64. Senate Select Committee on POW/MIA Affairs, *Report of the Select Committee on POW/MIA Affairs*, 103rd Cong., 1st sess., 13 January 1993, S. Rep. 103–1, 141–42; Davis, *The Long Road Home*, 374–76; Deposition of Roger Shields, 24 March 1992, Transcripts of Depositions, Records of the Senate Select Committee on POW/MIA Affairs, 102nd Congress, 1991–1993, Records of the U.S. Senate, RG 46, National Archives, Washingon, D.C., 249.

65. Memo from Neal Kravitz to Frances Zwenig, 4 October 1992, Cora Weiss, Box 6, Investigator's Case Files, Neal E. Kravitz, Records of the Senate Select Committee on POW/MIA Affairs, 102nd Congress, 1991–1993, Records of the U.S. Senate, RG 46, National Archives, Washington, D.C.

66. Letter from COLIAFAM to classified family member, 7 April 1970, folder 2, Box 4, Records Received: State Department, Selected Records of Frank A. Sieverts, Records of the Senate Select Committee on POW/MIA Affairs, 102nd Congress, 1991–1993, Records of the U.S. Senate, RG 46, National Archives, Washington, D.C.

67. Davis, *The Long Road Home*, 244.

68. Stockdale and Stockdale, *In Love and War*, 244.

69. Ambrose, *Nixon*, 429.

70. Richard Nixon, *Public Papers of the Presidents of the United States: Richard Nixon, 1971* (Washington, D.C.: U.S. Government Printing Office, 1972), 541.

71. Memo from Frank Sieverts to Elliot Richardson, 4 June 1970, folder 3, Box 8, Records Received: State Department, Selected Records of Frank A. Sieverts, Records of the Senate Select Committee on POW/MIA Affairs, 102nd Congress, 1991–1993, Records of the U.S. Senate, RG 46, National Archives, Washington, D.C.

72. Berman, *No Peace, No Honor*, 77; Intelligence Brief, 17 September 1970, Folder North Vietnam—Negotiations 1968–1973 (4), Box 10, National Security Adviser, NSC Vietnam Information Group: Intelligence and Other Reports, 1967–1975, Gerald R. Ford Presidential Library, Ann Arbor, Michigan.

73. Anthony Lewis, "Hanoi Aide Says P.O.W. Agreement Can Be Separate," *New York Times*, 7 July 1971, A1, A14; Chalmers Roberts, "N. Viets Demand Aid End," *Washington Post*, 9 June 1971, A1, A10.

74. Kimball, *Nixon's Vietnam War*, 273.

75. Ibid., 263–75; Berman, *No Peace, No Honor*, chapter 4.

76. Quoted in Murrey Marder, "The POWs in Political Crossfire," *Washington Post*, 21 May 1971, A22.

77. Letter from Mrs. Tom Beyer to Richard Nixon, 30 March 1971, folder 1, Box 21, Records Received: State Department, Selected Records of Frank A. Sieverts, Records of the Senate Select Committee on POW/MIA Affairs, 102nd Congress, 1991–1993, Records of the U.S. Senate, RG 46, National Archives, Washington, D.C. (emphasis in original).

78. Mullen Keenan, *Every Effort*, 141.

79. Letter from Barbara Mullen to Melvin Laird, 31 October 1971, and responding letter from Laird to Mullen, n.d., folder 207D, Box 3, Records Received: Department of Defense, Office of Secretary of Defense, Policy Files, Records of the Senate Select Committee on POW/MIA Affairs, 102nd Congress, 1991–1993, Records of the U.S. Senate, RG 46, National Archives, Washington, D.C.

80. "Please Mr. President," *Washington Post*, 27 May 1971, A4.

81. "Some 'POW' Relatives Say They Are Misled by American Officials," *Wall Street Journal*, 30 September 1971, 1, 27.

82. Cronin quoted in a letter from Robert Leggett to Members of Congress, 24 January 1972, folder 2, Box 21, Records Received: State Department, Selected Records of Frank A. Sieverts, Records of the Senate Select Committee on POW/MIA Affairs, 102nd Congress, 1991–1993, Records of the U.S. Senate, RG 46, National Archives, Washington, D.C. (emphasis in original).

83. Letter from Charles Bennett to Richard Nixon, 9 June 1971, folder: Ex ND 18-3/CO 165 [1 January 1971–31 December 1972], Box 2, White House Central Files, Nixon Presidential Materials Staff, National Archives at College Park, Maryland.

84. Joseph Lelyveld, "P.O.W. Arithmetic," *New York Times*, 3 October 1971, 60.

85. Jonathan Schell, "Reflections—The Nixon Years, Part IV," *New Yorker*, 23 June 1975, 76.

86. Don McLeod, "Kin of Missing and Captive GIs Urge War's End," *Washington Post*, 29 May 1971, A12.

87. Taylor Branch, "Prisoners of War, Prisoners of Peace," *Washington Monthly*, August 1972, 11F.

88. Another Mother for Peace pamphlet, February 1971, folder 207D, Box 3, Records Received: Department of Defense, Office of Secretary of Defense, Policy Files, Records of the Senate Select Committee on POW/MIA Affairs, 102nd Congress, 1991–1993, Records of the U.S. Senate, RG 46, National Archives, Washington, D.C.

89. Senate Select Committee, *Report of the Select Committee on POW/MIA Affairs*, 30.

90. Luu Van Loi and Nguyen Anh Vu, *Le Duc Tho–Kissinger Negotiations in Paris* (Hanoi: Gioi, 1996).

91. Franklin, *M.I.A.*, 54.

92. H. R. Haldeman with Joseph DiMona, *The Ends of Power* (New York: Times Books, 1978), 324.

OFFICIAL HISTORY, REVISIONIST
HISTORY, AND WILD HISTORY

DAVID W. P. ELLIOTT

In the course of many years of research and writing on the Vietnam War, I have become increasingly aware of the pitfalls of writing a "winner's history" that mainly examines the actions of the victors of a conflict. Most of the writings on the Vietnam War have examined in detail the plans, strategies, motivations, and perceptions of the revolutionary side of the conflict.[1] This chapter does not address in detail the related but separate question of American centered histories of the war (which privilege a "loser's" perspective) but concentrates on the way the Vietnamese dimension of the "Vietnam War" is depicted by foreigners writing on the war and the way Vietnamese sources on the war have been employed by them. We should also take note of recent attempts in American scholarship to portray the US effort in Vietnam as a "should-have-been" victory in which the war was fundamentally won before political factors turned success into failure, which has produced a kind of hypothetical or fictional "winner's history" that reduces the importance of taking the revolutionary side and its own accounts of the war seriously.

The focus on the revolutionary side is critically important, but in the process of redressing the American-centered portrayal of the war, we must be careful to avoid an equally imbalanced focus on the "other side's" depiction of this complex historical period. Winner's history is "official history," a long-standing tradition in both the Chinese and Vietnamese cultures that translates political power into control over the interpretation of past events. At the same time, in the face of postmodernist challenges to what once seemed like a very clear historical outcome after a long period of revolution and external intervention, we might do well to remind ourselves that, complex as it is, the twentieth-century history of Vietnam does have discernible contours.

This chapter is about the main challenges to the official history of the revolution: revisionist history and "wild history." Revisionist history as a generic term simply means a challenge to whatever is the current orthodoxy in the interpretation of historical eras and events. In the American context, the phrase was popularized by a group of scholars critical of the mainstream view of the Cold War as a reluctant response by a fundamentally reactive and defensive United States to a communist plan for global domination. Many revisionists were among the first to criticize American aims and objectives in Vietnam, and their criticisms were often accompanied by a more nuanced or even sympathetic portrayal of the revolutionary side (Hanoi and the National Liberation Front). Since that time, the revisionists have themselves been "revised," and the term has lost its clear point of reference. In this context, I use "revisionist" to refer to the post–Cold War generation of scholars who have taken the first generation of revisionists to task and asserted that the American intervention in Vietnam was justified—even if it ultimately failed. Some of the more recent revisionists even argue that the apparent triumph of the revolutionary side in 1975 was, in the final analysis, illusory. I have argued that the victory of the revolution was attained at a very high price and that the dislocations of the war led to serious unintended consequences to the victors. But the events of 1975 did produce clear winners and losers—a point which many of the new revisionists are unwilling or unable to fully explain.[2]

Wild history (a traditional Chinese and Vietnamese term for informal or unofficial history) is an approach to historical understanding that does not easily fall within the revisionist-counterrevisionist cycle. In terms of sources and motives, it is the opposite of official history and refers to unsanctioned, informal, bottom-up perspectives that subvert or (perhaps even more important) ignore the official version of events produced by the controlling authority. It can refer not only to the sources used by the historian (not from official archives or "authorized" interpreters of events) but also to the impressions and "gut feelings" that lie barely submerged beneath the surface authority of the historian's documentation, replete with footnotes and the conventional scholarly apparatus of research. Wild history has been employed to deconstruct such key concepts as Vietnamese nationalism—and even the idea of a "Vietnamese" identity. In this essay, I suggest that a variant of wild history—my own experiences and impressions while conducting a more formal and structured inquiry into the Vietnamese revolution—can also serve to cast some light on the more conventional story of Vietnam in the mid-twentieth century.

The perils of subjectivity inherent in relying on personal impressions should caution us against elevating this variant of wild history to a privileged position, however. Scholars of great eminence, such as Cornell's Keith Taylor, have arrived at conclusions about the Vietnam War significantly different from those that I offer here, also based in part on personal experience.[3] Taylor has provided a useful definition of what I will call the "corollaries" of the "Vietnam conflict era conventional wisdom" (defined below). In his personal reflection on the Vietnam War, Taylor outlined "three axioms in the dominant interpretation of the U.S.–Vietnam War that were established by the antiwar movement during the late 1960s and subsequently taken up by teachers at most schools and universities as the basis for explaining the war."[4] These axioms, examined later in this chapter, deal with the legitimacy of the Saigon government and the U.S. intervention in Vietnam, and the inevitability of victory by the revolutionary side. Later in this essay, I will briefly relate some of my own personal experiences in wartime Vietnam, which led me to accept the axioms that Taylor has challenged, despite my initial support for the war.

The Vietnamese Perspective

Clearly, the winner's history perspective is an essential part of the story we are examining. Much of the writing on the Vietnam War has focused mainly on the American perspective. Indeed, the "Vietnam War" has come to mean what Americans did in Vietnam (or even at home in the United States) and what was done to them. Robert McMahon has observed that the writing on the war is "overwhelmingly produced by Americans, asking American-oriented questions and seeking answers in documents produced by other Americans."[5] George Herring, who has written one of the standard histories of the Vietnam War, chided a colleague for writing yet another American-centric history of the war in which the more deeply America becomes involved, the more the Vietnamese recede into the background, becoming shadowy figures whose actions remain obscure. He adds:

> Like most American writing on Vietnam [this book]...does not fully bridge the chasm of ignorance that separated us from our Vietnamese allies and enemies at the time. Our inability as a nation to make this cultural leap is of more than academic importance. There is little indication in recent political debates on possible American intervention in the world that we have learned

an essential lesson of Vietnam: the need to understand and respect the history, cultural, and local dynamics of places where we contemplate involvement.[6]

Ronald Spector takes yet another recent work on the Vietnam War to task for its "ethnocentrism" and the "assumption of American omnipotence" and for ignoring the "ideas, plans and actions of the Vietnamese."[7] In short, Americans will never learn the elusive lessons of Vietnam by looking only in the mirror.

One example of the importance of taking the revolutionary perspective seriously is the belated discovery by Robert McNamara that one of the incidents that prompted the full intervention of the United States into the Vietnam War—the attack on an airfield in Central Vietnam—did not mean what he and other American officials assumed at the time. McNamara writes that, in February 1965, "there was little doubt in Washington that Hanoi had ordered the attack in Pleiku specifically to send a signal of its own to the United States while the Bundy team [national security advisor McGeorge Bundy] was visiting Saigon." In Washington's view, the incident meant that "Hanoi did indeed 'seek a wider war' via attacks such as were carried out at Pleiku." At a conference in Hanoi long after the end of the war, however, McNamara discovered that the Pleiku attack was ordered by local revolutionary commanders "who had no idea that Bundy was in Saigon or that [Soviet premier Alexei] Kosygin was in Hanoi…[and] *were unaware that U.S. personnel were present at the time of the attack!* In other words, the Pleiku attack was not targeted at Americans, was not ordered by Hanoi, and was not designed by Hanoi to send a signal of any kind to anybody."[8]

The Vietnamese have an evocative term for attributing one's own prejudices to others, *suy bung ta ra bung nguoi* (to project our own thoughts and motives onto others). As the coauthors of McNamara's book *Argument without End* conclude:

> It appears that the U.S. decisionmakers running the air war from the White House—including President Johnson, who was centrally involved—came to believe that the NLF's war on the ground was being run *with the same degree of detailed control* from the leadership headquarters in Hanoi. It was not. Thus, strictly speaking, Pleiku and Qui Nhon [another NLF attack that followed the one on Pleiku] did not pull the "trigger" that initiated the American war. Washington pulled the trigger itself—it took the momentous step, based on a misunderstanding of NLF command and control procedures, thinking that their counterparts in Hanoi had *already* done so.[9]

McNamara and other leading officials of the Kennedy-Johnson era later ruefully confessed that they had not understood the mindset of their opponents. Listing the "lessons of Vietnam" in his 1995 book, *In Retrospect*, McNamara writes:

> We misjudged then—as we have since the geopolitical intentions of our adversaries.... We viewed the people and leaders of South Vietnam in terms of our own experience. We saw in them a thirst for—and a determination to fight for—freedom and democracy. We totally misjudged the political forces within the country. We underestimated the power of nationalism to motivate a people (in this case the North Vietnamese and Vietcong) to fight and die for their beliefs and values—and we continue to do so today in many parts of the world.[10]

Maxwell Taylor, once John F. Kennedy's chief military advisor on Vietnam and then ambassador in 1964–1965, added:

> First, we didn't know ourselves. We thought we were going into another Korean War, but this was a different country. Secondly, we didn't know our South Vietnamese allies. We never understood them,... and we knew even less about North Vietnam.... So, until we know the enemy and know our allies and know ourselves, we'd better keep out of this dirty kind of business.[11]

It is noteworthy that McNamara and Taylor came to embrace some of the views of the antiwar critics—which ultimately became the "Vietnam conflict era conventional wisdom" among scholars and specialists on Vietnam. Of course, some important points are glossed over in the McNamara-Taylor reflections. It wasn't just that the U.S. decision makers didn't know either their allies or their opponents. Fundamentally, the "best and the brightest," as David Halberstam labeled the Vietnam War advisors of Kennedy and Johnson, thought that the Vietnamese were irrelevant to the big picture in which they had placed Vietnam. The United States, having already been complicit in the overthrow of Ngo Dinh Diem, an ally of nine years' standing, thought so little of its nominal host, the government of the Republic of South Vietnam, that it did not even bother to inform its own ally that America would escalate the war and send in combat troops. "They are landing on the beaches right now. They are already ashore," exclaimed the astonished Premier Phan Huy Quat as the marines disembarked on the beaches of Danang in March 1965.[12] What is even more remarkable is that a recent generation of scholars is engaged in debunking the Vietnam conflict era conventional wisdom that McNamara and Taylor eventually came to embrace.[13]

Thus, there is some value in revisiting the Vietnam conflict era conventional wisdom. But instead of concentrating on the official history of the revolution and on accounts of the obvious strategic turning points of the war, such as the launching of the insurgency in 1959–1960 and the Tet Offensive in 1968, I would like to urge consideration of a few somewhat neglected issues: the extent to which socioeconomic change from 1963 to early 1965, *prior* to the major U.S. military intervention, may have influenced both the outcome and the aftermath of the conflict, and the question of what was actually happening in Vietnam in the latter years of the war (1970–1971), which some recent revisionist historians have alleged was the point at which the South Vietnamese government had essentially won the war.

Temporal Perspectives and Patterns of Causation

The "Vietnamese perspective" deals with the definition of the subject of analysis and the point of view of the analyst. The temporal dimension of events is equally important and problematic. Periodization, the attempt to identify distinctive historical eras or segments of time, may be likened to organizing chapters of a book, each of which contains a distinctive portion of the larger story. As I will argue below, the main pitfall in dividing history into temporal segments lies in treating the larger story as a seamless narrative, with a clear beginning, a middle, and a conclusion that follows inevitably from the earlier chapters of the story. So we must be careful not to let the end of the story dictate our analysis and determine how we structure and present the earlier chapters of the narrative.

A related point is how we link the parts or chapters of the story and imply a cause-and-effect relationship between earlier and later events. An example is the pattern of causality asserted by the Cold War conventional wisdom: an aggressive Soviet Union provoked a reluctant response from an otherwise passive United States. The protorevisionist argument was that the United States also contributed to the escalation of the Cold War and that the pattern was not simply Soviet provocation and American response. Similar issues are involved in the various generations of revisionist interpretations of the Vietnam War. The original orthodoxy was the official U.S. position that the war was initiated by "aggression from North Vietnam." Soon, a first-generation or protorevisionist interpretation challenged this by emphasizing American intervention in Vietnam's politics and the southern origins of the insurgency. Later generations of scholars have, in turn, questioned this interpretation.

In this section, I will examine not the origins of the insurgency, but the escalation of 1963–1964 that led to full-scale U.S. military intervention. Though my research generally supports the first-generation revisionist emphasis on the southern origins of the insurgency and Hanoi's reluctance to launch a conflict in 1959–1960, it also suggests that Hanoi contributed to the American escalation of 1964–1965 by a crucial decision made in December 1963.

In assessing how approaches to periodization and the analysis of causation affect our understanding of the Vietnam War, we might consider the following:

1. Historians need to compensate for the loss of eyewitness and participant accounts. This inevitably results in less original research and more focus on reinterpretation and recycling of existing evidence rather than attempting to dig deeper into what actually happened during the war. There is thus a built-in bias toward revisionism rather than attempts to reconstruct the past. As time passes, participant accounts produced long after the events become more unreliable. Scholars of the Vietnam War should put a premium on searching out sources that were produced contemporaneously.

2. Analysts need to compensate for the fact that we know how the war turned out and are tempted to read what came later into the earlier periods of the conflict. "History is lived forward but is written in retrospect," wrote the late British historian C. V. Wedgwood. "We know the end before we consider the beginning, and we can never wholly recapture what it was to know the beginning only."[14] The war is often viewed through the images of its final act—North Vietnamese tanks crashing through the gates of the Presidential Palace—which give the impression that the war was essentially a military conquest of the South by the North.

3. There are, however, some benefits of the perspective that comes from knowing the outcome and attaining more historical distance from the events. More attention needs to be paid to accurately identifying the crucial turning points in the conflict, which were not evident at the time. It is mainly in retrospect that we can see the December 1963 Ninth Plenum resolution in Hanoi as a fateful turning point. Resolution 9 shifted the revolution's approach to the conflict from a guerrilla war strategy that placed equal emphasis on political and military

struggle to an all-out attempt to defeat Saigon's forces militarily before the United States could intervene. It also marked a temporary shift toward China in the Sino-Soviet dispute.[15]

In addition to changing the international dynamics of the war (by moving closer to China and by ordering a high-risk challenge to U.S. policy interests), the December 1963 debate over strategy produced a high-level internal split in Vietnam, as Vu Thu Hien argues in his extraordinary book *Dem Giua Ban Ngay*, or *Darkness at Noon*.[16] It also set in motion mobilization politics which profoundly affected the relationship between the southern revolutionary movement and the rural population by imposing forced conscription and heavy taxes on the peasantry—not long after building strong support by land distribution. The shift in strategic focus away from the Mekong Delta to battlefields more suited for big unit operations also had a major impact on the war. The big push to end the war before the United States could intervene did bring the ARVN nearly to collapse, but it also provoked the very U.S. intervention it was designed to preempt. This might lead to speculation about whether a continuation of a predominantly guerrilla strategy could have led to a different outcome, but such a historical counterfactual argumentation is inherently fruitless. We would do better to try to understand what actually did happen and why it happened in the way it did, rather than diverting attention to the road not taken.

The aftermath of Resolution 9 raises the question not only of turning points construed as discrete events, which triggered transformations of the conflict, but also can serve as a way to reexamine the conflict dynamic itself, in this case the action-reaction cycle which led to the escalation of the war. The American-centered approach tends to put the spotlight on Lyndon Johnson and his advisors as the initiators, while downplaying the role played by the revolutionary leadership (and the Saigon government). While this may be more satisfying to critics of the U.S. intervention, it also tends to deny agency to the Vietnamese side of the conflict and glosses over the role that decisions taken by the Vietnamese had on the war. It is ironic that the most critical assessment of the wisdom and motives of decisions taken by top party leaders in Hanoi has come from within the ranks of the revolution, including Vu Thu Hien and various postwar memoirs by southern revolutionary leaders.

One could argue that Resolution 9 did not initially advocate a go-for-broke strategy, but that the escalation evolved from the seeds planted by the resolution. Gareth Porter maintains in his provocative book *Perils of Dominance* that "contrary to the interpretation of the Ninth Plenum as authorizing a strategy of striving for quick victory, the text of the resolution shows that Hanoi's leaders had not in fact decided on such a strategy."[17] This may be true, but the situation in the Mekong Delta could certainly support another view, an example of the importance of local history in clarifying important controversies about the war. Bui Tin, a colonel in the North Vietnamese army,[18] reported to Hanoi in the spring of 1964 that PLAF regiments were not big enough or strong enough to fight American forces (though this leaves open the question of whether they could have successfully overwhelmed ARVN forces as they did in the key battle of Binh Gia in late 1964, which showed that the ARVN could not cope with the new scale of conflict). Bui Tin concluded that it would not be possible to liberate the South without deploying northern units in the South—which is exactly what happened.

Was Bui Tin's view shared by all in the politburo (we have strong evidence from Vu Thu Hien and others of significant disagreements at the highest political levels in the North)? Did the Central Office for South Vietnam (COSVN), Hanoi's command headquarters in the South, agree? What about the regional commands in critical areas like the Mekong Delta? Did North Vietnam activate contingency plans for escalation only in response to American provocations or was the script already written into Resolution 9 in December 1963? Porter cites a politburo resolution of September 1964, which stated that the " 'best method to win victory for the South Vietnamese revolution' was to rapidly build up military forces in the South and partly destroy the ARVN in an effort to 'completely defeat the puppet army before the United States jumps into the war.' " But, he adds, "the document later explained that winning a 'decisive victory' in the South could only be accomplished 'within a few years.' "[19] I argued in *The Vietnamese War* that, by early 1965, Le Duan, the party leader in the North, had concluded that it was now possible to finish the war off by bold action.[20]

I think Porter has it right in arguing that Le Duan's plan for ending the war was based not so much on defeating the Saigon government militarily, but on doing enough damage to the ARVN to discourage Washington from believing in a military solution.[21] Washington fundamentally misunderstood the strategic assumptions of Hanoi, which were assumed to be a copy of the Maoist "three-stage war," or an unfolding plan of military escalation from defensive guerrilla war to large-scale conventional battles. It was the fear that this plan was reaching its final stage that may have panicked Washington into intervening to change the military balance of forces enough to postpone defeat. In reality, Hanoi had adopted a defensive strategic framework that aimed at exhausting the strategic options of the ultimate opponent (the United States) rather than relying on military victory. This misperception, which is not widely noted in the literature on the war, also had a major impact on U.S. interpretations of the 1968 Tet Offensive.[22] Nevertheless, what happened in the Mekong Delta following Resolution 9 strongly suggests that it led to a fateful go-for-broke military push that, in turn, led to U.S. military intervention.

Much of the analysis of this key turning point in the Vietnam War has been based on official texts, such as party resolutions on strategy and postwar authorized histories. These sources do not, however, provide conclusive evidence about the underlying motives for the decision or even what the decision actually was. For one thing, the official documents have been selectively released for public consumption, and there are certainly many more documents in Hanoi's archives which might throw additional light on the subject. There is also a largely untapped reservoir of captured "Viet Cong" documents preserved on microfilm at various U.S. libraries, which could be considered a part of the quasi-official record, since the documents were official but have not been screened or redacted to form an "authorized" account. There are also nonofficial sources which can be useful in understanding the ambiguities of important actions and decisions taken by Hanoi and the southern revolutionaries during the war. The unauthorized memoirs of Bui Tin and Vu Thu Hien are one example. Another is the oral histories of people who lived the events in question—especially those that were recorded contemporaneously. The deeper the scholar digs into official records, the clearer is the need to supplement them with other sources.

Official History and Wild History

There are two conflicting traditions in Vietnamese and Chinese historiography: the *chinh thong (chinh su)*, or "official" or "authorized" history commissioned and vetted by the power holders in society, and the *da su*—"wild history" or "field history." (The term *da* refers to uncultivated terrain "in the wild.") Unlike the official or court history, which is largely based on official archival documents, wild history is unauthorized and based on nonofficial sources. The Vietnamese dictionary definition of *da su* is "a kind of orally transmitted history that reflects the concepts and attitudes of the ordinary people toward historical events and figures, in contrast with *chinh su.*"[23] Other dictionaries simply define *da su* as history written by private individuals in contrast to official history.

The use of interviews with lower-level participants in the conflict represents one source for a wild history of the war. My book *The Vietnamese War* relied heavily on interviews done with "Viet Cong" prisoners and defectors under the auspices of the Rand Corporation during the war. For all of the obvious defects of these interviews (done under official American auspices in a highly constrained environment), they do have the following merits as sources: they were done contemporaneously and capture a snapshot of each period of the war; they were views on the ground and not from a higher or more distant vantage; despite the clear incentives to tailor responses to serve the personal interests of each interview subject, the general assessments of the actions and motives of others tended to be surprisingly objective and often against the interest of the subject; there were a large number of interviews, providing a basis for cross-checking for plausibility; and they were in-depth interviews most often recorded verbatim, offering the possibility of retrieving nuances of signification even from a considerable historical distance. Semi-authorized biographies of midlevel revolutionary leaders are a kind of hybrid between wild history and official history. These are valuable sources for understanding the gap between revolutionary vision and situational reality during the war, especially with respect to such key episodes as the Tet Offensive of 1968 and the spring offensive of 1972. The combination of ground-level interviews (and low-level documents such as those in the massive Combined Document Exploitation Center, or CDEC Collection),[24] the midlevel semi-authorized biographies of revolutionary leaders, and the official histories produced by the revolutionary movement can give us a deeper understanding of the heterogeneity of what has often been portrayed as a monolith (by its critics) or an infallible and historical predestined undertaking (by its leaders).

The lack of contemporaneous sources about adherents of the anticommunist position is a crucial void in the history of the conflict. This is the most obvious consequence of the tendency to write a winner's history. Some important work is being done by younger scholars to fill this vacuum, especially with regard to the Diem years.[25] As Mark Bradley has shown, wild history can be extracted from archival sources, usually considered the main locus of official history.[26] His book *Imagining Vietnam and America: The Making of Postcolonial Vietnam, 1919–1950* is a model of rigorous and empathetic recreation of mindsets of the past and an attempt at understanding how the world looked to those who did not know the end of the story.

Of course, the spirit of wild history would imply that the more marginal, subversive, and peripheral to the main lines of authority, on both sides of the conflict, are the voices, the more authentic. Thus the Holy Grail of wild history would be the recollections of those at the margins of politics and society, who could provide a more distanced and ambiguous picture of a complex, even fragmented reality. It is true that those at the margins of the conflict are largely unheard in postwar histories. These would include large segments of the peasantry and the politically demobilized urban underclass, many of them refugees from the countryside focused only on coping with surviving in an alien environment.

The Vietnamese War argues that in some ways the most important political divide in Vietnam was not between revolutionaries and their opponents, but between the entire "political class" on both sides of this divide, who were risk takers and "plunged" (*dan than*) into politics, and the risk averse, whose constant refrain was "do whatever you like, I'll still be a simple citizen" (*lam gi lam, toi van la dan*)—using the age-old distinction between a passive "subject" of authority (*dan*) and those who belong to the political class.

Some might argue that the so-called Third Force, a loosely connected group of primarily urban middle-class people who did not support either the Saigon government or the revolutionary side, is a significant exception to this. My own view is that though the Third Force did not like the political choices they faced, they were unable to change the political parameters of Vietnamese society at the time. There is much to be said for the concept of the Third Force as a more "authentic" Vietnamese voice than the official contenders, but it is also probably true that from a winner's history vantage, the Third Force did not have a significant impact on the outcome of the war beyond destabilizing the Saigon government. The complex legitimacy issues which the Third Force raised are, however, worth extended examination. They viewed the Saigon government as not only repressive (the revolution was far more so) but also as a tool of foreign intervention. However grudgingly, the Third Force implicitly acknowledged the more credible nationalist credentials of the revolutionary side. In the context of this chapter, however, the most important aspect of the Third Force may be to reinforce the idea that there was a broadly accepted view of Vietnamese identity, on which this concept of nationalist legitimacy was based—a view which has been contested.

Revisionist and Postmodern Views of Vietnamese Nationalism

In reaction to the monolithic and destined-to-succeed views of the revolutionary movement, recent trends in Western scholarship on Vietnam have not only downplayed the dominant role of the revolutionary movement in shaping modern Vietnamese history, but have also challenged the notions of

Vietnamese identity and Vietnamese nationalism that it proclaimed.[27] This view of identity was largely shared by the anticommunists as well (the only question was which side best represented the vision of a unified and cohesive Vietnam). But the conventional understanding of the basic nature of the Vietnamese conflict has now been "problematized," to use the language of the postmodernist critics.

Broadly speaking, there are two schools of thought on the elusive subject of Vietnamese nationalism, which we could call the "Vietnam conflict era conventional wisdom" and "postwar postmodernism." Keith Taylor, the author of a path-breaking study of the formation of Vietnamese identity, has written about a long-standing scholarly consensus on depicting a "unified Vietnam, a Confucian Vietnam, and a revolutionary Vietnam." This is especially problematic, some scholars feel, because the Vietnam War unfolded in the southern part of Vietnam, a region with a quite distinctive history. Victor Lieberman notes that "in recent years scholarly research has focused ever more insistently on the polyphonic, localizing, fragmenting implications of post-1550 southern settlement in what Pierre Gourou as early as 1936 termed 'the least coherent territory in the world.'"[28]

Gourou's comment, of course, refers mainly to the Mekong Delta. If there is any validity to the dominant consensus among foreign scholars during the Vietnam War (Vietnam conflict era conventional wisdom) of Vietnamese nationalism as a fusion of commitment to the ideal of national unity and resistance to foreign intervention as espoused by the revolutionaries whose leaders were, in Alexander Woodside's memorable term, Confucian-influenced "proletarian mandarins,"[29] the most challenging test would be to apply this model of Vietnamese nationalism to "the least coherent territory in the world."

The Vietnamese revolutionaries themselves promulgated this view of Vietnamese nationalism as a combination of a seamlessly unified Vietnamese population and territory with a visceral and historically derived impulse to resist foreign interference in Vietnam. There is some ambiguity about the role that China's influence on Vietnam has had in forging this sense of unity both by giving Vietnam the tools of statecraft to build effective institutions and an ideology that provided cohesion for the ruling elite in the precolonial era,[30] and also by providing a unifying threat that would consolidate a distinct Vietnamese identity. North Vietnam's leading intellectual publicist during the conflict, Nguyen Khac Vien, frankly acknowledged the Confucian legacy[31] even while Vietnamese revolutionary leaders were trying to construct a more indigenous model.[32] It should be noted that the Confucian legacy was much more pronounced in northern Vietnam and tended to recede as one moved farther south, which would thus support the postwar postmodernist view of a more fragmented Vietnamese identity. The central issue for understanding what politically motivated large numbers of Vietnamese in the Mekong Delta to engage in a struggle for national unification under the guidance of a distant leadership based in North Vietnam requires that we explore the extent to which their vision of national identity—whatever its actual historical accuracy—was internalized by the revolutionaries in the South.

Hanoi's own historians have, in recent years, acknowledged the great differences between the society in the Mekong Delta and other parts of Vietnam stemming from the frontier character of this area, the last major territory brought under unified Vietnamese control, and the related factors of prolonged civil war and ethnic as well as cultural diversity. To some Vietnamese scholars, the pluralism of Mekong Delta society is a distinctive and enriching feature of Vietnamese identity, but is nevertheless encompassed by it.[33]

Developments inside Vietnam since the end of the Vietnam War and shifting academic fashions in the world outside Vietnam have combined to challenge the view of a cohesive Vietnamese nationalism or even a well-defined Vietnamese national identity. The failure to impose the revolution's model of northern socialism on the South and the ultimate disillusionment with that model are two factors. Another is the way southern revolutionaries were shunted aside from positions of leadership after the conflict. The vogue of deconstructionism and postmodernism in Western academic circles is yet another factor.

Perhaps the necessary counterpart to the postmodern urge to deconstruct is the attempt to understand why communities and political movements cohere, and how they construct identities through common experience. Anthropologist Charles Keyes writes:

> In reflecting on "national integration" it is still useful, I believe, to begin with the seminal work in the effort to understand the nature of the problems attendant on national integration—Clifford Geertz's 1963 essay, "The Integrative Revolution: Primordial Sentiments and Civil Politics in the New States." Geertz stressed that if a new state was to succeed as a nation-state, means must be found to establish a "civil" order that transcended the existing "primordial" differences between the peoples living within the boundaries of the state. Finding such a means was neither obvious nor the same from case to case. There is a direct line, I believe, between Geertz's ideas and those of Benedict Anderson, Ernest Gellner, Eric Hobsbawm, Terence Ranger and others who have shaped the contemporary approach to problems of

"nation-building" and "national integration." Today we speak of the "imagining," "invention" and "construction" of national communities out of the diversity that is found within the politically recognized boundaries of states.[34]

Keith Taylor has asserted that a "'common history' lies in the realm of mythology and indoctrination."[35] The Vietnamese revolutionaries would not necessarily disagree, and it is perhaps a tribute to the energy of their propagandists that they were so successful in purveying their party-sanctioned mythology through extensive indoctrination. Indeed, all nations are built in one way or another on constructed visions. Civil societies are built largely by forging consensus on shared visions of community. The same could be said about revolutionary movements. The outcome and ultimate form of successful revolutions are not preordained by the elements that form a revolutionary movement, but painfully forged in a common experience of struggle. In Vietnam's case, this also resulted in postrevolutionary complacency along with arbitrary and oppressive rule based on a sense of victor's entitlement, which undermined much of the initial promise of the revolution and has led some to question not only its original purposes, but also its very historical substance. But the historical record of the revolutionary movement in Vietnam is concrete and clearly visible—thanks to the voluminous records of contemporary sources from which its actions and social impact can be reconstructed.

Personal Reflections

Let us recall the corollaries of what I have called the Vietnam War era conventional wisdom as stated by Keith Taylor: there was never a legitimate noncommunist government in Saigon; the United States had no legitimate reason to be involved in Vietnamese affairs; and the United States could not have won the war under any circumstances. I would like to conclude this chapter with some personal reminiscences drawn from the six years I spent in Vietnam between 1963 and 1973.

When I first arrived in Vietnam as a trained Vietnamese linguist in the army in October 1963, I fully subscribed to the Cold War orthodoxy as it applied to Vietnam, which was undergirded with the idealism of youth fueled by the rhetoric of President John F. Kennedy. In addition, I was already engaged to be married to a Vietnamese graduate of Georgetown University whose immediate family (with the exception of her oldest sister, who was a committed follower of the revolutionary movement) had fled communism in North Vietnam in 1954 and were strong supporters of America's policy in Vietnam.[36] During the course of the war, I came to believe that it was unwinnable and, eventually, that it was futile to prolong it—especially after it became clear that the original reasons for American involvement had been repudiated by American officials. In addition to the revelations in the Pentagon Papers, Henry Kissinger conceded in his famous *Foreign Affairs* article of 1968 that the original policy rationale for the Vietnam intervention was obsolete and, in his memoirs, said dismissively, "Our predecessors had entered in innocence, convinced that the cruel civil war represented the cutting edge of some global design."[37]

With respect to Keith Taylor's three corollaries of the Vietnam War era conventional wisdom, therefore, I agree with what I think is the central point of the three items: the United States could not have won the war under any circumstances. I won't repeat my detailed arguments on this point, presented in books and papers referred to earlier, but will simply state a conclusion drawn from personal experience and observation in Vietnam: the Vietnamese noncommunists could not have won without the United States, but could not have won by dependence on the United States either.

To me, the first point is self-evident. Without the United States, there would have been no Republic of South Vietnam, and even if a noncommunist entity had somehow come into existence after 1954 without the United States, it would have collapsed in 1965 without direct and massive U.S. military intervention. But this intervention came at a cost. First, the United States had already undermined the fragile basis of a legitimate South Vietnamese government by supporting the overthrow of Ngo Dinh Diem in November 1963. This action also marked the end of any pretense that America's main objective was to preserve South Vietnam's right to determine its own political future. This was the decisive turning point in America's involvement in the conflict. As Stanley Karnow put it, "America's responsibility for Diem's death haunted U.S. leaders during the years ahead, prompting them to assume a larger burden in Vietnam."[38] If President Kennedy had found that there was no longer any common ground or shared interest with the government of Ngo Dinh Diem, that would have been the time to declare a parting of the ways. Instead, the United States, by supporting a coup against Diem, made itself politically and morally responsible for the aftermath. But at some point, mistakes must be rectified, not compounded, and this culpability in the Diem coup is not a sufficient argument for staying the course, whatever the costs or consequences.

A second corollary of the Vietnam War era conventional wisdom is the belief that there was never a legitimate noncommunist government in

Saigon. "Legitimacy" is one of the most elusive concepts in the lexicon of political science. Here, the best testimony comes from the anticommunist nationalists in Vietnam. Even the top leadership of Saigon's Republic of Vietnam (RVN) felt that its overwhelming dependence on foreign assistance was a major political handicap. In a Rand study of the views of top Vietnamese officials on the war, done shortly after the conflict ended, one former RVN general said:

> Since the dependence and subordination of the Vietnam government was so obviously demonstrated by the predominant presence and power of the Americans, the Vietnamese general public could not refrain from viewing their government as a puppet deprived of all national prestige, lacking in a national mandate and thus being untrustworthy.

The study concluded that in such "a highly ideological struggle as the Vietnam war, this aspect had a strong negative impact and worked much to the detriment of the RVN cause. Moreover, reacting to the negative attitude of the Vietnam[ese] public, RVN officials were unwilling or afraid to take any initiative and were thus reduced to adopting a defensive attitude." The Rand study noted that the "long list of negative statements made by former South Vietnamese leaders about their own leadership was punctuated only rarely by positive statements about anyone, military or civilian, although some senior commanders were praised."[39] Bui Diem, a former South Vietnamese ambassador to the United States and a perceptive observer of Vietnamese politics, wrote:

> Caught in the middle of these powerful forces, Vietnamese nationalists found themselves in a succession of precarious situations. In most cases they were forced to choose among unpalatable alternatives; often, indeed, they saw no choice at all. With their survival at stake they were forced to take refuge in a series of uneasy and uncomfortable compromises that little by little eroded their legitimacy.[40]

Although there was corruption during the Diem period, it was not as institutionalized as it became under his successors. The heads of regions, provinces, and districts all had to purchase their positions under the Thieu regime, and paying back the investment mean that they, in turn, had to demand kickbacks from their subordinates. In addition to the obvious fact that this put a premium on connections over efficiency (which accounts for the ineffective use of the lavish military resources provided by the

United States), the culture of corruption fatally wounded the Republic of South Vietnam by turning on its most capable officers and officials. The most remarkable officer I met in South Vietnam was a dynamic district chief whose brilliant career was cut short by a mysterious criminal conviction which was almost certainly the result of bribery and corruption and very likely initiated by the revolutionary side to get rid of a dangerously effective opponent.[41] Another outstanding officer, once equal in rank to Thieu, survived an assassination attempt caused by his refusal to engage in the pervasive network of corruption. As many observers have noted, the problem posed by people like this was more than a simple refusal to provide money to corrupt superiors. Clean hands could not be tolerated because they threatened the entire system. To a degree, the United States was the enabler of this system, because the easy money provided the temptation, and the American prop disguised the consequences of trading efficiency for cash—until it was too late; the money dried up and the prop disappeared. It was not only the origins of the government of the Republic of South Vietnam that raised legitimacy questions but its nature and behavior, and corruption was perhaps the leading reason that the Saigon government and its officials were not held in high regard, even by their own peers. Perhaps this also explains why, when the moment of truth came, the majority of South Vietnam's officers and officials were not willing to defend it to the death.

It has been argued that corruption is rife under the current communist regime and that it is therefore unfair to blame the Saigon government for what seems to be an endemic Vietnamese—indeed, human—problem. And it is tempting in retrospect to smile at the naïveté of the antiwar writers who felt that the "cleansing flame of revolution" was about to forever rid the land of corruption.[42] Certainly, corruption is a major issue in Vietnam today, but the corruption does not appear to be built into the system as it was during the war era, and the current regime is not fighting for its very existence. But the fact of continuing corruption in Vietnam today also raises the question of how much the outcome of the war has made a permanent impact on Vietnamese society.

I worked closely with Vietnamese who had been passionate supporters of Ngo Dinh Diem, and have great admiration for their abilities and their political idealism. Also on our small team of Rand researchers were two individuals who had been jailed by the Diem regime for their fierce opposition to his authoritarian rule. My own research suggests that the Diem regime was terminal, in the Mekong Delta at least, and had painted itself into a political corner, where it had fatally antagonized the patron that was its only hope of survival and, at the same time, had alienated much of its natural anticommunist political base by autocratic political behavior.

In my early years in Vietnam, I also heard stories from former Saigon high officials about military advice from the United States in the Eisenhower and Kennedy periods that had molded South Vietnam's security forces in the American image, rendering them incapable of responding to the escalating insurgency, for example, insisting that the Civil Guard be equipped with U.S. 2½-ton trucks rather than with the requested modified three-wheeled Lambretta vehicles that were common throughout Vietnam during the period. The Lambrettas could carry a squad of rural militia along village and hamlet paths and could be inexpensively maintained by any village mechanic. The trucks were sent over the objections of the Civil Guard commander and were, as he had predicted, parked in the provincial capital for ease of management and maintenance. As their transportation pulled out of the countryside, so did the Civil Guard. This is one of many instances where the United States ended up hurting the people it was trying to help.

The examples of inappropriate U.S. advice to the South Vietnamese government and self-serving deception are multiple. The deceptions of Vietnam eroded our democracy and destroyed much of the early idealism that Kennedy had instilled in my generation. From this I learned that self-deception is the surest road to disaster.[43] But the main reason I concluded that the U.S. presence was damaging to Americans as well as to the people we were trying to help was that for America, the Vietnam War was never about Vietnam, but always about some larger abstraction of concern to the United States—containing China, dominos, credibility. The false premises of U.S. involvement in Vietnam eventually seriously undermined other critical areas of our global security during the Cold War.

Taylor's third corollary of the Vietnam War era conventional wisdom is that the United States had no legitimate reason to be involved in Vietnamese affairs. I wouldn't put it this way, but I also find it hard, in retrospect, to view America's involvement in Vietnam as a noble venture precisely because it was not intended to benefit the Vietnamese, but manipulated the Vietnamese for American ends. In the final analysis, even America's own interests in Vietnam were undermined by its casual indifference to the Vietnamese and the realities of their situation.

One of the most revealing documents about the Vietnam War is a hybrid of official history and wild history. I refer to a note jotted by John McNaughton in 1964, which was not intended as an official document but as a reminder to himself of what American interests in Vietnam were. McNaughton, Robert McNamara's chief deputy for the Vietnam War, gave short shrift to

296 Wars End and Endless Wars

the importance of local allies in U.S. calculations. He observed that U.S. aims were:

> 70 percent—To avoid a humiliating defeat (to our reputation as a guarantor). 20 percent—To keep SVN (and then adjacent) territory from Chinese hands. 10 percent—To permit the people of SVN to enjoy a better, freer way of life. ALSO—to emerge from crisis without an unacceptable taint from methods used. NOT—to "help a friend," although it would be hard to stay in if asked out.[44]

I was, of course, deeply affected by the prisoners and defectors from the revolutionary movement whom I met in the course of my work with the Rand Corporation. The genuine idealism and courage of most of these one-time members of the revolution left a deep impression on me, even as they recounted countless examples of the ruthlessness and brutality of the movement. These were extraordinary individuals who did exceptional things in unusual times, and it does them a great disservice to lump them together with the opportunistic and often corrupt cadres that many recent visitors to Vietnam have found so off-putting.

Not much attention has been paid to the final years of the conflict in Vietnam. This is somewhat surprising in view of the fact that one of the main tenets of some of the new revisionists is that the war was essentially won by the United States and Saigon in 1970 or 1971. On my return in 1971 after my earlier departure to continue graduate study in 1968, I was struck by the depth of anti-American sentiment in the cities, especially among the middle class. In part, this was a backlash of frustration and resentment against the Americans who were withdrawing as they had entered—indifferent to the fate of their Vietnamese allies. In part, it was due to the extensive social disintegration of a society dislocated by war, which appalled many anticommunist conservatives of the older generation. American cars were being burned in the streets of Saigon. The strains and tensions in urban South Vietnamese society have been largely forgotten in postwar histories of the conflict, but they are an important part of the story of this period as are, of course, the vast rural dislocations, which also tend to be downplayed in revisionist accounts. The extent of the damage to "Vietnamization" and Saigon control by the 1972 Easter Offensive has also been underplayed in some of more recent scholarship on the war.

Although the My Lai massacre is the most familiar of the Vietnam era depredations against civilians, there is a lesser known episode which in many ways is even more disturbing because it was a product of official policy, condoned and even encouraged at a high level of military command. This was Operation Speedy Express, which took place from December 1968 to June 1969, during which large numbers of civilians were killed by indiscriminate firepower from the U.S. Ninth Division as an organic element of the operation's design. I briefly discuss this in *The Vietnamese War*, but even the extensive interviews conducted several years after these events would not have grasped the full moral magnitude of this tragedy had it not been for an alert *Newsweek* stringer (Alex Shimkin, later killed during the 1972 Easter Offensive), who deduced what was going on sometime after the fact, and the later writing of Colonel David Hackworth, who was a battalion commander in the Ninth Division and was appalled by the methods advocated by his superiors.[45] It is a sad commentary on our collective historical recall that these methods are now being repackaged as clever military pacification tactics ("clear and hold") and advocated as the solution for the insurgency in Iraq.[46]

The Thieu government was widely unpopular, especially as Thieu ran in a one-man election in 1971 with the acquiescence of the American ambassador. Although America's limitations in shaping the political face of South Vietnam were always evident, this was a particularly clear example of the noncommunist nationalists' dilemma outlined by Bui Diem: they couldn't win with the United States and couldn't win without it.[47] The logic of Henry Kissinger's "decent interval" was all too clear to the noncommunist nationalists; they would be left holding the bag after having made an unwise bet on the Americans' determination to stay the course.[48]

Much of the postwar revision of the Vietnam War era conventional wisdom is the result of the bleak aftermath of the conflict—repression, refugees, poverty. But it is a long step from acknowledging that the 1975 victory of the revolutionary forces was followed by a painful aftermath, to the further attempt to reformulate this historical outcome or to interpret the entire Vietnamese revolution through the lens of the post-1975 period. It would certainly have been desirable to have a more flexible, competent, and humane government running Vietnam's affairs after 1975, but a large part of the reasons for the failures of post-1975 go back to the long conflict itself. Revolutions are shaped by the forces that produce them. Britain's relatively lighter colonial touch produced Fabian socialist postindependence regimes in many cases. French rule in Vietnam helped to shape an independence movement that was as rigid and authoritarian as the repression that it was forced to confront.

On the occasion of the thirtieth anniversary of the end of the Vietnam War, *Los Angeles Times* journalist David Lamb wrote an article titled "War

Is History for Vibrant Vietnam," which opened by stating, "Thirty years after the fall of Saigon, the firmly communist nation has a flourishing economy, social freedom and deep ties with the U.S. Half the nearly 83 million people in Vietnam were born after Saigon fell." His article posed the question, "So what have the decades since brought to a country that Air Force Gen. Curtis LeMay once suggested the United States should bomb 'back to the Stone Age?'" His answer was:

> Ironically, if you took away the still-ruling Communist Party and discounted the perilous decade after the war, the Vietnam of today is not much different from the country U.S. policymakers wanted to create in the 1960s. It is a peaceful, stable presence in the Pacific Basin, with an army that has been whittled down to 484,000 troops. Its economy, a mix of Karl Marx and Adam Smith, has the highest growth rate in Southeast Asia. Private enterprise is flourishing, a middle class is growing, poverty rates are falling. The United States is a major trading partner, and Americans are welcomed with a warmth that belies the two countries' history.[49]

During my many trips to Vietnam since the end of the Cold War and the initiation of its economic reforms, I have been struck by the same thought expressed by Lamb, that no matter who won the Vietnam War, the result would not be fundamentally different from today's realities in Vietnam. One significant exception, of course, is that although Vietnam's leadership has jettisoned Marxism, it has maintained its tightly controlled Leninist political system. It might be that Jeanne Kirkpatrick was right in saying that authoritarian systems (like South Vietnam's Diem and Thieu regimes) were different from totalitarian systems, like those in the communist world, because they were transitional regimes moving toward more openness and democracy, while totalitarian regimes are forever. One can only speculate how the South Vietnamese regime might have evolved if it had survived, but it is at least possible that it could have become as much of a democracy as Thailand. Alternatively, it might have relapsed into the sad spectacle of threatened coups and bread-and-circus governments that has tarnished the democratic legacy of the Philippines.

But all of this lies in the realm of hypothetical scenarios. For historians, what counts is what happened and when it happened. As I have written elsewhere:

> Many postwar studies of the Vietnam War contend that "if only" certain tactics, programs, or weaponry had been applied in timely fashion, the outcome

of the war would have been different. However, the conflict unfolded in historical "real time." There was always a reason why these panaceas were never employed when they might have made a difference. To take two examples; land reform and smart weapons. Saigon's "land to the tiller" might have had an impact on the peasantry had it been done in the 1950s in the place of the Diem reforms (which backfired). But, of course, it would have been unthinkable and politically impossible for Diem to do this—and far more outlandish to think of the French acting along these lines in the late 1940s when the first Viet Minh land reforms were consolidating a base of support for the revolution. It is true that smart bombs and other advanced weapons technology might have been more effective than the less sophisticated weaponry used earlier on by the United States and the Government of Vietnam, but there would have been few targets for them in this phase of dispersed guerrilla war. The revolutionaries did not stand still either. Starting with sharpened stakes and machetes in 1945, which were adequate for the job at the time, they graduated to SAMs in the 1970s. Of course these were supplied by China and the Soviet Union, but the point is that the conflict was a dialectic unfolding of action and reaction, in which every new innovation in counter-revolution produced a corresponding racheting up of revolutionary capabilities. The "what if" scenarios are ahistorical and fruitless. What mattered was what happened at the time it was happening and the relative strengths of each side at that precise moment.[50]

There is a profound insight in C. V. Wedgwood's observation that "[w]e know the end before we consider the beginning, and we can never wholly recapture what it was to know the beginning only." The most difficult task for future historians of the Vietnam War will be to strip away the many layers of history that have been superimposed on the events they will reexamine, and try to see how they were understood at the time. Recapturing the sense of contingency is a way of correcting both the tendency to assume a predetermined outcome, which is rightly criticized by Keith Taylor, and the tendency to indulge in revisionism for merely contrarian reasons. Those who lived the history they write about have problems in gaining the detachment essential to objectivity. But distance from the events does not necessarily guarantee objectivity either. I am struck by how few of the recent revisionist reformulations of the Vietnam War try to come to grips with an essential element of the historical method—an examination of the evidence. Whether this takes the form of official history or wild history, evidence should be the ultimate arbiter of interpretation.

NOTES

1. See, for example, my following writings: "Hanoi's Strategy in the Vietnam War," in Jayne Werner, ed., *The Vietnam War: Vietnamese and American Perspectives* (Armonk, N.Y.: Sharpe, 1993); "Vietnam: Tradition under Challenge," in Russell Trood and Ken Booth, eds., *Strategic Cultures in the Asia-Pacific Region* (New York: St. Martin's, 1999); "Wag the Dog: Vietnam and the Cold War," in Arthur L. Rosenbaum and Chae-Jin Lee, eds., *The Cold War: Reassessments* (Claremont, Calif.: Keck Center for International and Strategic Studies of Claremont McKenna College, 2000).

2. I have presented a version of this argument in David W. P. Elliott, *The Vietnamese War: Revolution and Social Change in the Mekong Delta 1930–1975*, 2 vols. (Armonk, N.Y.: Sharpe, 2002).

3. Keith W Taylor, "How I Began to Teach about the Vietnam War," *Michigan Quarterly Review* 43.4 (Fall 2004): 637–47.

4. Taylor comments, "It took me many years to step free of these axioms and to see them as ideological debris of the antiwar movement rather than as sustainable views supported by evidence and logic. What enabled me to do this was that I finally came to terms with my own experience." Ibid., 637.

5. *Los Angeles Times*, 11 May, 1997.

6. George C. Herring, "The Big Muddy," book review of Robert D. Shulzinger's *A Time for War: The United States and Vietnam, 1941–1975* (New York: Oxford University Press, 1997), *Los Angeles Times Book Review*, 11 May 1997, 7.

7. Ronald Spector, "Cooking Up a Quagmire," book review of H. R. McMaster's *Dereliction of Duty* (New York: HarperCollins, 1997), *New York Times*, 20 July 1997, section 7, 31.

8. Robert S. McNamara with James Blight, Robert Brigham, Thomas Biersteker, and Col. Herbert Schandler, *Argument without End: In Search of Answers to the Vietnam Tragedy* (New York: Public Affairs Press, 1999), 173.

9. Ibid., 174.

10. Robert S. McNamara, *In Retrospect* (New York: Random House, 1995), 221–22.

11. Quoted in Stanley Karnow, *Vietnam: A History* (New York: Penguin, 1984), 19.

12. Bui Diem, *In the Jaws of History* (Boston: Houghton Mifflin, 1987), 132.

13. The most sweeping revisionist account is Mark Moyar, *Triumph Forsaken: The Vietnam War, 1954–1965* (New York: Cambridge University Press, 2006).

14. Quoted in Dean Acheson, *Present at the Creation* (W.W. Norton, 1987), xvii.

15. Elliott, *The Vietnamese War*, 1:613.

16. Vu Thu Hien, *Dem Giua Ban Ngay* (California: Van Nghe, 1997). He is the son of a long-time revolutionary who was once the personal secretary of Ho Chi Minh. Hien, who had extensive contacts among the top Vietnamese leadership through his father, was jailed for many years on spurious political charges. His account is largely based on informal conversations within this network of contacts. The book is consciously titled after *Darkness at Noon*, Arthur Koestler's 1940 account of his break with communism.

17. Gareth Porter, *Perils of Dominance: Imbalance of Power and the Road to War in Vietnam*, (Berkeley: University of California Press, 2005), 128.

18. Bui Tin also became an iconic figure in the "final act" of the war by accompanying North Vietnamese tanks crashing through the gates of the Presidential Palace. Stanley Karnow ends his acclaimed book *Vietnam: A History* with Bui Tin who, after having witnessed the surrender of the Saigon government, stretched out on the grass in front of the Presidential Palace in Saigon and "gazed at the sky, exalted" (684). This depiction of the concluding act of the Vietnam War now takes on a slightly different coloration with the subsequent knowledge that Bui Tin later became a political dissident and now resides in Paris.

19. Porter, *Perils of Dominance* 132.

20. Elliott, *The Vietnamese War*, 2:739.

21. Porter, *Perils of Dominance*, 135.

22. Some U.S. officials argued at the time that the Tet Offensive was a desperate gamble or a propaganda stunt by Hanoi. Most subsequent historians have concluded that the offensive turned into a major military defeat for the revolutionary side because no urban uprisings occurred, and the attackers were driven out of the cities with heavy losses which crippled the southern component of its regular military forces. Among those who acknowledge that Tet ended in a military setback for the revolutionary forces, many also agree that in a strategic sense this was the major turning point in the war, because it led to the conclusion in Washington that the war was stalemated and could not be won militarily. Still others agree that Tet was decisive because of this political impact, but assert that the war was still winnable after Tet.

23. Nguyen Nhu Y, chief ed., *Dai Tu Dien Tieng Viet [Great Dictionary of the Vietnamese Language]* (Ho Chi Minh City: NXB Van Hoa-Thong Tin, 1999), 504.

24. The CDEC is part of the J-2 (intelligence) branch of the Military Assistance Command, Vietnam (MAC-V). This is where documents captured from revolutionary forces were collected, screened, summarized, sometimes translated, analyzed, and later microfilmed. See the discussion on the Vietnam Studies Group listserv, http://www.lib.washington.edu/Southeastasia/vsg/guides/cdec.html.

25. See, for instance, the essay by Edward Miller in this volume and the suggested readings at the end of this book.

26. Mark Philip Bradley, *Imagining Vietnam and America: The Making of Postcolonial Vietnam, 1919–1950* (Chapel Hill: University of North Carolina Press, 2000).

27. A more extensive version of this section can be found in the paperback concise edition of my *The Vietnamese War* (Armonk: M.E. Sharpe, 2006).

28. The Taylor quote and following comment are in Victor Lieberman, *Strange Parallels: Southeast Asia in Global Context, c. 800–1830*, vol. 1: *Integration on the Mainland* (Cambridge: Cambridge University Press, 2003), 342–43.

29. Alexander B. Woodside, *Community and Revolution in Modern Vietnam* (Boston: Houghton Mifflin, 1976).

30. See especially the writings of John Whitmore, including *Essays into Vietnamese Pasts*, co-edited with K. W. Taylor (Ithaca, N.Y.: Cornell University

Southeast Asia Program, 1991); *Vietnam, Ho Quy Ly, and the Ming, 1371–1421* (New Haven, Conn.: Yale University Southeast Asia Program, 1985); and *An Introduction to Indochinese History, Culture, Language, and Life* (which he edited) (Ann Arbor: University of Michigan Center for South and Southeast Asian Studies, 1976).

31. See Nguyen Khac Vien's classic essay "Confucianism and Marxism," in David Marr and Jayne Werner, eds., *Tradition and Revolution in Vietnam* (Washington, D.C.: Indochina Resource Center, 1974), 15–52.

32. See Charles F. Keyes, "Ethnicity and the Nation-State: Asian Perspective," paper given at the North Carolina State University Center for International Ethnicity Studies, 17 January 2003. Available: http://www2.chass.ncsu.edu/CIES/KeyesPaper.htm.

33. See, for example, Nguyen Cong Binh et al., *Van Hoa Va Cu Dan Dong Bang Song Cuu Long [Culture and People of the Mekong Delta]* (Ha Noi: Nha Xuat Ban Xa Hoi Hoc, 1990), 41.

34. Keyes, "Ethnicity." See also Benedict R. O'G. Anderson, *Imagined Communities: Reflections on the Origin and Spread of Nationalism*, 2nd ed. (London: Verso, 1991); Ernest Gellner, *Nations and Nationalism* (Oxford: Blackwell, 1983); Eric J. Hobsbawm, *Nations and Nationalism since 1780: Programme, Myth, Reality* (Cambridge: Cambridge University Press, 1990); and Hobsbawm and Terence Ranger, *The Invention of Tradition* (Cambridge: Cambridge University Press, 1984).

35. Keith Taylor, "Surface Orientations in Vietnam: Beyond Histories of Nation and Region," *Journal of Asian Studies* 57.4 (November 1998): 972.

36. See Duong Van Mai Elliott, *The Sacred Willow: Four Generations in the Life of a Vietnamese Family* (New York: Oxford University Press, 1999).

37. Cited in Henry Kissinger, *White House Years* (Boston: Little, Brown, 1979), 226.

38. Karnow, *Vietnam: A History*, 294.

39. Hosmer et al., *The Fall of South Vietnam*, (New York: Crane, Russak and Co., 1980) 74. See also the discussion of corruption in Gabriel Kolko, *Anatomy of a War* (New York: New Press, 1985), 208–13.

40. Bui Diem, *Jaws of History*, 335.

41. The story is told in my *The Vietnamese War*, 2:900–902.

42. Frances Fitzgerald argues:

[B]ehind the dam of American troops and American money, the pressure is building toward one of those sudden historical shifts when "individualism" and its attendant corruption gives way to the discipline of the revolutionary community. When this shift takes place, the American officials will find it hard to recognize their former proteges [*sic*]. They may well conclude that the "hard core Communists" have brainwashed and terrorized them into submission, but they will be wrong. It will simply mean that the moment has arrived for the narrow flame of revolution to cleanse the lake of Vietnamese society from the corruption and disorder of the American war. (Fitzgerald, *Fire in the Lake* [New York: Random House, 1973], 590)

I deal with the issue of local corruption among revolutionary cadres in my *The Vietnamese War*, 2:95–98. While not uncommon, it was not systematized as it was in the RVN and was a result of gaining official position and therefore power on merit, rather than a means of obtaining official position, and was severely punished when uncovered.

43. I recently learned that the misrepresentations of the Gulf of Tonkin incident, which provided Johnson with a "blank check" to go to war, were largely due to an attempt to cover up a translation error of a signal intercept. Scott Shane, "Vietnam Study, Casting Doubts, Remains Secret," *New York Times*, 31 October 2005. I had received orders to go to the Army Security Agency base at Phu Bai outside of Hue, and almost certainly would have been involved with the translation had I not been transferred to MAC-V because I announced my intention to marry a Vietnamese national and therefore lost my cryptographic clearance.

44. Quoted in Marilyn B. Young, *The Vietnam Wars: 1954–1990* (New York: Harper Perennial, 1991), 135.

45. *The Vietnamese War*, 2:1161–62. Even the increasingly optimistic John Paul Vann criticized General Julian Ewell, commander of the Ninth Division for inflicting excessive civilian casualties in his quest for increasing the "body count," and the highly decorated Colonel David Hackworth, a battalion commander in this division, stated, "I knew Vann was right. Americans should never have been deployed in the Delta—especially under the command of 'the Butcher of the Mekong Delta,' with his insatiable appetite for body counts." Ewell had clearly caught on to the new "catch the fish" approach. Hackworth describes him as "a tightly wrapped, thin-lipped, hard charging West Pointer who meant to drain the Delta before the Delta pulled the plug on him." David H. Hackworth, *Steel My Soldiers' Hearts* (New York: Touchstone, 2002), 370.

46. See my paper "Parallel Wars? Can 'Lessons of Vietnam' Be Applied to Iraq?" delivered at the Southeast Asia Forum at the Walter H. Shorenstein Asia-Pacific Research Center, Stanford University, 8 May 2006, and published under that title in Lloyd C. Gardner and Marilyn B. Young, eds., *Iraq and the Lessons of Vietnam* (New York: New Press, 2007).

47. Bui Diem quotes Kissinger as feeling that Thieu's autocratic methods were "unwise" but concluding that there was nothing to be done: "We considered support for the political structure of Saigon not as a favor done to Thieu but an imperative of our national interest." Diem's comment on the 1971 one-man election of Thieu was:

At this point, the dual track of South Vietnamese political development halted abruptly. In these pre-election events the democratic process, even in its roisterous and imperfect Vietnamese mode, received the kiss of death.... Outside South Vietnam, as well as inside, the image of the Thieu regime as a corrupt and repressive dictatorship got a rousing confirmation. (*Jaws of History*, 292–93)

48. The most authoritative research on this subject has been done by Jeffrey Kimball; see "The Case of the 'Decent Interval': Do We Now Have a Smoking Gun?" Available: http://www.ohiou.edu/shafr/news/2001/sep/internal.htm.

49. David Lamb, "War Is History for Vibrant Vietnam," *Los Angeles Times*, 30 April 2005.

50. Elliott, *The Vietnamese War*, 2:1390.

SUGGESTED READINGS

PART I: *American Intervention and the Cold War Consensus*

MARK ATWOOD LAWRENCE, *"Explaining the Early Decisions: The United States and the French War, 1945–1954"*

Anderson, David L. *Trapped by Success: The Eisenhower Administration and Vietnam, 1953–1961* (New York: Columbia University Press, 1991).

Bradley, Mark Philip. *Imagining Vietnam and America: The Making of Postcolonial Vietnam, 1919–1950* (Chapel Hill: University of North Carolina Press, 2000).

Gardner, Lloyd C. *Approaching Vietnam: From World War II through Dienbienphu* (New York: Norton, 1988).

Hess, Gary R. *The United States' Emergence as a Southeast Asian Power, 1940–1950* (New York: Columbia University Press, 1987).

Lawrence, Mark Atwood. *Assuming the Burden: Europe and the American Commitment to War in Vietnam* (Berkeley: University of California Press, 2005).

Lawrence, Mark Atwood, and Fredrik Logevall, eds. *The First Vietnam War: Colonial Conflict and Cold War Crisis* (Cambridge, Mass.: Harvard University Press, 2007).

Rotter, Andrew J. *The Path to Vietnam: Origins of the American Commitment to Southeast Asia* (Ithaca, N.Y.: Cornell University Press, 1987).

SETH JACOBS, *" 'No Place to Fight a War': Laos and the Evolution of U.S. Policy toward Vietnam, 1954–1963"*

Dommen, Arthur. *Conflict in Laos: The Politics of Neutralization* (New York: Praeger, 1964).

Kochavi, Noam. "Limited Accommodation, Perpetuated Conflict: Kennedy, China, and the Laos Crisis, 1961–1963," *Diplomatic History* 26 (Winter 2002): 95–135.

Pelz, Stephen E. " 'When Do I Have Time to Think?': John F. Kennedy, Roger Hilsman, and the Laotian Crisis of 1962," *Diplomatic History* 3 (Spring 1979): 215–29.

Stevenson, Charles. *The End of Nowhere: American Policy toward Laos since 1954* (Boston: Beacon, 1972).

GARETH PORTER, *"Explaining the Vietnam War: Dominant and Contending Paradigms"; Fredrik Logevall, " 'There Ain't No Daylight': Lyndon Johnson and the Politics of Escalation"*

Freedman, Lawrence. *Kennedy's Wars: Berlin, Cuba, Laos, and Vietnam* (New York: Oxford University Press, 2000).

Gardner, Lloyd. *Pay Any Price: Lyndon Johnson and the Wars for Vietnam* (Chicago: Dee, 1995).

Halberstam, David. *The Best and the Brightest* (New York: Random House, 1972).

Kahin, George McT. *Intervention: How America Became Involved in Vietnam* (Garden City, N.Y.: Doubleday, 1987).

Kaiser, David. *American Tragedy: Kennedy, Johnson and the Origins of the Vietnam War* (Cambridge, Mass.: Harvard University Press, 2000).

Kattenberg, Paul. *The Vietnam Trauma in American Foreign Policy, 1945–1975* (New Brunswick, N.J.: Transaction, 1980).

Logevall, Fredrik. *Choosing War: The Lost Chance for Peace and the Escalation of the War in Vietnam* (Berkeley: University of California Press, 1999).

McNamara, Robert, et al. *Argument without End: In Search of Answers to the Vietnam Tragedy* (New York: Public Affairs, 1999).

Porter, Gareth. *Perils of Dominance: Imbalance of Power and the Road to War in Vietnam* (Berkeley: University of California Press, 2006).

Preston, Andrew. *The War Council: McGeorge Bundy, the NSC, and Vietnam* (Cambridge, Mass.: Harvard University Press, 2006).

PART II: *The Coming of War in Vietnam*

SOPHIE QUINN-JUDGE, *"Through a Glass Darkly: Reading the History of the Vietnamese Communist Party, 1945–1975"*

Brocheux, Pierre. *Ho Chi Minh: A Biography* (New York: Cambridge University Press, 2007).

Duiker, William. *Ho Chi Minh: A Life* (New York: Hyperion, 2000).

Gaiduk, Ilya. *The Soviet Union and the Vietnam War* (Chicago: Dee, 1996).

Kerkvliet, Benedict. *The Power of Everyday Politics: How Vietnamese Peasants Transformed National Policy* (Ithaca, N.Y.: Cornell University Press, 2005).

Marr, David G. *Vietnam 1945: Quest for Power* (Berkeley: University of California Press, 1995).

Quinn-Judge, Sophie. *Ho Chi Minh: The Missing Years* (Berkeley: University of California Press, 2003).

Shaplen, Robert. *Lost Revolution* (New York: Harper & Row, 1965).

Zhai Qiang. *China and the Vietnam Wars, 1950–1975* (Chapel Hill: University of North Carolina Press, 2000).

EDWARD MILLER, *"Vision, Power, and Agency: The Ascent of Ngo Dinh Diem, 1945–1954"*

Anderson, David. *Trapped by Success: The Eisenhower Administration and Vietnam, 1953–1961* (New York: Columbia University Press, 1991).

Catton, Philip. *Diem's Final Failure: Prelude to America's War in Vietnam* (Lawrence: University Press of Kansas, 2002).

Chapman, Jessica. "Staging Democracy: South Vietnam's 1955 Referendum to Depose Bao Dai," *Diplomatic History* 30.44 (September 2006): 671–703.

Hammer, Ellen. *A Death in November: America in Vietnam, 1963* (New York: Dutton, 1987).

Jacobs, Seth. *America's Miracle Man in Vietnam: Ngo Dinh Diem, Religion, Race, and U.S. Intervention in Southeast Asia, 1950–1957* (Durham, N.C.: Duke University Press, 2004).

DAVID HUNT, *"Taking Notice of the Everyday"*

Elliott, David W. P. *The Vietnamese War: Revolution and Social Change in the Mekong Delta, 1930–1975* (Armonk, N.Y.: Sharpe, 2006).

Hendry, James. *The Small World of Khanh Hau* (Chicago: Aldine, 1964).

Hickey, Gerald. *Village in Vietnam* (New Haven, Conn.: Yale University Press, 1967).

Race, Jeffrey. *War Comes to Long An* (Berkeley: University of California Press, 1972).

Sansom, Robert. *The Economics of Insurgency in the Mekong Delta of Vietnam* (Cambridge, Mass.: MIT Press, 1970).

Taylor, Philip. *Fragments of the Present: Searching for Modernity in Vietnam's South* (Honolulu: University of Hawaii Press, 2001).

———. *Goddess on the Rise: Pilgrimage and Popular Religion in Vietnam* (Honolulu: University of Hawaii Press, 2004).

HEONIK KWON, *"Co So Cach Mang and the Social Network of War"*

Brigham, Robert K. *ARVN: Life and Death in the South Vietnamese Army* (Lawrence: University Press of Kansas, 2006).

Duiker, William J. *Sacred War: Nationalism and Revolution in a Divided Vietnam* (Boston: McGraw-Hill, 1995).

Heonik Kwon. *After the Massacre: Commemoration and Consolation in Ha My and My Lai* (Berkeley: University of California Press, 2006).

———. *The Ghosts of War in Vietnam* (Cambridge: Cambridge University Press, 2007).

Hy Van Luong. *Revolution in the Village: Tradition and Transformation in North Vietnam, 1925–1988* (Honolulu: University of Hawaii Press, 1992).

Pike, Douglas E. *Viet Cong: The Organization and Techniques of the National Liberation Front of South Vietnam* (Cambridge, Mass.: MIT Press, 1966).

Trullinger, James W. *Village at War: An Account of Conflict in Vietnam* (Stanford, Calif.: Stanford University Press, 1994).

PART III: *War's End and Endless Wars*

LIEN-HANG T. NGUYEN, *"Cold War Contradictions: Toward an International History of the Second Indochina War, 1969–1973"*

Asselin, Pierre. *A Bitter Peace: Washington, Hanoi, and the Making of the Paris Agreement* (Chapel Hill: University of North Carolina Press, 2002).

Berman, Larry. *No Peace, No Honor: Nixon, Kissinger, and Betrayal in Vietnam* (New York: Simon & Schuster, 2002).

Bui Diem. *In the Jaws of History* (Bloomington: Indiana University Press, 1999).

Kimball, Jeffrey. *Nixon's Vietnam War* (Lawrence: University Press of Kansas, 1998).

Luu Van Loi, and Nguyen Anh Vu. *Le Duc Tho–Kissinger Negotiations in Paris* (Hanoi: Gioi 1996).

Mai Van Bo. *Ha Noi–Paris: Hoi ky ngoai giao cua Mai Van Bo* [*Hanoi–Paris: The Diplomatic Memoir of Mai Van Bo*] (Ho Chi Minh City: Nha Xuat Ban Van Nghe Thanh Pho Ho Chi Minh, 1993).

Phu Duc Nguyen,. *The Viet Nam Peace Negotiations: Saigon's Side of the Story* (Christiansburg: Dalley Book Services, 2005).

Porter, Gareth. *A Peace Denied: United States, Vietnam, and the Paris Agreement* (Bloomington: Indiana University Press, 1975).

MICHAEL J. ALLEN, " '*Help Us Tell the Truth about Vietnam*': *POW/MIA Politics and the End of the American War*"

Davis, Vernon E. *The Long Road Home: U.S. Prisoner of War Policy and Planning in Southeast Asia* (Washington, D.C.: Office of the Secretary of Defense, 2001).

Franklin, H. Bruce. *M.I.A.; or, Mythmaking in America* (New Brunswick, N.J.: Rutgers University Press, 1993).

Keenan, Barbara Mullen. *Every Effort: A True Story* (New York: St. Martin's, 1986).

Rochester, Stuart I., and Frederick Kiley. *Honor Bound: The History of American Prisoners of War in Southeast Asia, 1961–1973* (Annapolis, Md.: Naval Institute Press, 1999).

Senate Select Committee on POW/MIA Affairs. *Report of the Select Committee on POW/MIA Affairs*. 103rd Cong., 1st sess., 13 January 1993, S. Rep. 103-1.

INDEX

Acheson, Dean, 31
Agnew, Spiro, 263, 266
Allen, Michael J., 15–16
Alsop, Joseph, 99
American war with Vietnam
  civilian deaths in, 296–97
  Cold War consensus paradigm on
    U.S. motives for, 69–73
  domestic American opposition to,
    251, 257–58, 259, 260, 263–64,
    265, 266–68
  French criticism of, 104–5
  and Gulf of Tonkin incident, 78, 255
  internationalization of, 220, 227, 238
  legacy of in Vietnam, 212, 214
  military desertion in, 205–6
  Ninth Plenum resolution as turning
    point in, 117, 126, 283–86
  as noble war, 7, 16
  and phased withdrawal of troops
    under John F. Kennedy, 77
  reenactments of, 3, 4–5
  revisionist U.S. history of, 277–78,
    282–83, 297
  role of Vietnamese mothers in,
    205–6
  role of Vietnamese social networks
    in, 199–215
  role of U.S. national security
    bureaucracy in, 76–80
  Tet Offensive during, 15, 112, 117,
    219, 220, 221, 222, 281, 287
  unofficial Vietnamese history of,
    277, 278, 286–88
  See also Democratic Republic
    of Vietnam; Johnson, Lyndon;

Kennedy, John F.; Kissinger,
  Henry; National Liberation Front;
  Nixon, Richard; prisoners of war;
  U.S. Congress; Viet Cong
Anderson, Benedict, 290
Anderson, David L., 37
Army of the Republic of Vietnam
  (ARVN), 180, 192, 202, 205, 211,
  285
  counterinsurgency activities of, 201,
  210
Asselin, Pierre, 226
Aubrac, Raymond, 130

Ball, George, 91, 104
Bao Dai, 29, 138, 144, 145, 148
  discrediting of, 154–58
  relationship with Ngo Dinh Diem,
    139–40, 150
  role of in establishing post-WWII
    government in Vietnam, 141–42
  See also Bao Dai solution; Elysée
    accords; Ngo Dinh Diem
Bao Dai solution, 34, 141–43, 145
Berman, Larry, 68, 223, 269
Berman, Marshall, 172
Betts, Richard, 7, 38, 70
Bidault, Georges, 27
Billings-Yun, Melanie, 36–37
Binh Xuyen, 155, 159
Bowles, Chester, 61
Bradley, Mark, 28–29, 131, 287
Braudel, Fernand, 173
Brezhnev, Leonid, 235
Bridges, Styles, 60–61. *See also* U.S.
  Congress

Mao Zedong, 31, 112, 113, 125, 231, 234
  endorsement of Ho Chi Minh, 124
  influence over DRV, 117, 129
  See also China; Kissinger, Henry; Nixon, Richard; Sino-Soviet split
Marcovitch, Herbert, 130
Marr, David, 11
McCarthy, Eugene, 256
McCarthyism, 31, 35, 146
McClintock, Robert, 48
McClure, Claude, 251, 255, 257
McCone, John, 81
McGovern, George, 256, 259
McHale, Shawn, 12
McMahon, Robert, 279
McMaster, H. R., 73
McNamara, Robert, 70, 95, 102
  doubts about escalation of Vietnam War, 96, 106
  on Laos, 45–46, 60
  misreading of Vietnamese, 96, 98, 280–81
  pressure on Johnson to escalate war, 78–79, 81–83, 106
  role in Kennedy's phased withdrawal plan, 77–78
  See also Johnson, Lyndon; Kennedy, John F.
McNaughton, John, 97, 295–96
Meeker, Oden, 51
MI6, 123
Miller, Edward, 13
Modernization theory, 172, 191–92
Moise, Edwin, 86
Morgenthau, Hans, 95
Mounier, Emmanuel, 150–51
Movement for National Union and Peace, 155
Moyar, Mark, 7

National League of Families of American Prisoners and Missing

in Southeast Asia, 261–63, 267.
  See also Prisoners of war
National Liberation Front, 10, 14, 172, 174, 177, 179, 186, 201, 267, 224
  defections from, 192–94
  political uses of U.S. POWs by, 251, 254–55, 257, 258, 265
  promotion within, 188–89
  recruitment for, 181–82, 183, 187–88
  role of women in, 189–91
  See also American war in Vietnam
National Mobilization Committee to End the War in Vietnam, 258
National Security Council, 48, 60, 74, 77, 78, 82, 86
Ne Win, 98
Newman, John, 72
Ngo Dinh Can, 149–50
Ngo Dinh Diem, 6, 13, 38, 45, 58, 75
  advocacy for a Third Force in Vietnam, 145, 148, 152
  American exile of, 143–48
  anti-French attitude of, 145
  Catholicism of, 137–38, 145, 146, 148–49
  correspondence with Kennedy on Laos, 47–48
  discrediting of Bao Dai by, 154–58
  early struggle for power, 135–43
  family of, 137, 143–45, 146, 149–54
  overthrow of, 281, 292
  post-WWII vision for Vietnamese society, 142
  relations with Viet Minh, 139–40, 142
  rise to power of, 158–61
  split with Bao Dai, 142
  Viet Minh assassination plans for, 143
Ngo Dinh Kha, 137
Ngo Dinh Khoi, 137, 139
Ngo Dinh Luyen, 149–50
Ngo Dinh Nhu, 149–54, 159, 160
  role in Diem's rise to power, 154–57
Ngo Dinh Thuc, 137, 143–45, 146

Qiang Zhai, 115
Quinn-Judge, Sophie, 13, 14

Race, Jeffrey, 11
Radford, Arthur, 36
Rand Corporation, 287, 293, 295, 296
    study on defectors from the National
        Liberation Front, 172–194
Ranger, Terrence, 290
Reagan, Ronald, 7, 262
Republic of [South] Vietnam (RVN;
        also referred to as Government of
        Vietnam, GVN)
    betrayal of by U.S., 234
    competition with NLF for military
        recruits, 173, 175, 184, 186,
        187–88, 190, 191–194;
    corruption in, 293–94
    dependence on U.S., 292–93
    lack of scholarly interest in, 219
    role in negotiations to end American
        war in Vietnam, 220, 222, 224,
        226, 237–39
    See also American war with
        Vietnam; Army of the Republic
        of Vietnam; Kissinger, Richard;
        Nixon, Richard
Reston, James, 263–64
Richardson, Elliot, 263, 266
Roberts, Chalmers, 35–36, 37
Roosevelt, Franklin D.
    anticolonialism of, 25, 39
    support for international trusteeship
        for Indochina, 5, 24–29
Rostow, Walt, 76, 80
Rotter, Andrew, 32
Royal Lao Army, 47, 49–50, 52–54,
    56–59, 61
Royal Lao government, 45, 49
Rusk, Dean, 50, 62, 78, 81, 82, 95, 103,
    106
Russell, Richard, 60–61, 93, 95, 101, 106,
    256, 257. See also U.S. Congress

Sarit Thanarat, 47
Schaller, Michael, 33
Schandler, Herbert, 70
Schecter, Jerrold, 53, 225
Schell, Jonathan, 268
Schlesinger, Arthur, 6–7, 50, 54
Schulzinger, Robert, 71
Second Indochina War. See American
    war with Vietnam
Shackford, R.H., 52
Shaplen, Robert, 131
Sheehan, Neil, 252
Sieverts, Frank, 256–57, 266
Sino-Soviet split, 15, 96, 97, 100, 125,
    284
    exploitation of by the Nixon
        administration, 222, 228–29
Smith, George, 251, 255, 257
Smith, Walter Bedell, 80
Sorenson, Theodore, 50
Southeast Asia Treaty Organization
    (SEATO), 38, 72
Souvanna Phouma, 46, 55, 62
Soviet Union, 5, 30, 31, 102
    breakdown of relations with
        Vietnamese Communist Party,
        125–26
    collapse of, 7
    détente with U.S., 94, 97, 128, 221,
        227, 231, 234–36, 238
    deterioration of relations with
        U.S., 27
    hesitance to support DRV in conflict
        with U.S., 94
    imbalance of power with U.S., 8–9,
        74–76, 82–84
    reluctance to support Ho Chi Minh,
        124
    role in partition of Vietnam, 75
    role of in peace talks to end
        American war in Vietnam, 227, 239
    support for DRV, 75, 93–94, 122,
        127, 143

CPSIA information can be obtained at www.ICGtesting.com
Printed in the USA
LVOW10s1931130915

453994LV00001B/228/P